Contents

UTAH 78

THE SOUTHWEST

NEW MEXICO 100

ARIZONA 122

THE FAR WEST

NEVADA 144

CALIFORNIA 166

- *over 237,000 acres of scenic isolation, and 50 crystal-clear lakes* — Marble Mountain Wilderness 168
- *circle tour to the top of the famous peak and Lassen Volcanic National Park* — Shasta Country 170
- *raucous, oft-burned mining town restored complete with Wells Fargo and Company Express office* — Columbia 172
- *most spectacular view of San Francisco in the entire Bay area* — Mount Tamalpais 174
- *remnant of a basaltic lava flow that originated 915,000 years ago carved by glacial action into symmetrical columns* — Devils Postpile 176
- *adventure trails crisscross 10,000 acres of jagged peaks* — Pinnacles 178
- *rugged, desert land and the remains of a violent mining town on the edge of Death Valley* — Panamint City 180
- *one of the most beautiful circle trips in southern California* — Ojai Valley 182
- *exploring this once inhabited desert wonderland by foot trails and auto tours* — Joshua Tree National Monument 184
- *state park preserving desert wilderness intact with fossil footprints made by giant mastodons* — Anza-Borrego Desert State Park 186

THE NORTHWEST

WASHINGTON 188

- *"America's most beautiful boat trip" leads to a fascinating paradise* — San Juan Islands 190
- *see gray whales at play at the most northwesterly point on the U.S. mainland* — Cape Flattery 192
- *follow the route of fur traders and prospectors in a country of badlands and saw-toothed mountain pinnacles* — Okanogan Country 194
- *over 600 miles of trails through rain forests and a glacier wonderland* — Olympic National Park 196
- *spectacular entry to America's newest national park and its more than 150 active glaciers* — North Cascades 198
- *skeleton of a waterfall once 100 times more powerful than Niagara* — Dry Falls 200
- *geological wonder formed 10 million years ago* — Ginkgo Petrified Forest 202
- *to the top of one of the largest extinct volcanoes in the United States* — Mount Rainier 204
- *myriad fishing streams in the land where legend turned Indians into mountains* — Tieton Recreation Area 206
- *sportsman's playground hallowed in Indian legend* — Spirit Lake 208

OREGON 210

IDAHO 232

PREFACE

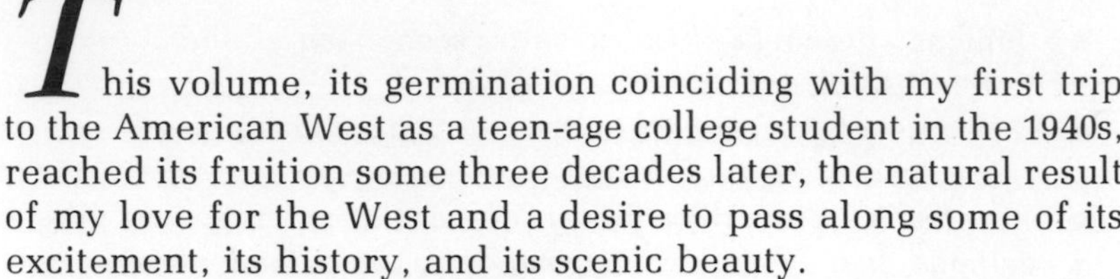

This volume, its germination coinciding with my first trip to the American West as a teen-age college student in the 1940s, reached its fruition some three decades later, the natural result of my love for the West and a desire to pass along some of its excitement, its history, and its scenic beauty.

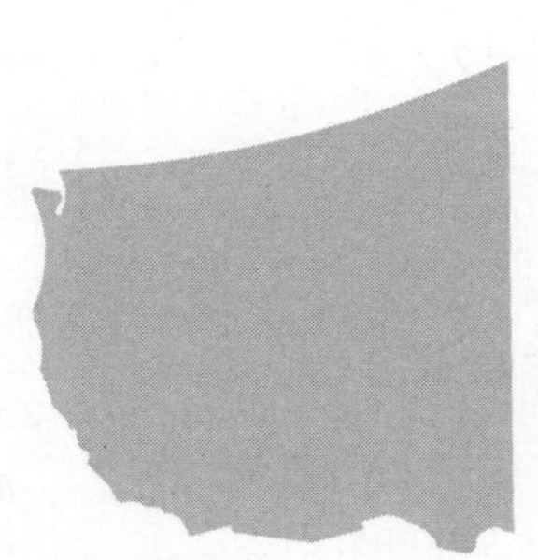

I wish to express my appreciation to those many individuals in the National Park Service and the U.S. Forest Service who cooperated generously, and to the various state agencies concerned with tourism, and to the many chambers of commerce and historical societies that provided graphics as well as assistance with the text.

Of the greatest help—and without whom the deadlines could not have been met—was my research assistant, Yvonne Shepardson. I am also grateful to another western traveler, Jon Bower, who read the manuscript and offered many worthwhile and important suggestions.

ACKNOWLEDGMENTS

The author wishes to thank the individuals and agencies listed below for permission to reproduce the photographs appearing on the pages specified: Ronald F. Ruhoff, p. 30; Wyoming Travel Commission, pp. 35, 37, 38, 40, 42, 45, 46, 51, 53; National Park Service, pp. 56, 167, 168, 171, 176, 179, 180, 184-185, 205; Utah Travel Council, pp. 79, 84, 91, 93, 98; Utah Tourist and Publicity Council (Forest Service), 82; Utah Tourist and Publicity Council (Hal Rumel), 86, 92; Utah Tourist and Publicity Council (Frank Jensen), 95, 99; Utah Tourist and Publicity Council (Parker Hamilton), 97; Idaho Department of Commerce and Development, 233, 235, 236, 240, 244-245, 248; Idaho Department of Parks (W. M. Beckert), 250; Allan E. Miller, 49; Montana Highway Commission, 59, 63, 66, 68, 71, 77; U. S. Forest Service, 60, 73, 74, 196, 223, 239, 253; New Mexico Department of Development, 107, 119; Arizona State Department of Economic Planning and Development, 124, 126, 129, 137, 138, 141, 142; Flagstaff Chamber of Commerce, 130; Nevada State News Bureau, State Department of Economic Development, 146; Reno News Bureau, 148, 149; Las Vegas News Bureau, 153, 161, 165; California Office of Tourism, 172, 187; Washington State Department of Commerce and Economic Development, 190, 191, 195, 197, 199, 201, 202, 207, 208; Charlie and Jo Larson, 209; Oregon State Highway Department, 212, 213, 215, 216, 219, 221, 225, 226, 228, 231; Oregon State Highway Commission, 218; Boyd Thomas, 246-247. Maps are by Gene Coulter.

INTRODUCTION

We are in a land of superlatives, of ghosts and giants, of great orange sunsets, of snow-laden peaks, of wild rivers in mile-deep canyons, of shadowy caverns cloaked in mystery and legend, of crashing surf against knifelike cliffs, of forests deep and silent, of cool, azure lakes cushioned in the lap of mountain valleys and vast horizon-to-horizon high-country parks.

We are in the many million-acred land of the American West, extending from the fast-rising foothills of the Colorado Rockies through the canyons and deserts of Utah to the sharp face of the Sierra, across the lush and fertile valley of California to the variegated shore of the Pacific. It is, in New Mexico, the land of enchantment; in Colorado, the land of the fragile columbine; in Montana, the big sky country. Then, too, there is wonderful Wyoming or California, the Golden State. It is a land where a man can still be lonely, where he can stand on a mountain peak and look for a hundred miles without a village, a town, a megalopolis, a television antenna, or a multicolored billboard to interrupt his view. It is a place where a man can walk for a week in the wilderness, where the only sounds are blue jay screams, chipmunk chattering, mountain stream laughter, or wind whispering through the pines. It is a place where man can visit the past, and observe the Indians at home in their pueblos, or tending their sheep in Monument Valley. He can struggle up the ladders into the cliff dwellings at Mesa Verde and stroll along the street in front of the O.K. Corral in Tombstone or pan gold in Clear Creek on his approach to Central City, or hike for miles along the Oregon Trail and read the names of pioneers on monuments and gravestone markers.

The American West is a geographical giant. The eleven states included in this book represent more than one-third of the land area of the forty-eight contiguous states, but only 16 percent of their population (and 10 percent of this is represented by California's 20 million). A mere century ago the West was frontier country, much of it unexplored and still in territorial status, with a vigilante style of law and order, and prospectors leading burros into the rugged mountains to seek their fortunes in gold and silver. The Indians were ever present, determined to defend their rights to the land that had always been their hunting grounds. John Wesley Powell had barely explored the canyons of the Colorado, and Ferdinand Hayden's party of stalwart surveyors, accompanied by photographer William Henry Jackson, were fording rushing rivers and climbing rugged peaks to record the nature of the land for the United States government.

This is a young country, in white man's terms, drenched with history and cloaked in beauty. It is too vast, too varied, too expansive to be covered in a single volume, and certainly too gigantic to be absorbed by the traveler in a week, a month, or a year.

I've lived in the West for twenty-five years, a transplanted easterner, as are most of my generation who are now westerners. I've traveled the eleven western states, crisscrossing some of them perhaps a dozen times, spending years in a few and months in several. But I'm not an expert on the West, for there is no such animal. And I have not tried, in this book, to classify the West or to suggest a ten-day tour from point to point. It's an informal approach, a personal kind of guide about places that have some special appeal—sometimes historical, sometimes scenic, sometimes as a favorite fishing or hunting spot.

The selection of ten points of interest in each of the eleven states, as well as the restriction to eleven states, was an arbitrary choice in part, but with validity, for this book is intended as a companion volume to other more comprehensive guidebooks available for each of the states. It provided a challenge, that of choosing the most spectacular, the most unusual, the most exciting, or the most enjoyable places to visit. In many cases, I've suggested various side trips to other nearby points, not for the obvious reason that they were in the vicinity, but because they are worthwhile attractions in themselves.

The reader will soon discover that most of the trips are designed for family enjoyment, with occasional inclusion of places for those individuals with special interests: fishing, hunting, rock hunting, cave exploring, white water running, backpacking, or mountain climbing. Transcending these specifics is the appeal of the dramatic, beautiful, history-laden American West to those who are intrigued by travel and who love the grandeur of the limitless outdoors.

To tour the West is to be the adventurer, the Lewis and Clark or the Escalante of yesterday, and retracing the footsteps of the pioneer and the prospector provides a warm handclasp with our American heritage.

roaming in

Colorful Colorado is a state that boasts of deep blue mountain skies all the year round. Here masses of rich, golden aspen burst into full color in September and October, brilliant green carpets gently rolling meadows at altitudes above 10,000 feet, and white billows of clouds portend a brief, high-country shower. A 400-mile range of snow-capped peaks towers above all; while in the furrows and the valleys lie clear, deep, azure lakes inhabited by flashing rainbow trout. From a lonely pinnacle, the visitor sees a vast panorama of multihued wild flowers: deep reds, purples, yellows, pinks, lavenders.

Colorado is the land of rugged mountains, the heart of the Rockies, with 1,143 peaks reaching higher than 10,000 feet and with more than fifty giants towering above the 14,000-foot level.

This is a land of legend—of gold and silver and ghosts. Ever widening highways wind through and around the historic towns of Georgetown, Leadville, Steamboat Springs, Durango, Cortez, and Silverton. And byroads snake uneasily along mountain shelves to Tincup and Cripple Creek and Victor, to Creede and Central City and Blackhawk. This is the land of the men who struck it rich, the land of Haw Tabor and Baby Doe and the Face on the Barroom Floor.

Here the adventurer can seek out the wilderness in Routt National Forest or in the Uncompahgre Scenic Region, or wind his way up the precarious Virginia Canyon Road to Central City. Traveling east to west along the southern part of the state, the wanderer can visit huge mountains of shifting sand (the Great Sand Dunes) and continue to Durango for a trip into yesterday via the Durango to Silverton narrow-gauge railroad. Just a few miles west of Durango he can explore the most famous Indian ruins in the United States at Mesa Verde National Park.

This is Colorado, the colorful state.

Fish Creek Falls near Steamboat Springs, Colora

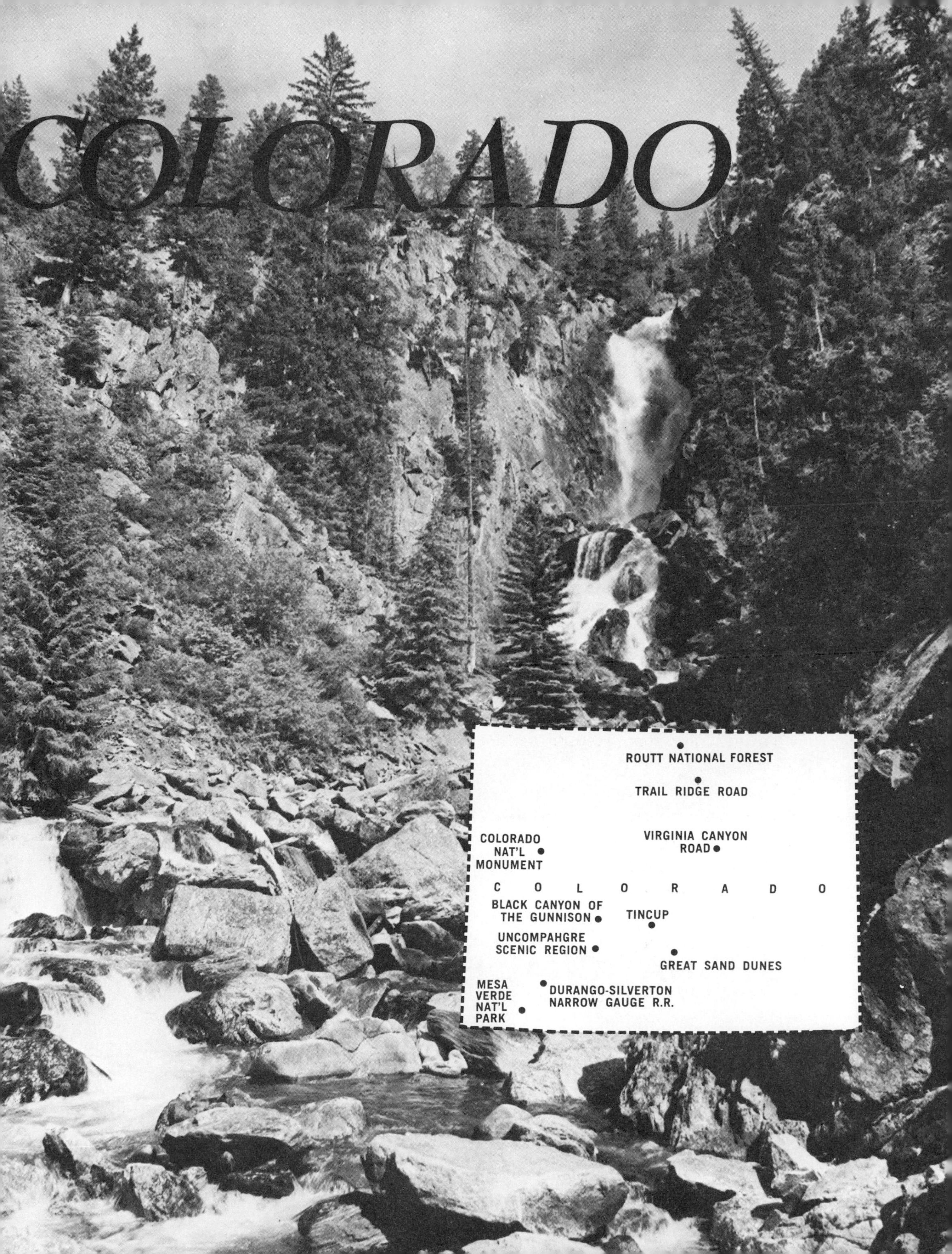
COLORADO
ROUTT NATIONAL FOREST
TRAIL RIDGE ROAD
COLORADO NAT'L MONUMENT
VIRGINIA CANYON ROAD
C O L O R A D O
BLACK CANYON OF THE GUNNISON
TINCUP
UNCOMPAHGRE SCENIC REGION
GREAT SAND DUNES
MESA VERDE NAT'L PARK
DURANGO-SILVERTON NARROW GAUGE R.R.

Elk River in Box Canyon, Colorado

hunting and trapping land of the mountain man

ROUTT NATIONAL FOREST

The stepping-stone to the rugged isolation of Routt National Forest is Steamboat Springs in northern Colorado. From Denver, take U.S. 40 west, through Idaho Springs and over Berthoud Pass (11,314 feet), descend into the broad valley of the Fraser River and Middle Park. At Granby the highway swings west again, then winds its way through narrow Byers Canyon at the base of spectacular orange cliffs. The route crosses the Continental Divide for the second time at Muddy Pass and starts its ascent to a third crossing at Rabbit Ears Pass (9,680 feet), named for the long, earlike formation at the top of Rabbit Ears Peak. From this point the highway starts its descent into Yampa Valley, affording some tremendous views as the road switchbacks its way down the long slope, crossing the eastern boundary of Routt National Forest en route.

At 160 miles the highway enters Steamboat Springs, a sleepy mountain town that comes to life when the snow begins to fall and where children are taught to ski on the slopes of Mt. Werner and Howelsen Hill as soon as they have learned to walk. In the immediate vicinity are some 150 medicinal springs, with water temperatures varying from 58 to 152 degrees. The town was named when early pioneers, hearing the sounds of the bubbling springs, compared them to the chugging of a steamboat.

In summer, Steamboat Springs is the heart of some of the best trout fishing in the state and in the fall is the gateway to excellent deer and elk hunting country.

The region of Routt National Forest was Indian country. Long before the coming of the white man, many Indian tribes ventured into the Yampa Valley to drink the mineral spring water, to hunt, fish, and trap. The mountain men came to the forests teeming with wildlife, the many streams and alpine lakes creating ideal conditions for beaver. Between 1825 and 1842 William Ashley, William and Milton Sublette, Pegleg Smith, Jim Baker, Kit Carson, and Jim Bridger were explorers of this wild land.

In 1862, when Joseph Hahn discovered gold north of Steamboat Springs, the first permanent settlers moved into the area. But it was not gold country and prospectors gave way to ranchers and farmers who found the rich Yampa Valley to their liking.

Within Routt National Forest is the Mt. Zirkel-Dome Peak Wilderness Area, some 80 square miles of spectacular alpine scenery, and dozens of high country lakes. As decreed by Congress, this region remains in its natural wild and primitive state, untouched by man's power-driven mechanical machines. There are no roads and no motor vehicles are permitted. Only trails have been developed by the Forest Service so that the area can be used and enjoyed, but not destroyed.

One of the more accessible campgrounds and a takeoff point for some exciting trails into the Wilderness Area is Seedhouse, located 28 miles north and east of Steamboat Springs. Take U.S. 40 west for 2 miles and turn right. The route

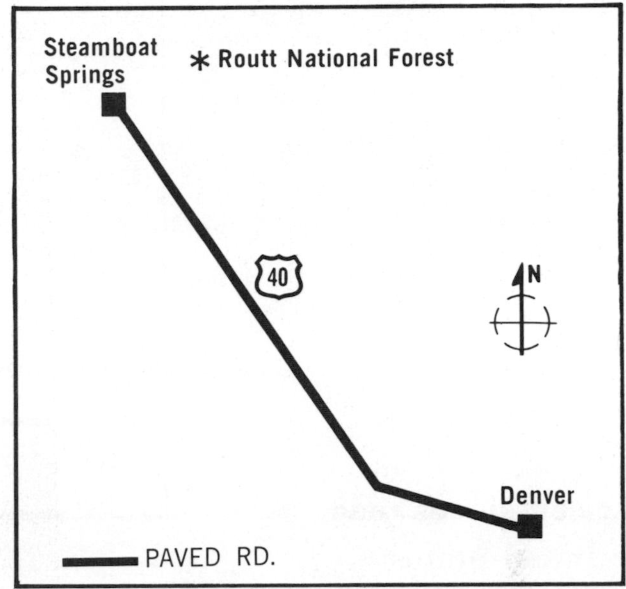

follows the Elk River up the canyon toward Hahn's Peak. At 20 miles (from Steamboat Springs), turn right on Forest Service road 1951 and continue approximately 8 miles to Seedhouse Campground. From here trails take off to the north along the North Fork of the Elk River, crossing into the Wilderness at Diamond Park and continuing to Dome Peak; and east to Mica Lake and Big Agnes Mountain. There are numerous opportunities for excellent fishing all along the trail.

Two trails across the Continental Divide are located in the Forest. One, about 12 miles long, starts at the Continental Divide on Rabbit Ears Pass, going north to Buffalo Pass. The other, some 25 miles long, starts at Buffalo Pass and proceeds north along the Divide to Three Island Lake and on to Seedhouse Campground.

An interesting trip by passenger car can be taken by continuing north past the junction with Forest Road 1951 to Hahn's Peak country, one of the best hunting and fishing areas in the state. The town of Hahn's Peak, at the foot of the mountain by the same name, was named for Joseph Hahn, a prospector who perished while attempting to cross the Gore Range in 1866. With the discovery of gold, Hahn's Peak became the most important community and was selected as the seat of Routt County in 1879. The county seat was moved to Steamboat Springs in 1912, after the decline in gold activity ended the boom in Hahn's Peak.

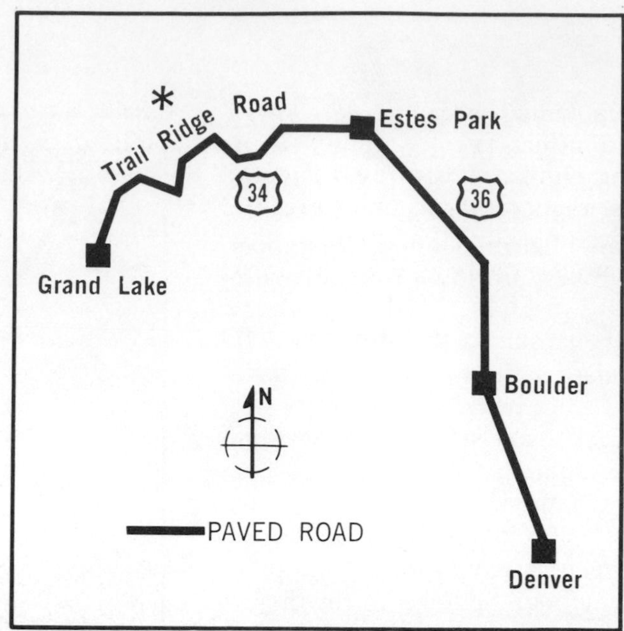

highest continuous road in the United States

TRAIL RIDGE ROAD

Trail Ridge Road, the highest continuous automobile road in the United States, winds its way through Rocky Mountain National Park from Estes Park on the east to Grand Lake on the west. From Denver, take the Denver-Boulder Turnpike (U.S. 36) to Boulder (27 miles), continuing on U.S. 36 through Lyons to Estes Park (38 miles). There is a junction here with U.S. 34, which leads to the Fall River entrance and the starting point for Trail Ridge Road. An alternate route from Estes Park is via State 36 to the Beaver Meadows entrance.

Climbing over 5,000 feet from the valley at Estes Park to 12,183 feet, the road's highest point, it is one of the most spectacular highways on the North American continent. Originally an old Indian trail used by the Ute and Cheyenne on hunting expeditions, Trail Ridge was opened to automobile traffic in the early 1930s. As it winds and twists its way ever upward, the panoramic views of the jagged peaks of the Never Summer Mountains and the Mummy Range become ever more dramatic. Once past timberline, the route emerges into the windswept tundra, a carpet of delicate wild flowers covering the high, rocky soil.

From Forest Canyon Overlook the deep, forested gorge is a sweeping vista, dotted here and there by beautiful, blue mountain lakes, unspoiled by the hand of man. As the route nears the summit, there is a parking area high above Iceberg Lake, so called because it is at least partially covered with ice all year long. Then, a half-mile farther on, the road reaches 12,183 feet and starts its descent. At the junction with Fall River Road is the Trail Ridge visitor center, with information concerning the park, a restaurant, and a gift shop.

From this point, the road drops quickly, making a series of tight switchbacks along the ledge cut into the mountainside. The view of the valley below is unforgettable, with the pine-covered slopes encompassing the flat, green meadows, dotted with beaver dams along the meandering headwaters of the North Fork of the Colorado River.

At Timber Creek Campground the floor of the valley is reached and the road becomes fairly level as it parallels the Colorado, sometimes at its side, sometimes winding through a tree-lined wilderness.

Grand Lake, Colorado's largest natural body of water, is just outside the park. It is a popular resort, with boating and water-skiing facilities.

As spectacular as Trail Ridge Road may be, hiking affords an opportunity to visit scenic spots not seen from the highway. The Bear Lake and Glacier Gorge areas are both good starting points for short hikes into the numerous lakes. Other trails which are not difficult start from the Cub Lake and Fern Lake trailheads.

Over the years, Rocky Mountain National Park has become increasingly popular with mountain climbers. Longs Peak, 14,256 feet high, is a favorite and offers several routes to its summit, providing climbs of varying difficulty. All climbers must register at the chief ranger's office, and no solo climbs are permitted.

Seven campgrounds are located in the park, with stays limited to 14 days. Fishing is permitted in most of the streams and lakes, but a Colorado license is required.

The park is open all year, but Trail Ridge Road is closed beyond Hidden Valley, a popular ski area, from late October to the end of May.

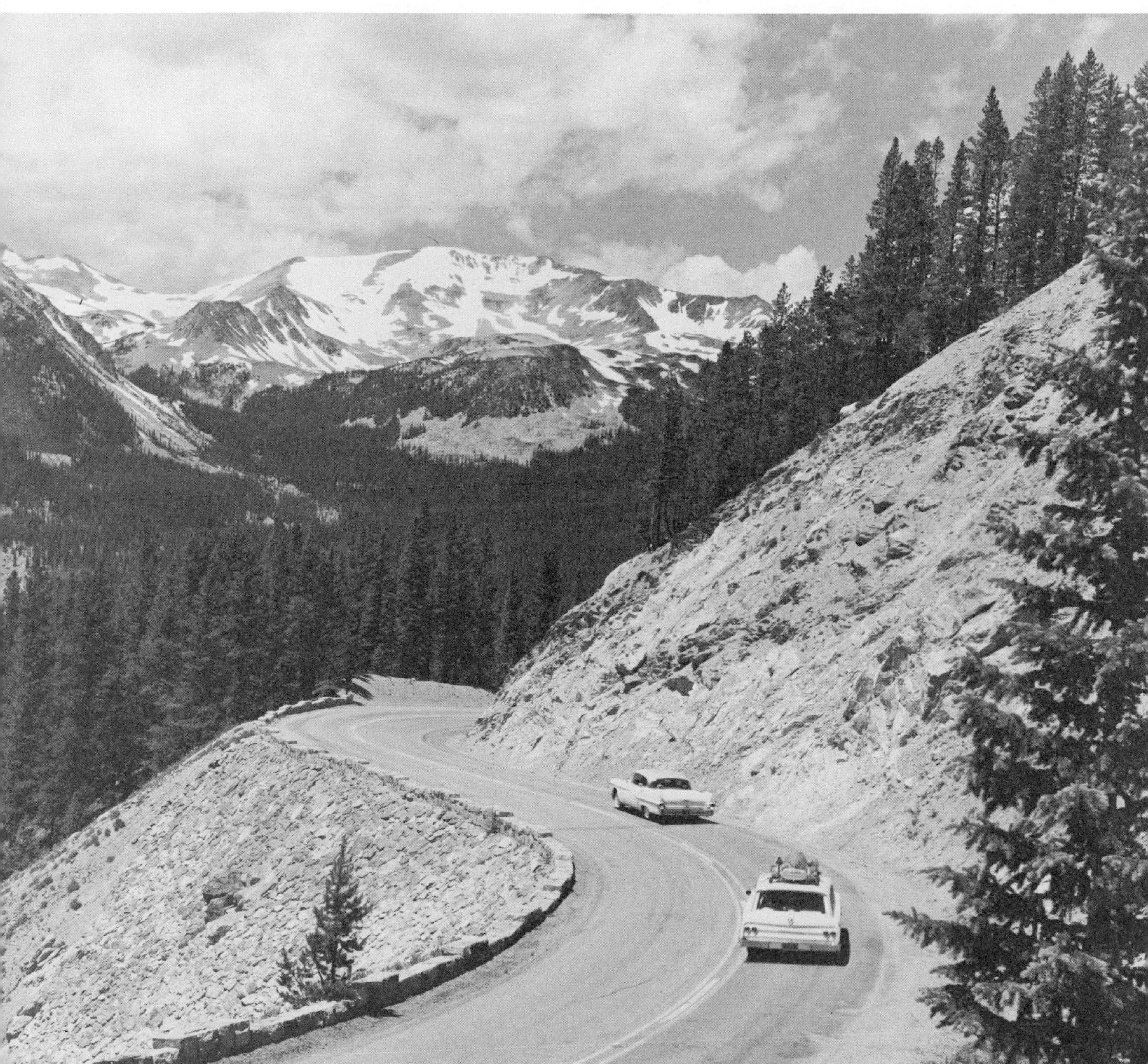

Trail Ridge Road, Colorado

stamping ground of dinosaurs and prehistoric Indians

COLORADO NATIONAL MONUMENT

Colorado National Monument in the western part of the state is a short drive west from Grand Junction on State 340 (4 miles).

Including 27 square miles of sheer-walled canyons, giant monoliths, and weirdly shaped formations of deep red sandstone, the monument also offers spectacular views of distant Grand Mesa and the fertile valleys surrounding

Colorado National Monument

Miracle Rock in Glade Park

Grand Junction. The road twists its way around and sometimes through massive 500-foot cliffs, and along winding canyon rims over a thousand feet above the valley floor.

Known scientifically as the Uncompahgre Highland, the monument is a result of a great upwarp in the earth's crust which subsequently has been worn down by the erosive forces of wind, water, heat, and cold. As the highland was eaten away, streams and winds carried sediments into the lowlands or seas on either side. It was this slow, persistent action over the centuries that formed the corridorlike canyons lined with sheer cliffs, the towering monoliths, and the strange rock formations. In the process, dinosaur bones over 100 million years old have been exposed, petrified logs laid bare, and colorful stones washed out. Evidence has been found on the canyon floors that prehistoric Indians once wandered about the area.

Several short foot trails are located in the monument, one of the most rewarding leading from Rim Rock Drive to Liberty Cap, a peak providing a spectacular view to the east. A trail also starts at Coke Ovens, continuing along Monument Canyon past the Monolith Parade, Kissing Couple, and Independence Monument.

The Ute Indians were the first modern inhabitants of the monument, and possibly the first white men to observe it were members of the Escalante expedition, which, according to Escalante's journal, passed near the site about August 27, 1776.

How it became a national monument is a story that belongs to John Otto, a trailblazer who built roads and trails throughout the area, then turned to publicizing the wonders of the place by writing hundreds of letters, both to individuals and newspapers, urging that it be set aside as a scenic area. By 1907 he had aroused sufficient interest for a petition to the Secretary of the Interior, and in 1911 President Taft signed the proclamation, naming John Otto as its first custodian.

Another unusual wonder of nature, Miracle Rock, is reached by leaving Rim Rock Drive near the east entrance at Cold Shivers Point and driving west for 6 miles to Glade Park. An unpaved road leads to Miracle Rock, a tremendous reddish formation balanced precariously on an impossibly small point. So top-heavy does it appear that the awe-struck observer is convinced that this 12,000-ton boulder will tumble down the sheer canyon walls at any moment. The Rock is 60 to 70 feet tall, and overlooks from its 1,000-foot-high perch on the edge of a precipice, a rich and fertile valley extending north as far as the sandstone walls of the Colorado Monument.

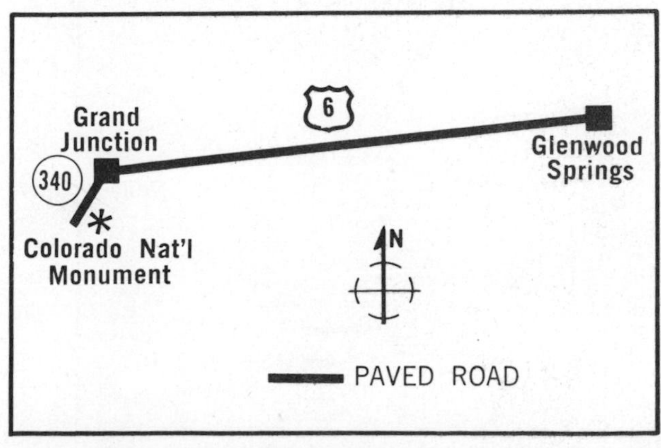

a harrowing

one-time stagecoach route

VIRGINIA CANYON

With Denver as the starting point for the adventure tour of the old Virginia Canyon stagecoach route between Idaho Springs and Central City, take U.S. 6 west to Idaho Springs, a forty-minute jaunt over the foothills of the Rockies. From the top of Floyd Hill the snow-capped panorama of the front range comes into view. Take the first Idaho Springs exit from U.S. 6, continue into the historic mining town, and turn right up a graded street. Almost immediately, the route starts its steep ascent up the mountain slope, a serpentine gash in the gold-filled hills. It's a hair-raising trip, even for the natives, but is safe enough for a passenger car with a careful driver.

The road is narrow, with a continuous series of sharp switchbacks and with no guard rails. The shelf road runs between steep rocky cliffs on one side and a sheer dropoff into Virginia Canyon on the other. Staying to the right, even on the outside, is prudent, for it is a two-way road. Sounding the horn at each of the blind, reverse turns around the mountain slopes is also recommended. Fortunately, the road is seldom used and rarely do two cars moving in opposite directions meet. In this event, it's necessary to look for a turnout area, since most of the route is too narrow to allow safe passing.

As the road continues upward the view constantly changes, the vistas becoming more sweeping and more spectacular. The road twists higher and higher, and the town of Idaho Springs, directly below, appears smaller and smaller with each new turn.

Toward the top of Pewabic Mountain are dozens of old gold mines, none of which are in business today. Some are hardly more than a simple man-size opening, painfully and tediously dug out by a lonely prospector who trudged up this same trail with a burro at his side. But there are the remains, too, of elaborate, million-dollar producers that have left behind great reddish yellow mine tailings spilling down hundreds of feet from the mine above, scars of a flourishing yesterday.

There are occasional pulloff parking areas close to some of the diggings, offering an opportunity for some exploring and some rock collecting from the environs of the mine. The open tunnels and shafts should be avoided, however. From the trails to the mines a mighty mountain range looms behind the valley, dominated by 14,264-foot Mount Evans, which can be conquered via the highest automobile road in the United States.

After crossing the ridge of Pewabic Mountain, the road dips down the Russell Gulch, the site of one of the earliest gold discoveries in this "richest square mile on earth." From this point on, the road is literally paved with gold, since it was surfaced using materials from the hundreds of gold dumps in the region.

Minutes later the up-and-down fabulous Central City unfolds, presenting an adventure in itself. One of the most famous of Colorado's mining towns, it has been restored and is noted for its summer opera and play festivals, featuring world-renowned artists. A walk up Eureka Street is strenuous, but enlightening, as virtually every building includes a plaque describing its history. The highlights are the Opera House and the Teller House, with its noted *Face on the Barroom Floor*, painted on the Teller bar floor in 1936 by Herndon Davis, who was inspired by Hugh Antoine d'Arcy's ballad, "The Face Upon the Floor." It has become a part of Central City's legend.

Not as harrowing, but offering some spectacular scenery, the route back (State 119) leads to Blackhawk, then down North Clear Creek Canyon to the junction with U.S. 6 and 40 in Denver.

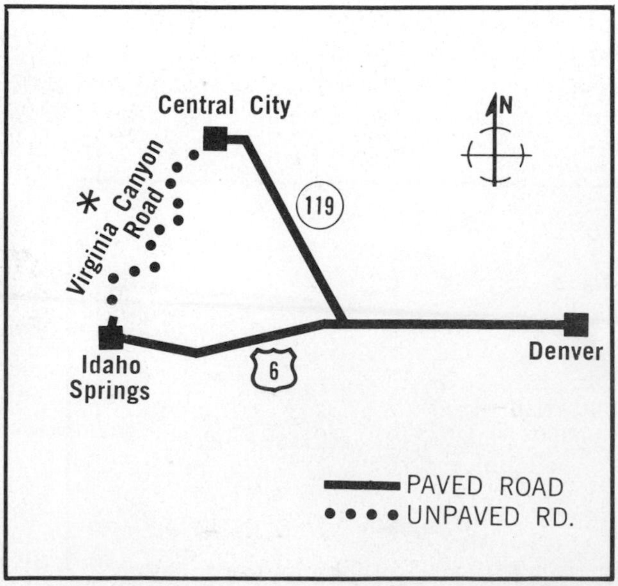

Central City
N
Virginia Canyon Road
119
Idaho Springs
6
Denver
PAVED ROAD
UNPAVED RD.

Central City, Colorado

TELLER HOUSE
MACHINERY CO
OWL

rough-and-ready
boom town
of the gold rush days

TINCUP

From Gunnison, couched at the footsteps to the towering San Juans, the trip to the ghost town of Tincup is 35 miles. Swing northeast on State 135 proceeding to Almont. Turn right at the trading post and push along the winding, graveled byway ever upward, paralleling in serpentine fashion the rushing Taylor River to Tincup (originally Tin Cup).

Some residents still live in the semideserted town that vibrated with the raucous sounds of a booming mining camp in 1885, when it boasted a population of 6,000 along with its gold and silver veins that made rags-to-riches dreams come true almost daily. The constant throb of activity centered around Frenchie's saloon, where the gambling stakes were high, the girls pretty, and the whiskey plentiful. Miners from the entire Gunnison area migrated to Tincup on Friday nights to shake the dust off their boots at a dance or to gamble away the rich rewards of a week's diggings.

The town's fame as a rowdy brat among mountain settlements grew until it challenged Leadville and Creede, two of Colorado's wildest camps of the period. Gangsters staffed the city offices with their stooges, and each new sheriff —there were several short-lived careers—was on notice that his term in office would end abruptly if he arrested anyone whose name appeared on the "protected" list.

First called Tin Cup Camp, a moniker bestowed after a miner was observed carrying his hoard of gold dust in a tin cup, the community was incorporated under the name of Virginia City. Almost immediately the hue and cry was heard throughout the San Juans to change the name, the main argument being that another Virginia City already existed in Colorado. A meeting of the town board was called, but the hot-tempered miners could come to no agreement. Finally the United States Post Office Department ended the rift by approving the name Tin Cup. At its peak, the town was considered the silver and gold mining center of southwest Colorado. The Gold Cup mine, which produced over $7,000,000 during its reign, was the wealthiest. But prosperity came and went, the population rising and falling with the opening or closing of the mines.

A few year-round residents who now keep this tiny community from becoming a true ghost town are hardy individuals, much like the early settlers who bored into the rich mountainsides of the San Isabel National Forest for treasures of silver and gold.

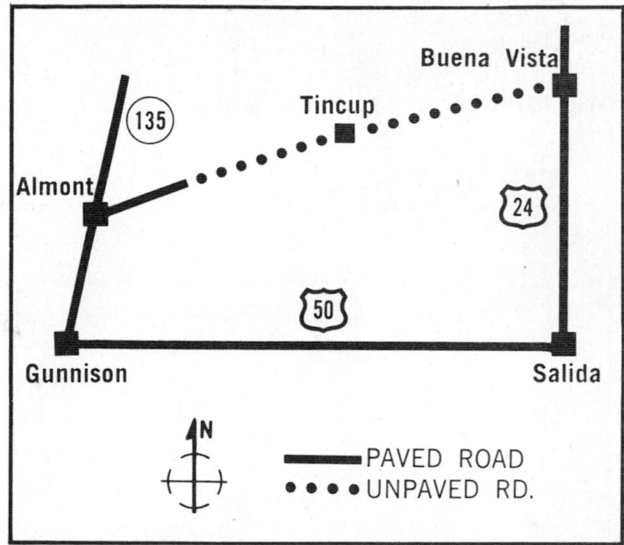

Most of the early cabins, business houses, saloons, and bawdy establishments have disappeared, but a few buildings still stand in tribute to Tincup's colorful past. Perhaps the most interesting remnant of bygone days is the cemetery south of the community. The graveyard is located on four knolls, including one each for the Protestant, Catholic, and Jewish faiths. The fourth—and by far the most popular—was for those who had no religion except survival and, ultimately, lost even that.

For exciting variety, the rugged country around Tincup offers over 100 miles of unposted trout fishing streams. Without venturing out of sight of the town, some excellent catches can be made in Willow Creek, running behind the town's main street. But, to get away from it all, the adventurer-angler can hike deep into the mountains in virtually any direction and bring back his limit of brook or rainbow.

On the return trip, there are options for those who prefer the excitement and grandeur of rugged Cumberland Pass, with an opportunity to visit the ghost towns of Pitkin and Ohio City before joining U.S. 50 a few miles east of Gunnison.

A third route, for the four-wheeler only, is over Tincup Pass, past Mirror Lake and over the summit into the ghost town of St. Elmo, continuing to drop down on Chaffee County Road 90 to Mt. Princeton Hot Springs, eventually joining U.S. 285 at Nathrop, a few miles south of Buena Vista.

one of the great wild gorges of the world

BLACK CANYON OF THE GUNNISON

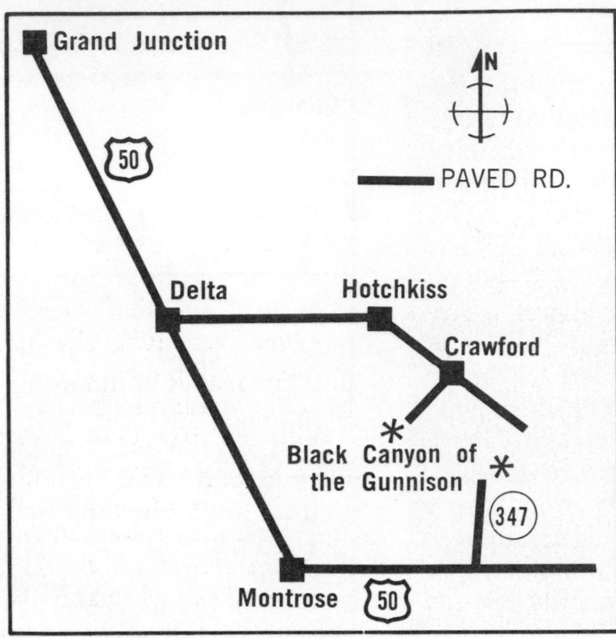

Black Canyon of the Gunnison, Colorado

The Black Canyon of the Gunnison, one of the most rugged and spectacular canyons in the West, has two approaches—one leading to the north rim and the other to the south rim. From Grand Junction, proceed southeast on U.S. 50 to Delta (41 miles), turn left on State 92, continuing through Hotchkiss (16 miles) and bearing right to Crawford (12 miles). Approximately 1.5 miles beyond, a side road (right) leads to the Black Canyon on the north rim. To reach the south rim, continue on U.S. 50 through Delta to Montrose (21 miles), turn left and continue on U.S. 50 to State 347 (6 miles), then left for 5 miles to the Black Canyon.

Starting near Sapinero in western Colorado, an ever deepening gorge cut by the Gunnison River extends westward for about 50 miles. The deepest and most spectacular part of this gorge lies within Black Canyon of the Gunnison National Monument.

One of the great wild canyons of the world, the depth ranges from 1,730 feet to 2,425 feet, while the width narrows to 1,300 feet at the rim and as little as 40 feet at the bottom. The rim drive, along a good portion of its 10-mile length, includes numerous exciting overlooks with excellent photographic possibilities. Several foot trails lead from the rim to the bottom of the Black Canyon, so named because of the lichen-covered, black-stained walls that in places are never touched by the sun because of the depth of the narrow canyon.

The starkness of the canyon walls is emphasized by the abundance of vegetation on the rim. Most of the monument is characterized by a cover of mountain brush, especially Gambel oak and serviceberry, but there are also several well-developed stands of pinyon-juniper woodland in the higher sections. Gnarled old pinyons and junipers on the rims have been estimated to be from 467 to 742 years old, with one giant pinyon on the north rim near Serpent Point which is probably even older.

The monument area is one of the last strongholds in Colorado of the Rocky Mountain big-

horn sheep and occasionally (it is a sight to remember), they may be observed fleet-footing along the precipitous ledges of the gorge. Mule deer are abundant, and muskrat, mink, and beaver live along the river. There are also coyotes and bobcats, and occasionally a black bear or cougar may be seen.

With the discovery of Folsom spear points in the Uncompahgre Valley and of ancient petroglyphs in the nearby countryside, archeologists are convinced that prehistoric Indians lived in the vicinity of the canyon.

Ute Indians were camping and hunting in the area when the white man arrived, but seldom went into the canyon.

Juan Maria de Rivera visited the area as early as 1765, claiming it for Spain. After the Mexican War (1847-48) this entire region became United States territory. Captain John Gunnison led an expedition through the country in 1853, but he purposely avoided the canyon itself. In 1874 an expedition of the Hayden Surveys explored the north rim, establishing several survey stations within the boundaries of the present monument.

Geologically the canyon and the surrounding terrain are a study in contrasts. For several million years the Gunnison River has been cutting through the Pre-Cambrian rock, the oldest matter in geologic time, while the hills surrounding the canyon are much more recent. During the interval of time represented, life developed from the single cell to the mammoth dinosaur.

Two campgrounds are found within the monument, one on each rim, with limited water and wood supply. Light lunches, souvenirs, and information are available at Rim House on the south rim. The monument is open all year, with park rangers stationed on both rims during the summer months.

land of waterfalls
and glacial basins

UNCOMPAHGRE SCENIC REGION

The Uncompahgre Scenic Region, encompassing some of the most rugged and beautiful country in the state, is bisected by U.S. 550 and can be reached via this highway from Durango on the south and via U.S. 50 and U.S. 550 from Grand Junction on the north. The heart of the area is located in the Silverton-Ouray-Telluride region.

Including about 10,000 acres, the scenic region is roughly one-tenth of the entire Uncompahgre National Forest. Within its boundaries are three major peaks—Mount Sneffles west of Ouray and Uncompahgre and Wetterhorn to the east, all over 14,000 feet in elevation.

Numerous trails and secondary roads wind through the entire region, offering a rare opportunity for the entire family to explore a rugged

land still virtually untouched by civilization.

The Horse Thief Trail, named for the outlaws who in frontier days drove stolen horses over this route from Colorado to Utah, rises abruptly from just north of Ouray toward a high crest of the San Juan Mountain Range. Four miles from the starting point it traverses the Bridge of Heaven, a narrow hogback that slopes very steeply nearly 2,000 feet to the floor of the valley. From this point the trail ascends to American Flats, skirts the south shoulder of the Wild Horse Peak, then descends through a forest of spruce and fir to Lake City.

The trail as far as the Bridge of Heaven is a pleasant 2-hour climb on horseback and offers a spectacular vista of the eastern edge of the region, dominated by Uncompahgre Peak. The Red Mountains, near Silverton to the south, are also visible.

Another short but extremely rugged trip takes off from Ouray to Yankee Boy Basin, named for one of the many rich mines that once operated in the area. Mountain peaks rise on three sides from 12,000 to 14,000 feet, while the cold, clear streams that drain the region cascade in a series of beautifully formed waterfalls before disappearing into the precipitous canyons above Ouray. The final leg of the 8-mile trip tests the muscle of four-wheel drive vehicles (the trip can be made on horseback), which must climb over the moraine left behind by an ancient glacier.

Yankee Boy is typical of the glacier-carved basins of the San Juan Range. A jagged line of peaks tower above the small, ice-gouged saucer. The talus slopes of weathered and disintegrated rock that cover the mountainside descend to the edge of a sapphire-colored lake fed year-round by melting snow. A trail on one side of the basin leads to an abandoned mine, while another follows a serpentine course to the top of the ridge, where it is possible to look down on Ridgeway and the Uncompahgre Valley.

An extremely interesting, though hazardous for the inexperienced, loop trip can be taken from Ouray to Telluride via the East Ridge and Black Bear Basin, then to U.S. 550 and Ouray over Ophir Pass. It is a full day's trip and can be made only by a four-wheel drive vehicle. Leaving the Million Dollar Highway (U.S. 550) at Red Mountain Pass, the road climbs quickly to East Ridge, 13,000 feet, and then descends into Black Bear Basin, named for Black Bear Mine.

From this point on, the trip is extremely hazardous and can be ended here by the less adventurous or inexperienced mountain driver. During its final descent into Telluride, the road clings to the side of a 2,000-foot escarpment. The hairpin turns are sharp and frequent, requiring exceptional skill to manipulate successfully. The face of this cliff is sprayed by water from Bridal Veil Falls, the drop being so long that the falling stream dissipates into a fine mist before reaching the bottom of the falls.

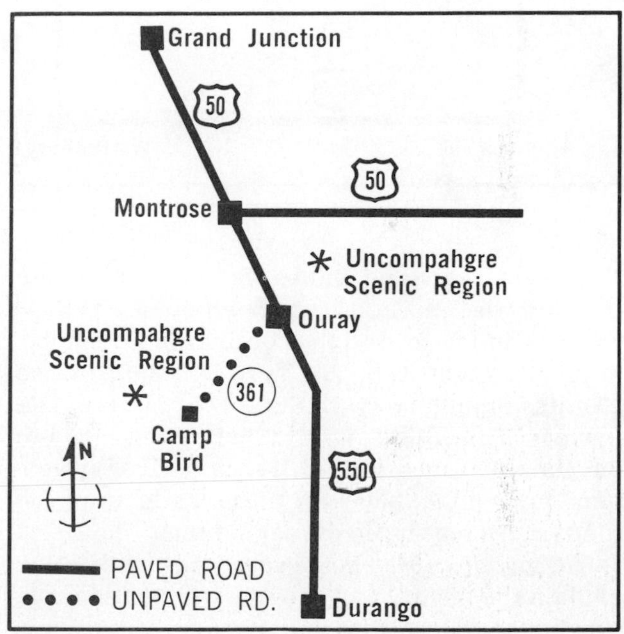

A must trip for the adventurer to Uncompahgre is the road following the Poughkeepsie Gulch and Miners Creek to Engineer Mountain, used as an early-day supply route between Lake City, Silverton, and Ouray. It skirts an old mine known as the San Juan Chief, then climbs higher into lush, open meadows. The grass is gradually replaced by alpine tundra as the road ascends Engineer Mountain. From the summit, 13,218 feet above sea level, the entire panorama of the Uncompahgre Scenic Region comes into full view. Fourteen peaks in the San Juan Range rise over 14,000 feet, and a number of them—including Uncompahgre, Wetterhorn, and Mount Sneffles—are visible from this elevated pinnacle, one of the most spectacular views in all America.

land of moving mountains

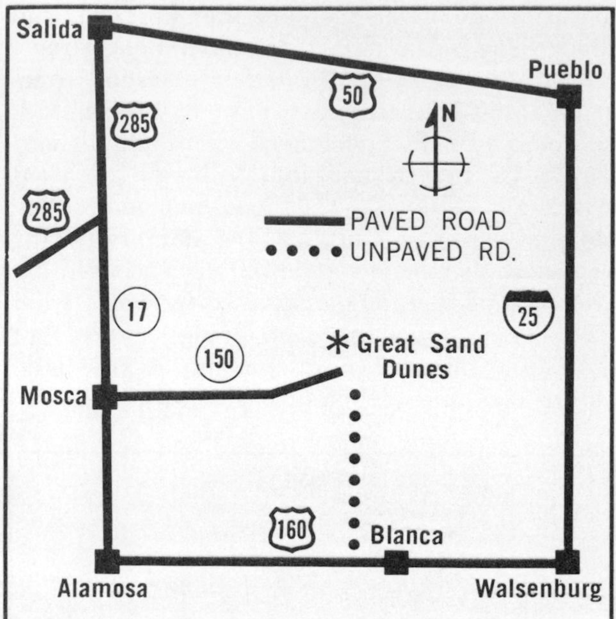

To reach Great Sand Dunes National Monument in southern Colorado from Pueblo, take U.S. 50 west 97 miles to Salida, continuing five miles to junction with U.S. 285. Turn left and proceed 27 miles to junction with State 17 at Mineral Hot Springs. Take State 17 for 35 miles and turn left on State 150 to the sand dunes. From Walsenburg, take U.S. 160 west 56 miles to unpaved road (right) leading to the sand dunes.

The visitor center has a series of exhibits that explain the history and provide information concerning the Great Sand Dunes, dedicated as a national monument in 1932.

The San Luis Valley, in which the dunes are located, is a desert receiving less than 8 inches of moisture a year. East and northeast of the valley is the abrupt wall of the Sangre de Cristo Mountains, to the west the volcanic San Juan Mountains, and to the south the San Juan Hills. At the eastern edge of this broad valley are some of the world's tallest sand dunes, piled to heights of over 700 feet.

Fed by melting snow, streams from the nearby mountains have carried sand, silt, and gravel into this arid basin for thousands of years. The desert floor of the valley, covered only sparsely with vegetation, does little to hold the light, sandy soil. Once in this mountain-ringed region, the sand and silt are exposed to the prevailing southwesterly winds which have blown the grains of sand toward the Sangre de Cristos. Reaching this barrier, the sand-filled wind sweeps upward, but the sand is too heavy to be carried on and is piled at the foot of the mountain passes.

The ceaseless winds change and constantly reshape the dunes, sometimes shifting the ridgetops of the dunes until they seem at times to lean over backwards. Day-to-day changes can be seen in the lacelike ripples that stretch across the ridges and troughs, but the dunes themselves change very little over the years.

Archeologists believe this region was occupied about 10,000 years ago by nomadic hunters. Two of their campsites which have been excavated yielded Folsom points, as well as bones from an extinct species of bison. During more recent times the Ute Indians largely controlled the valley, although Pueblos, the Apache from the south, and the Comanche, Cheyenne, and Arapaho from the east and north periodically appeared in the area.

Spaniards reached the San Luis Valley in 1779, and Lieutenant Zebulon Pike entered the Valley in the winter of 1806-07, including a description of the dune area in his journal.

A hike to the top of the dunes from the picnic area takes about three hours for the round trip, with early mornings and late afternoons most pleasant, since the sand may get hot during the middle of the day. During the summer, park naturalists give campfire programs on the natural history of the monument, and each morning they conduct nature walks to the dunes.

Accommodations within the monument are limited to a campground and a picnic area with water and a wood supply. During the summer, provisions and gasoline are available at the Dunes Outpost, one mile south of the monument.

Great Sand Dunes, Colorad

GREAT SAND DUNES

Train on the Durango-Silverton Line

traveling frontier-style in the twentieth century

DURANGO-SILVERTON NARROW GAUGE

To reach Durango, home of the depot for the Silverton train, the only narrow-gauge passenger train operating in the United States, take U.S. 160 west from Walsenburg over LaVeta Pass (9,382 feet elevation), through Alamosa and Del Norte to Durango (223 miles from Walsenburg).

A journey on the Silverton train is a scenic adventure unmatched anywhere else in the world. It is also an adventure back in time, for the entire train, from caboose to the coal-fired engine, is a part of the western frontier. And the vastness of the mountains seen from the narrow-windowed coaches would be as familiar to the hardy pioneers who rode the train in 1882 as to today's adventurer. It was in 1882 that the narrow-gauge track reached Silverton, fastest growing mining camp in the treasure-filled San Juans. In an amazing feat of construction, the tracks had been laid the 44 miles from Durango in nine months and five days, working through the howling blizzards of a high-country winter.

By the 1950s, abandonments had reduced the little frontier lines to a handful, including the Silverton, and finally it became the only narrow-gauge line carrying passengers.

For the greater part of its journey, the train traverses the center of the 2,000,000-acre San Juan National Forest, running on a daily schedule from June through early October. Following the narrow canyon of the El Rio de Las Animas (The River of Lost Souls), the Silverton provides a bewildering, minute-by-minute succession of scenic thrills—deep, silent forests, crags and canyons, sparkling waterfalls, cliffs within an arm's length on one side, and sheer drops to the river hundreds of feet below on the other.

The first train leaves each morning at 8:30, and the second train (operating only during peak periods) leaves at 9:30 A.M. Almost at once the terrain becomes rugged, isolated mountain country. At 17 miles is Rockwood, an old lumber camp and stagecoach stop, now sometimes used by winter mountain climbers trying the ascent of a triumvirate of peaks nearby: Windom (14,087 feet), Mt. Eolus (14,084 feet), and Sunlight (14,059 feet). The Silverton enters Animas Canyon Gorge at 19 miles, and begins its serpentine route along the "high line," a narrow shelf blasted out of the red granite cliffs. The river at this point is nearly 400 feet below the track.

At 22 miles is the Ah Wilderness Ranch stop. The only access to this guest ranch is by the Silverton train, on foot, or on horseback. Frequently guests at the ranch follow the train through the narrow valley on horseback for a few hundred yards. The train stops here on signal.

The train makes another stop at 23 miles to take on water at Tank Creek, and to provide the passengers an opportunity to take a brief look at the scenery and snap a few pictures.

At noon the first train arrives at Silverton, with plenty of time for lunch and sightseeing in this historic mining town. Blair Street is one of the highlights, a two-block strip that at one time boasted 40 gambling and sporting houses in operation, employing nearly 300 dance hall girls. Blair Street, with its original buildings, has been used as location for many movies.

Silverton, which can also be reached from the north by the Million Dollar Highway and from the south via U.S. 550, has become a winter playground, with thousands of acres of exciting snowmobile country, and the Kendall Mountain Ski Area located at the edge of town, noted for its nighttime skiing.

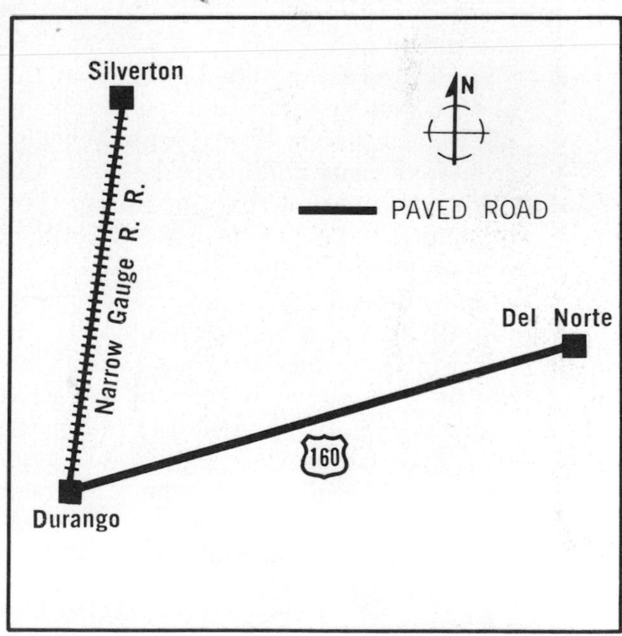

abode of the ancient cliff dwellers

From Durango in southwestern Colorado, the entrance to Mesa Verde National Park, the most significant Indian cliff dwellings in America, is 36 miles west via U.S. 160. From Cortez, the entrance is 9 miles east on U.S. 160.

For approximately 1,300 years, beginning about the time of the birth of Christ, Indians lived in and around Mesa Verde, farming, fashioning tools and household utensils, and trading with other Indian tribes. The first culture was that of the Basket Makers, from Christ's birth to A.D. 450. The second group was called the Modified Basket Makers (A.D. 450 to 750), the third the Developmental Pueblo (A.D. 750 to 1100), and fourth, the Classic Pueblo (A.D. 1100 to 1300).

The earliest Indians were a primitive people living in the Mesa Verde caves, doing some weaving and making simple tools, and growing corn and squash on the mesa. Toward the latter part of the 8th century, houses were built on the surface, on top of the mesa, although circular kivas were built underground and were used for ceremonial purposes. Pottery became more sophisticated and a crude system of irrigation was developed.

For some reason, largely unknown, the Pueblo people moved from their mesa-top pueblos to the caves about 1200, probably to achieve greater security and less risk from attack. It was during this period that the Indians began construction of the great cliff dwellings which remain today. There was a migratory movement in the 13th century, and by the end of A.D. 1300, the cliff dwellings had been completely deserted.

There is a complete road system throughout the park, enabling visitors to see many of the excavated ruins with short, self-guided hikes from the parking areas. Along the entrance road are the following five numbered stops (to avoid crossing traffic lanes, stops 1 and 2 should be made on the way in, and stops 3, 4, and 5 on the way out):

Stop 1. The Montezuma Valley Overlook provides an outstanding panoramic view of the valley and mountains to the north and west.

Stop 2. Park Point, halfway between the entrance and park headquarters, affords superb views of the entire Four Corners region (the

MESA VERDE

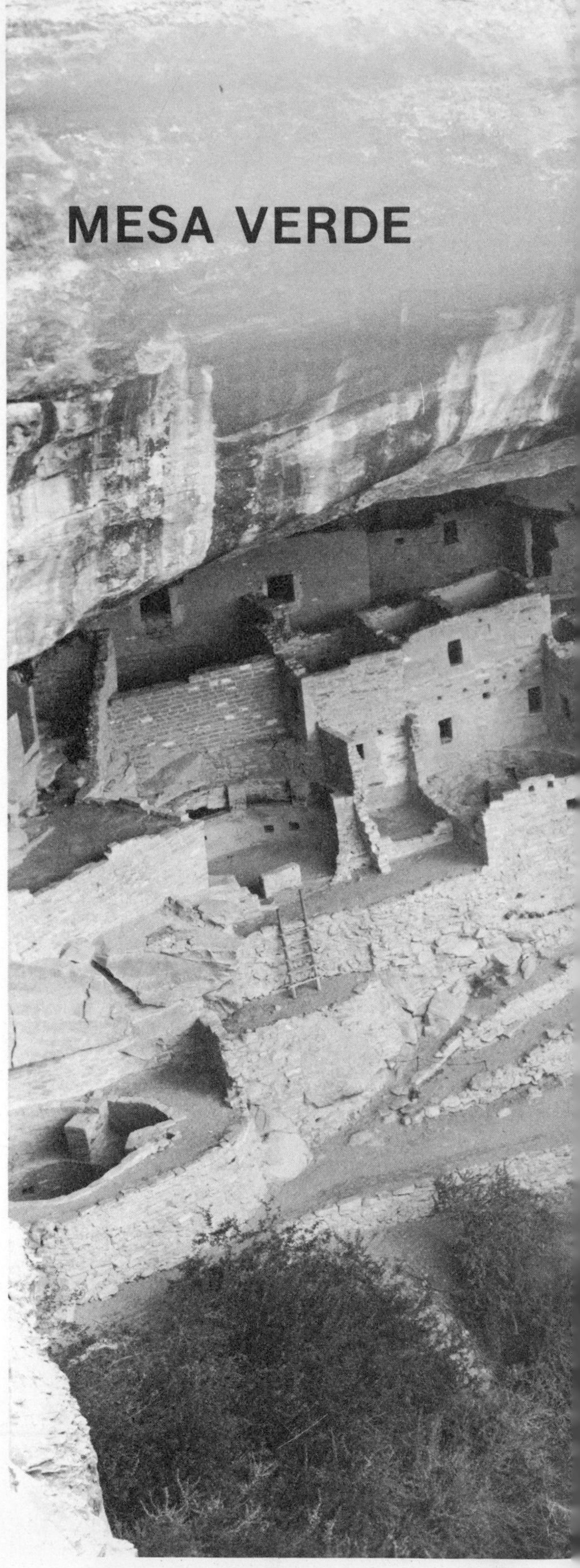

Mesa Verde Cliff Dwellings, Colorado

only place in the United States where four states—Colorado, New Mexico, Utah, and Arizona—join at a common point).

Stop 3. Cedar Tree Tower, a ceremonial structure, is reached by a half-mile hike, just north of park headquarters.

Stop 4. Far View House and Pipe Shrine House are a short distance from the main road, 4 miles north of the park headquarters. These two large mesa-top pueblos date between A.D. 1000 and 1200.

Stop 5. Mancos Valley Overlook is below Point Lookout, the towering promontory observed when entering the park.

There are two self-guiding loops of the Ruins Road Drive, totaling 12 miles. Some 10 excavated mesa-top ruins can be visited on this tour, and numerous cliff dwellings can be viewed from canyon rim vantage points.

During the summer season, park rangers conduct trips through several of the cliff dwellings, but in winter only Spruce Tree House may be visited. Campfire programs are conducted each evening from early June to September, dealing with prehistoric and modern Indians of the Southwest, as well as with the archeology, history, and natural history of the area. Hiking within the park is limited, but horseback rides to some of the lesser-known points can be arranged at Morfield Campground during the summer.

Inside the park, the Mesa Verde Company manages Far View Lodge at Navajo Hill, providing cabins and motel units from mid-May to mid-October. Morfield Campground is available for both tent and trailer camping and offers complete facilities except for utility hookups.

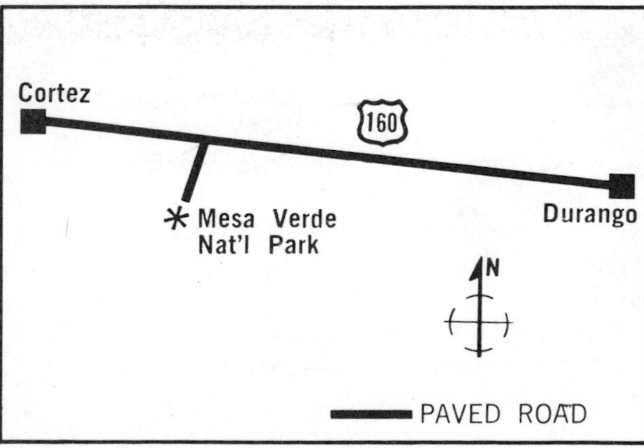

Wyoming is Big Country, a land of wide open spaces where antelope and wild horses roam and the rare golden trout abound in the lakes of the high-country wilderness. The state is the site of famous Indian battles, old forts and stagecoach stops, and gold, silver, and copper mines that yielded rich treasure until borasca overtook them. In Wyoming, the traveler can follow the rutted wagon tracks along the Oregon Trail and participate in a re-creation of the wild and woolly West at Cheyenne's fantastic Frontier Days celebration.

Averaging only four persons for each of its 97,914 square miles, Wyoming spreads across broad and lonesome prairies in the eastern part of the state, the terrain rising in the west as the Bighorns thrust skyward. And beyond, the mighty Tetons, sculptured into sheer peaks, razorlike ridges, and perilous canyons. When John C. Frémont first viewed Teton country, he wrote in his journal, "It seemed as if nature had collected all her beauties together in this one chosen place."

In the northeastern part of Wyoming rises an awesome landmark, Devils Tower, the nation's most spectacular volcanic neck. Farther south Ayers Natural Bridge spans La Prele Creek, a wonder described by Dr. Hayden as "a perfect natural bridge" when he observed it in 1870. In the northern section, close to the Montana border, the traveler discovers an exciting blend of history and scenic splendor in the Bighorn Recreation Area. With the recent completion of Yellowtail Dam, a great water highway was created, opening up via boat or rubber raft a wild and spectacular region previously seen only by the most rugged and experienced outdoorsman.

Tucked away in the extreme northwest corner of the state is Yellowstone, America's first and perhaps greatest national park, encompassing more than 2 million acres. It is a land of miracles, from its most famous landmark, Old Faithful, to its hundreds of other geysers, bubbling mud volcanoes, and the beautiful Lower Falls of the Yellowstone River.

Wyoming, the Equality State, has elbow room and western hospitality to spare.

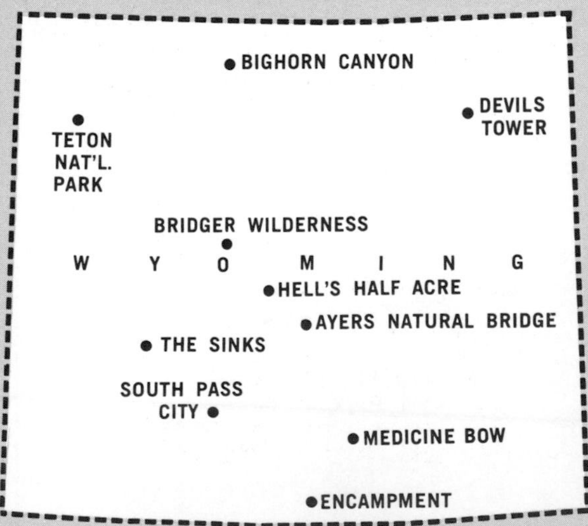

Grand Teton National P

roaming

in WYOMING

site of bloody frontier battles

The Bighorn Recreation Area in northern Wyoming and southern Montana is reached from Sheridan via U.S. 14 west 44 miles to Burgess Junction, then U.S. 14A for 54 miles, and turning right on a paved road and continuing for 12 miles. From Lovell, take U.S. 14A east for 3 miles and turn left, then proceed as above.

BIGHORN COUNTRY

Located in the heart of the Bighorn National Forest, this recreation area was established following the completion of Yellowtail Dam on the Bighorn River near the mouth of Bighorn Canyon and 45 miles southwest of Hardin, Montana. The dam formed a reservoir 71 miles long, a great water highway within rugged Bighorn Canyon, whose steep walls tower hundreds of feet above the man-made lake. For the first time, via boats or rubber rafts, this primitive backcountry can be seen and enjoyed by the average family with a flair for adventure.

The Bighorn Canyon is one of the most famous deep, water-cut gorges of the West. It was known by the white man even before William Clark of the Lewis and Clark Expedition camped at the mouth of the Bighorn in July of 1806. In the following decades fur traders used the river and canyon as part of their water route for transporting beaver and otter pelts to St. Louis. In 1866 the United States Army established Fort Smith near the mouth of the canyon to guard the Bozeman Trail. Although the dam is in Montana, most of the land area in the Yellowtail project (61 percent) is in Wyoming.

Yellowtail has proven to be one of the finest fishing areas in the Rocky Mountain West, stocked primarily with a variety of trout. Other activities available include boat trips (float trips are especially exciting), hiking, backpacking, scenic drives, and exploration of nearby caves.

All of this is within Bighorn National Forest, an area of rugged wilderness some 80 miles long and 30 miles wide, with an abundance of wild game, numerous natural and man-made lakes, and rushing, trout-filled streams. There are 58 camp and picnic grounds in the forest, most of which are accessible by car.

Before the settlement of the white man, the Sioux, Crow, and Cheyenne Indian tribes lived and hunted around the Bighorn Mountains (so named by the Indians impressed by the large numbers of Rocky Mountain sheep called bighorns because of the size of their great horns). The resentment by the Indians of the white man's intrusion led to some of the bloodiest battles of the American frontier. It was just north of the Bighorn National Forest that General Custer and his command were exterminated in the famous battle of the Little Bighorn. And in 1866 Captain Fetterman and his 81 soldiers were ambushed and slain by Red Cloud and his Ogallala Sioux in this area.

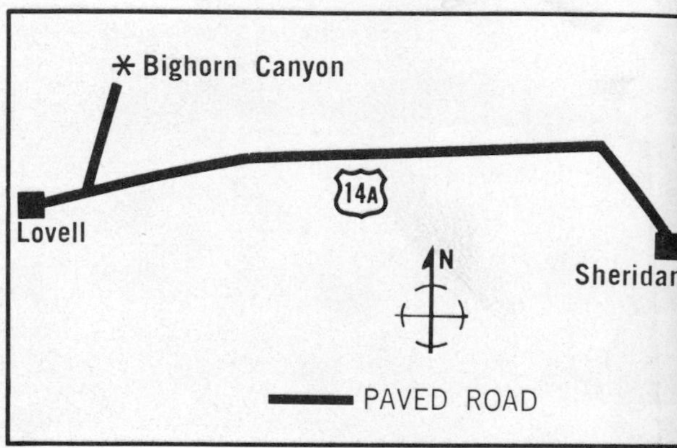

One of the great mysteries found in the forest is the prehistoric Medicine Wheel located on Medicine Mountain, reached by taking a forest service road from U.S. 14A north to 28 miles east of Lovell. This strange relic is constructed of stones laid side by side, forming an almost perfect circle 70 feet in diameter. Around the rim of the wheel are six small cairns about 2.5 feet high. In the center of the wheel is a hub, 12 feet in diameter, and around the outer edge is a circular wall two and a half feet thick. No one knows when the wheel was constructed, or what exact purpose it had, although most students of Indian history believe it had some religious significance and was a part of an Indian ritual.

Bighorn Canyon

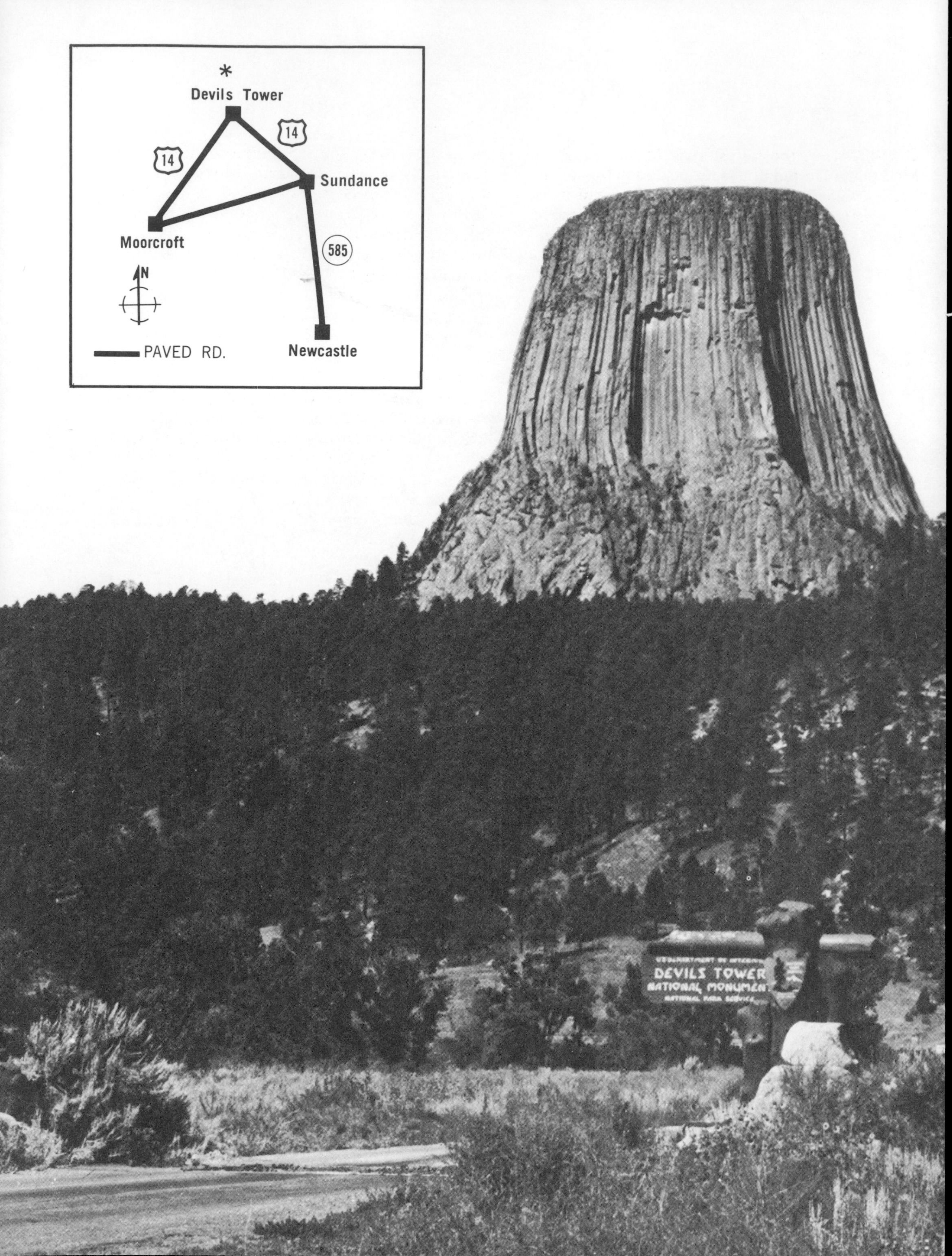

Devils Tower
14
14
Sundance
Moorcroft
585
N
PAVED RD.
Newcastle
DEVILS TOWER
NATIONAL MONUMENT

Devils Tower, the tallest rock formation of its kind in the United States, is located in the northeast corner of the state. It can be reached from Newcastle via U.S. 85 north to Four Corners (18 miles), then turning left on State 585 to Sundance (28 miles) and the junction with U.S. 14. Take U.S. 14 west to Devils Tower Junction; then go right on State 24 for six miles to Devils Tower National Monument. An alternate route from Newcastle is via U.S. 16 northwest to Moorcroft, then U.S. 14 north to Devils Tower Junction, proceeding on State 24 to the tower.

DEVILS TOWER

landmark to explorers and travelers

This gigantic stump-shaped cluster of rock columns looming over the Belle Fourche River at a meeting place of the pine forests of the Black Hills with the grasslands of the rolling plains, rises 865 feet above its wooded base and 1,280 feet above the river. Its diameter at the bottom measures 1,000 feet and that at the top 275 feet.

For centuries Devils Tower played an important role in the legend and folklore of Indian tribes. Later it became a landmark to explorers and travelers pushing their way west from the Black Hills region. And, finally, it was the first national monument in the United States, so proclaimed on September 24, 1906.

According to geologists, the tower is composed of igneous rock formed directly by the cooling and crystallization of once molten materials. One of its most striking features is its fluted form, appearing to be made of a mass of vertical, polygonal columns. In the middle part of the tower the columns are bounded by well-developed, open joints or cracks, but as the columns taper upward, the joints are more tightly compressed, the result of contraction that occurred as the rock cooled from its molten state. Erosion, principally by the Belle Fourche River, has since uncovered the tower by wearing away the softer rocks that once enveloped it.

An added attraction at the monument are the prairie dogs, living in a prairie dog town about a half-mile from the entrance and spending most of their lives around the monument enjoying the tourists.

At the visitor center are exhibits explaining the geology, history, and natural environment of the tower. A self-guiding nature trail encircles the monument, providing an opportunity to observe the tower from all directions. It is about an easy hour's walk along a trail just over a mile long.

Campsites are available in the monument, and restaurants, a general store, and post office are located within a mile from the entrance.

Devils Tower National Monument

The Grand Tetons and the Snake River

land of dramatic peaks and sightseeing trails

To reach the Grant Teton country, highlighted by one of the most spectacular mountain ranges in the world, from Rock Springs take U.S. 187 north for 188 miles, through Farson, Pinedale, and Jackson to Moose, headquarters and visitor center for Grand Teton National Park.

This 40-mile range of jagged peaks rises with dramatic suddenness out of the rolling plains of the Snake River Valley. Approaching from the south toward Jenny Lake, the meadow is a colorful wonderland of wild flowers, with broad splashes of crimson, yellow, deep purple, and brilliant green. The valley is covered with such flowers as Indian paintbrush, larkspur, scarlet gilia, balsamroot, lupine, bitterbrush, pentstemon, and purple fringe.

A circle trip can be taken by following the Jackson Hole Highway to Moran Junction (east entrance to the Park), turning left to Jackson Lake Lodge, then going south on Teton Park

Road to Moose. Rather than returning to Moose, it is possible to continue north on U.S. 287 along beautiful Jackson Lake to the north entrance and to Yellowstone National Park. As spectacular as this drive is, the best way to see the Teton country is by way of the more than 200 miles of well-maintained hiking trails, most of which start from the Jenny Lake area.

One of the more popular trails starts at the flagpole on the west side of the lake and leads to Lake Solitude. It is possible to walk around from the parking area (southeast side), but most adventurers prefer to take the motorboat that leaves from a dock near the parking area. The trail climbs upward 1,000 feet in the first four miles, to the junction of the north and south forks of Cascade Creek, with most of the climbing at the beginning. The trail then levels out as it meanders through forests and meadows. The trail roughly follows the north fork, rising steeply over the next three miles until it reaches Lake Solitude (9,024 feet). From the lake is a spectacular view of the Cathedral Group of the Tetons—Teewinot, Grand Teton, and Mt. Owen.

The Amphitheater Lake Trail from Jenny Lake is also popular, with some spectacular sweeping panoramic views of Jackson Hole en route. The trail, reached by traveling across Cottonwood Creek and continuing toward the mountains until it ends at the parking area, is about 4.5 miles long, but with a climb of 3,150 feet.

Another way of exploring the Tetons, less strenuous than hiking, is by taking the 6-hour guided raft trip 30 miles down the Snake River. Arrangements can be made through the Grand Teton Lodge Company at Moran.

All of the trail trips can be made on horseback, as part of a guided tour, and arrangements can be made at the stables at Jenny Lake.

For the experienced climber, any of the mountains in the Cathedral Group offer an exciting challenge. Climbers must register at the Jenny Lake Ranger Station, and solo climbs are not permitted.

In addition to sightseeing, the park offers excellent fishing in both the mountain streams and the many alpine lakes. Camping facilities are available in the park, and excellent accommodations are available at the Grand Teton Lodge.

At Jackson Hole is Wyoming's finest ski resort and deluxe accommodations at Teton Village. Summer or winter, the Jackson Hole aerial tramway, with a vertical rise of 4,000 feet in 2.5 miles, provides an exciting 100-mile view into three of the Rocky Mountain states—Wyoming, Montana, and Idaho.

GRAND TETON COUNTRY

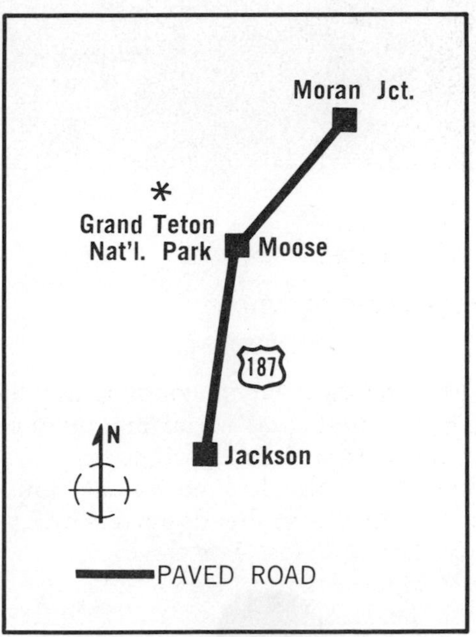

awesome bottom
of an ancient sea

HELL'S HALF ACRE

With Casper as the starting point to the adventure tour of Hell's Half Acre, a weird maze of sandstone badlands, take U.S. 20 west 40 miles to the entrance (left) to Hell's Half Acre. From Riverton proceed northeast on U.S. 26 through Shoshoni (22 miles), continuing approximately 4 miles beyond Waltman and turning right to entrance.

Though much of this 320-acre chasm of fantastic shapes lies close to the highway, it generally goes unnoticed by the motorist, since it lies several hundred feet below the horizon. Located in the flat wilderness country of central Wyoming, the region includes deep caverns, crevices, and pits as well as towers, spires, and castlelike formations.

The eastern portion, called the Devil's Kitchen, is the roughest section and at the same time the most spectacular.

Indians regarded the strange depression with superstitious awe, especially the sulphurous odors and steam originating from underground hot springs. They named it "burning mountain" and avoided it whenever possible as being a place cursed by the gods.

According to geologists Hell's Half Acre was thrust up into a surrounding sandstone formation some 60 million years ago. After centuries of erosion, the softer sandstone was eaten away, leaving the grotesque and brightly hued spires and escarpments.

There was a time in some prehistoric era when the area was the bottom of a great sea. Near its shores wandered animals long since extinct, and as they were killed or died their bones remained untouched and bleached by the sun. Fossils and skeletons have been found of beavers the size of mice, of a miniature horse with five toes, and numerous other prehistoric animals.

When Captain Bonneville first saw Hell's Half Acre, he wrote, "Here the earth is hot and cracked, in many places emitting smoke and sulphurous vapors, as if covering concealed fires."

The region cannot be fully appreciated by a casual observation. A series of foot trails wind among the strange and mystic spires and into the caverns and around the bases of the giant toadstoollike monuments and the goblin figures of rock.

Continuing west to Moneta (33 miles), a dirt road (left) leads to Castle Gardens (18 miles), another strange geologic formation with white-ledged cliffs and varicolored sandstone cones, minarets, and campaniles that rise almost 100 feet. The cliff walls are covered with Indian picture writing, some of the best preserved in existence.

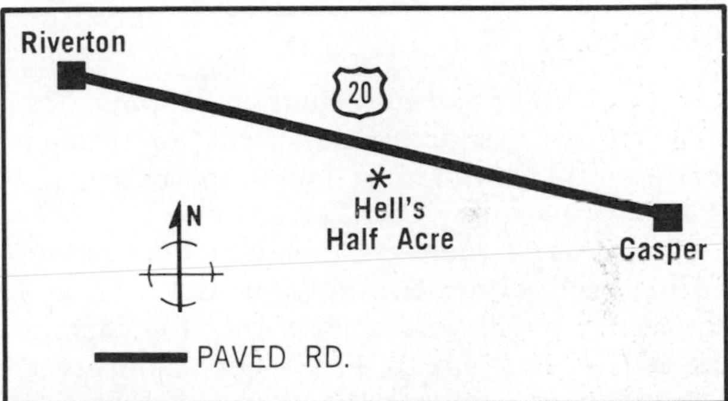

beauty from a few million years of erosion

To reach Ayers Natural Bridge, one of the most beautiful arches in the West, from Douglas, take Interstate 25 west 12 miles; then go 4 miles south on an oiled road to the bridge, located in Ayers Park. From Casper, proceed on Interstate 25

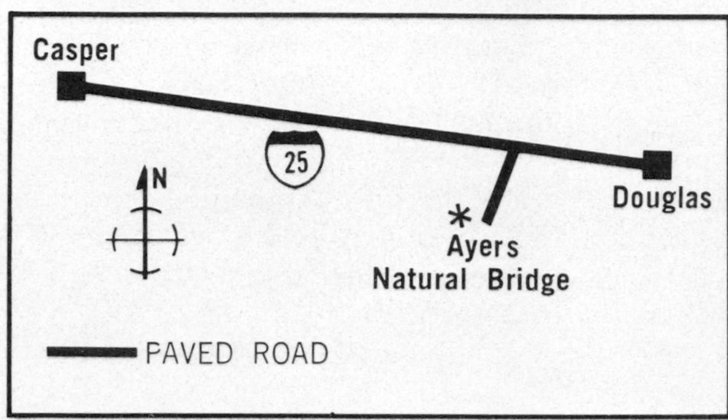

east for 32 miles and turn south to the park. The road into the area is pleasant, winding through gentle, sage-covered hills, then dropping sharply as it nears the valley of La Prele Creek.

Thousands of pioneers traveling the Oregon Trail passed within two miles of the arch and apparently never saw it. Not until the famous surveyor of the West, Dr. F. V. Hayden, observed it in 1870 is there any indication that the white man had been there. "On the morning of August 17," he wrote, "we made a short side trip from Fort Fetterman up the valley to the canyon of La Prele Creek. Lieutenant O'Brien and Captain Wells accompanied us to point out the location of a remarkable natural bridge. We found it even more wonderful than we had anticipated. It is certainly as perfect a natural bridge as could be desired."

The first pictures were taken by the expedition's official photographer, William H. Jackson, 100 years ago. From that time to this, no geological or physical changes have occurred that are apparent to the casual observer.

The arch, 150 feet long, 30 feet high and 50 feet wide, was formed in the last few million years, the result of shady La Prele Creek, on its route from the mountains high in the Medicine Bow Range, slowly wearing a passageway through the thick stone, gradually eroding away more and more of the sandstone, constantly increasing the opening.

The arch supports hundreds of tons of rugged sandstone rocks above the river, and a short trail leads up the steep sides to the top of the arch.

Since its establishment as a park, fireplaces and picnic tables have been provided in the shade of the cool cottonwoods, and camping is permitted in the area.

At the junction of La Prele Creek and the North Platte, reached by proceeding from Douglas 11 miles northwest, is historical Fort Fetterman, first established as a military post in July of 1867. The fort was named after Captain Fetterman, who was killed along with all 81 members of his command by Red Cloud and his Ogallala Sioux in the Bighorn Canyon country.

In 1882, after the conquered Plains Indians had been confined to reservations, it was abandoned. Later, cattlemen took over the fort and turned it into a wild, roaring frontier town. After the founding of Casper and Douglas the town was eventually deserted. The only buildings still remaining are a restored officers' quarters, now serving as a museum, and an ordnance building.

Ayers Natural Bridge

AYERS NATURAL BRIDGE

Square Top Mountain in Bridger National Forest

hiking and hunting in the
footsteps of Oregon Trail pioneers

BRIDGER WILDERNESS

The Bridger Wilderness Area, a part of Bridger National Forest in western Wyoming, is reached from Rock Springs via U.S. 187 north 100 miles to Pinedale, one of the stepping stones to the Wilderness Area itself. Other routes, leading to unpaved roads to the edge of the Wilderness at Green River Lakes, start at Cora, reached by taking U.S. 187 west from Pinedale 6 miles, then turning right and continuing for 4 miles.

The area is named for Jim Bridger, famous mountain man, explorer, and partner in the Rocky Mountain Fur Company which flourished during the early part of the 19th century. Established as Bridger National Forest by President Theodore Roosevelt in 1908, it contains 1,700,028 acres, of which 383,300 acres are included in the Bridger Wilderness.

More than 1,300 lakes dot the rugged landscape, with trout—rainbow, Eastern brook, and native cutthroat—plentiful in virtually all of them. The rare golden trout is found in 29 of the lakes at higher elevations.

Outstanding amid the spectacular scenery of the Wilderness is Gannett Peak, the highest point in the state, towering 13,785 feet above sea level.

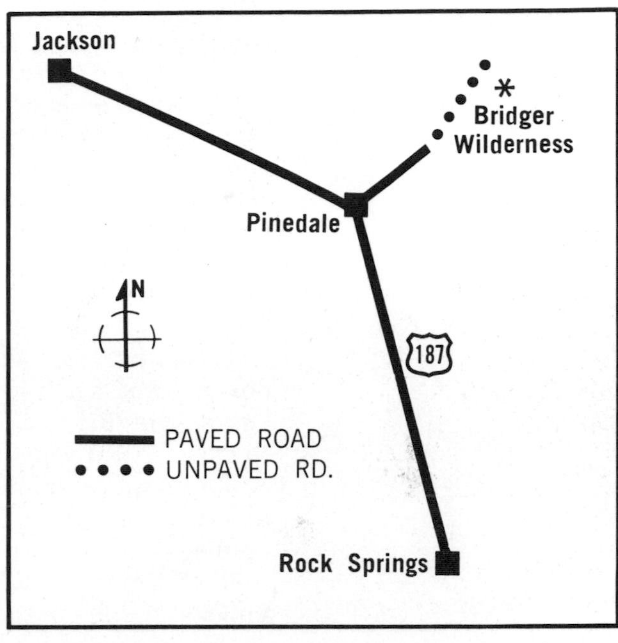

Motorized traffic is prohibited in the Wilderness, but the 500 miles of trails provide opportunities to visit virtually every portion of its 90-mile length. The five main entrance takeoff points—Lower Green River Lake, New Fork Lake, Elkhart Park, Boulder Lake, and Big Sandy—are accessible by roads.

Lower Green River Lake, with 11,679-foot Square Top Mountain in the background, is one of the most spectacular features in Bridger National Forest. Scenic trails encircle the lower lake and provide a leisurely 3- to 4-hour hike within the Wilderness. The same trails join at the upper end of the lake with others for extended trips into the Wilderness Area. Horse corrals and a loading ramp are located near the 23-unit campground. Both rental horses and outfitters' services are available.

Another easy trail leads to a unique spring about five miles east of Afton (located on U.S. 89). During the latter part of the summer the spring completely shuts off every 18 minutes, then turns on again and slowly builds to a thundering, surging, ice-cold torrent. The canyon leading to this spring that breathes is unusually scenic.

Fremont Lake, located 4 miles from Pinedale and available by conventional vehicles, is the second largest natural lake in Wyoming—12 miles long and a half-mile wide. A popular site for boating, camping, and swimming, the lake is particularly famous for its large fish, including record-breaking mackinaw more than 40 pounds in weight.

The Lander cutoff of the Oregon Trail goes through the Forest, starting at South Pass and continuing to Fort Hall, Idaho. Bronze plaques embedded in concrete posts mark the route. Many dates, names, and initials can still be seen, and graves have been marked and identified wherever possible.

Found in Bridger National Forest is a wide variety of wildlife, including moose, deer, elk, antelope, bighorn sheep, and bear, all of which are hunted successfully.

Snowmobiling is permitted in certain areas within the Forest (but not in the Wilderness Area), opening up a wonderful winter wonderland never available to the sightseeing public before. A danger from avalanches does exist, and snowmobilers should check with district rangers to determine safe routes.

THE SINKS

this mysterious river disappears and rises again

The Sinks of the Popo Agie (pronounced pope-ah-gee), a mysterious disappearing river, are reached from Riverton via State 789 to Lander (24 miles), and continuing for nine miles on the Sinks Canyon road. From Casper, proceed west for 75 miles on State 220, then west on U.S. 287 for 75 miles to Lander. Continue as above.

Cascading from the Wind River Mountains down to the southwest, the Middle Fork of the Popo Agie River is like any other mountain stream until it seemingly flows into the side of a mountain, completely disappearing, finally emerging as a waterfall several hundred yards below.

The point of its disappearance is called The Sinks of the Popo Agie, and the placid blue pool at the bottom of the waterfall is known as The Rise of The Sinks, some 200 feet below the river's point of entry.

There is some evidence that the Indians centuries ago related The Sinks to their legends and

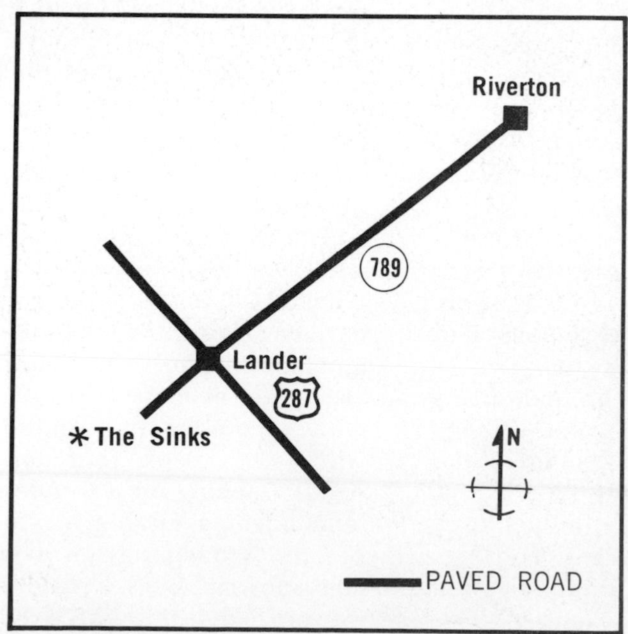

The Sinks of the Popo Agie

mythology. When it was discovered by white men is not known, but the French-Canadian fur trappers probably visited the phenomenon around 1743. Mountain men like Jim Bridger, Bill Sublette, and Joe Meek hunted and trapped in the area which flourishes with game and is a hunter's paradise even today. Their journals report that the great annual rendezvous, traditional time for bringing in the furs, was frequently held on the banks of the Popo Agie.

Geologically, The Sinks are located in a common gray limestone known as the Madison formation, estimated to be 275 million years old. On a much smaller scale, the cavern system formed by the Popo Agie is similar to that of Mammoth Cave in Kentucky and the Carlsbad Caverns in New Mexico. The Sinks have never been fully explored and therefore the size and extent of the cavity, and the course of the river as it flows underground, are unknown.

After reappearing, the river continues a northeasterly course in its regular stream bed until its confluence with the Little Popo Agie and the North Fork Popo Agie, tributaries of the Wind River and, ultimately, the Big Horn River.

Visitors to The Sinks can walk for a short distance into the cavern alongside the river at its point of disappearance, and can follow a trail at The Rise to an observation walk way above the waterfall and pool.

The Bridger Wilderness Area, offering myriad opportunities for adventure, is nearby, and the town of Lander is noted for its annual One-Shot Antelope Hunt. The participants include various notables such as movie stars, sports figures, astronauts, senators, and governors.

battleground of prospectors, Indians, women's rights

South Pass City, a gold-mining ghost town and the birthplace of the women's suffrage movement in Wyoming, can be reached from Rock Springs by taking U.S. 187 north to Farson (40 miles), then turning right on State 28 for approximately 38 miles to the dirt road turnoff (right) leading to South Pass City. From Lander, take State 28 south 40 miles to the dirt road turnoff.

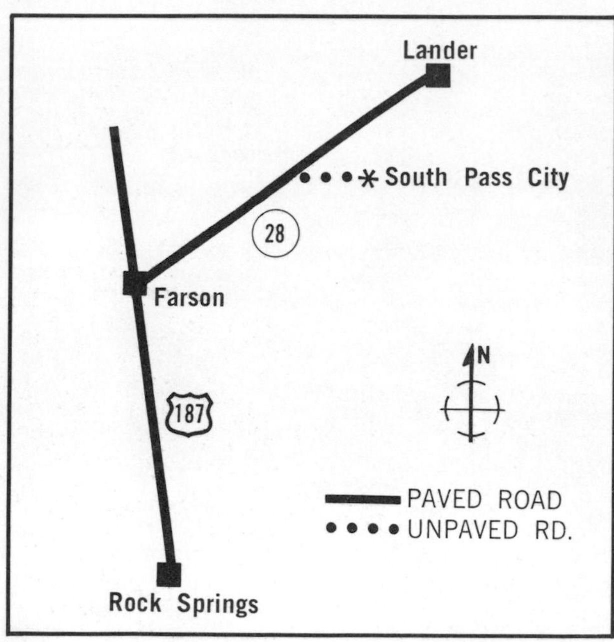

The first gold strike in the South Pass area was reported by a self-styled miner from Georgia who told some friends that he was going to stake a claim at the head of the Sweetwater River. But before he achieved this goal, he was killed by Indians, and only the rumor of his find persisted. In 1855 another group of prospectors worked several areas along the Sweetwater and found small amounts of gold. But they were under almost constant attack by the Indians and eventually left the territory.

Finally, in 1867, spurred on by the recurring reports of riches in the Sweetwater district, prospecting activity increased. One group, led by Captain J. W. Lawrence, set out on a concentrated search and on June 8 located the Carissa Lode, rich beyond anything previously discovered. Lawrence and some of his men were subsequently attacked by Indians and he was killed. But fantastic reports of the gold find spread and prospectors poured into the area in spite of the Indian threat.

The population started to grow and mines were being opened by the dozens—Miner's Delight, King Solomon's, Northern Light, Lone Star State, Jim Crow, and Hoosier Boy were some of the colorful names of the diggings.

The Indians, resenting the white invasion of their hunting grounds, continued their attacks on the miners, usually in the isolated camps near their claims, but occasionally making a raid on the settlement of South Pass itself.

By 1870 the population of South Pass City was 4,000 and its main street was half a mile long. Carter County was created and the newly established mining town was named as its county seat. A sawmill started operations and two stage lines began to serve the community. Businesses flourished, and South Pass City boasted 13 saloons, 3 meat markets, a weekly newspaper, 5 hotels, 4 law firms, and a shooting and bowling alley.

But as was typical of most of the boom towns of the period, the rich veins played out, giving way to new discoveries in other places, and the population disappeared until, by December of 1873, the town was deserted and the county seat moved to Green River.

One of South Pass City's claims to fame is that Esther Morris, with her husband and three children, moved to the town in 1869 and became one of the leading crusaders for equal rights for women. She is credited with having exerted considerable pressure on William H. Bright, another South Pass City resident, to propose the his-

SOUTH PASS CITY

South Pass City

toric women's suffrage bill in the Wyoming Territorial Legislature. Treated lightly by the lawmakers at first, the bill was eventually passed on December 10, 1889, giving to all "women at the age of twenty-one years residing in this territory" the right to cast their votes and to hold office. Following the bill's passage, Mrs. Morris was named as the first female justice of the peace.

Today, South Pass City is a conglomeration of crumbling log cabins, clapboard houses, and false-front stores. Funds were appropriated in 1969 by the state legislature to restore the historic ghost town.

from mountain men's rendezvous to copper boom to ghost town

ENCAMPMENT

The old mining town of Encampment in southern Wyoming is reached from Laramie via State 130 west across Snowy Range Pass (10,800 feet) to the junction with State 230 (71 miles). Turn left and proceed through Riverside to Encampment (10 miles).

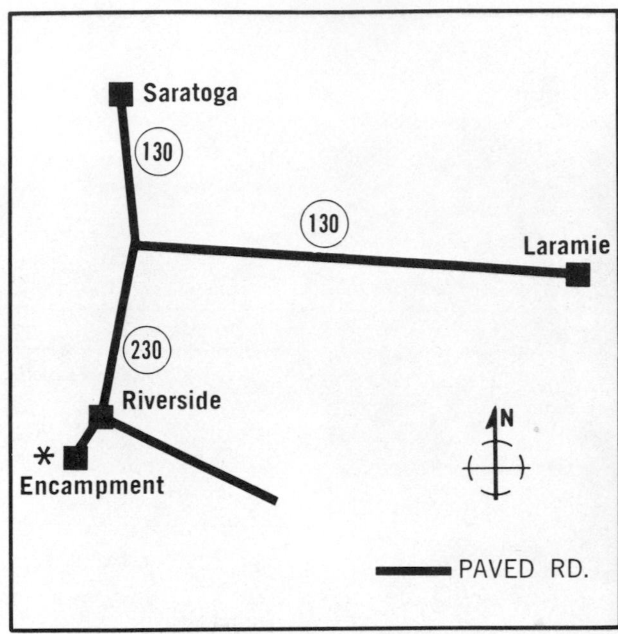

Originally the site of a trappers' rendezvous in 1851, the area was called Grand Encampment, but it did not develop into a mining camp until Ed Haggarty, a prospector, found outcroppings of copper ore near Bridger Peak in 1896. Haggarty and a group of partners developed the Rudefeha mine. The town was founded the following year by Willis George Emerson, who formed the North American Copper Company, purchased the Rudefeha, and renamed it the Ferris-Haggarty.

Emerson established a smelter on the banks of the Encampment River and performed one of the great engineering feats of that day, the erection of a 16-mile aerial tramway from the Ferris-Haggarty to the smelter.

With the encouragement of the Encampment newspaper proclaiming to the world its newfound wealth, new settlers rushed into the valley. By 1901 Encampment had a population of 2,000 and more than 260 companies were in operation. By 1908 over $2,000,000 worth of ore had been taken out, but the value of the metal in a declining market was not sufficient to meet expenses and the population dropped to a handful. The surrounding "Hamlets of Grand Encampment" became lost in the wilderness, and Encampment barely survived.

In recent years, amid the tired and weathered shacks and old business establishments relegated to history, the visitor sees a trim, modernistic structure called the Doc Culleton Memorial Building, built by one of the old-timers who believed that the memory of Encampment should be preserved. The building is a museum, with fascinating displays and historical documents of Encampment as it was in its heyday. This is the beginning of a museum complex which eventually will include a carriage house, a frontier village, and elaborate mining and ranching exhibits.

Encampment has become a popular center for sportsmen, the base for hunting, fishing, scenic trips, camping, and dude ranching. The town has a grocery, hardware, clothing and novelty stores, as well as a motel and restaurant.

The Encampment Woodchoppers' Jamboree is held annually the latter part of June. This unique celebration features log-cutting contests, axe-chopping contests, parades, street dancing and the Woodchoppers' Ball.

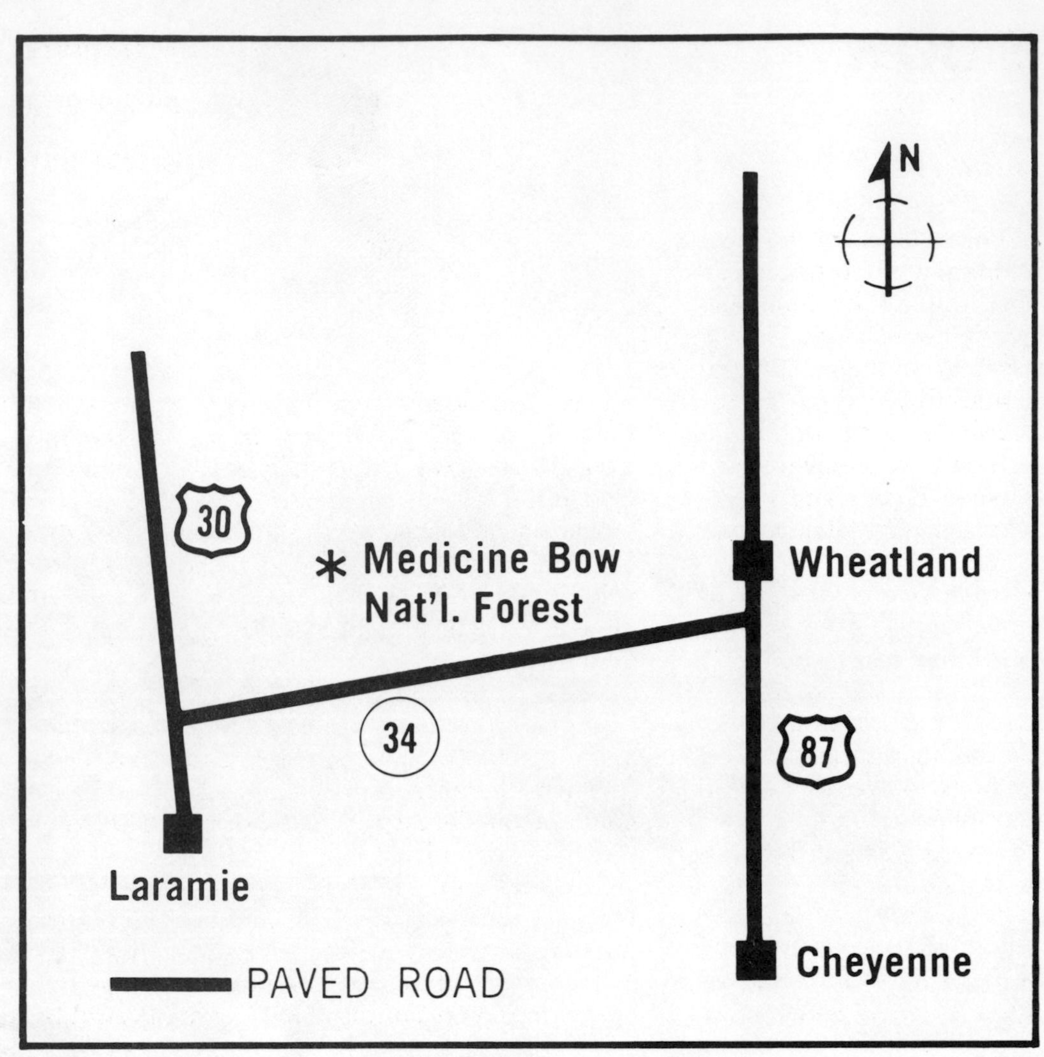
N
30
Medicine Bow
Nat'l. Forest
Wheatland
34
87
Laramie
Cheyenne
PAVED ROAD

MEDICINE BOW

Valhalla for hunters, fishermen, and water sportsmen

Medicine Bow National Forest is one of the most accessible areas in Wyoming, while retaining its primitive isolation from the civilization surrounding it. Reached from Cheyenne via U.S. 87 north to takeoff points at Wheatland, Glendo, or Douglas, access to and through the forest is also available from Laramie, north on U.S. 30 to State 34. Farther north on U.S. 30 several unpaved roads (right) between Bosler and Medicine Bow wind back through this picturesque sportsman's paradise.

The trapper and fur trader were the first to follow the Indians into Laramie Peak country, as the forest is called. Of these hardy pioneers, Jacques La Ramie, a French-Canadian fur trader, entered the area in 1820. Laramie Peak, 10,272 feet elevation and the highest point in the United States east of the Rockies, was named for him, as was the city of Laramie.

Numerous trails crisscross the forest, leading to many lakes and streams, and others provide pleasant hikes into some beautiful, isolated backcountry. La Bonte Creek, reached via county road 61 from the Rock River area, offers an excellent stretch of trout fishing water with good public access.

Mule deer is the most abundant big game animal in the Laramie Peak district, and it is not difficult for the ardent hunter to bag a trophy buck. Elk hunting ranks second to mule deer, with hunting improved since the addition of a small resident herd by the Forest Service and Wyoming State Game and Fish Department.

An interesting automobile trip can be taken by proceeding north from Medicine Bow on State 487 to a junction (right) with the old Casper-Medicine Bow Road (approximately 16 miles), designated as county road 62. Remain on 62, passing through the La Prele work center and then paralleling La Prele Creek for several miles, veering east near Point of Rocks, skirting the edge of La Prele Reservoir, past Ayers Natural Bridge (see above under Wyoming) into Douglas.

One of the most renowned fossil beds, discovered in 1877, is located at Como Bluff, midway between Medicine Bow and Rock River near U.S. 287. It is known locally as the Dinosaur Graveyard.

A rather extensive network of unpaved roads is found within the Medicine Bow Forest boundaries, but most of these are passable only with four-wheel vehicles. Local inquiry should be made of the forest ranger before attempting to travel these roads.

At Glendo, on the eastern edge of the forest, is a state park and the Glendo Reservoir, offering 12,500 acres of water for rainbow trout fishing, boating, skiing, and swimming. A marina, boat ramps, and camping facilities are available.

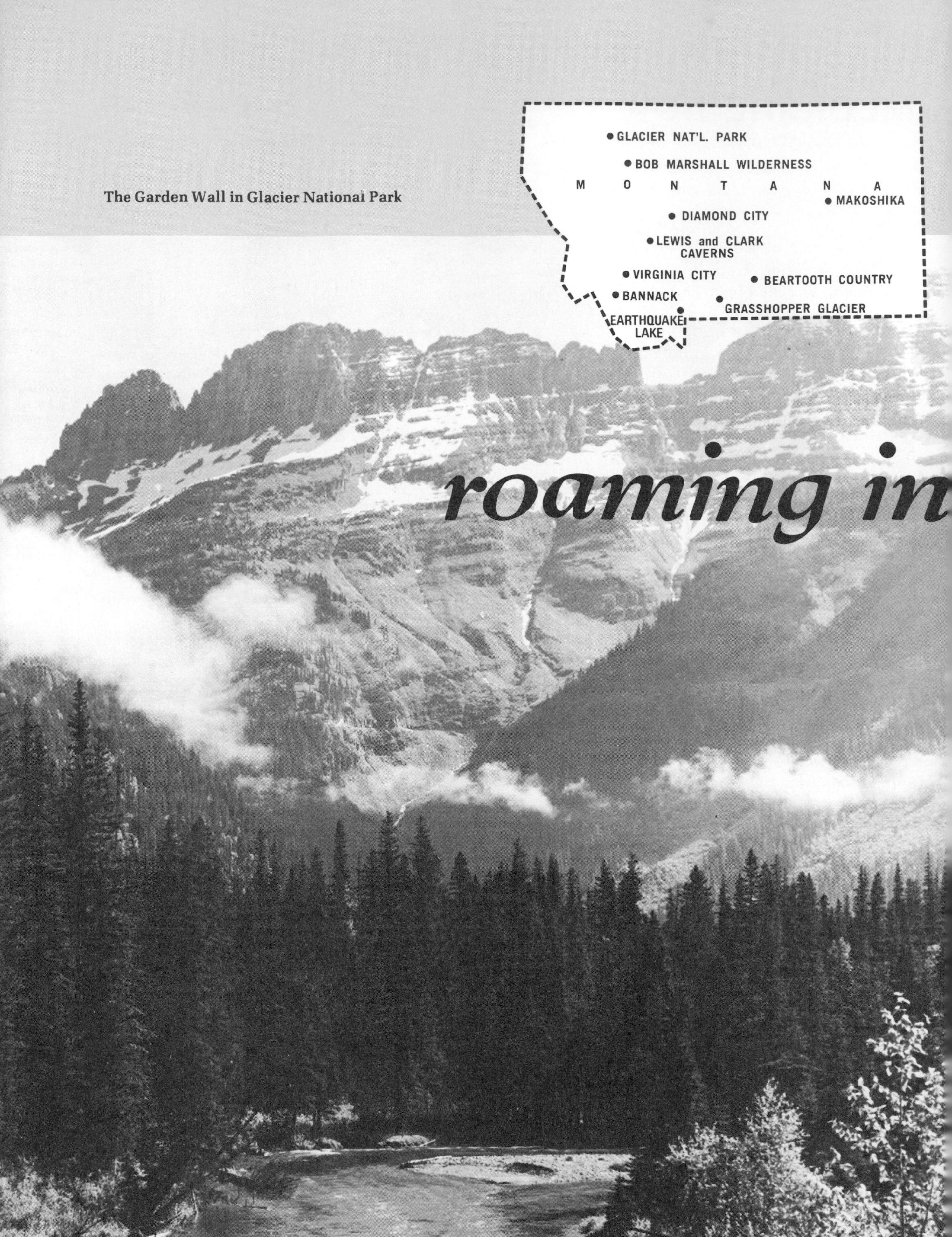

The Garden Wall in Glacier National Park

roaming in

Montana, the Land of Shining Mountains, spreads deep and wide across the Rocky Mountain West, from Wyoming to the Canadian border and from the Dakotas to Idaho. It is a country filled with riches; gold and silver and copper were its seedlings, nurtured and worshipped by the nineteenth-century prospectors in Virginia City, Bannack, Snowshoe Gulch, and Diamond City. Scenic riches abound, too; witness the lofty beauty of Glacier National Park, crowning the continent across the Rocky Mountains of the Northwest. Montana is a land hallowed by the labor and struggles of brave men—the Lewis and Clark expedition through the heart of the land, the Indian wars and Custer's Last Stand at Bighorn, and the warm and timeless paintings of Charles Russell.

MONTANA

Montana is a land of dramatic contrasts. Rolling, lush valleys press against heavily forested, snow-covered peaks; and rising from the banks of the meandering Missouri are the strange and magnificent White Cliffs. In the heart of some of the richest mineral deposits in the world lurk the mysterious Lewis and Clark Caverns. In a southeasterly direction, along the western edge of the Madison range, lies Hebgen Lake and its satellite descendant, Earthquake Lake, formed by a shattering earth movement during the summer of 1959. Beyond, to the east, is Yellowstone, and north of the park, cradled by the soaring peaks of Beartooth country, is Grasshopper Glacier, an unusual phenomenon of nature in the shadow of 12,799-foot Granite Peak, the highest point in Montana.

For the sportsman, the Bob Marshall Wilderness offers almost a million acres virtually untouched by the mechanized hand of man—an untold number of rugged peaks, alpine lakes, meandering rivers, and rushing mountain streams. Fishing, hunting, canoeing, hiking, mountaineering, or scenic solitude are all available in this Valhalla.

Throughout the western half of this giant of a state the history buff will discover ghost towns by the dozens among the Big Belt Mountains east of the wide Missouri, and in the Garnet, the Bitterroot, the Tobacco Root, and Pioneer ranges to the west. He can hike his way across the Lewis and Clark Pass or take a float trip through the same country explored by this expedition in 1804-06.

A land of beauty, a land of legend—this is Montana, Big Sky country.

GLACIER NATIONAL PARK

a spectacular from the Ice Age

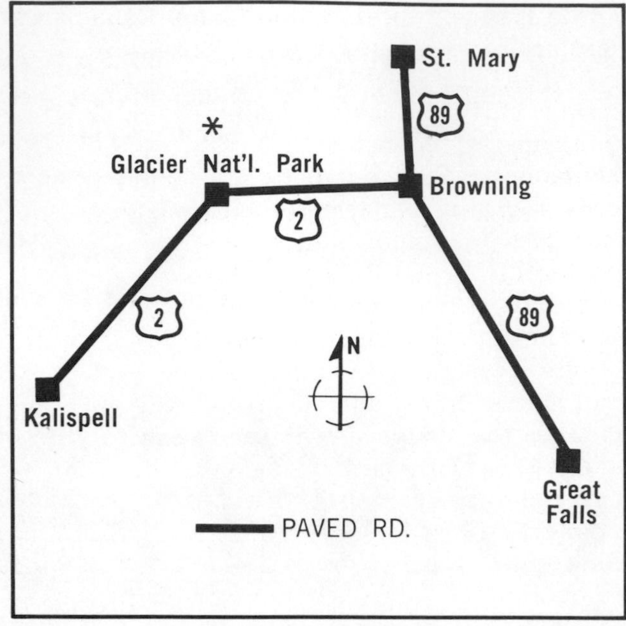

Glacier National Park in northwestern Montana is reached from Kalispell via U.S. 2 east for 7 miles, then north for 26 miles to Apgar, and left for 2 miles to the entrance at West Glacier. From Great Falls, proceed west on U.S. 89 123 miles to Browning. Turn left on U.S. 2 to East Glacier, or continue to West Glacier entrance. To reach the visitor center at St. Mary, continue on U.S. 89 through Browning and continue 31 miles to St. Mary.

Established in 1910 and including 1,583 square miles, Glacier National Park is one of the outstanding wilderness areas still remaining in the United States. Although there are only 70 miles of improved roads within the park, several excellent routes encompass the perimeter.

Starting from the visitor center at St. Mary, Going-to-the-Sun Highway cuts through the heart of the park, ending at West Glacier (51 miles). The route skirts the northern edge of Upper St. Mary Lake, reaching at four miles Triple Divide Peak. From this peak water flows into three drainages: through the Columbia system to the Pacific, through the Mississippi system to the Atlantic, and through the Saskatchewan-Nelson system to Hudson Bay and the Arctic. Directly across the lake are Divide, Kootenai, Red Eagle, and Little Chief mountains on the left. Singleshot, Whitefish, Goat, and Going-to-the-Sun mountains are on the right.

A road at 6.4 miles to the right leads to a campground area. Another half-mile on the main road is the Narrows, a narrow valley leading into the broader St. Mary Valley. At 10.5 miles a footpath leads to Sunrift Gorge, a spectacular cleft in red argillite hardly 10 feet wide, with 25- to 50-foot vertical walls, formed by a slip along a fault and eroded into fantastic shapes by wind and water.

The road continues steadily upward around Going-to-the-Sun Mountain, swinging across a tributary of Reynolds Creek to the side of Piegan Mountain. Across the forested slopes is Mount Reynolds. On a lower point of Mount Reynolds is a lookout station that overlooks the St. Mary Valley.

Seventeen miles farther is a 408-foot tunnel through Piegan Mountain, completed in 1933 after 12 years of hazardous construction. At the opening ceremony in Logan Pass, Indians from the west met the Blackfeet from the east and ceremoniously ended the centuries-old feud between them.

Logan Pass (18.3 miles) is a favorite stopping point. An attractive visitors center is located here, with naturalists on duty to provide information and answer questions. From Logan Pass, the Hidden Lake Overlook Trail starts. This 2-mile self-guided nature trail winds across the terraces of the Hanging Gardens and, at 1 mile climbs the lateral moraine of a glacier not seen from the trail. The footpath continues to the edge of a precipitous cliff overlooking sapphire-blue Hidden Lake some 800 feet below.

After leaving Logan Pass, a parking area at 26 miles affords a spectacular vista of McDonald Valley, some 2,500 feet below, and a panorama of peaks in the Livingston Range to the north. The road enters a second tunnel at 26.7 miles, with two openings overlooking McDonald Valley. The route drops rapidly into the heavy forest of tall spruce, pine, and fir on the west side. At 33 miles the evidence of a tremendous avalanche in 1953-54 can be seen to the east. The swath cut by the avalanche swept trees, rocks, and everything else that happened to be in its way down the mountainside.

Lake McDonald (38.5 miles) is the largest lake in the Park, 10 miles long and more than a mile wide. Maximum depth is 437 feet. Fly-fishing is excellent in the deep water near the bank.

Another example of the damage caused by forest fires can be seen shortly before arriving at West Entrance station. The new growth between the aspen is mostly lodgepole pine.

An interesting drive around the park perimeter starts from East Glacier Park, continuing through St. Mary on the Blackfeet Highway to the Canadian border (59 miles).

The most satisfying way to see Glacier National Park is on foot or on horseback. Boasting one of the best trail systems in the United States, the park has more than 1,000 miles of wilderness trails. Some are short 15-minute walks, and others, deep into the backcountry, require several days. Visitors are invited to join the park naturalists on 2-hour, half-day, all-day, and overnight trips. Except for the expenses of meals and lodging in connection with the overnights, there is no charge for the guide service. Professional park-approved outfitters also operate camping trips, including the services of a guide, cook, and pack animals.

There is excellent fishing at dozens of spots throughout the park, and adequate camping facilities in picturesque wilderness. Hotels are also open at Glacier and Waterton Lakes from June 15 to September 15.

sportsmen's bounties

astride the Continental Divide

BOB MARSHALL WILDERNESS

A vast 950,000 acres of land (larger than Rhode Island) virtually untouched by the hand of man, the Bob Marshall Wilderness Area is easily reached from Great Falls via U.S. 89 west to Choteau (50 miles), then left on U.S. 287 for less than a mile to an unpaved road (right) to Gibson Reservoir. The area can also be reached from Kalispell, Missoula, and Helena. In addition to Choteau, ranger stations are located at Condon, Seeley Lake, Lincoln, Spotted Bear, and Augusta. Big Prairie ranger station is located within the Wilderness.

Bob Marshall, born in New York City, was nevertheless dedicated to the concept of a need

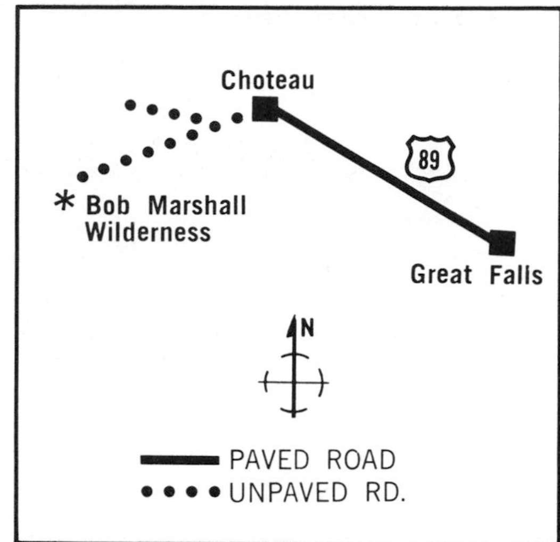

for the wilderness. "In the forest," he said, "men temporarily abandon a life to which they cannot become wholly reconciled." By the time he was 36, he had taken more than 200 wilderness hikes of 30 miles, 51 hikes of 40 miles, and several up to 70 miles. It was Marshall who recommended in 1935 that Congress set aside areas as wilderness, an idea which in 1964 became a reality as the National Wilderness Preservation System.

The Bob Marshall Wilderness includes rugged peaks and alpine lakes, mountain valleys, open meadows, and meandering rivers. Elevations range from 4,000 feet along the valley floors to more than 9,000 feet atop the serpentine Continental Divide. Crisp high-country air, timbered slopes with towering trees, quiet mountain lakes, and the cheery sound of songbirds in concert are a part of a land removed from the pressures of civilization.

Ponderosa pine stands grow along the South Fork of the Flathead River Valley, with Douglas fir, larch, and pines dominating the forest. And as the trails move higher, the tall sentinels give way, at last, to a few dwarfed alpine firs at timberline.

Activities are as varied as the outdoorsman wishes to make them. Fishing and hunting take on a new dimension in the Wilderness, and there are opportunities for canoeing, rafting, photography, hiking, mountaineering, and horseback riding. Or, in a quieter vein, wildlife and botanical observation or geological and fossil study add to the multi-appeal of this great country.

Numerous trails and backpack trips are available throughout the Wilderness, varying from a single day to 10, from a few miles to 75. Extensive wilderness trips should be planned with the help of one of the forest rangers, and commercial outfitters and guides make wilderness adventures safer and more exciting, as well as more pleasant. A list of licensed outfitters and guides is available from the Montana Fish and Game Department at Helena 59601.

Lakes and streams in the Bob Marshall Wilderness provide excellent fishing. Cutthroat trout are common in most streams, and occasionally rainbow are taken above Salmon Lake.

For the big-game hunter, the Wilderness is a paradise, with plenty of elk, grizzly bear, mule deer, white-tailed deer, black bear, bighorn sheep, and mountain goats.

Bird hunters will have opportunities to bag ruffed, Franklin, and blue grouse. And small game includes badger, beaver, muskrat, porcupine, hoary marmot, woodchuck, and snowshoe rabbit.

The fossil hunter will enjoy a hike up Kevan Mountain (8,400 feet), for on its slopes can be found trilobites, fossils of a prehistoric arthropod that was about two inches long and lived about 200 million years ago. At Bullet Nose Mountain, in addition to spectacular scenery, the adventurer has an opportunity to explore ice caves which remain all year long.

Geologically, the mountains of the area were elevated from an ancient sea bottom. And eons later glaciers rasped their way downward, leaving U-shaped troughs which can be readily observed in the White River Area downstream from the junction of the North Fork and the South Fork.

Excellent trail maps and comprehensive informational literature are available from the U.S. Forest Service at Missoula, Montana.

earl Basin from the Continental Divide, Bob Marshall Wilderness

where strange monoliths dominate "Hell Cooled Over"

MAKOSHIKA

With Billings as the starting point for the adventure tour of Makoshika State Park, an area of strange natural wonders in eastern Montana, take Interstate 94 northeast 220 miles to Glendive, then turn south to Makoshika. The highway, following the wide sweep of the Yellowstone River, winds through lonely badland country, with brown, buff, and gray buttes rising along the riverbanks. As the route continues northeasterly, the country becomes more desolate, the low, rolling hills reaching endlessly to the horizon.

The old highway (U.S. 10) passes through Miles City, once a wild and woolly frontier town, now transformed into a quiet cow town, remembering its colorful past by holding an annual rodeo, usually on July 4. In the old days, the south side of Main Street was a solid block of saloons, gambling dens, and brothels, with the north side reserved for the "decent" people.

At Glendive, an excellent long-range view of the Makoshika formations is obtained by taking an easy hike to the top of Hungry Joe, a massive butte.

Makoshika was created over the centuries by the erosive action of wind, water, heat, and cold on the relatively soft shales and sandstone. This weirdly fantastic region is dominated by tall columns of sandstone rising singly and then capped with overhanging rocks, appearing like giant mushrooms. Other rocks have taken the shapes of camels, castles, ships, or Indian chiefs.

The park is, perhaps, most spectacular in the early morning or dusk. The combination of the slanting orange rays and lengthening shadows seems to create an ever changing configuration throughout the 760 acres of Makoshika.

A drive through the area is possible, but far greater satisfaction results by hiking down into the narrow, deep washes of the multicolored layers of shale, rock, and sandstone.

This was virtually an unknown region until Dawson County gave 160 acres of the land to Montana in 1953 and it became a state park. Another 600 acres, under a lease arrangement with the Bureau of Land Management, was added in 1958.

The community of Glendive proceeded to donate both time and money to develop roads, scenic turnouts, and picnic facilities. Some years ago an amphitheater was constructed overlooking some of the more spectacular portions of the park.

How it received the name Makoshika remains a mystery. Some say it's a Dakota Sioux word meaning badland, or bad earth. And others are convinced the name is a synonym for "Hell Cooled Over."

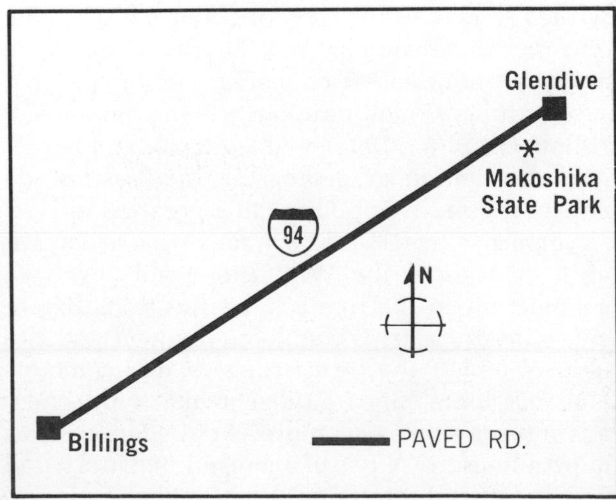

Makoshika State Park

remnants of a fabulous mining town

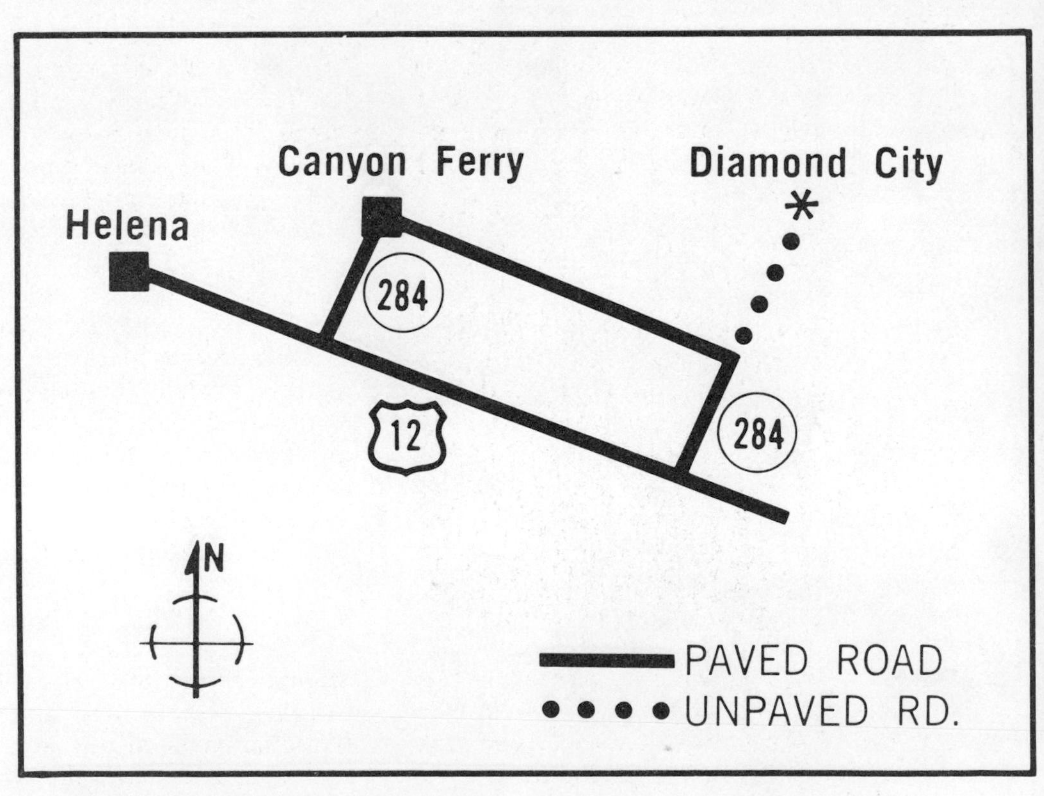

To reach Diamond City, one of Montana's most fabulous old mining towns, from Helena, take U.S. 12 east for 9 miles to junction with State 284. Turn left and cross Canyon Ferry Lake at the dam. Bear right and continue 15 miles from Canyon Ferry, turning left on an unimproved road and continue for eight miles to Diamond

DIAMOND CITY

City. The adventure point can also be reached from Townsend by going east two miles on U.S. 12 and turning left on State 284, passing the first unpaved road (right) and continuing to the second (21 miles from Townsend), then proceeding to Diamond City.

The entire mining area, known as Confederate Gulch, was so named as the result of three exiled Confederate soldiers deciding they'd rather pan gold after the Civil War than return home. The very first pan of gold was worth ten cents, and this was the beginning of the rush. Prospectors of all kinds poured in; many veterans from California and Colorado came, but many were amateurs who arrived enraptured by the talk of gold practically lying around on the mountainside waiting to be picked up.

One of the more naive prospectors, not knowing how or where to look, asked an old-timer to suggest a place for him to prospect. The old-timer, grinning from ear to ear, pointed to the most unlikely spot. "Try that bar—you might find somethin'." The rank amateur took the advice and staked the claim on Montana Bar, one of the richest ever found.

With every new strike, Diamond City increased in size until the population reached 10,000. During the boom years the streets seethed with excitement and activity, and soon the usual influx of bars, gambling dens, and brothels became a part of the way of life. Houses had to be placed on stilts to save them from burial beneath the avalanche of tailings that swept down the gulch.

In less than a decade the gold was gone and those who had not struck it rich moved on to try again, while others, like John Schonneman, Alex Campbell, and Charles Fredericks, who had located the richest portions, sacked their few millions and left happily as the teams hauled the gold to Fort Benton. Over $10,000,000 had been taken from the Big Belt Mountains before it was over. But the 1870 the population had thinned to 255 and by 1883 only 4 families remained. Finally these, too, departed, and today the boom-bust community of Diamond City consists of a few crumbling foundations amid the desolation.

En route back to Helena, an interesting stop can be made at Canyon Ferry Dam. The name originated in 1865 when John Oakes started ferrying miners and prospectors across the Missouri River at this point. The present dam, replacing one originally built a mile upstream in 1898, was completed in 1954 and has resulted in an excellent recreation area on and around Canyon Ferry Lake, 25 miles long and from 3 to 6 miles wide. Camping, picnic facilities, and boat launching ramps are available at several sites along the lake shore.

mineral organ pipes in the Northwest's largest caves

LEWIS AND CLARK CAVERNS

To reach the Lewis and Clark Caverns from Butte, proceed east on Interstate 90 or U.S. 10 to the juncture of the routes at Cardwell. From this point continue 11 miles and turn left on side road that leads to the caverns. From Bozeman take Interstate 90 or U.S. 10 to Three Forks, then continue west for 14 miles to side road and turn right to the caverns.

The caverns, located in a limestone formation at the base of a high cliff were discovered in 1902 by Daniel Morrison, who was engaged in surveying the countryside. Exceeded in size only by Mammoth Cave in Kentucky and Carlsbad Caverns in New Mexico, Lewis and Clark Caverns are the largest in the Northwest and are unique in many respects. The caves are a succession of vaulted chambers and passageways thickly hung with stalactites and studded with stalagmites.

Originally it was necessary to hike the half-mile from the parking area to the cave entrance, but today this is accomplished by means of a jeep railway and tram lift. In the first chamber, opaque and almost flawless, stalagmites and stalactites form fluted pillars. Continuing on, the path leads to the Deepest Room, noteworthy for the one large stalagmite in the process of formation, with water dripping into it from above. A spring makes a clear pool in the center of the floor and the ceiling rises to a curved dome almost mosaic in design.

The Brown Waterfall is so named for the cascade of rocks that appears to tumble down the chamber wall from a rocky ledge above. A corridor leads on to the Organ Room. This chamber is dominated by a mass of pipelike columns, which, when struck by a piece of broken rock, give off strange musical sounds.

Many of the corridors and chambers vary widely both in formation and coloring, with the walls of some delicately filigreed, others appearing to be hiding behind a weirdly patterned drapery.

Surface water, seeping down the bedding planes of the Madison limestone, hollowed out the cave by gradually dissolving the limestone at successive levels. The cave is dry, except at its lowest point, which is about 300 feet below the entrance.

The town of Three Forks, nearest to Lewis and Clark Caverns State Park, was an ancient battleground of the Crow and Blackfeet Indians and was visited by Lewis and Clark in 1805.

Trappers sent out by the Missouri Fur Company attempted to establish a trading post in 1810, building a stockade on a neck of land between the Jefferson and Madison rivers some two miles above the confluence. But, before the year had ended, the Blackfeet had driven them out, killing some 20 men in the process. Andrew Henry, one of the founders, moved on across the mountains to the Snake and established a post there while the other founder, Pierre Menard, took the main party and returned to the safety of St. Louis.

Finally, in 1864 a group of Missourians laid out Gallatin City at what they believed was the head of navigation on the Missouri. But when they discovered that the Great Falls of the Missouri prevented navigation far upstream, they abandoned it. A town was finally established when the railroad was built.

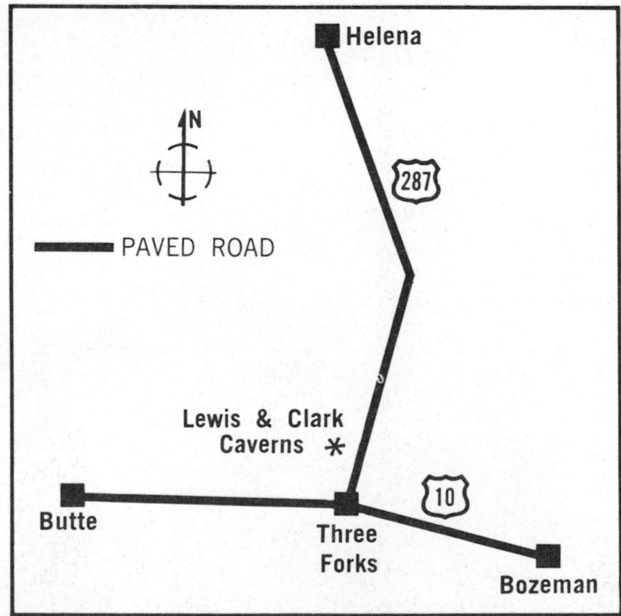

Lewis and Clark Caverns

VIRGINIA CITY

most famous ghost town

lives again

Virginia City, Montana's most widely known ghost town, can be reached from Bozeman by taking State 289 west for 36 miles to junction with U.S. 287, turning left and continuing to Ennis (16 miles). Turn right on State 287 and proceed 14 miles to Virginia City.

The first incorporated town in Montana, Virginia City was also the second territorial capital, replacing another mining boom town, Bannack, in 1865. After a bitter election, Helena became the capital in 1875. Though today Vir-

ginia City has only a fraction of the population that crowded the streets when gold was flowing freely in Alder Gulch, the town has remained in existence continuously since its beginning in 1863. It was in May of that year that six prospectors camped near an alder-banked stream in the Tobacco Root Mountains. Two of them, left to watch the horses while the others went prospecting, saw some likely looking gravel and panned it out. What they found kept them there another day and then sent them rushing to Bannack for supplies. The six men, led by Bill Fairweather, had struck it rich. By the end of the first day they had panned out about $180.

Less than six months later, thousands of miners were working along the banks of Alder Gulch. Within a year an estimated 35,000 people were living in Virginia City, Nevada City, Summit, and other camps near the discovery point.

In the beginning there was no safe way of shipping out the millions in gold that the Alder Gulch placers yielded ($10,000,000 the first year). The only stage route was the one to Bannack, and money was sent to the nearest express office in private hands. It was only natural that outlaws were attracted by such conditions. Under the leadership of Henry Plummer, who had managed to be elected sheriff by the miners, an organization of thieves and gunmen was formed, complete with officers, secretary, and informers. Coaches were plundered and scores of men were murdered. There was no formal law and order, with the nearest court being 400 miles away. Finally, with the robbery and murder of a quiet and inoffensive Dutchman, Nicholas Thiebalt, for $200 in gold dust, the irate miners reached the boiling point, and the first vigilante group was formed. George Ives was apprehended for the crime, tried by a miners' court, and hanged. During the next six weeks, starting in December of 1863, the vigilantes were a busy bunch, hanging at least 21 men, including Plummer, and scaring the rest of the outlaws out of the country.

The site of the vigilante hangings is at the corner of Wallace and Van Buren streets. Here five road agents were strung up on January 14, 1864, and were buried in a row on Boot Hill (the graves can be seen at the cemetery, 0.4 miles north of town).

Today Virginia City is a blend of the old and the new, a mining camp with a wealth of history as a heritage. The authentic reconstruction of Nevada City on its original site down the gulch adds to the charm of this slice of the Old West. The historic buildings have been restored with painstaking authenticity.

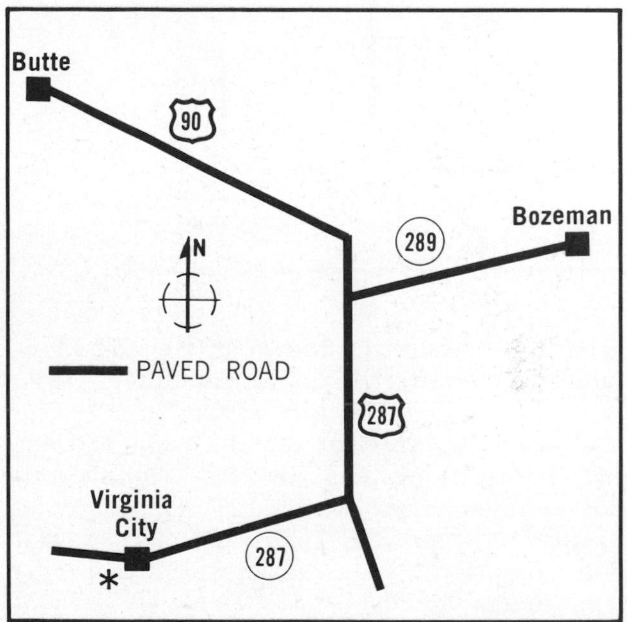

The old Salisbury stage station of the Ruby Valley has been moved to Nevada City and is now being operated as a modern hotel. Virginia City has established two historical museums. There is also a drugstore museum, and an old brewery has been restored, complete with the wooden vats as they stood when used for making beer.

Although no railroad was ever built into Virginia City in the gold rush days, the Virginia City Trading Company has constructed a replica of an early railroad, which is now used to carry visitors the one mile between Nevada City and Virginia City.

dio in Virginia City

desperado capital of the West

BANNACK

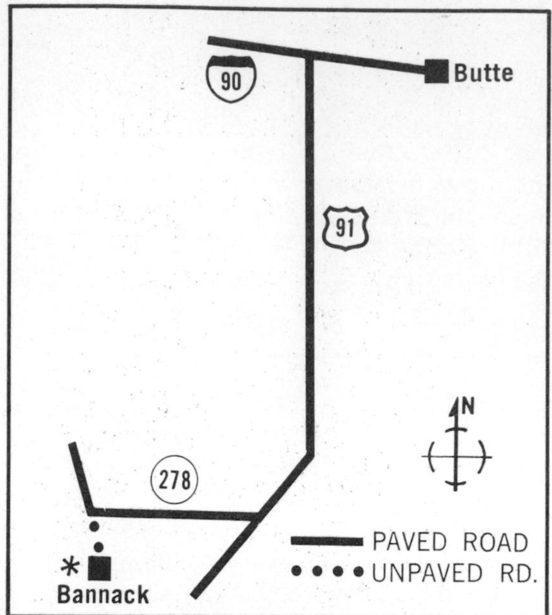

From Butte to the ghost town of Bannack, Montana's first territorial capital, take Interstate 90 west for 7 miles and turn left on U.S. 91. The route crosses the Continental Divide at Deer Lodge Pass (elevation 5,902 feet), then drops down in Beaverhead Valley to Dillon. Continue 5 miles to State 278. Turn right and proceed approximately 18 miles. An unpaved road (left) leads to Bannack.

Gold was originally discovered in Montana at Gold Creek in 1856, but the first big strike came on Grasshopper Creek, at Bannack, July 28, 1862 by John White and a small party of prospectors. The fever spread; in a few months the country was overrun by prospectors, and a roaring, vigorous tent, shack, and log-cabin village began to grow, straddling the gold-laden Grasshopper Creek.

The initial rush bringing in about 1,000 men ended after the first year with new discoveries on Alder Gulch (see Virginia City under Montana) whetting the miners' gold-hungry appetites. Bannack remained almost deserted until 1866, when a miner's ditch was built to increase the water supply so necessary for placer operations. Additional companies came into Grasshopper Creek to provide ditches, one being 44 miles long. After a year or so the shallow reserves gave out and once again Bannack became the place the world forgot. At intervals it showed signs of life, but when the post office was closed in 1938 it became, unofficially at least, a ghost town.

During its early days, particularly in 1862-63, it probably harbored more desperadoes and infamous characters than did any other mining town in the West. It was between this point and Virginia City that Sheriff Henry Plummer and his band of road agents preyed on the slow-moving stages and their innocent passengers until the Alder Gulch vigilantes ended the outlaws' careers at the end of a rope.

Remnants of the town are still there, with tall trees shading weathered and crumbling log cabins, half-hidden by sagebrush and greasewood. A few false-fronted stores are located behind the cabins, and another 50 or so feet up the street is a deserted church. One building, almost out of place, was built of red brick and is identified as the first Territorial Capitol of Montana.

Though this was gold country in the beginning, Beaverhead County still has a mining industry, with commercial quantities of silver, lead, talc, manganese, bentonite, phosphate, graphite, iron, and tungsten. However, its most important industry is agriculture, with ranching and farming producing most of its income.

A substantial part of Beaverhead National Forest's 2,216,634 acres of rugged mountains, timberland, and wilderness lies within Beaverhead County, offering exciting recreational opportunities. Fishing in high-country lakes or in the Big Hole and Beaverhead rivers is a satisfying experience. There are excellent areas for hunting, either for big game—elk, deer, antelope, bear—or for game birds—sage hens and pheasants.

GRASSHOPPER GLACIER

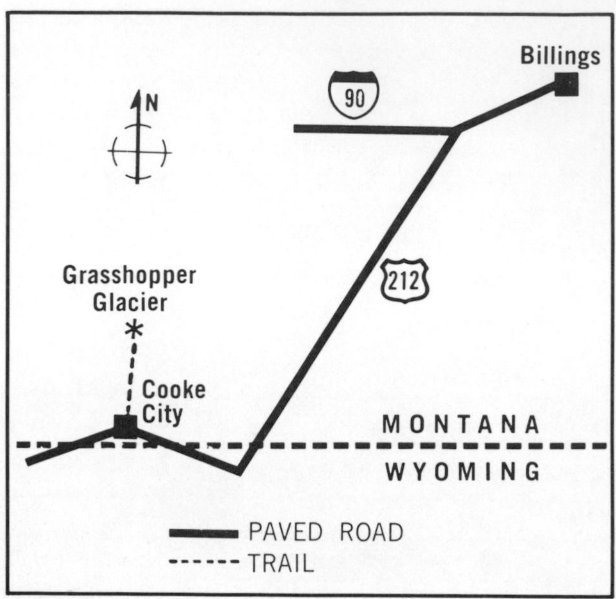

where grasshoppers two centuries old are embedded in ice

Grasshopper Glacier, on the southern edge of the Beartooth Primitive Area in Custer National Forest, is reached from Billings via U.S. 212 over Beartooth Pass (10,940 feet) to Cooke City (123 miles). Turn north on an unpaved road until the road terminates at the upper end of Goose Lake (13 miles). Only the first two miles are passable by regular passenger car, with a four-wheel drive vehicle required for the remaining 11 miles.

After an ascent of 2,300 feet from Cooke City to Goose Lake, a steep, rough trail continues toward the glacier. A saddle between two peaks is approached and provides a view of a vast snowfield, not to be confused with Grasshopper Glacier. The trail goes to the right, winding up to the crest of a rock ridge. At this point is the first view of the glacier.

This rare natural wonder is in the heart of rugged, picturesque peaks of the Beartooth Mountain Range. The glacier is a field of ice approximately a mile long and a half-mile wide at an elevation of 11,000 feet. At one time it was more than 4 miles in length, and several small glaciers in the same area were a part of it.

Within a radius of several miles the headwaters of four principal streams rise and flow into the Yellowstone River. The trail descends into the West Rosebud drainage and follows the Sawtooth Ridge to the north of the saddle for about one-half mile. From this point to the northeast is a dramatic view of 12,799-foot Granite Peak, the highest point in Montana.

Grasshopper Glacier actually has millions of grasshoppers buried in its thick layer of ice. In times past, visitors to the spot could dig perfectly preserved specimens from the ice, but following the unusually hot summer of 1919, the surface of the glacier was melted and many of the grasshoppers were exposed to the atmosphere and decomposed.

Dr. J. P. Kimball, a mining geologist, is credited with the discovery and first scientific exploration of the glacier. A number of the grasshopper specimens have been studied by entomologists. They are migratory locusts, members of the species *Melanoplus spretus, Thomas*, common many, many years ago in the West. It

Granite P

is estimated that the grasshoppers embedded in the glacier are two centuries old, and evidence indicates that they became embedded in the ice when, as they passed over the high mountain range, they were caught in a severe storm and dashed to the surface of the forming glacier.

Nearby Granite Peak offers a challenging climb to those with stamina and experience. To reach a starting point, climbers may turn south off Interstate 90 at Columbus on State 307 through Absarokee, proceeding to the Montana Power Plant at the end of the West Rosebud Road and leaving the vehicles at this point. However, no climb should be attempted without first contacting the ranger and arranging for an experienced guide.

There are numerous backpack trips in the Beartooth Primitive Area suitable for families. Guide and packer services are available, and names can be obtained from the Forest Service offices or ranger stations.

Earthquake Lake

lake formed by an earthquake with the power of 2,500 atomic bombs

EARTHQUAKE LAKE

Earthquake Lake, one of nature's strange creations and a feature attraction in the Madison River Canyon Earthquake Area, can be reached from Butte by taking Interstate 90 (some portions of this highway are still U.S. 10) east to the junction with U.S. 287. Turn right and continue for 76 miles to the visitor center. An interesting circle trip may be enjoyed by continuing on U.S. 287

to the junction with U.S. 191 (23 miles) and turning left, proceeding to junction with Interstate 90 10 miles west of Bozeman (92 miles from junction to junction). Access to all points of interest is possible by the main highway and a new road constructed in the area, or by short hikes.

The visitor center includes a beautiful observatory, a working seismograph, and intriguing displays. Talks are given at intervals to explain the occurrence of the earthquake and its consequence in the geology of the region.

The Hebgen Lake Earthquake, one of the strongest ever recorded in the United States, happened near midnight on August 17, 1959. The violent impact was felt in an eight-state area, with the heaviest damage in the Gallatin National Forest in southwestern Montana.

A year later the Madison River Canyon Earthquake Area was dedicated by Dr. Richard E. McArdle, former Forest Service chief, "in memory of the events which took place here . . . as a dramatic example of earth-shaping forces . . . and for all its values . . . its resources, its geologic history and its deep human meanings."

The most spectacular single feature left by the earthquake is the huge slide across the Madison River near the west end of the area. Enough rocks and earth smashed down into the Canyon to fill the entire Rose Bowl stadium ten times, with quite a few rocks left over. A paved road leads to Vista Point and displays on top of the slide.

As the result of this jumbled mass of rocks and the blocking of the River, a completely new lake was formed, now called Earthquake Lake. During the period before a channel could be cut through the slide, the new lake was a potential flood threat to the towns and ranches downstream. Earthquake Lake can be viewed from the slide, from Beaver Creek Campground, and from U.S. 287 as it follows its north shore.

Upstream from the slide and the site of Earthquake Lake, violent shocks lowered the north shore of old Hebgen Lake, a long-time favorite with sportsmen. The violent jolt created great waves which swept across the lake and over Hebgen Dam at the west end. Large sections of the highway plunged into the lake before the night of terror had ended. Fault scarps, where the earth fractured and dropped, parallel the northeast lake shore for several miles. At Cabin Creek, downstream from the dam, an excellent closeup view of the Hebgen Lake fault scarp is possible. The road, reconstructed around the washed-out portions, follows the length of Hebgen Lake.

In total, the power of the earthquake was equal to that of 2,500 atomic bombs, with surface damage extending from near Old Faithful in Yellowstone National Park westward for about 50 miles. Soon after the main shock at 11:37 the night of August 17, escape from the canyon was blocked, starting a night of fear for the hundreds

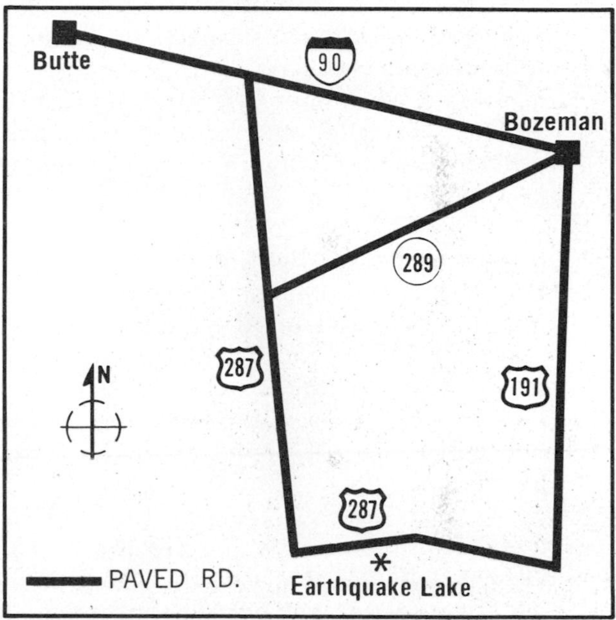

of vacationers in tents, campers, trailers, and lodges near Hebgen Lake and along the Madison River.

In addition to its recent claim to fame as the epicenter of the great earthquake, the Madison River Canyon is the heart of a popular recreation area, boasting some of the finest fishing in the West, numerous trails through the vast wilderness, and a timeless scenic splendor unequalled in dramatic ruggedness.

Accommodations are available in the vicinity of the earthquake site, with restaurants, motels, and stores at various towns a short distance away. The Beaver Creek Campground, located in the area itself, is one of the most complete. Several other camping areas are found on the south shore of Hebgen Lake or within a few miles to the east or west.

hanging valleys and alpine plateaus

BEARTOOTH COUNTRY

Beartooth Country, a giant land of raw, natural beauty, starts at Red Lodge, 59 miles southwest of Billings and reached via U.S. 212.

More than 25 mountain peaks rise higher than 12,000 feet, flanked by glaciers and overlooking more than 300 lakes and 5,000 waterfalls. And everywhere is a profusion of tiny flowers, splashing color against snowbanks and across alpine meadows.

Isolated, secluded, far removed from civilization, this wild land is easily reached and easily observed with the construction of the Beartooth Highway. Few mountain roads in the world provide such spectacular scenery at every turn. Beartooth Highway reaches from Red Lodge into Yellowstone National Park in Wyoming. From the valley floor at its start it climbs above timberline and into Wyoming, then roams westward over the Beartooth Plateau, turns back into Montana, and passes through the tiny towns of Cooke City and Silvergate before dipping into fabulous Yellowstone Park.

Beartooth Country offers something for everybody. Hunting and fishing are the best in the various wilderness areas. Big game animals—deer, moose, bear, bighorn sheep, and mountain goat—are plentiful in the foothills and mountains. For the fisherman, hundreds of streams and lakes offer choice fighting fish—Rocky Mountain whitefish, the rare grayling, and rainbow, brown, brook, and golden trout.

Good skiing is available in the Custer National Forest at Grizzly Peak near Red Lodge, with double chairlifts with a vertical rise exceeding 2,000 feet. In summer, the lifts offer excellent sight-seeing opportunities.

For rock hounds, some of the best hunting grounds are near old mines like McLaren Mine, 5 miles into the mountains north of Cooke City. Geologically, the rocks exposed along the Beartooth Highway are among the oldest known to man, perhaps going back in time for 2.7 billion years or longer. The rocks are identified today as granite gneiss, hornblende gneiss, mica schist, and quartzite.

At about 12 miles from Red Lodge is Rock Creek Vista Point, a railing-enclosed observation platform reached by an easy 800-foot walk. Far below is glaciated Rock Creek Valley and, rising to the sky, are the majestic Beartooth Mountains. Also visible are hanging valleys and alpine plateaus.

After crossing into Wyoming, the highway passes Twin Lakes, two blue gems some 700 feet below the road and surrounded by towering cliffs. Beyond the lakes is part of Rock Creek Valley and, above it, Hellroaring Plateau. Just above Twin Lakes is a cirque lake, situated in a rock-walled amphitheater that was cut into the valley's head by glacial action.

The highway crosses Beartooth Pass (10,940 feet), highest point on the route, then reaches Beartooth Plateau, a broad expanse of grassy tableland, a top-of-the-world landscape of colorful flowers, melting snowbanks, picturesque rocks and lakes.

Another few miles and the road passes Beartooth Butte, rising abruptly 1,500 feet above

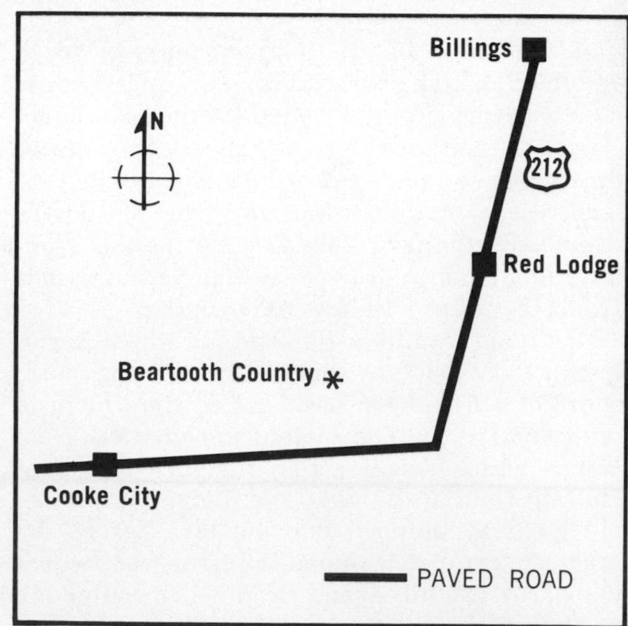

Beartooth Mountains

Beartooth Lake. In the red layer of rocks near its top are fossils of primitive, armor-plated fish and plants. The lake has a 4.5-mile shoreline and is stocked with rainbow, cutthroat, and brook trout. Cabins and horse rentals are available here.

Forest Service campgrounds are open from June until sometime in September. Campsites are filled on a first-come, first-served basis and length of stay is not limited.

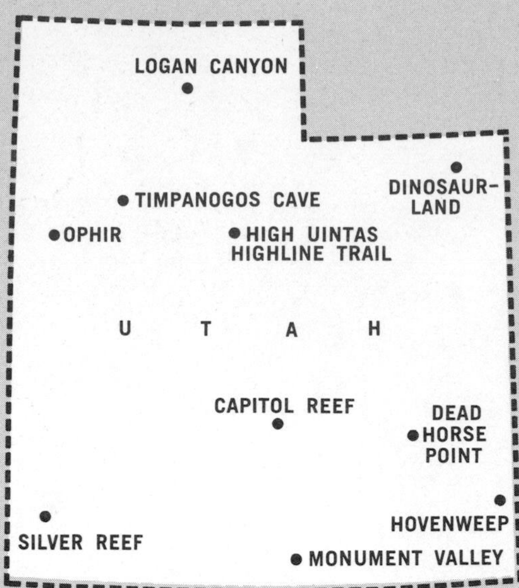

roaming

Utah is a land of contrasts: thousands of miles of deserts carved into segments by deep, red-rock canyons and fiery orange reefs and pinnacles; heavily timbered mountain ranges topped by snow-capped peaks; beautifully mysterious waters like the Great Salt Lake, emerald-hued Bear Lake, and the Flaming Gorge and man-made Lake Powell; dinosaur fossils in a wilderness and the cryptic towers of Hovenweep; Butch Cassidy's hideout at Robbers' Roost and legendary Timpanogos Cave and Dead Horse Point.

Utah is a land of moods—of soul-stirring thrills created by the crimson fire of a canyon sunset, the majestic silence of desert grandeur, the sudden charm of a small town nestled against a rugged mountain backdrop, or the peacefulness of a long, western twilight.

Adventure opportunities in the Beehive State abound, from the excitement of a river float trip down the Green, retracing Powell's famous expedition, or observing the excavation of dinosaur remains or exploring the High Uintas, the only mountain range running east and west in the United States. Hiking trails are numerous throughout this Primitive Area, providing the backpacker with unforgettable views of hundreds of high-country lakes, and offering the fisherman some of the best stream fishing for rainbow trout in the West.

For the family photographer, scenic views prevail mile after mile throughout the state. Logan Canyon is one of the most beautiful gorges in America. Dead Horse Point overlooks some 5,000 square miles of the Colorado River plateau and canyonlands. Spectacular, though isolated, Monument Valley is one of the most photographed areas in the great American West.

The ghost town addict's appetite will be satiated as he travels north to south in the central part of Utah—from Ophir, where Indians were using gold to make trinkets before the white man discovered it, to Silver Reef, where silver was first found interspersed in sandstone formations, disproving the old wives' tale that the two elements could not exist together.

This is Dinosaurland, Mountainland, Canyonland, Panoramaland. This is the different world of Utah.

Tony Lake in Logan Can

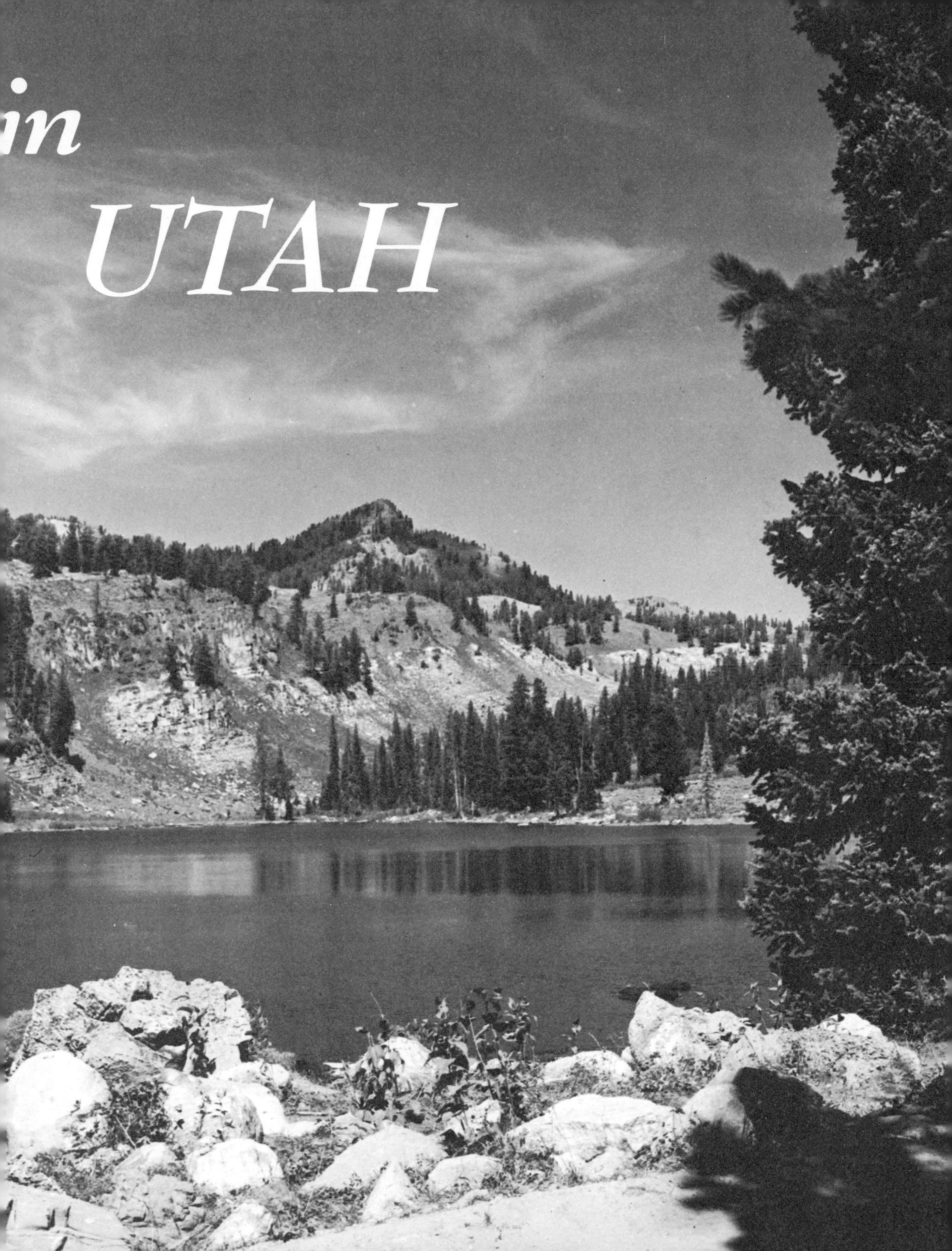
in
UTAH

LOGAN CANYON

32-mile drive through the most picturesque gorges

The takeoff point for the adventure tour of Logan Canyon and Bear Lake is Ogden, Utah's second largest city and a great hub of history of the Frontier West. U.S. 89 proceeds north through Brigham City (21 miles) and northeast 22 miles to Logan.

Logan Canyon extends from its mouth approximately 2.5 miles west and continues eastward through the Bear River Range for 32 miles to the Bear Lake Overlook. At 12 miles, about a tenth of a mile off the highway, is Logan Cave, a double-mouthed cavern nearly 2,000 feet in length. It is inhabited by bats, and can be explored if caution and a flashlight are used.

Thirteen miles east of the canyon origin is a 1.5-mile foot trail leading to Juniper Jardine, the oldest tree in Utah and considered by many to be the oldest juniper in the world as well as the largest. More than 3,000 years old, the tree is 44 feet high and more than 8 feet in diameter.

Not only is the canyon one of the most beautiful gorges in America, but the Logan River is one of Utah's best fishing streams. The entire area is sprinkled with exciting trails and mirror-like glacial lakes. Once out of the canyon depths, the road starts to climb, eventually reaching the Overlook providing a tremendous panorama of unique Bear Lake and beautiful Bear Valley. The lake, over 20 miles long and 6 miles wide, lies half in Utah and half in Idaho and is entirely surrounded by rugged mountains. Garden City is the main resort center for the lake, and the activities include fishing, swimming at the white sand beaches, boating, and water-skiing. On nearby Beaver Mountain is a major ski area, with slopes from 7,500 to 8,500 feet, double chair-lifts, a lodge, ski school, and snow rangers head-quarters. Other winter sports in the area include ice skating, ice fishing, and cutter races, a modern version of Roman chariot racing but with a new twist: they are run over snow.

There is a legendary sea monster supposedly observed by the Indians in Bear Lake. The Shoshone myth referred to "a great beast," which disappeared after extinction of the buffalo in the region by snowstorms in 1830. But the *Deseret News* on July 27, 1868 reported additional testimony as to the existence of a monster in the

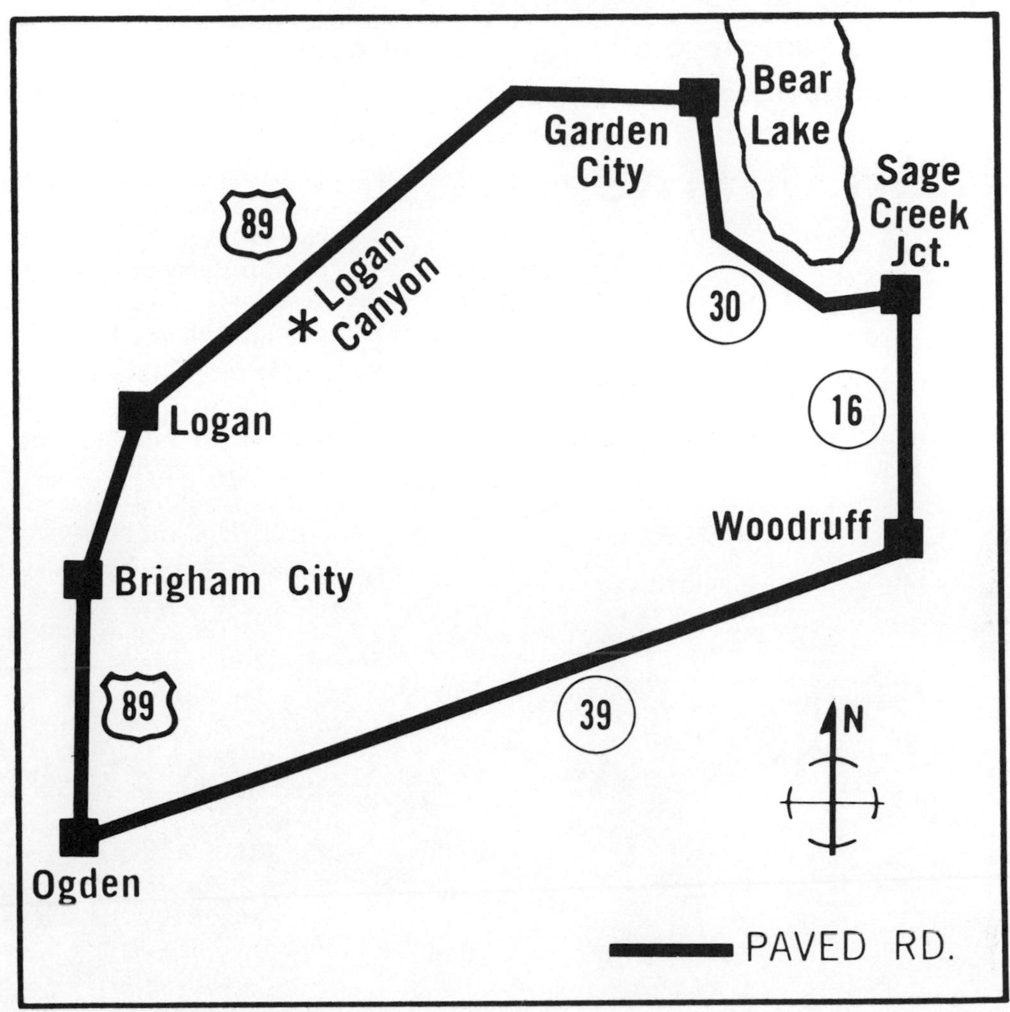

lake. S. M. Johnson of nearby South Eden stated that he saw the head of the animal rising from the lake. The next day, says the newspaper account, four people saw a large animal that "swam much faster than a horse could run on land." Another observer, Thomas Slight, said he "distinctly saw the sides of a very large animal that he would suppose to be not less than 90 feet in length." And Mr. Allen Davis stated that he "never saw a locomotive travel faster." But in the past century the monster of Bear Lake has remained invisible and there have been no more sightings reported.

The Bear River valley stretches south and east of Bear Lake, a richly developed farm land in the shadow of the high peaks of the mighty Wasatch Range.

An interesting circle route from Bear Lake to Ogden starts at Garden City. Take State 30 through Bear Lake valley to Sage Creek Junction (25 miles), then right on State 16 to Woodruff, one of the coldest spots in Utah (officially recorded temperature of 50 below zero). Turn right on State 39, across the Wasatch Range through Cache National Forest to Ogden (70 miles).

From Woodruff the highway passes through Walton Canyon, past the Monte Cristo Recreation Area and over the highest point, 9,008 feet, near Monte Cristo Peak. State 39 continues through Huntsville, a typical Mormon village, and reaches Ogden through Ogden Canyon, a dramatic narrow passage between towering, vertical cliffs.

site of the Highline Trail and the only mountain range running east and west in the United States

HIGH UINTAS

The High Uintas Primitive Area, with its 244,000 acres of mountains, lakes, timber, and streams, is less than three hours' driving time from the heart of busy Salt Lake City. The route proceeds east on U.S. 40 to Silver Creek Junction (28 miles), then left on U.S. 189 to Wanship (8 miles).

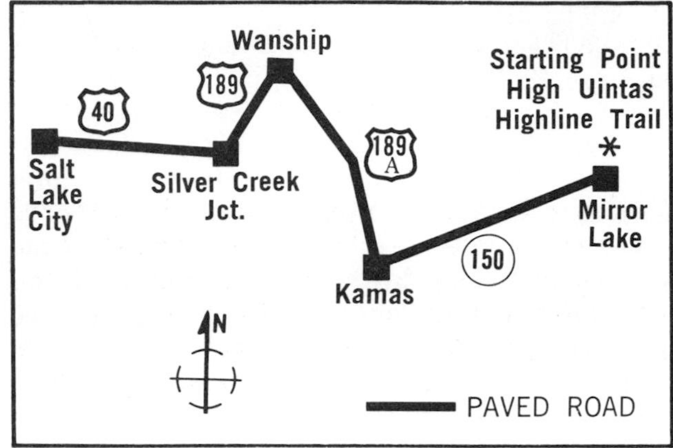

Take U.S. 189A south to Kamas. State 150 (left) continues to Mirror Lake (29 miles) at the western edge of the Primitive Area.

Extending along the crest of the Uinta Mountains from Mirror Lake eastward to King's Peak (13,498 feet), highest in Utah, the area is geologically unique, for this is the only mountain range running east and west in the United States. Besides King's Peak, the High Uintas include four other peaks more than 13,000 feet high. As the result of the Ice Age thousands of years ago, hundreds of small depressions were created which have now become crystal-clear alpine lakes. Most of the larger lakes are stocked with trout offering the angler that exciting combination of good fishing and a backdrop of magnificent scenery.

Because it is a Primitive Area, no roads or other provisions for motor transportation are available, and no man-made structures exist, except those which were already in place at the time the Primitive Area was established. Here the adventurer can enjoy the unspoiled beauty of the West, a wilderness that still exists unchanged from the days of the mountain man and the rugged frontier explorer.

Hiking trails and pack trips on horseback are not difficult and offer the only method of exploring the High Uintas Primitive Area. The Highline Trail starts from Mirror Lake, touching the south edge of Bonny Lake (2.5 miles), noted for its excellent rainbow trout fishing. Continuing east through tall forests and colorful mountain meadows, the trail winds its way to Scutter Lake (6 miles) and then crosses the North Fork of the Duchesne River (8 miles), another ideal fishing stream. A mile beyond, a second trail leads to the right to Four Lake Basin (4 miles), the heart of a region including perhaps a dozen lakes, all well stocked with native and rainbow trout.

Winding generally eastward, the Highline Trail crosses Rocky Sea Pass, and the hiker experiences some of the most difficult terrain—rough, steep, and rocky. At 18 miles the trail circumvents a towering rock point and winds north to a small lake crowded between two solid rock cliffs and fed by small springs gushing forth from the cliff face.

Twenty-four miles farther, at the summit of Red Knob Pass, is one of the more magnificent panoramas of bleak, craggy peaks, with Mt. Lovenia (13,277 feet) towering over all, and to the east are dense forests dotted with dozens of lakes. At the summit of Anderson Pass (42 miles), just north of King's Peak, a path leads to the highest point on the trail, where the register of those who have taken the trail is kept.

The route crosses Gunsight Pass, down through lush meadows and heavy timber to Henry's Fork Park (56 miles), the eastern terminus of the Highline Trail. Several good campsites maintained by the U.S. Forest Service are located here.

A detailed map showing trails through the High Uintas Primitive Area is available from the U.S. Forest Service in Salt Lake City. Names of experienced guides and information concerning pack trips may be obtained through the Utah Tourist and Publicity Council at Salt Lake City.

Numerous graded and dirt roads may be taken around the perimeter of the Primitive Area, many of these leading to various campgrounds or dude ranches. From Vernal, on U.S. 40, an interesting 79-mile scenic drive around the Red Cloud Loop may be taken by conventional vehicles. Take State 44 north from Vernal 22.1 miles, turning left on a graded road into Ashley National Forest. Three miles from the highway is Iron Springs Campground, from which a foot trail leads approximately one-half mile to Big Brush Creek Cave, an ice-filled cavern penetrating several hundred feet into the mountainside.

The road loops back to Vernal through Dry Fork Canyon, one of the most spectacular drives in the High Uintas. Many good to excellent campgrounds and picnic areas are located along the route.

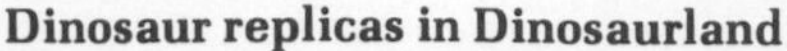

Dinosaur replicas in Dinosaurland

fossilized dinosaur bones exposed in canyon country

DINOSAURLAND

Dinosaur National Monument, located in the northeastern corner of Utah and northwestern Colorado, is part of an adventurers' paradise known as Dinosaurland. The traveler may follow Major John Wesley Powell's original footsteps from Green River, Wyoming, south on State 530 for 44 miles (route changes to State 43 at Utah line). Turn left at junction with State 44 at Manila, continuing 70 miles to Vernal. Turn left on U.S. 40 and proceed to Jensen and junction with State 149. Turn left and continue 6 miles to the Quarry Visitor Center.

From Salt Lake City, take U.S. 40 east for 184 miles to Jensen and proceed as above.

Part of Dinosaurland includes the high, craggy peaks of the Uinta Mountains and a vast, unspoiled wilderness, with some 800 crystal-clear mountain lakes. Teeming with trout, the lakes are scattered throughout the primitive area of the Wasatch and Ashley national forests.

Vernal marks the focal point for raft trips on the meandering Green River, an adventurous journey through exciting rapids, but safe for the entire family.

The Dinosaur Quarry can be observed from the Visitor Center—a remarkable view of scores of fossilized dinosaur bones that have been partially carved out of the rock in bas-relief to show how they existed at the exact moment of their burial some 140 million years ago. The quarry is approximately 40 feet high, 400 feet long, and 40 feet wide. The entire monument envelops 320 square miles of rugged, multicolored canyons and mesas, most of which can be observed close up through the use of river boats on the Green River or by driving the secondary dirt roads that twist through the countryside.

Part of the canyon section—including Lodore, Whirlpool, and Split Mountain canyons of the Green River and the Bear Canyon of the Yampa—is located primarily in Colorado. All are breathtaking gorges up to 3,000 feet deep, exposing multicolored strata eroded and cut away over the past thousands of centuries.

Today a great desert highland, there was a time—100 million years ago—when this land was a rich valley through which broad streams meandered, teeming with crocodiles, fish, and amphibians. On the land, verdant with ferns, grasses, and giant trees, huge beasts wallowed through the marshy swamplands and reptiles of every size and shape lived in abundance. Some were small, no larger than a rat, and others, the dinosaurs, were over 100 feet in length and weighed as much as 40 tons.

One of the most vivid descriptions of Dinosaurland was written a century ago by Major Powell during his first expedition. Today, the

Dinosaur National Monument in northwestern Colorad

view from the summit on the east side of Split Mountain Canyon remains as he described it:

"We are standing three thousand feet above its waters, which are troubled with billows and white with foam. Its walls are set with crags and peaks, and buttressed towers, and overhanging domes. Turning to the right, the park is below us, with its island groves reflected by the deep, quiet water.

"Rich meadows stretch out on either hand to the verge of a sloping plain, that comes down from the distant mountains. These plains are of almost naked rocks, in strange contrast to the meadows; blue and lilac colored rocks, buff and pink, vermilion and brown, and all these colors clear and bright. A dozen little creeks, dry the greater part of the year, run down through the half-circle of exposed formations, radiating from the island-center to the rim of the basin. Each creek has its system of side streams . . . Beds of different colored formations run in parallel bands on either side. The perspective, modified by the undulations, give the bands a waved appearance, and the high colors gleam in the midday sun with the luster of satin. We are tempted to call this Rainbow Park.

"Away beyond these beds are the Uinta and Wasatch mountains, with their pine forests and snowfields and naked peaks. Now we turn to the right and look up Whirlpool Canyon, a deep gorge with a river in the bottom—a gloomy chasm, where mad waves roar; but, at this distance and altitude, the river is but a rippling brook, and the chasm a narrow cleft. The top of the mountain on which we stand is a broad, grassy table, and a herd of deer is feeding in the distance. Walking over to the southeast, we look down into the valley of White River, and beyond that see the far distant Rocky Mountains, in mellow, perspective haze, through which snowfields shine."

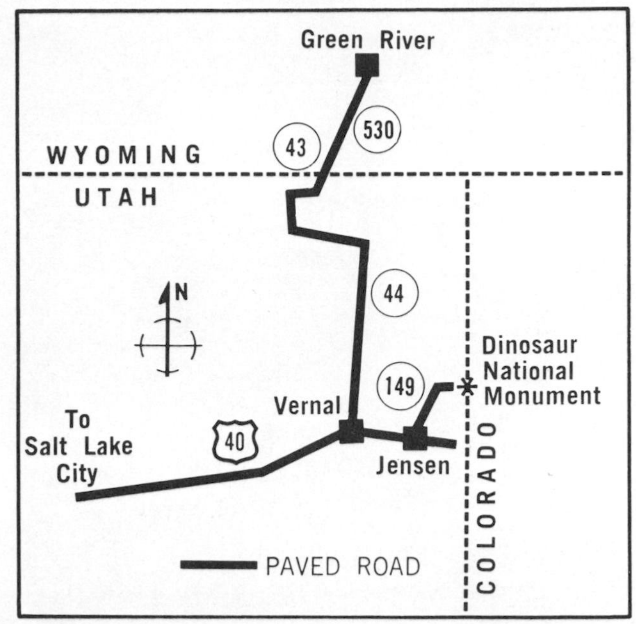

There are camping and picnic areas at Split Mountain and Green River, but there are no lodging facilities or supplies available at the monument.

hidden lake and caverns where nature's sculpture is still at work

TIMPANOGOS CAVE

From Salt Lake City, the trip to mysterious Timpanogos Cave National Monument is a short 27 miles, via U.S. 91 for 17 miles to the junction with State 80. Turn left and proceed 9.8 miles to the parking area. For a spectacular circle tour, continue on State 80 to the junction with U.S. 189. Go north to Heber City (and junction with U.S. 40) for trip back to Salt Lake City.

Timpanogos Cave lies hidden on the precipitous north slope of Mount Timpanogos in the dramatic Wasatch Range. Normally the cave, 1,000 feet above the road and reached by a 1.5-mile foot trail, is open during the daylight hours from May 1 to October 31.

Timpanogos is actually a series of three small caves connected by man-made tunnels, the first of which was discovered by Martin Hansen in 1887 and is called Hansen Cave. The others were not discovered until 1921.

Along the hour-long trail the Utah Valley and American Fork Canyon stretch below, offering a spectacular panorama. Much of the cave interiors are covered by a filigree of pink and white translucent crystals which glow like expensive jewels in the subdued light. An 85-foot arched tunnel leads from Hansen to Middle Cave. This is a narrow, winding tunnel with a vaulted ceiling, reaching a height of 125 feet. A series of winding passages, stairs, and grilled footways lead from one portion of the cave to another. Colors range from pure white to lemon yellow, ivory, brown, coral, and mauve.

Timpanogos Cave, connected to Middle Cave by a 190-foot tunnel, is the most dramatic. There is a hidden lake and hundreds of formations in the cave that bear resemblances to camels, chickens, or human hearts, as the imagination dictates. There are feathery boas, braided wreaths, and needlelike stalactites among the myriads of nature's wonders.

Formation of dripstone is still taking place. From the tips of the stalactites hang sparkling drops of water, each of which leaves behind an infinitesimal layer of limestone before it drops to the floor, where another bit of calcium carbonate is deposited. So slow is the process that it may require 100 years to add a single inch to a stalactite or stalagmite.

With the temperature inside the cave at 43 degrees, a light sweater will add to the visitor's comfort. A brief stop at the visitor center will provide interesting details concerning the formation and history of the cave.

After completing a tour of the cave, the adventurer will find dramatic vistas and exciting trails in the Mount Timpanogos Scenic Area, an area of 10,750 acres in the Uinta National Forest set aside as wilderness. The region abounds with wildlife: mule deer, rodents, golden eagle, bobcat, porcupine, and a variety of birdlife.

Once each year, in July, Brigham Young University sponsors a hike to the top of Mount Timpanogos. Approximately 4,000 people participate in the event, although only 2,000 usually complete the 12-mile hike to the 12,008-foot peak.

Continuing east on State 80, the route winds toward Aspen Grove, and joins U.S. 189 at Wildwood, turning north into beautiful Heber Valley, often called the Switzerland of America. Completely encircled by mountains, it is rich farming and dairy country. Adjoining the valley is Wasatch Mountain State Park, encompassing 22,000 acres of wooded mountain slopes and canyons.

U.S. 40 connects at Heber and continues through Hailstone, Kimball, and Parleys Canyon to Salt Lake City.

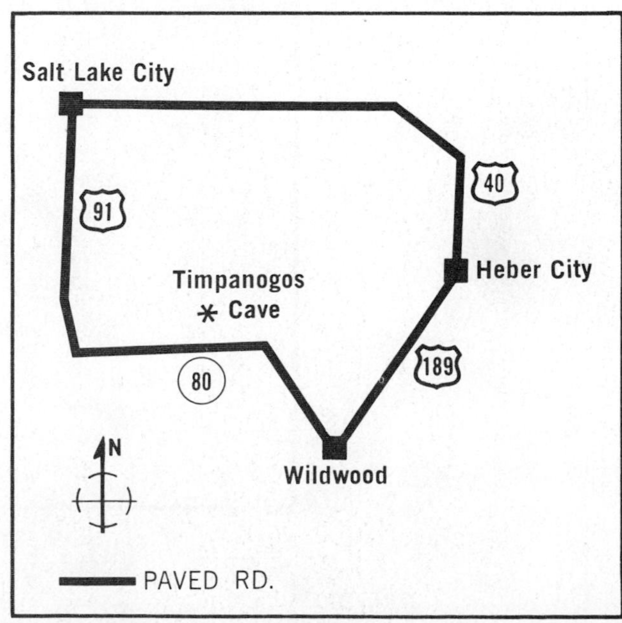

where Indians mined silver and gold long before the white man

To reach the adventure point of Ophir, an old ghost town nestled in the Oquirrh Canyon, leave Salt Lake City on U.S. 40 west 25 miles to Mills Junction. State 36 leads south, paralleling the rich, mineral-producing Oquirrh Mountains to the east and the Stansbury Mountains to the west. Continue through Tooele (9 miles) and the worn-out old town of Stockton (7 miles), coming

OPHIR

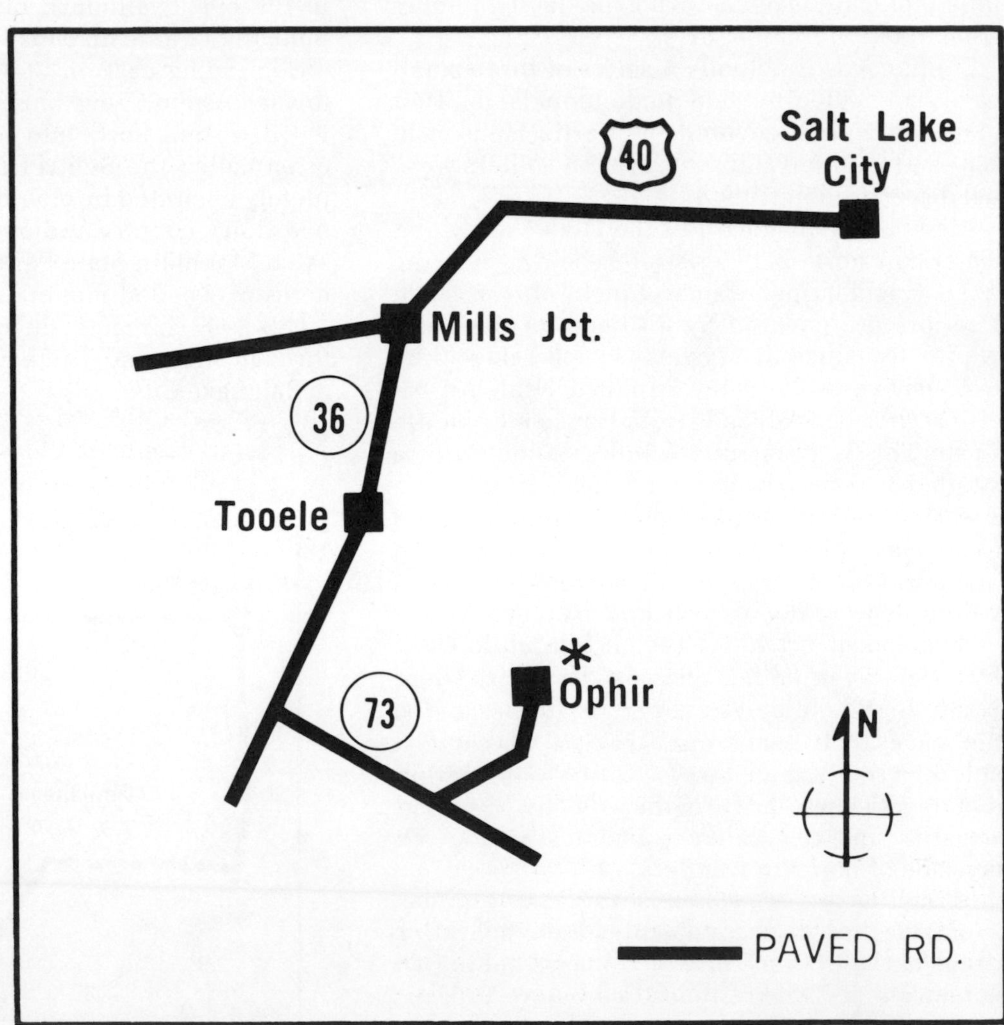

to the junction with State 73 (4 miles). Turn left and proceed for 5.1 miles to an unmarked paved road leading north. Continue on this road for 3 miles to Ophir.

Centuries ago Indians mined silver and gold for trinkets in this deep, narrow canyon until Colonel Patrick Connor's men heard of the activity and moved in, staked the St. Louis Lode claim in 1865, and named the town for the fabulous mines of King Solomon (contrary to the old-timers' version that when they first saw the area the soldiers shouted, "Oh fer God's sake").

When news of success leaked out, other prospectors made their way along the bottom of the rugged limestone cliffs toward the isolated canyon and staked claims to be known as the Wild Delirium, the Pocatello, the Ophir, the Miner's Delight, and the Velocipede. By the 1870s the entire area was booming. The Pioneer Mill was built by the Walker Brothers of Salt Lake City and was producing 30 tons of ore a day. Soon other mills sprang up: the Ophir, the Brevoort, the Faucett, and Enterprise.

Mack Gisborn, an old prospector who made it big at nearby Mercur and turned entrepreneur, built a toll road from Ophir to Stockton. From there the ore was hauled north to Lake Point on the Great Salt Lake and then boated to Corinee and the newly constructed railroad. The town was booming and rows of shacks appeared almost overnight to house the miners and the promoters and gamblers who became a part of every mining camp. Saloons lined the streets, interspersed with dance halls, brothels, and gambling halls.

One dramatic poker game between Digger Mike and Frank Payton is recounted in the *Park City Record*, as related by an eyewitness: "I walked over to the corner table and took a position where I could watch the players. Digger had about $5000 in front of him while Payton had about $7,000. Both men played cautiously for awhile, or until there was a jackpot which Digger opened with a bag of gold dust. Payton stayed and raised him $250, which the Digger saw and went him $500 better. Payton just called him and then threw five hundred of his dust into the pot remarking, 'I don't need any.'

"Payton skinned his hand again and after going through the usual motions of looking at his antagonist for a few minutes he saw the five hundred and went it five hundred better. Digger was more prompt in raising this four bags of dust and Payton even more promptly saw the raise and went it two thousand better. They continued to raise each other until the Digger shouted for a showdown, saying he couldn't call another cent. Both hands went down on the board at the same moment and then Payton reached over and began to scoop in the gold dust and chips. He had a pair of fours, while Digger had been bluffing on a kelter (absolutely nothing). 'I didn't think you had enough nerve to follow me, Frank,' was all he said as he got up from the table to leave the place to go back to the diggings to toil for more gold dust."

The aftermath: Payton left the saloon and that was the last time he was seen until his body was found a week later in a ravine. His skull was crushed and his money was gone.

Ophir was the springboard for Marcus Daly, the Montana copper king who staked the Zella claim during the Ophir boom and used the profits to start the giant Anaconda Copper Corporation. Ophir also produced one of the largest silver nuggets ever found. It was sent to the St. Louis World's Fair in 1904.

By 1880 the boom days were over and virtually all of the mines were abandoned, although in the 1930s deeper shafts were sunk in the area and some production was resumed. But, except for a few tumbling stone buildings, marking the firehouse and the post office, the wild bloom that was once Ophir has faded and died.

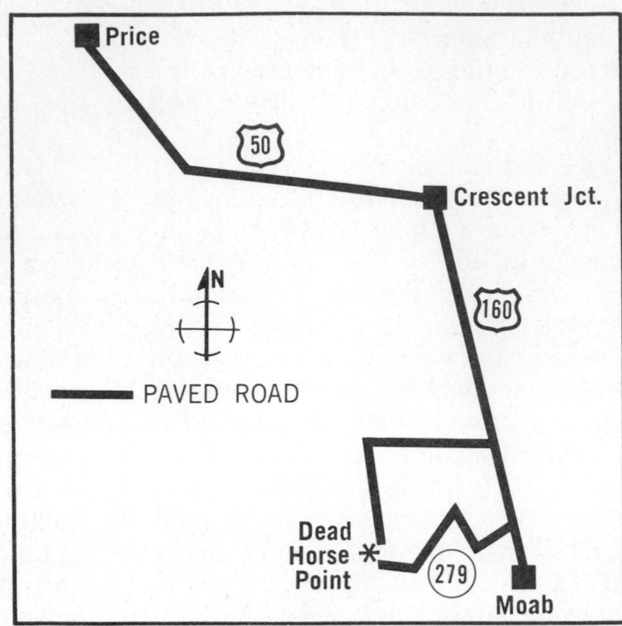

overlooking 5,000 square miles of breathtaking canyons

DEAD HORSE POINT

From Price, the adventure starting point, to Dead Horse Point is 126 miles, via U.S. 50 southeast to Crescent Junction. Turn right on U.S. 160 and proceed 21 miles to the junction with a paved, unmarked road. Turn right and continue 10 miles, then sharp left, remaining on paved road for 13 miles to Dead Horse Point.

An alternate route, offering more thrills and excitement, starts from Moab along State 279 following the north bank of the Colorado River. The road passes a potash mining complex (visitors welcome) and then switchbacks up Shafer Trail to the top of the plateau and Dead Horse Point. This should only be attempted in good weather and must be driven with extreme care.

A short trail through a grove of cedars growing out of the red sandstone formation leads to the Point, overlooking a great bend in the Colorado River shaped roughly like an arrowhead. From this spot, the entire Canyonlands region sweeps in a full circle, encompassing fantastic cliffs, buttes, gorges, and mesas, and all in varying shades of reddish colors, from deep vermilion to subtle pink hues.

Dead Horse Point is virtually the gateway to the recently created Canyonlands National Park, which is still in the young stage of development but will eventually be a fabulous Utah attraction.

From Dead Horse Point the view overlooks some 5,000 square miles of the rugged Colorado Plateau. The panorama extends east to the La Sal Mountains, south to the Abajo Mountains, southwest to the Henry Mountains, and west to the Acuarious Plateau. And, 2,500 feet below, the Colorado River winds sinuously, snaking its way in great loops through a maze of buttes and mesas, visible from the Point at a dozen different places.

According to Indian legend, which is probably true, the name originated as a logical consequence of events. A band of wild desert ponies was herded on the Point, with the best of them being taken for the Indians' own and the remainder left on the high; peninsulalike mesa. Bewildered by the strange surroundings, the wild horses wandered in circles, some of them eventually falling to their deaths in the canyon below, others dying of thirst, unable to reach the great Colorado, only a half-mile away, but straight down.

Dead Horse Point

The Point is a state park, with a headquarters building, shelter, protective fence, water, and campground facilities.

It is only a short distance to Grandview Point (in Canyonlands National Park), offering a view straight down into Monument Canyon, a gigantic bowl eroded out of the White Rim and including innumerable free-standing pinnacles and weirdly shaped buttresses.

Moab itself is the takeoff point for numerous river trips. Pleasure cruises are available from Moab, and launch facilities are excellent for those who have their own boats. In May and June, hundreds of people assemble from all over the country to participate in the Friendship Cruise (held in May) and the River Marathon (held in June) between Green River City and Moab.

from prehistory—petrified forests, petroglyphs, and pictographs

CAPITOL REEF

From Provo, the spectacular rainbow-rocked region of sheer-walled canyons known as Capitol Reef is reached by taking U.S. 89 south for 107 miles to Sigurd, at the junction of State 24, and proceeding southeasterly for 71 miles.

The small town of Fruita is located in the Capitol Reef National Monument, and both horses and guides are available for extensive tours of this dramatic wonderland. Although lesser known, Capitol Reef has combined the fantasy of Bryce with its steep scarps, carved pinnacles, and gorges, and the grandeur of Zion, but surpassing both in the brilliant colors of its carved pinnacles and dramatic canyon walls.

The reef extends for 20 miles and is visible for miles, thrusting upward for hundreds of feet above the surrounding terrain. The reef is part of the Waterpocket Fold, so named because of numerous natural pockets which hold thousands of gallons of water in the spring. The fold reveals a thousand feet of varied rock strata, pushing upward toward the west and disappearing beneath the ground in a great curving arc to the east.

Parallel to the eastern slope of the Waterpocket Fold is a dry-weather road extending from Notom to the Bullfrog Recreation Area bordering recently developed Lake Powell.

Petrified forests that flourished millions of years ago abound throughout the monument, particularly in the area north from Cathedral Cliffs to Chimney Rock.

Both prehistoric Basket Makers and Pueblo Indians have carved petroglyphs and painted pictographs on many of the cliff walls, and occasional remnants of adobe granaries have been found.

East of the reef the Fremont River, which has cut its deep gorge through the monument, meanders through a landscape substantially different from that on the west of the reef. Except for an occasional oasis, like the tiny town of Caineville, the land is endless desert, multi-

colored in subdued hues of yellows, grays, and browns, with occasional pockets of variegated shale or clay.

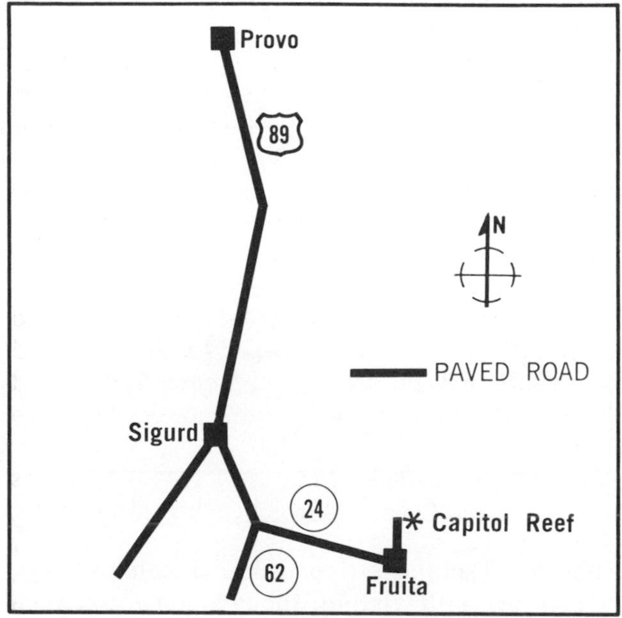

It is possible to explore by horseback the deep river gorge of the Fremont, leading from Fruita to Broad Arch (3 miles). The massive arch of pink and white sandstone is 15 feet thick at the narrowest point and 133 feet from rim to rim. En route to the arch the trail passes a well-preserved cliff dwelling and a tiny natural bridge.

Historically, the area near Capitol Reef offered within its many deep canyons ideal hide-outs for many of the West's notorious outlaws, particularly Butch Cassidy and the Wild Bunch, who virtually claimed an area in the vicinity—Robbers Roost—as their private sanctuary.

Desert and semidesert plants grow profusely in the Capitol Reef Monument. By late spring and early summer, a dozen or more varieties of desert wild flowers are in bloom. The land also supports cactus, cedar, and juniper trees. Some of the flowering plants include Indian paintbrush, desert geraniums, and Spanish bayonets, with some yucca and scattered clumps of grama grass. At one time herds of wild horses roamed the area, but most animal life today is confined to ground squirrels, chipmunks, coyotes, and lizards.

The main road continues east through Grand Wash for several miles, then to Capitol Gorge, with castellated formations set high on sloping purple bases, with summits 1,200 feet above the canyon floor. The gorge is walled by red and tan-colored cliffs, as well as an endless variety of magnificently colored monoliths and pinnacles.

A few miles beyond, the canyon pinches to a width of 18 feet, its walls towering to heights nearing 1,000 feet. At the eastern end of the Narrows, natural tanks were formed ages ago and were used as watering places by the Indians. From this point to the end of the Capitol Reef National Monument, the cliff walls are lower, though multicolored. And as the highway emerges, passing The Golden Throne Mountain, the magic fairyland is left behind and the rolling desert hills stretch endlessly ahead.

apitol Reef National Monument

With Cedar City in southwestern Utah as a starting point, U.S. 91 south touches Kanarraville (named for a Paiute Indian chief), passes through Anderson Junction, and intersects a gravel road to the right (36 miles), less than a mile before reaching Leeds. Proceed on this road for 1.2 miles and turn left on a dirt road at the base of a red reef to the deserted, ghostly town of Silver Reef.

The discovery of silver in the sandstone formations near the town disproved the popular theory of the day that "silver is never found in sandstone." Silver Reef ranks as one of the most fabulous of the early mining camps, flourishing during the 1870s and 1880s and even threatening nearby St. George as the county seat before the air was let out of the silver bubble.

Today, covered by weeds and sage, the old streets still wind along the ridge, and the crumbling foundations of the gambling dens,

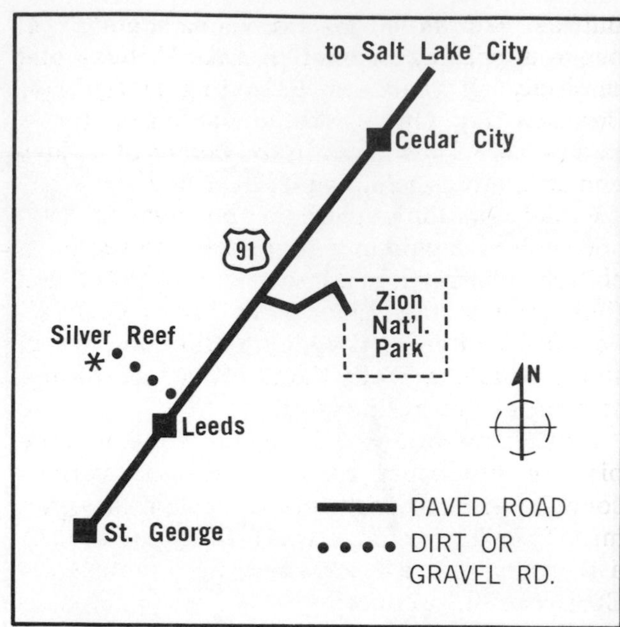

boom-and-bust site of spectacular silver strike in the 1870s

SILVER REEF

churches, schools, dance halls, saloons, and homes are still visible, though more a part of nature than of man. Only two complete buildings remain, having withstood for a century the assaults of the elements and the ghost town treasure hunters.

Stories of the discovery of silver are varied, some maintaining that the Spaniards once mined in the area, others insisting that an unknown passerby made the first discovery. It is known that the first claims were filed by John Kemple, a prospector, who originally explored the area in 1866 and returned with a party of men in 1870 to file on a white reef a few miles north of town. Kemple named it the Harrisburg Mining District, but very little was accomplished until the Walker Brothers, Salt Lake City bankers, sent William Tecumseh Barbee, Ed Maynard, and Thomas McNally to the area to check on Kemple's find.

Barbee's enthusiasm was boundless, and he sent back glowing reports of finding silver everywhere, even in petrified wood, and proceeded to locate 22 claims on Tecumseh Ridge. After a quick trip to Salt Lake City for supplies, he returned to establish "Bonanza City."

His companions were skeptical, pointing out to the Walkers that silver just did not occur in sandstone. On the basis of this report, the bankers bowed out, turning over all claims to

Barbee. Stories of the fantastic silver finds began appearing in the *Salt Lake Tribune* and suddenly all roads were leading to Barbee's Bonanza City. One of the new arrivals, Hyrum Jacobs, set up his camp in the center of a ridge and officially proclaimed it Silver Reef.

Father Scanlan arrived in the town in 1877, and under his guidance funds were raised for a church, a hospital, and a school. Also in 1877 the first issue of the *Silver Reef Echo* appeared. Soon Silver Reef had added a mile-long line of stores, hotels, a Wells Fargo office, a brewery, saloons, and gambling halls.

By 1880 operations were at full scale, with the big ore producers consolidated into various companies, each with its own amalgam stamp mill. The Buckeye mine was turning out, in 1877, a thousand-ounce brick every day. In 1878 the Christy mill produced 10,249 tons valued at $302,597.

But the boom was nearing its end, and a combination of falling silver prices and water in the mines created a crisis for the operators. Wages were cut from $4 to $3.50 per day, and the 300 miners in the area refused to accept the pay cut and left the mines. Eventually, after the union ringleaders ran Colonel Allen, superintendent of one of the mines, out of town, there were wholesale arrests of the miners and activities in Silver Reef soon came to a standstill.

All companies had ceased operating by 1891, although there was a revival the following year that lasted until 1903, when silver dropped to $.65 an ounce. In 1916 Alex Collbath organized the Silver Reef Consolidated Company, which led to a flurry of activity that continued through World War I. But with silver prices dropping to $.25 an ounce, all hope for Silver Reef was lost, and today it remains as a rather shabby monument to a fabulous past.

HOVENWEEP

Hovenweep, a national monument located in one of the most remote parts of Utah's canyonlands, is reached from Provo via U.S. 50 southeast for 147 miles, right on U.S. 160 (at Crescent Junction) for 84 miles to Monticello and a junction with State 47 through Blanding (22 miles), continuing for 15 miles to junction with State 262. Turn left. At approximately 9 miles, State 262 turns right, but a graveled road continues straight ahead 14 miles to Hovenweep.

Hovenweep can be approached from Cortez, Colorado, by traveling south on State 106 for 4 miles and turning right on graveled road, continuing 29 miles to the entrance. All roads are passable in dry weather.

The ruins of Hovenweep, dating back at least 800 years, were originally built by the Pueblo Indians with a highly developed culture. Abandoned by the Pueblos around A.D. 1300 after a drought that lasted a quarter of a century, the ruins were passed by when Padres Escalante and Dominquez went through the region in 1776 and were not actually discovered by the white man until the time of the Hayden expedition a hundred years later.

The Monument includes four large canyons, the principal ruins being located in Ruin and Cajon canyons in Utah, and in Hackberry and Keely canyons in Colorado. Most impressive of the ruins is the Square Tower Canyon cluster, part of the south fork of Ruin Canyon. The main canyon appears suddenly, without warning, some 300 to 500 feet deep, an abrupt drop from the mesa top. Along the canyon walls are found Hovenweep House, at the head of Square Tower Canyon. At one time this large semicircular structure housed 50 or more families and included several kivas (underground ceremonial rooms) and a large tower rising from the approximate center of the dwelling.

Below Hovenweep House, dug out of the steep cliff wall, are the remains of Square Tower. On the north rim of Square Tower Canyon is Hovenweep Castle, well preserved, with massive walls built of rock and mud mortar, some of them rising for 20 feet.

A short hike from Hovenweep Castle leads to a large, circular kiva surrounded by rectangular rooms known as Unit Type House. In Cajon Canyon, southwest of Ruin, is a major ruin called Cool Spring House. Directly east from Ruin, across the Colorado line, are Hackberry Castle and Horseshoe House.

The original builders of Hovenweep migrated, apparently, from the north, learning as they went. When they first settled along the tributaries of the Colorado River, they were far more primitive, living in simple pit dwellings. But as they continued south, they built more complex structures, developed the art of pottery making, began to farm the land, and established permanent communities.

Evidence exists at Hovenweep that the Indians constructed dams and irrigation ditches. Three-story houses were built, and the technique of raftering each floor with cedar logs was used.

The functions of the mysterious towers have been variously explained as lookout towers, storage bins, or religious temples. Most archeologists believe that they were used for all of these purposes.

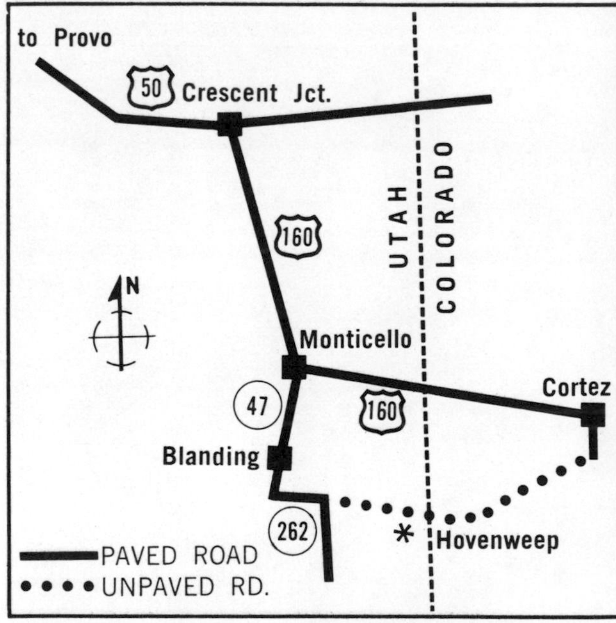

Another mystery surrounds the disappearance of the people. One Indian legend tells of an invasion by the Navajos living south of the San Juan River. Following an invasion, the Navajos drove the Hovenweep people into the rivers, where they were changed into fish. More logical is the explanation that, as the communities grew in size, arable lands were no longer able to support the population explosion and the people were forced to migrate southward.

Pueblo ruins in Square Tower Canyon, Hovenwee

mysterious ruins
of the Pueblo civilization

remote land of giant monoliths

MONUMENT VALLEY

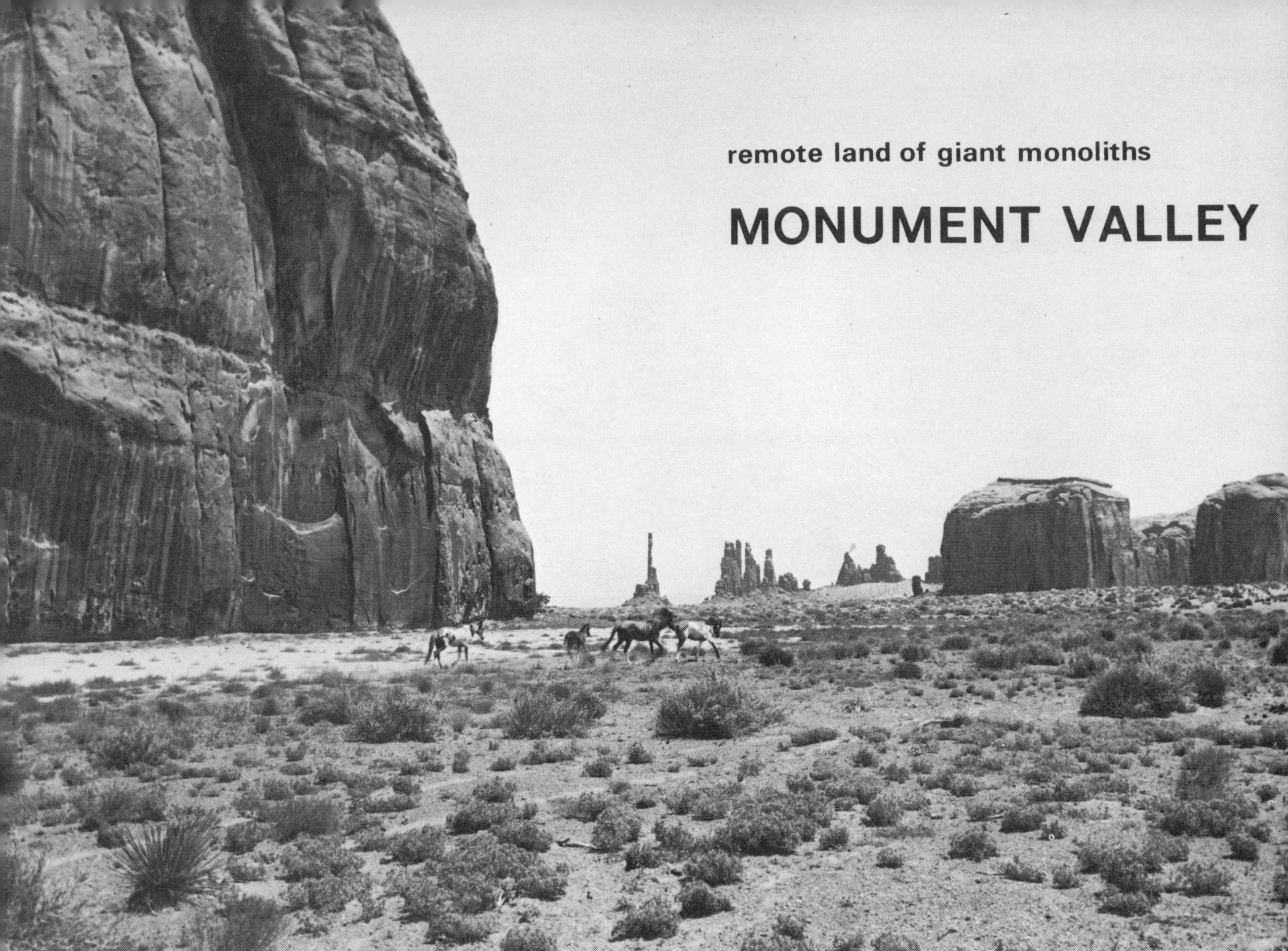

Monument Valley, one of the most photographed scenic areas in western America, is also one of the most remote. Located on the southern border of Utah and actually extending into Arizona, it is most easily approached from Monticello, some 90 miles to the northeast. From Monticello, take State 47 through Blanding (22 miles), the small town of Bluff (48 miles, population 70), Mexican Hat (73 miles), and into the vast and colorful Monument Valley.

The Valley is located on the Navajo Indian Reservation, where the Navajo still herd their sheep and goats and many still dwell in the traditional hogan (a rounded cabin of logs covered with red mud), although the ancestral dress and customs are gradually disappearing. Monument Valley remains virtually untouched by the outside world. Its great red cliffs extend endlessly toward the horizon, and fingerlike monoliths, extending a thousand or more feet skyward, dot the arid plain.

One of the unique attractions in the Valley is Rainbow Bridge, the largest and most beautifully formed natural bridge in the world. The Bridge, with a span measuring 278 feet, arches a canyon in the primitive arid country between Navajo Mountain and Glen Canyon. Rainbow Bridge, now a national monument, is accessible by overland trail or from Lake Powell.

The Navajos moved into the Southwest about 500 years ago and were, according to Spanish records, a warlike people. In 1863 Kit Carson was assigned to round up all the tribe and move them to Fort Sumner, New Mexico. Four years later they were released and allowed to return to their valley. Today, although the men continue to raise sheep and goats, the Navajo are noted for their excellent handwoven rugs.

All rug weaving is done by women, using wool from their own sheep and processed by their own hands. The value of a rug is determined by the closeness of the weave, the complexity of the

The Mittens, Monument Valle

design, and the weight.

A visit should be made to Goulding's Trading Post, reached by a paved road to the right just before reaching the Arizona line. Goulding himself is revered by the Indians and was influential in interesting Hollywood in the use of Monument Valley as a location for several movies, including the original *Stagecoach*.

The Navajo for many years have brought their wool, rugs, and silverwork to the trading post, and the traveler can be assured that the merchandise is authentic. Pack trips into the far reaches of the valley can also be arranged by Goulding.

Continuing on State 47 along the floor of the valley, several unusual monoliths are viewed to the left, including one of the Mittens and Merrick Butte. At the point of crossing into Arizona, Tuba City is 93 miles to the southwest via Arizona State 464 to Kayenta and the junction with U.S. 164, turning left and continuing 72 miles.

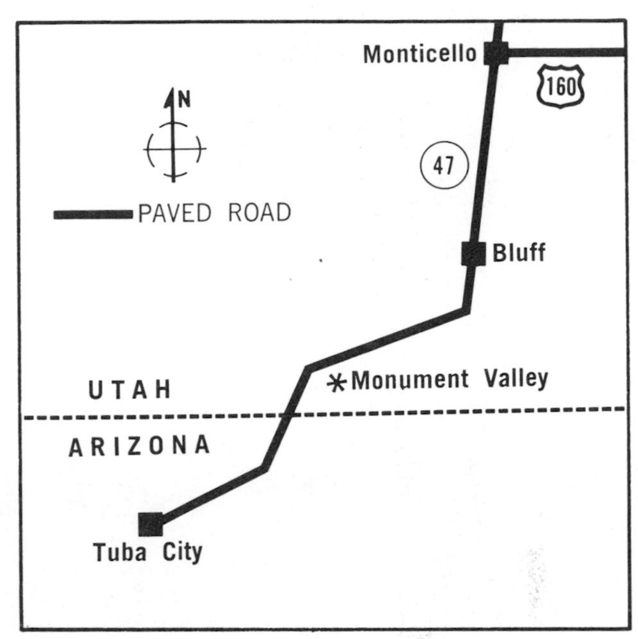

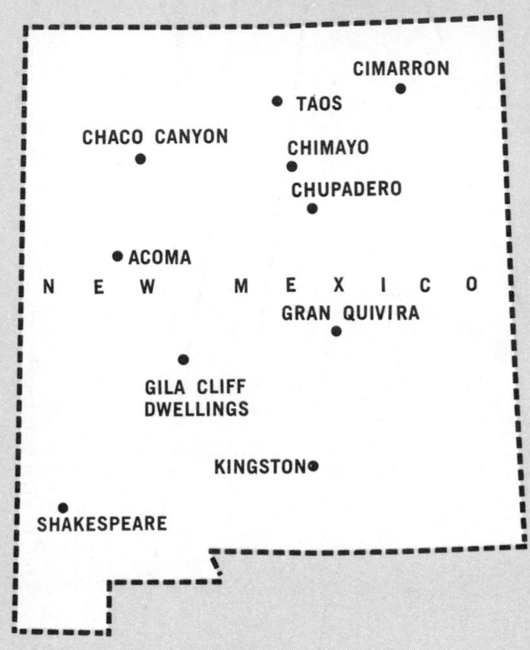

roaming ir

New Mexico is a state of diversity, culturally, politically, and geographically, but with an underlying mystique that pervades the land from the Four Corners on the north to the Mexican border on the south. Snow-capped mountains push southward from the Colorado line, flattening out to rolling hills and, finally, the desert and sage of the great Southwest. Deep forests beautify the slopes of the Sangre de Cristo range in varying hues of green until the fall, when splashes of golden aspen overwhelm the mountainsides. Slicing through the state is the life-supporting Rio Grande, cutting a deep and spectacular gorge between Taos and Santa Fe, eventually widening as it meanders through the rich, agricultural lands.

New Mexico is an old land, as measured by the white man, for it was the early sixteenth century when the Spaniards invaded the region on their search for golden treasure in the Seven Cities of Cibola, and the name New Mexico appears on maps as early as 1583—almost 300 years before the discovery of gold in California. And in the four centuries that

NEW MEXICO

followed, the territory of New Mexico has known three flags: Spanish, Mexican, and American. Where, except at the Taos Pueblo, can one find an apartment dwelling that has been lived in continuously for more than 800 years? In Chimayo, over a few hills from Santa Fe, the Tiwa Indians are practicing arts handed down from generation to generation —and the beginning was beyond the memory of man. In dozens of villages, a few hundred yards off the black-topped highways, the Pueblo people live, work, play, and dress as though time had stood still.

In other towns, like Cimarron, the remnants of the western frontier still breathe through crumbling walls and faded facades, and improbable places like Shakespeare, Kingston, and Hillsboro still echo the golden dreams men sought and died for less than a century ago.

New Mexico has a flavor, unique and unforgettable. New Mexico is a land of endless sky, sage, butte, and mesa and mountaintop. It is truly the Land of Enchantment.

Cimarron Canyon

CIMARRON

hangout for the fastest guns in the Wes

A circle trip to Cimarron country, with Santa Fe as a starting point, provides a full day of excitement and spectacular scenery through some of New Mexico's oldest and most historic areas. Take U.S. 64 north to Taos (see the next attraction under New Mexico), continuing through Eagle Nest and Ute Park to Cimarron (124 miles). The circle is completed by going east on State 58 to the junction with U.S. 85 and turning right through Springer, Wagon Mound, Las Vegas, and Glorieta to Santa Fe (156 miles).

Cimarron (meaning wild) is divided into two parts by the Cimarron River. New Town, located directly on U.S. Highway 64, dates from 1905 and includes a present population of approximately 1,000. To reach "Old" Cimarron, turn right (south) on State 21. To the north and west rise the dramatic Sangre de Cristo Mountains, while to the south and east are two of New Mexico's most fertile valleys.

Old Cimarron had its beginning about 1849 when Lucien Maxwell, a hunter and trapper who had accompanied General Fremont on two of his expeditions, settled on the land. By 1865 Maxwell and his wife were the sole owners of 1,714,765 acres, a territory some three times as large as Rhode Island. The grant originally awarded by Governor Armijo to Carlos Beaubein, Maxwell's father-in-law, extended on the east to Springer and Maxwell, west to Ute Park, and as far north as Stonewall in Colorado.

Maxwell enjoyed the finer things in life, living lavishly, gambling, drinking, and creating excitement when there was none. In his most prosperous days he had 500 peons working on the grant, grazing thousands of cattle and sheep, and keeping thousands of acres of his land under cultivation.

In 1860-62 Maxwell joined with Buffalo Bill Cody in a goat and sheep ranch operation near Cimarron. In 1867, disaster struck the one-time trapper as he dropped a fortune in a gold mining venture and was forced to sell a substantial portion of his grant for $750,000. In 1870 he founded the First National Bank of Santa Fe, but again he was unsuccessful. He sold out for $250,000, investing the proceeds in bonds for construction of the Texas Pacific Railroad. This venture wiped him out, and he died in 1875 in comparative poverty.

The Maxwell House, now in ruins in Old Cimarron, was at one time as large as a city block, housing a gambling room, billiard room, and dance hall. In the late 1860s and 1870s, Maxwell's became the principal stopping place for travelers on the Santa Fe Trail and the rendezvous for prospectors, hunters, trappers, cowboys, and outlaws. Its guests included Kit Carson, Ceran St. Vrain, Jesus Abreu, Davy Crockett, Clay Allison, Charles Bent, and Buffalo Bill.

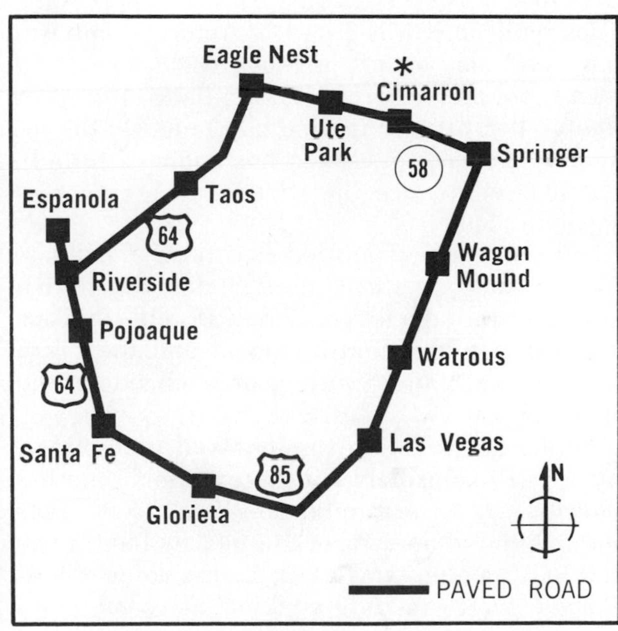

Across from the Maxwell House the St. James Hotel was built in the 1870s (it is now the Don Diego) by Henry Lambert, one-time chef for General Grant and President Lincoln. The St. James was the primary hangout for gunmen, and 26 killings were recorded there. According to legend, whenever a man was shot in the hotel the townspeople would say, "Lambert had a man for breakfast." The *Las Vegas* (New Mexico) *Gazette* once noted, "Everything is quiet in Cimarron. Nobody has been killed for three days."

Clay Allison, sometimes referred to as Cimarron's most notorious gunman, frequented the St. James, and one of his encounters has become a legend in Cimarron country. Pancho Griego had been dealing monte for some Negro soldiers when an argument started. Griego dashed the money to the floor and in the ensuing confusion he drew his gun and killed two of the soldiers, then took care of the third with his Bowie knife. It was a short time later that Pancho Griego decided he could likewise take on the infamous Allison. He started an argument with the gunman, at the same time fanning himself with his sombrero, holding it so as to shield his right hand as he attempted to slide the gun out of his holster. But Allison had stayed alive during his dangerous career by keeping alert. Before Griego could complete his maneuver, Allison had shot him twice through the head.

Saloon-keeper Lambert, in a desperate attempt to keep the peace, posted a sign which read: "Gents Will Please Leave Their Six-Guns Behind The Bar While In Town. This Will Lessen The Customary Collections for Burials."

Cimarron was the birthplace of Buffalo Bill's Wild West Shows, and he would frequently spend Christmas at the St. James Hotel, giving a party for all the children in town. On one occasion each child received a plush-seated tricycle; some of these valued treasures remain in existence today as priceless antiques.

Some of Cimarron's more interesting buildings include the Agency Warehouse, originally built in 1848 and now occupied as a residence; the county jail and courthouse, both built in 1854; the National Hotel built in 1858 (behind the Don Diego), and Swink's Gambling Hall, which rivaled Maxwell's as the best place in Cimarron to win or lose a fortune overnight (Swink's is now a garage).

Cimarron Canyon, west on U.S. 64, is a spectacular, narrow, twisting gorge whose sheer walls seem to overhang the highway. There are several good camping spots in this area between Cimarron and Ute Park (13 miles).

Taos Pueblo

TAOS

Taos (rhymes with house), 60 miles northeast of Santa Fe on U.S. 64, is the center of a way of life unique in America. The town itself, officially Don Fernando de Taos but shortened by the post office department to Taos before the turn of the century, has retained the charm, warmth, and architectural simplicity of a bygone era.

The one-story adobe stores of the village surround the grassy plaza shaded by the ancient cottonwoods. But if there is a similarity in the buildings, the inhabitants who live or work in Taos are as varied as the colors of a map. Indians from nearby Taos Pueblo, clothed in somber blankets, shuffle along the uneven sidewalks under the *portales*, contrasting with the light-skinned bearded Anglos, the Spanish cowboy with sombrero and cowboy boots, or the bewildered tourist in slacks and T-shirt.

Taos lies on a 7,000-foot mesa in the foothills of the Sangre de Cristo (Blood of Christ) mountain range, overlooking the awesome gorge of the Rio Grande. Its dramatic setting once prompted D. H. Lawrence to remark, after his first visit, "I think the skyline in Taos the most beautiful of all I have ever seen."

Captain Hernando de Alvarez, the first white man to enter this part of New Mexico, and his Spanish conquistadores first viewed Taos in 1540, when only the Taos Pueblo existed.

A general Pueblo revolt in 1680 forced the Spaniards to leave the country, but 16 years later, after continuous assaults, Don Diego de Vargas reconquered the territory for Spain. In all, Taos has been under three flags: the Spanish until the Spanish-Mexican war of 1821, then the Mexican and, after the United States' war with Mexico, the Stars and Stripes.

Taos throughout history has been a meeting place. In the beginning, it was a rendezvous point for the Plains and Pueblo Indians, for traders from Mexico and Old Spain. Later, the fabulous Mountain Men and the Indian fighters walked the sleepy streets: Bill Williams, Kit Carson, the Robidoux Brothers, Milton Sublette, the Bent Brothers, and Dick Wootton. And, starting in the 1880s and continuing today, Taos has been a meeting place and a home for dozens of artists, writers, sculptors, and other creative spirits. Taos is truly the art center of the Southwest. Frequent concerts, lectures, exhibitions, art films, symposiums, and dramatic productions are a part of Taos life. Nearly 100 artists are permanent residents of Taos, with scores of others arriving to spend their summer months in the pulsating atmosphere of creativity. Art is completely eclectic, varying in style from the traditional to the avant-garde.

The impact of art is immediately felt by every visitor. Every wall in Taos—be it hotel, motel, restaurant, service station, or public building—is adorned with original paintings. More than 30 art galleries are open on a year-round basis, and several of these are the display rooms of the artists themselves, who frequently, time permitting, describe their work to interested tourists.

But the Taos Pueblo, located 2.5 miles north of the town on State Highway 3, is also a part of the Taos syndrome. It is a part of America's ancient past, and also a part of the present. Occupied today by more than 1,400 Indians, the Taos Pueblo has been inhabited continuously for 800 years, and its appearance has changed little in the 400 years since the first Spanish explorers saw it in 1540.

Its two large, five-storied structures, the oldest "apartments" in the United States, are unlike any other Indian village. The Rio Pueblo de Taos cuts through the central plaza, and there are numerous private dwellings on each side of the river.

Adobe construction (mud mixed with straw) was used exclusively for the exteriors, and the interior walls are mud-plastered. The Taos Indians living here farm the nearby land, raise cattle or horses, and work in the town. Their special crafts include making moccasins and drums as well as a simple, micaceous pottery.

The Pueblo is self-governing, with an elected governor and a council of elders who handle

three cultures combine

in this historic art colony

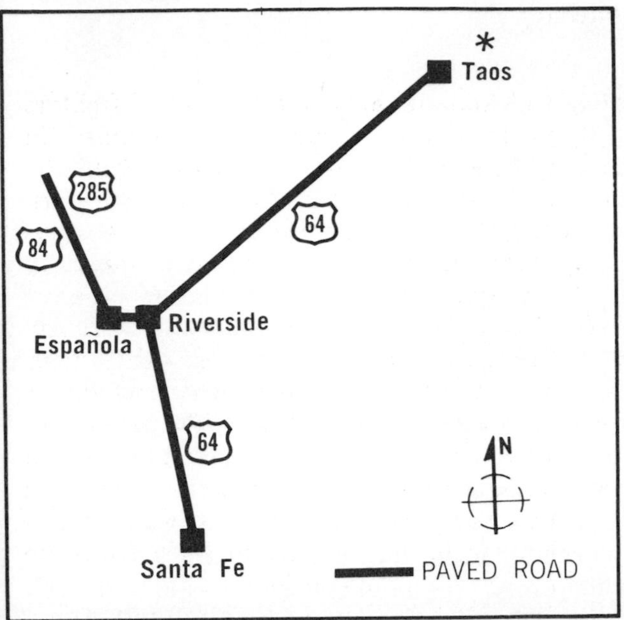

civic affairs. The *cacique* (priest) and the clan groups are historically instrumental in all the life of the Pueblo also, and ancestral ceremonials are still observed with traditional dances and songs.

Until about 1890 the only entrance to the terraced rooms on the upper levels was by means of ladders that led to hatchways in the roofs. As the danger of attack decreased, doors and windows were cut in the adobe walls, although ladders remain on the outside as the only access, since there are no inside stairways.

The dances are noted for their beauty and precision. The Deer, Buffalo, and Turtle dances are elaborate, combining dramatic symbolism with ritualistic movements.

Visitors are permitted to view many of the ceremonials through the courtesy of the Pueblo, but they must be observed with quiet respect. No picture-taking is permitted during the ceremonials. On nonceremonial days, pictures may be taken for fees ranging from $1.50 up, but no pictures may be taken of the Indians without their permission, and they may suggest a charge.

For the adventurer, the trip to Taos is not complete without visiting St. Francis of Assisi Mission Church at Ranchos de Taos, 4 miles south of town on U.S. 64. A massive, beautiful example of early Mission architecture, it is one of the oldest continuously used churches in the Southwest. Inside the church, which is surrounded by the traditional adobe wall, are numerous valuable religious objects as well as a mystery painting of Christ.

Within a short distance of Taos are numerous facilities for outdoor buffs: fishing, hunting, camping, hiking, and skiing. The Taos Ski Valley is reached through beautiful Rio Hondo Canyon (in summer, there are an abundance of camping and picnicking areas available). Take State 3 north, turn east on State 150 4 miles north of Taos, and follow the signs for 19 miles.

A 100-mile circle trip that offers opportunities for fishing and camping along the way starts by going north on State 3 for 25 miles to Questa, at the entrance to Cabresto and Red River canyons. Turn east on State 38 to the summer and winter resort of Red River, 13 miles. Continue to Eagle Nest, 18 miles, where beautiful Eagle Nest Lake nestles in the Merona Valley. Fishing is available without a license, but a charge is made for fish caught. Take U.S. 64 back to Taos, 30 miles, over spectacular Palo Flechado and through Taos Canyon.

There is year-round fishing in the Rio Grande and seasonal fishing in the many cold, flashing mountains streams and forested lakes. German brown and brook trout abound in Cabresto Lake, Hondo Canyon, Red River, Rio La Junta, Rio Pueblo, Santa Barbara, Taos Canyon, and Tres Ritos. Jeep and horseback trails to hidden waters deep in the forests provide even more challenging and rewarding experiences.

Deer hunting in the rolling country of Taos is prime, and near-record trophy heads are not unusual. In the vast hunting ground of the Carson National Forest, the big-game hunter can track majestic elk, antelope, bear, wild turkey, and mountain lion. Small game includes grouse, pheasant, quail, squirrels, and cottontail and snowshoe rabbits.

Taos Ski Valley

where the Tiwa Indians have handed down the art of fine weaving from generation to generation

CHIMAYO

The starting point for the adventure tour of the fascinating Indian community of Chimayo is Santa Fe. U.S. 64 winds northward through rich farming country. At Riverside, turn east on State 76 and continue on 9 miles. As the paved road dips down into this sleepy little village of adobe homes and giant cottonwood trees, the present is left far behind.

Chimayo lies in the heart of the area where the white man's civilization in the New World began. Two score years before the Pilgrims landed in New England, the first capital of New Spain was established at San Juan, just a few miles north of Chimayo. And nearby are dozens of Indian pueblos whose inhabitants are living today much as their forefathers did centuries ago. Ancient cliff dwellings are within easy driving distance, as are the peaceful old Spanish villages of Santa Cruz and Cordova.

Chimayo itself is on the site of a pueblo inhabited by a group of Tiwa Indians, whose singular talent is fine weaving, handed down from generation to generation. From 1598 to 1695, Chimayo was the eastern boundary of the Province of New Mexico. Today, the single main road that winds through the village is lined with lilac hedges, and the walls of the adobe homes are covered in summer with the yellow rose of Castile. In the fall long strings of flame-red chili adorn virtually every house. And during Lent processions of impassive Penitentes, their bare backs being scourged by the flailing yucca whips, may be observed creeping up to a cross on the top of a nearby hillside.

In the center of town is Ortega's Weaving Shop, providing the traveler a rare opportunity to watch the traditional craftsmen practice an art which spans some 300 or more years. Not only are Chimayo blankets loomed, but they are manufactured from native wool and dyed brilliant colors with local vegetable dyes. Although Ortega's is the most accessible to the visitor, practically every other home in Chimayo contains a hand loom, with mother, father, and children capable of using it.

At Chimayo is a junction with a secondary dirt road leading to El Santuario de Chimayo 1.3 miles away. The low, flat-roofed adobe church with its tapering front towers and twin belfries has the typical wall-enclosed garden and is surrounded by ancient cottonwoods. Built in 1816 by Don Bernardo Abeyta, it has been enhanced by time. Inside, in characteristic Spanish-Pueblo style, the ceiling consists of heavy timbers of closely spaced *vigas* supported by brackets joining the stark plaster walls. In front of the high altar is a chancel wall with perforated wooden balusters and behind is a high reredos, simply decorated with painted symbols having religious connotations.

A short distance beyond, .8 miles, is the Santa

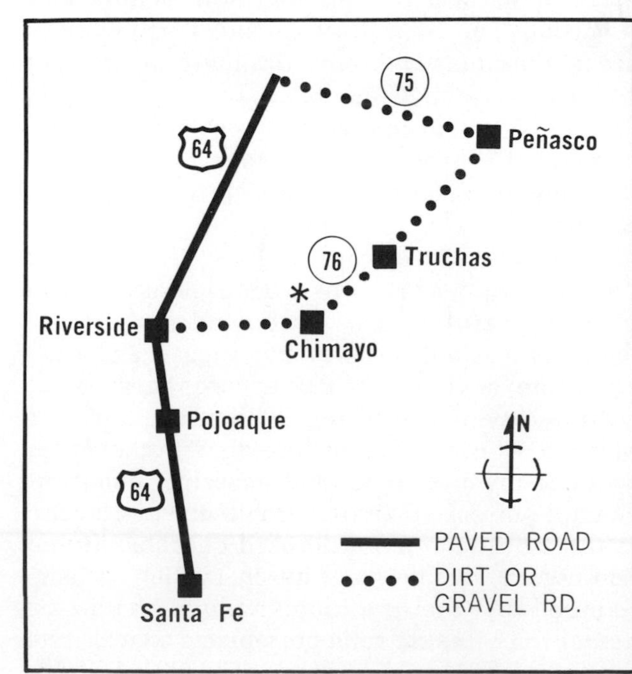

Cruz Reservoir, which is open to trout fishing.

State 76 continues through Chimayo, climbing along a hogback and affording a tremendous view of the Jemez Range to the left and New Mexico's highest mountain, Truchas Peak (13,306 feet) to the right. The village of Truchas is mentioned in a Spanish archive in 1752 as Nuestra Señora del Rosario de las Truchas. This is the center of Penitente country, and the stark, white *moradas* (churches) and crosses on the hillside are constant reminders of this medieval flagellant religious cult.

Numerous trails lead out from Truchas into the Carson National Forest, where hunting and fishing are excellent.

The road continues through the national forest, joining with State 75 at 14 miles. A left turn brings the adventurer to the junction with U.S. 64 at Embudo, leading back to Santa Fe (left) or to Taos (right).

From the ancient plaza in the heart of Santa Fe to Chupadero country, an adventure into the past that remains untouched by modern civilization, is only a few miles via U.S. 64 (Bishop's Lodge Road) north to Tesuque. Turn right and continue 6 miles through the foothills of the Sangre de Cristos to the tiny community of Chupadero. The route twists up piñon- and cedar-covered hills toward the gentle horizon.

CHUPADERO

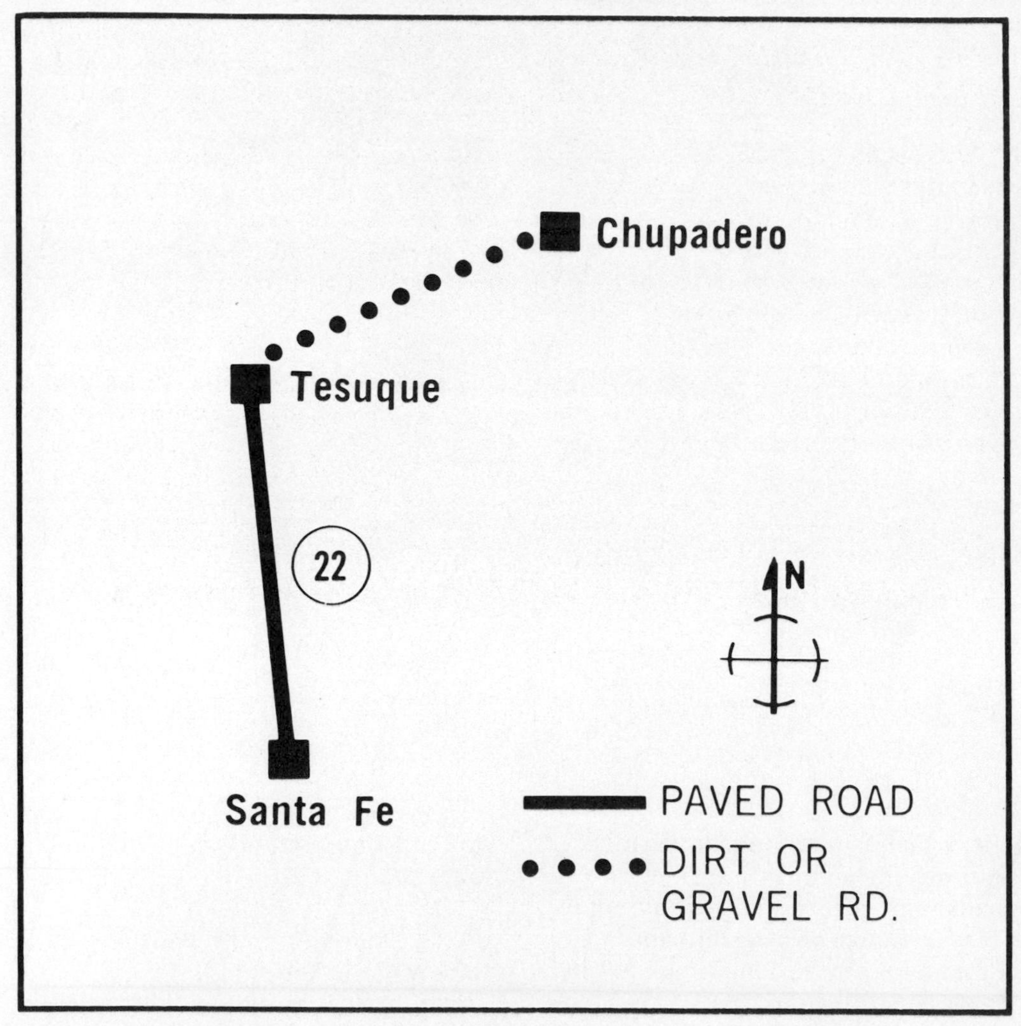

From the crest of the higher knolls are the unforgettable vistas of the Los Alamos and Jemez country. Everywhere there is history and legend, for this is Indian country and the land of the Spanish explorer, forerunner of the western pioneer.

Across the Española Valley stands the Black Mesa, rising up sharply from the Rio Grande. During the Pueblo Revolt of 1694 the San Ildefonso Indians repulsed de Vargas from the top of this flat and formidable formation. And it is legendary that the Black Mesa is the home of Savayo, the great giant who ate all the children of San Ildefonso. It is a remote country drenched in the mystery of an ageless past.

A turn to the left slashes through a hillock and below stretches out a long, narrow valley, forming a checkerboard pattern of small orchards and farms. This rich, fertile land—called Smokey Valley by the natives—grows abundant crops of peaches, pears, apples, apricots, chilies, cherries, corn, and beans. And amidst this abundance lies Chupadero, its dozen or so families living quietly in their adobe homes, far removed from the sound and fury of a busy world just over the horizon.

The village and its surroundings are as changeable as the seasons. The fragrant scent of fruit blossoms fills the air in springtime, and in the fall long lines of brilliant red chilies hang from the porches. Traditions, like threshing beans by hand, go back hundreds of years in time, as does their history in New Mexico. It was 1752 when Spain granted Juan de Gabaldon over 10,000 acres of land in the heart of a barren and "primitive land of enchantment." Today Chupadero is situated on this centuries-old tract.

No one knows why the forefathers of the present residents came to the place, whether they were restless wanderers who found the quiet valley to their liking, or were seeking the pot at the end of the Cibolan rainbow, or were merely the hippies of their day, seeking an escape from the ribald way of life in Santa Fe. Perhaps the warm sun, the big cottonwoods beside Chupadero Creek, the heaving rise of the green meadows, and the rich soil reminded them of some ancestral homeland. Whatever the reason, they are here, a colony unto themselves.

A mile and a half up the road is Rio en Medio, Chupadero's nearest neighbor, noted primarily for Our Lady of Sorrows, an untouched Spanish mission. Inside, the patron saint, Our Lady of Sorrow, wears a petite gold crown and a delicate gown of white satin and lace. Standing in her own private alcove, she presides over the other holy figures placed on the altar.

The old cemetery in front of the church offers an interesting opportunity for the cryptographer to decipher the faded lettering on the tired, weathered headstones, some of which are a century or more old.

through colorful Smokey Valley into the undisturbed past

The small town of Thoreau, 100 miles west of Albuquerque via U.S. 66, is the takeoff point for Chaco Canyon National Monument. State highway 56 leads north for 64 miles to the canyon entrance. Unpaved but graded, the road winds through a vast, remote, and semiarid land that centuries ago was the hub of Indian civilization and culture in the Southwest.

Almost at once great sandstone ridges border the road on the left. At 5.3 miles is the Antome

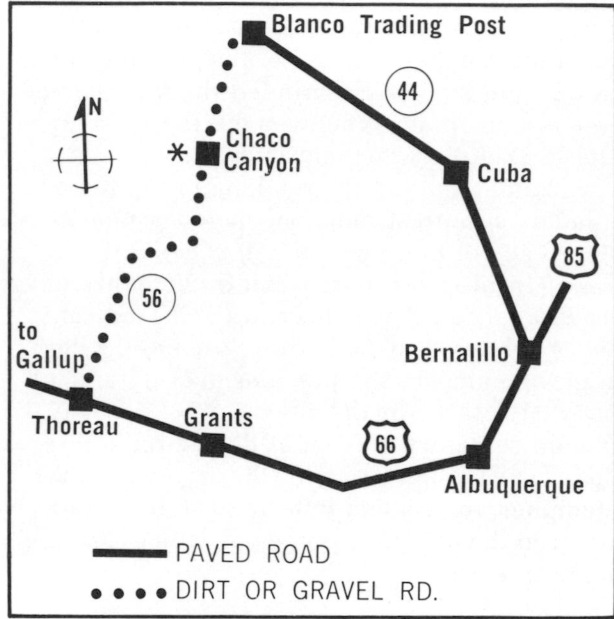

Indian Mission, and at 23.5 miles the towerlike Kin Yaah Ruin dominates the desolate countryside. Surrounding this ruin are the remains of a well-defined Navajo irrigation system, two reservoirs, and a main canal 25 to 30 feet wide.

State 56 runs a few miles east of the Navajo reservation, but the Indian hogans can be seen from the highway and frequently a lone Navajo can be seen riding his pony. Continuing northward, the road winds through country ever more rugged, ever more primitive.

The Chaco Canyon contains some of the greatest Indian surface ruins in the world—and also some of the most magnificent scenery. Roughly ten miles long and a mile wide, the deep cut of the valley gashes through a sandstone cap.

First stop for the adventurer is the visitor center to obtain maps of the trails leading to the 18

Chaco Canyon National Monument

CHACO CANYON

800-room pueblo dating back to A.D. 919

major ruins fully exposed and well preserved through the centuries in this arid climate.

The unique distinction of the prehistoric people who once inhabited the canyon lies in the massiveness of the buildings they constructed and the excellence of their masonry—achievements that took place during the 11th and 12th centuries, predating the later occupants, the Basket Makers, by 400 years.

One of the most exciting ruins, located close to the perpendicular north wall of the canyon, is Pueblo Bonito, first excavated in 1896-99. According to the experts, construction was started in A.D. 919, with additions being made over the next 200 years. This pueblo contained over 800 rooms and perhaps housed as many as 1,500 Indians at one time. Some of the rooms even today have retained their ancient timbered ceilings.

That Bonito was an exceptionally wealthy community is in accord with the Navajo myths of No-qoil-pi, the Great Gambler, who not only took over the possessions of the people, but enslaved them as well. Rich artifacts—turquoise beads, carved birds and insects, a frog of jet with eyes of inlaid turquoise—have been found; but the richest prize of all, the main burial grounds, has never been unearthed.

The setting is typical of vast portions of this land of enchantment, where the rolling wasteland barely supports stands of grama grass, rabbit brush, Indian ricegrass, and sagebrush. Occasionally, the traveler may catch a glimpse of a mule deer or a gray fox, but more often the wily bobcat or coyote.

By leaving the monument in midafternoon and traveling north, it is possible to reach the Colorado line and Mesa Verde National Park, where excellent accommodations are available (see under Colorado).

ACOMA PUEBLO

From Albuquerque, the starting point for the adventure tour of Acoma Pueblo (Sky City), take U.S. 66 west 50 miles, to the junction with State 23. Turn left and proceed 10 miles to the Enchanted Mesa, 4 miles from Acoma. The route crosses cultivated fields and gently rolling country sparsely covered with rabbit brush and juniper trees.

The Enchanted Mesa is a sandstone butte, 430 feet high, with precipitous walls and steep, spirelike pinnacles bursting out of the surrounding plains. The climb to the top is possible, but strenuous and dangerous for the unskilled mountaineer. According to legend, the ancestors of the Acoma Indians once lived on its top, but the only path leading to the mesa was closed by a storm. The aftermath was that those tending their fields on the plains below were not able to return to their homes, and those on the summit died of starvation.

Four miles beyond, on Acoma Rock, is the Acoma Pueblo, covering 70 acres atop a 357-foot mesa rising abruptly from the windswept sands. From its base well-defined trails lead to the formidable city, although some of the Indians prefer to ascend by the toe and finger-hole trails. Archeologists believe that the ladder trail on the northwestern side existed prior to 1629 and was, at one time, the only method of reaching the pueblo. To the right of the original trail is the one most frequently used today, especially by visitors. Although not difficult, it can be a hard climb if not taken at a leisurely pace.

The various buildings are 1,000 feet long and 40 feet high, constructed in three parallel lines of stone and adobe running east and west. The dwellings are terraced, with each of the three stories offset in the usual pueblo manner. A single trap door was the only method of access to the first story, which was used exclusively as a storeroom. Ladders reached from ground level to the second story, with the third story and roof reached by narrow outside steps built flush against the division wall.

Acoma today is largely unchanged in appearance and way of life from that day in 1540 when Captain Hernando de Alvarado of Coronado's army first discovered it. When the pueblo was built is still a mystery, although Indian tradition claims that it came into being following the destruction of the city on the Enchanted Mesa, centuries before the Spaniards. It existed in 1533, when Fray Marcos de Niza came to the area seeking the Seven Cities of Cibola. The Spanish first obtained a foothold in 1598 when the Akomi (as the inhabitants call themselves) submitted voluntarily to the Spanish crown. However, as the Spaniards were to discover, it had been part of a trick, with the Indians making a surprise attack on Don Juan de Zaldivar and his detachment of troops, killing all but four, who leaped off the rock to their deaths. This led to war and the subsequent capture and burning of the pueblo as well as the destruction of a large percentage of the Indian population.

The hatred of the Indians toward the Spaniards continued until 1629, when Franciscan Fray Juan Ramirez, the first permanent missionary, came to Acoma. According to legend, Father Ramirez walked alone from Santa Fe to Acoma and, upon arriving, was pelted by rocks and arrows as he tried to ascend. It happened that, in the confusion, a little Indian girl was accidentally pushed off the mesa and fell to a pointed rock some 60 feet below. Father Ramirez, ignoring his own safety, reached her, knelt and prayed, and then carried her unharmed to her parents. It was soon after this that the Indians became his followers and eventually helped him build the San Esteban Rey Mission, which still exists today, although it has been extensively remodeled through the centuries. One of the finest of all the old pueblo missions, it is 150 feet long and 40 feet wide, with walls 60 feet high and 10 feet thick. The construction feat is even more remarkable, considering that every bit of the material was carried up the steep trails on the backs of dedicated Indian women. The roof beams, 40 feet long and 14 inches square, were cut in the Cebollata Mountains, some 30 miles away, and were carried by the Indians to the top of Sky City.

Approximately 1,700 Indians live in the Acoma Pueblo today, living much as they have for the past 300 years. They still bake in the beehive-shaped ovens outside the dwellings. The men do most of the heavy construction when necessary, although the women sometimes build the adobe walls and do the plastering. Annually, as part of Saint Stephen's festival, the inside walls are painted; and garments of skins, blankets, jewelry, and trinkets are hung against them. Wool *colchones* (mattresses) are laid on the floor for sleeping at night and are rolled up and placed against the walls for seats during the day.

Sky City, an ancient Indian community, stands proudly atop a 357-foot mesa

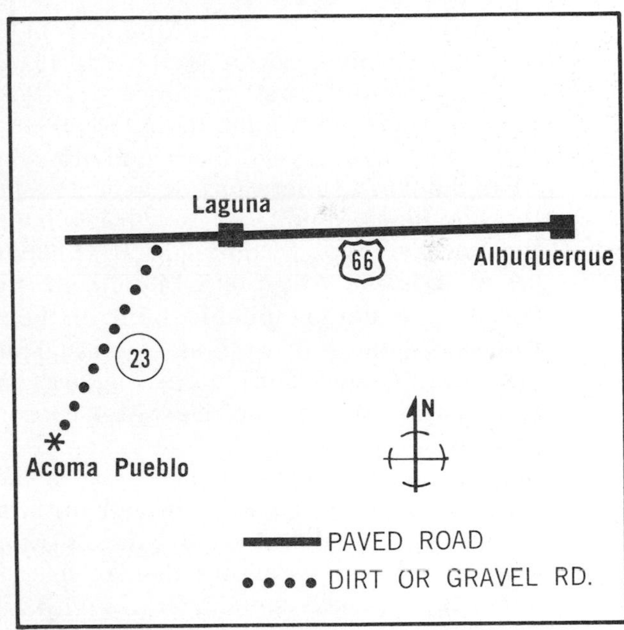

Acoma pottery is noted for its designs and geometric patterns, though it is less durable than other Indian pottery, such as the Zuñi.

Many of the Indians live in summer towns on the reservation, returning to their city in the sky only for ceremonies or festivities, not unlike a white American family returning home for a reunion at Christmas.

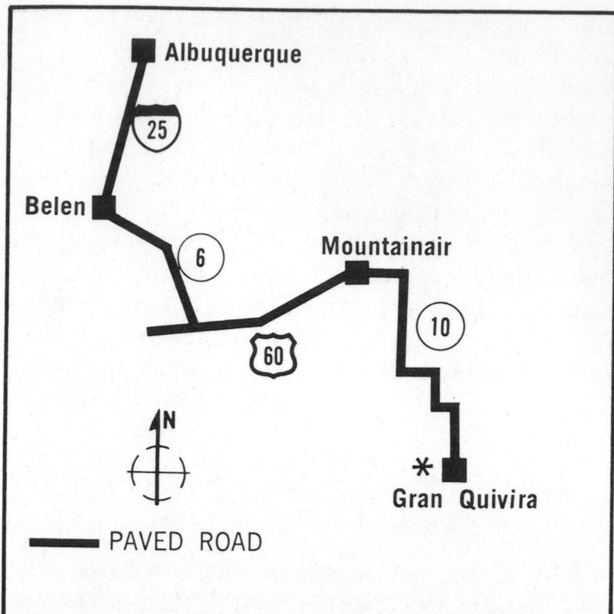

From the starting point of Albuquerque to the adventure stop at Gran Quivira is 102 miles. Take Interstate 25 south to Belen (33 miles), turn left on State 6 to Mountainair (44 miles), then south for 25 miles to Gran Quivira National Monument. The route passes over Abo Pass in the Los Pinos Mountains and drops down into the town of Abo. To the right at a distance of 0.8 mile is the Abo State Monument, the remains of a unique pueblo built on beautiful red sandstone with a kiva of unusual design. The Abo Mission church, built in 1646 and restored by the Museum of New Mexico, remains on the site.

Gran Quivira's visitor center provides information concerning trails through the area and archeological and historical exhibits. Standing atop one of the east-west ridges of the Chupadera Mesa, its rectangular features jutting above the skyline, is the long-abandoned 17th-century Franciscan church, San Buenaventura. Next to it and likewise silhouetted against the sky lies the Pueblo de las Humanas, surrounding San Isidro, another Franciscan church.

The earliest Indian community house, located on the south slope of the ridge, was constructed about A.D. 1300. It was a single-story rectangular coursed-masonry unit with a central plaza entered by a narrow passage at its eastern side. Later the house was abandoned and larger

where Spanish and Indian cultures met

GRAN QUIVIRA

multistoried units were constructed on the ridge.

It was during this period that black-on-white pottery became popular and the kiva (an underground ceremonial chamber) was adopted. The religion of the Indians was based on the beliefs that plants and animals, as well as man, had souls and that the forces of nature could be controlled by the proper performance of rites long ago taught to their forefathers by the spirits and handed down generation after generation.

By 1530, after Spain had colonized the area surrounding Mexico City, tales of vast wealth to the north circulated among the conquistadores, and it was not long until the lust to conquer was matched by the lust for gold. Under Coronado's leadership in 1540, exploring parties moved from present-day Albuquerque eastward in search of the reported riches of the land of Quivira. Finally, in October of 1598, a Spanish expedition visited Pueblo de las Humanas. The conquistadores thought they had reached the riches of the land of Quivira (which was actually in Kansas) and so named the place Gran Quivira. Spanish missionaries moved into the village and remained until the mid-1600s.

Archeologists have concluded that a severe drought during the years 1666-1670, accompanied by famine, pestilence, and increasing Apache Indian raids on the village, decimated the population. Evidence indicates that between 1672 and 1675 the pueblo was abandoned and the remaining Indians moved to the Rio Grande Valley in the vicinity of Socorro.

The Spanish padres were responsible for many changes. Stone and bone tools were replaced with copper and iron. Even the pottery styles changed with the introduction of candlesticks, soup plates, and cups with handles.

Through the centuries the ruins lost their identity, and near the end of the 19th century the name Gran Quivira was mistakenly assigned to the area.

Treasure seeker's shaft at Gran Quivira

GILA CLIFF DWELLINGS

The adventure trip to the Gila Cliff Dwellings starts at Las Cruces, New Mexico's fastest-growing boom town, resulting in part from its proximity to the Missile Development Center at Holloman Air Force Base and the White Sands Missile Range.

Interstate 10 leads west to Deming across flat

fourteenth-century Indian city in the crevasses of barely accessible canyons

farmland for 69 miles. U.S. 180 branches right, coursing through the Mimbres Valley, a land rich both in minerals and Indian lore. To the right of the highway the Cook Mountains stretch out of the valley. At 45.1 miles from Deming an unmarked road to Ft. Bayard (right fork) provides an interesting side trip, leading to the Cameron Creek Ruins, the remains of a Pueblo civilization.

Silver City, at 50.5 miles, is located in a beautiful setting at the foothills of the Pinos Altos Mountains and is the gateway to the Gila National Forest and the cliff dwellings. State 25 winds north through Gila National Forest, a total of 2.7 million acres of publicly-owned forest and range land, including more wilderness country than in any other place in the Southwest.

At 18 miles the road joins State 527 and continues north up Copperas Canyon to the vicinity of the cliff dwellings. The ruins themselves are located on a small tributary of the West Fork of the Gila River, in some of the most primitive land in all America.

This Indian community was occupied about 600 years ago, as evidenced by the kinds of pottery found in the ruins. Approximately 35 rooms, some of them giant-size, were built in four natural cavities in the face of a 150-foot-high grayish yellow cliff.

The largest cavity is 125 feet in diameter and nearly circular, with a natural rock roof about 20 feet above the floor. Natural archways lead into two tributary cavities which are divided into several rooms by walls built of adobe and flat stones from the surrounding area. The observant explorer can see, by careful examination, the finger imprints made in the adobe when the walls were built.

Another cavity, high on the face of the cliff, is in an excellent state of preservation, but is difficult to visit, since the cliff overhangs the cavity; it cannot be entered from above, and the sheer cliff below requires mountain climbing experience and equipment.

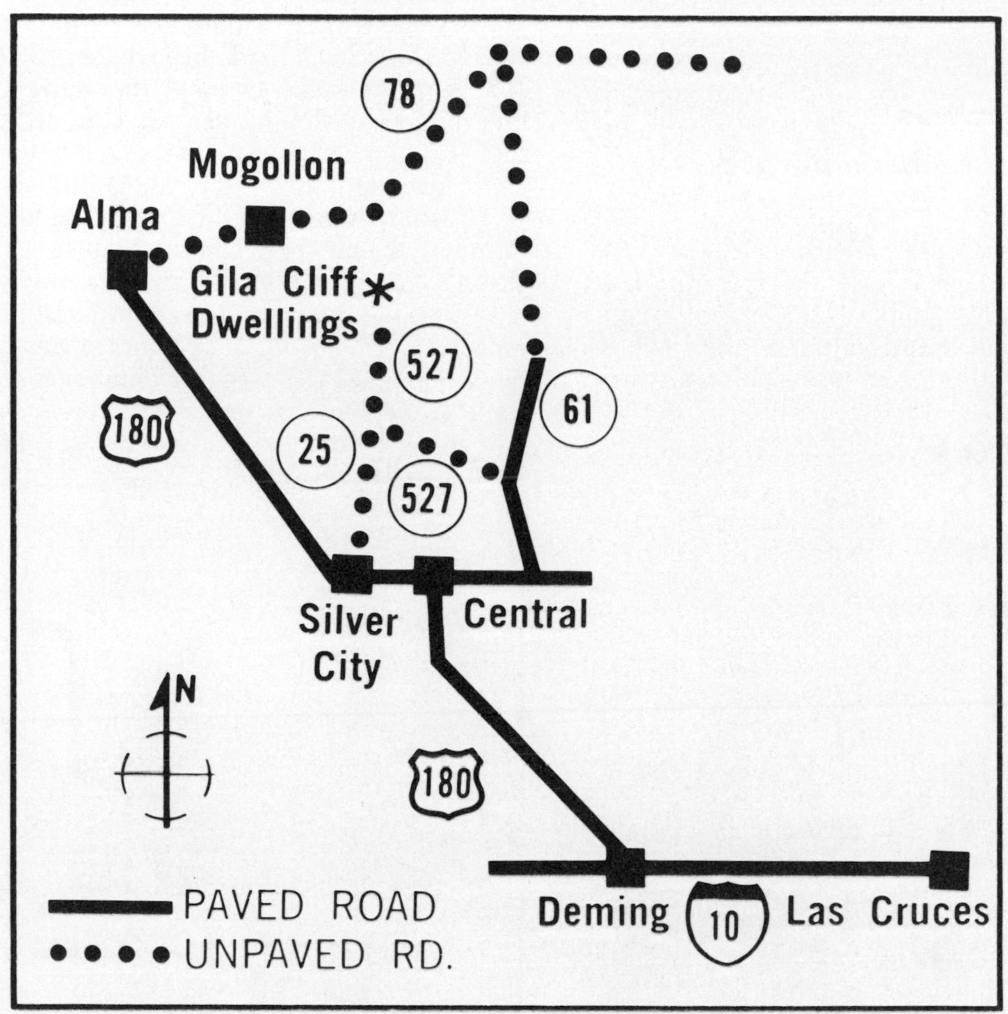

When first discovered in the 1870s by mining prospectors, some great architectural treasures—sandals, baskets, pottery, cooking utensils, and arrow shafts—were found.

The same road must be followed on returning from the cliff dwellings, but at the junction of State 527 and 25 (at Sapillo Creek) the left fork (State 527) leads east toward the Black Range and a junction with State 61 at 13 miles. By turning left on this graveled road a circle trip through Gila National Forest may be accomplished, with a return to Silver City. Length of the tour is approximately 180 miles.

Excellent fishing streams are plentiful, with the best trout fishing in the West and Middle forks of the Gila River within the Gila Wilderness and Primitive areas. Fishermen should be prepared to pack or hike into these streams since no motorized transportation is permitted.

Lake fishing is available at Wall Lake, a short hike to the east from State 61, and at Bear Canyon Reservoir, 2 miles north of Mimbres. Detailed forest service maps of the forest, showing camping, picnicking, and fishing areas, as well as trails and points of interest, are available at the ranger station in Silver City.

the route that was

a stagecoach robber's delight

KINGSTON

From Truth or Consequences to the historic ghost town of Kingston is a short 42-mile trip. Take Interstate 25 south 15 miles to Caballo, turn right on State 90 and continue through Hillsboro (18 miles) to the adventure point of Kingston (9 miles).

From Caballo, the country is vast and barren, stretching westward to the foothills of the Black Range. Hillsboro, like Kingston, started life as a mining camp. In 1877 two prospectors discovered gold in the nearby hills and shortly thereafter were joined by other miners working the mines in the Mimbres Mountains.

Everybody had his own suggestion for a name for the primitive community and it was finally agreed that they all would write their suggestions on slips of paper, drop them in a hat, and draw a winner. Originally the name was Hillsborough, later shortened to its present spelling. Early in its career about 1880, the town had 4 saloons, 4 grocery stores, and 4 companies of soldiers to protect the 300 inhabitants from the Apaches. Eventually Hillsboro had a population of 2,000 and became the county seat of Sierra County, complete with courthouse and jail, which was torn down in 1939.

Mostly deserted today, there are still a hotel and the Black Range Museum, filled with well-preserved mementos of Hillsboro's golden past. South of the town is the Lake Valley region, one of the richest ore producers of the frontier days. It was Lake Valley where the Apache chief Victorio made his home, striking fear and terror in the hearts of the Hillsboro miners. It was also Lake Valley where two miners struck an ore vein that they sold out for $100,000, thereby losing a fortune. Two days after the sale, the new owners discovered that the mine led into a subterranean room called Bridal Chamber that eventually produced over $3,000,000 in silver.

The route from Hillsboro to Kingston traverses the old stagecoach road, through Percha Canyon, a rugged nichelike channel that provided numerous ambush points for the legendary highwaymen and the Apaches. One of the stagecoach drivers, Sadie Orchard, continued to live in Hillsboro until she died in the 1940s. Sadie originally came from London in 1886, at a time when Kingston was a wild, shoot-'em-up town of 5,000 and the dance halls, saloons, and pleasure parlors were booming 24 hours a day. In her later years, her greatest enjoyment was retelling such experiences as her harrowing encounters with the Indians and the masked gunmen who lurked in the canyon.

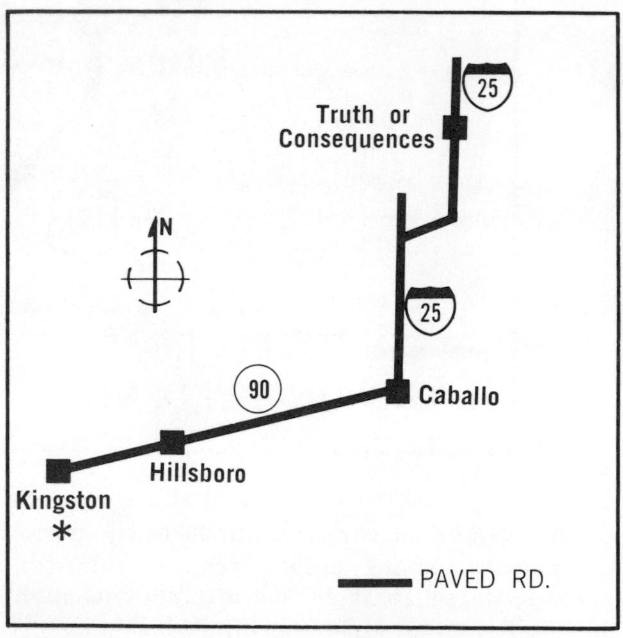

The remnants of the old town, except for a single ramshackle store building which can be seen from the highway, are hidden from the casual viewer by trees, although several landmarks remain, including the fire bell once used to summon the volunteers in cases of emergency, the Victorio Hotel (built in 1882), and the register, in use since 1887.

Kingston's humble beginning occurred in the fall of 1880 with the coming of two prospectors, Phillips and Elliott, who found silver in two mines, one named the Iron King and the other the Empire. But Apache Chief Victorio was on the warpath and it wasn't until 1882 that the town was actually created—a town that eventually became the hub of a $10,000,000 mining bonanza.

While the prospectors were digging in the hills for their fortunes in silver, A. A. Wise and W. W. Maxwell established the Kingston Townsite Company, buying up lots in June of 1882 for next to nothing, watching with anticipation the influx of the miners. By fall of 1882 the population was 1,800; within a year it reached 5,000 and eventually swelled to 7,500. By November of 1882, the lots which Wise and Maxwell had bought up for $25 were selling for $500, and in March of 1883 lots in the town brought $5,000 or more. Handbills and newspaper headlines throughout the West announced the great boom in New Mexico: "Fortune hunters, capitalists, poor men, sickly folks, all whose hearts are bowed down; and ye who would live long, be rich, healthy and happy; come to our sunny clime and see for yourselves!" People read and were convinced that the golden treasures of Cibola had finally been discovered. At the peak, nearly 30 mines were operating in the area; practically a caravan of ten-mule teams with high-sided wagons, heavy with ore, lurched up and down the canyons.

At its zenith, Kingston boasted 22 saloons, a brewery, an opera house, three hotels, three newspapers, 12 grocery stores, a church, and a schoolhouse.

Today the mines are silent, tributes to the glorious past. And the town itself, the few crumbling buildings, seems to be hiding amidst the pine trees, no longer proud or kingly.

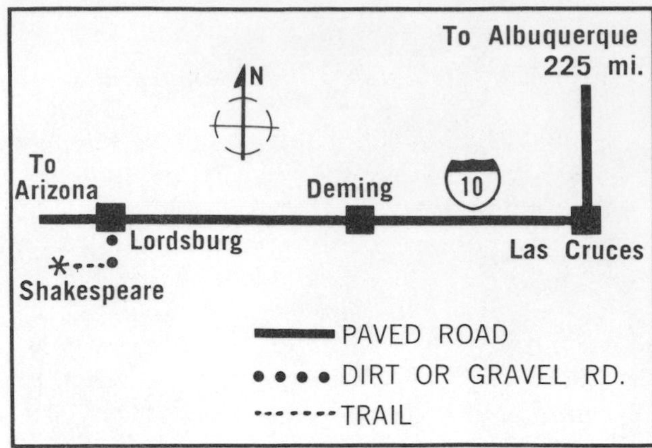

SHAKESPEARE

improbable ghost town with an improbable history restored for the adventurer

From Las Cruces, the starting point for this adventure trail, Interstate 10 follows the old California stagecoach trail across the Continental Divide to Lordsburg, 119 miles west.

At Lordsburg, a turn to the south on Main Street puts the traveler on his way to the ghost town of Shakespeare, a place with a history as much out of character as its name. At the end of the paved road, 2.5 miles, the road is graveled. Bear right for a few hundred feet to the town.

The few remaining adobe buildings stand silent and alone in the midst of a great expanse of sand, sage, and searing summer sun. To the north the distant Burro Mountains rise out of the purple haze. More than 100 years ago the wandering Apaches stopped at this spot to water their horses and refresh themselves. In the 1850s the stages bound for California paused at this watering hole and finally christened it Mexican Springs.

After the Civil War, Mexican Springs was renamed Grant by "Uncle" Johnny Evensen, who had opened up a stage station and was probably the town's first permanent resident. But fate and a San Francisco promoter, William C. Ralston, combined forces, and suddenly Grant became another boom town in the heart of New Mexico's mining district. A parttime prospector found silver ore that assayed 12,000 ounces to the ton, and Ralston suddenly became interested in this barren wide spot in the road.

Claims were staked throughout the nearby Pyramid Mountains, the town of Grant, renamed Ralston City, was platted, and construction of buildings for the town was started. Tents and adobe shacks of optimistic prospectors popped up overnight. Unfortunately, the miners soon discovered that most of the ore lay in small pockets and that most of it was too low-grade to be profitable. By the time lynching parties had been formed, Ralston had quietly moved out. The several hundred unhappy residents followed his example and Ralston City became a ghost town overnight—for awhile.

Hardly a year had passed before Johnny's Stage Station was again a beehive of activity, the deserted buildings were refurbished, and dozens of new businesses opened up along the main street. Ralston, spread the rumor, was the hub of the most fabulous diamond field in the world. Within weeks more than 3,000 people funneled into Ralston City, including Ralston himself, one of the founders of the new diamond mining company.

The great excitement continued until a government geologist decided to investigate the strike. He dug around and found some diamonds, some containing lapidary marks. Within two days after word of the great hoax had filtered back to the town, nobody was left in the settlement but Johnny Evensen, who maintained that it would rise again.

In 1879 Colonel William Boyle and his brother decided to re-establish some of the old mining claims in the area. But the name of Ralston City was synonymous with swindling; so it was changed to Shakespeare. Main Street became Avon Avenue and the principal hotel became the Stratford. Again the town began to boom. Wagonloads of silver ore were hauled out of the Pyramid Mines and the town's population grew to several hundred.

Stories of the wild events in Shakespeare became part of the legend of the West. Lawlessness was rampant and murders and hangings commonplace.

One night in 1881 a mob of 70 vigilantes decided to rid the world of two unsavory characters called Russian Bill and Sandy King. Using the wooden beam that spanned the dining room of Shakespeare's second hotel, the Grant House, they hanged the two men and walked away, leaving them to swing overnight. When the stage pulled in the next morning, a nervous passenger asked why they'd been hung. Uncle Johnny Evensen just nodded sagely and said, "Well, Russian Bill stole a horse, and Sandy King was just a damned nuisance." A few months later the postmaster received an inquiry from the mother of Russian Bill concerning her son's whereabouts. "Dear Madam," he wrote, "I'm sorry to report your son has died of throat trouble."

The panic of 1893 sounded the death knell for Shakespeare, and, except for a short gasp of life in 1907, it remained deserted until Frank Hill bought the town as part of an 11,000-acre ranch. He has preserved several of the old buildings. The Grant House still stands with bullet holes pitting the walls, and the heavy beam used to hang Russian Bill and Sandy King is still there. And Shakespeare's finest, the Stratford, remains as a mystic memento of a colorful past.

The Hills live in the old general store, with a portion of it converted to a museum full of relics. Some of the old-timers who've visited the town insist that it's haunted, that the ghosts of the old miners and the outlaws buried there still walk down Avon Avenue by night.

For the adventurer, exploring the old buildings and walking the deserted streets is an experience to remember, even if he fails to encounter an apparition out of Shakespeare's past.

Shakespeare

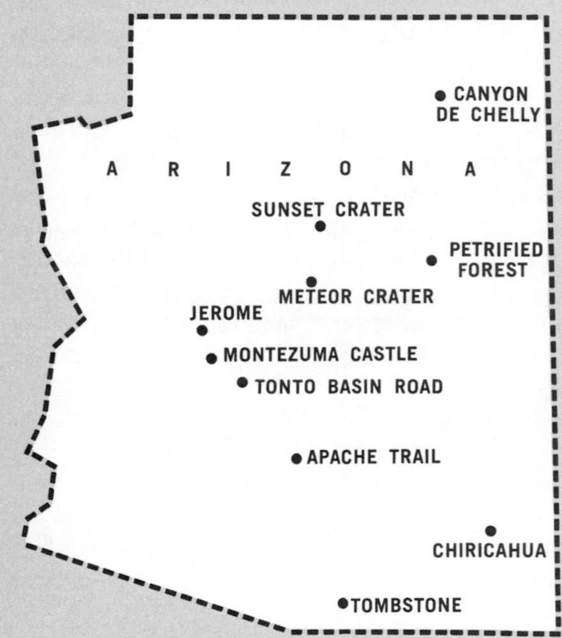

Arizona is the land of the sun, painted deserts and organpipe cactus silhouetted against the fiery orange sunset, endless reaches of deep blue western skies, spectacular red rock formations in Oak Creek Canyon en route to the resurrected ghost town of Jerome, living desert museums, and the greatest petrified forest in the world. Arizona contains the Grand Canyon of the Colorado and Glen Canyon Dam, the second highest in the United States, and Mogollon Rim, a precipitous 200-mile escarpment—not to mention ponderosa pine forests, spectacular Indian ruins, rodeos, Superstition Mountain, and the Lost Dutchman Gold Mine.

The Tonto Basin Road winds through 144 miles of wilderness, along the edge of the Mogollon Rim, twisting its way back to the valley at the base of the Mazatzal Mountains, eventually passing within a few miles of the pelican rookery at the northern end of Roosevelt Lake.

In the northeastern section of the state is the Canyon de Chelly, an ancestral stronghold of the Navajo in a dramatic setting of steep-walled canyons and flame-red sandstone

roaming in

cliffs. Near Flagstaff is one of nature's strange wonders, Sunset Crater, a perfectly symmetrical cone rising a thousand feet into the desert sky, formed when the earth erupted violently some 900 years ago. Far to the south, near the Mexican border towns of Naco and Agua Prieta, the frontier town of Tombstone lives on, re-creating memories of the O.K. Corral and the Earp-Clanton gunfight. Beyond, easterly, rise the Chiricahua Mountains, and nearby the range is the Chiricahua National Monument, a land of weird, grotesquely shaped multicolored monoliths and hundreds of other strange rock formations. This is the rugged country used as a stronghold by Cochise, the famous Apache chief, and frequented by the legendary Johnny Ringo, whose body was found in Turkey Creek

ARIZONA

Canyon with a bullet hole through the skull. For the spelunker, many passages of Crystal Cave, doubtless used as a hideout by the rowdy characters of the old West, remain to be explored.

Arizona, a country filled with Indian lore and history, the Grand Canyon and Painted Desert, a country of mountain meadows and high plateaus, is America's amazing sun and adventure land.

CANYON de CHELLY

exploring ruins of prehistoric Indian villages by foot and car

To reach Canyon de Chelly (pronounced d'shay), take U.S. 66 east from Flagstaff through Winslow and along the Little Colorado River to Holbrook. From Holbrook the route continues past the Painted Desert and Petrified Forest (see Petrified Forest under Arizona) to Chambers (49 miles). Turn left at Chambers and proceed north 40 miles to Ganado and a junction with State 264. Turn left, continuing for 7 miles and a junction with a paved road. Proceed north for 33 miles to Chinle at the entrance to Canyon de Chelly National Monument. From Gallup, New Mexico, take U.S. 666 north 4 miles to junction with State 264. Turn left, continue to Ganado, and proceed as above.

This monument includes awesome canyons which sheltered prehistoric Pueblo Indians for a thousand years and served as an ancestral stronghold of the Navajo. The beautiful, steep-walled canyons and the ruins of the dwellings cut into the high ledges are in startling contrast to the simple present-day Navajo Indian homes scattered along the canyon floor.

"De Chelly" is a Spanish corruption of the Navajo word "Tsegi," roughly translated as rock canyon. The Spanish name for the chief tributary of the main canyon, Canyon del Muerto, means "Canyon of the Dead." It received its name when James Stevenson, leading a Smithsonian expedition in 1882, found the remains of prehistoric Indian burials there. The canyons were officially discovered when Lieutenant James H. Simpson led an exploring expedition into the area in 1849. Actually, there is considerable evidence that Spanish settlers entered the canyon and fought the Navajo early in the 19th century.

Kit Carson's men marched the entire length of the canyon in 1863-64 as part of his campaign to remove the Navajo to the Bosque Redondo in New Mexico. By destroying their crops and attacking with great force and vigor, he successfully rounded up some 7,000 of the Indians.

The Rio de Chelly, which cuts through the canyon, rises near the Chuska Mountains and winds westward, emptying into the Chinle Wash just west of the monument. Streams in this region flow during the rainy season and during the spring runoff of snow from the nearby mountains. At other times they are dry.

In the canyons, ruins of several hundred prehistoric Indian villages exist, built between A.D. 350 and 1300. The earliest occupants built individual, circular pithouses. They grew maize and squash and made excellent baskets and sandals, but they did not make pottery.

As the centuries moved on, these Indians began making pottery, started using the bow and arrow, and moved out of their pits, building instead rectangular houses of stone masonry above the ground which were connected to form

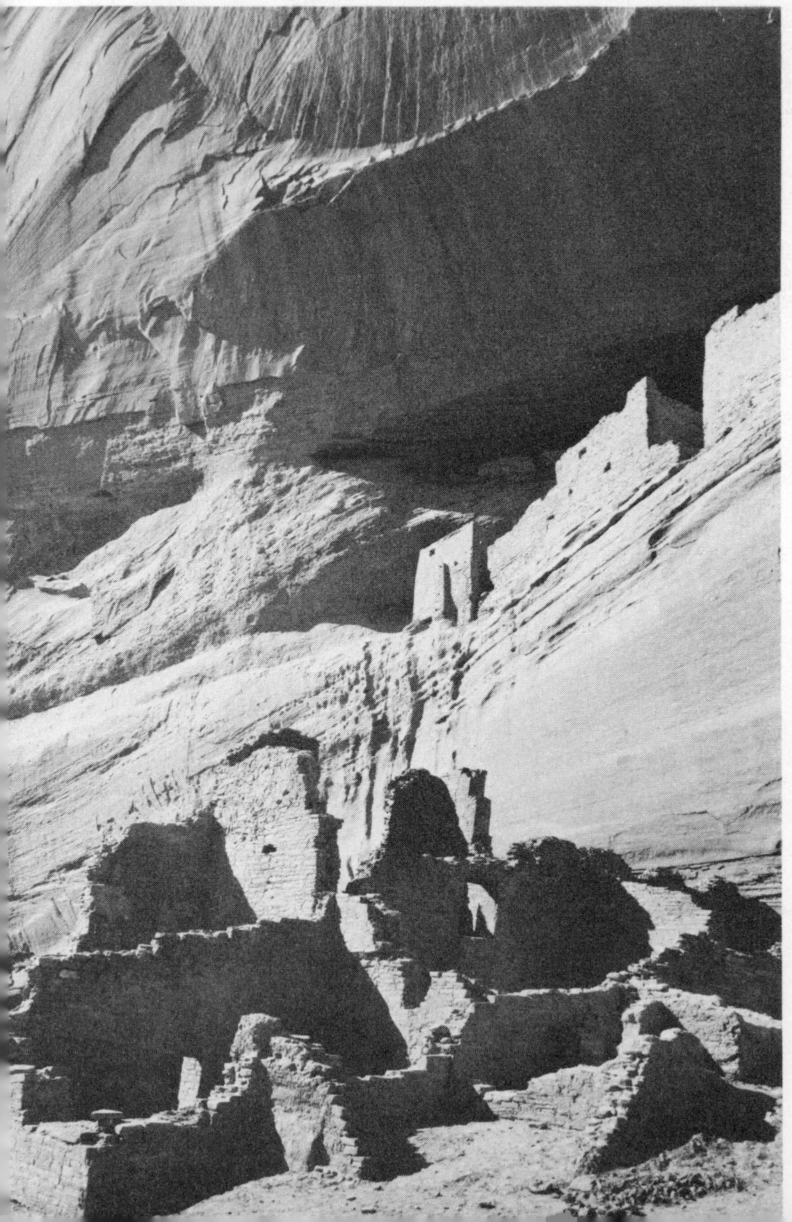

Canyon de Chelly

community villages, not unlike today's condominium concept. Most of the large cliff houses found in the canyon were built between 1100 and 1300.

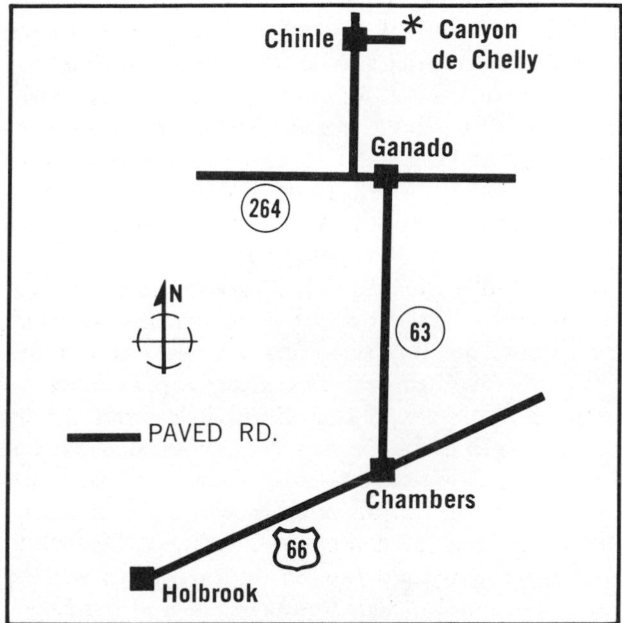

The great drought during the 1200s forced the people of the canyon to abandon their homes and scatter to other parts of the Southwest. About 1700 the Navajo Indians moved into Canyon de Chelly from northern New Mexico. An aggressive group related culturally and linguistically to the Apache, they made sporadic raids for 150 years on the Pueblo Indian villages and the Spanish settlements along the Rio Grande Valley, resulting in retaliation by successive governments of New Mexico—Spanish, Mexican, and the United States. The battles, with Canyon de Chelly as a major stronghold, did not end until Carson's removal of the Navajo.

A tour of the monument is best accompanied by a combination of driving and hiking. The Rim Drive, almost always passable, provides access to five scenic overlook points and also leads to the head of White House Trail, a mile long, leading to White House Ruin. When occupied, it was reached by ladders which could be hauled up in case of attack. A series of tiny depressions winding up the face of the red sandstone cliffs to the left of the ruin is a hand and toe trail used by the Indians.

Continuing on the Rim Drive, there is a stopping point at the junction of Canyon de Chelly and Monument Canyon for a view of Spider Rock, a spire of sandstone rising 800 feet above the canyon floor.

The Canyon de Chelly tour starts at Park Service Headquarters, branching northeast and entering the canyon mouth at 1 mile. At 4.1 miles is the First Ruin, high in the cliff and so perfectly protected that its walls remain practically intact.

Sliding Rock Ruin (7.5 miles) is gradually falling down into the canyon. So many of the walls of the old houses have fallen away that the number of dwellings once there is not known.

Beehive Ruins (10 miles), almost at the top of the left cliff, were somehow approached from the rim of the canyon rather than the bottom. It is impossible to get close to these ruins.

The Canyon del Muerto tour, which branches off from the Canyon de Chelly route at 4 miles, is even more impressive, the canyon walls being closer together and with such tremendous overhangs that from the canyon floor the sky appears as a narrow ribbon of deep blue.

At 3 miles is Antelope House, a large ruin located in a corner where the undercut cliff has protected it against the weather. Pictographs (including antelope) in brown and white appear on the wall to the left of the buildings.

The Mummy Cave Ruin (14 miles) is in an undercut cavern about 300 feet above the canyon floor. The buildings were three stories high. The western portion is 100 feet long and 75 feet deep, while the eastern portion is 200 feet long and 100 feet deep. Low buildings and a tower connect the two sections. A piece of charcoal with tree rings indicating that it dates from A.D. 348 was found on the slope directly below the ruin.

A mile upstream by foot is Massacre Cave, where Spanish raiders trapped a number of Navajos, including women and children, and shot them to death. The marks made by the ricocheting bullets are still visible.

Camping in the canyons is not permitted, but fireplaces, tables, and rest rooms are available at Cottonwood Campground near the monument headquarters. Gasoline and groceries can be obtained at nearby trading posts, and lodging and meals are available at Thunderbird Lodge in Chinle.

Sunset Crater

SUNSET CRATER

site of a fierce volcanic eruption 900 years ago

From Flagstaff to Sunset Crater, take U.S. 89 north 14 miles, turn right on Sunset Crater National Monument road, and proceed 4 miles to the visitor center. The paved road continues to Wupatki National Monument (14 miles) and back to U.S. 89.

The monument road passes the Bonito Lava Flow (3.5 miles) and the Ice Caves (4.1 miles), which were created by the mass of lava cooling at different rates and forming a crust on top while the material below was still molten. As the liquid drained, caves were formed in the lava that remained in a solid state. Since lava is a poor conductor of heat, the cold air at the bottom is protected, with the result that there is snow on the floors and ice clinging to the ceilings of the caves, regardless of the outside temperature.

Sunset Crater, appearing symmetrical and tranquil against the desert sky, was not always so serene. Some 900 years ago it violently erupted, and the Indians rushed away from the source of the weird phenomenon as ash clouded the sky and cinders rained down upon their primitive homes. By the time the eruption ceased, a cinder cone 1,000 feet high had been formed, with jagged lava flows at its base. The black ash, at first considered an evil sign from angry gods, covered hundreds of square miles and transformed the soil into rich farm country, drawing the Indians back into the area, where they constructed their communal homes, now preserved as part of nearby Wupatki National Monument.

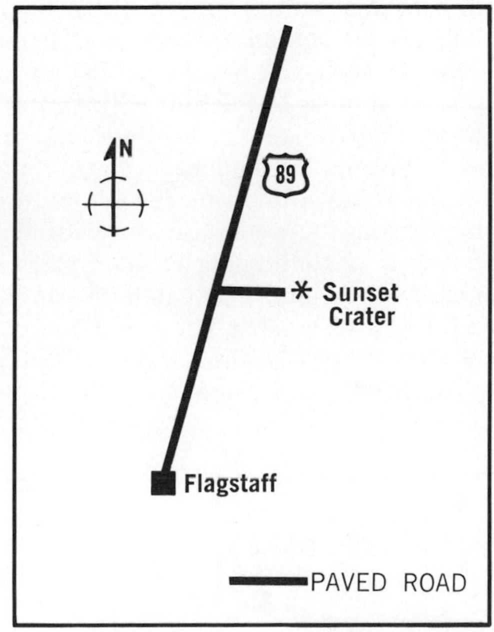

Prominent in north central Arizona are the San Francisco Peaks and the surrounding volcanic field, together covering 3,000 square miles. The area is studded with volcanic peaks, cinder cones, and lava flows indicating a long period of volcanic activity, starting perhaps 2 million years ago, and widely interrupted by intervals of quiet inactivity. With the eruption that formed Sunset Crater 900 years ago, another period of tranquility, still existing, began.

A foot trail winds up the side of Sunset Crater (allow one hour for round trip) to its crest, 8,000 feet above sea level and approximately 1,000 feet above the surrounding countryside. The crater's name reflects its many colors, the bright yellowish gold at the crest and a gradual change to varying shades of orange, then red and a base of black volcanic ash.

The Lava Flow Nature Trail will take you across some of the lava flow and a small lava cave and other interesting places which are described in a guidebook available at the register desk.

Continue on the monument road as it loops toward the Wupatki (pronounced Woo-pot-key) visitor center and site of the Wupatki Ruin.

This became one of the few areas in which various Indians of different cultures came together, the Pueblo comingling with the Hohokam, the Mogollon coming together with the Cohonina, all settling down to farm the newly enriched soil.

Villages were established throughout the area, with one of the first being Wupatki, the Hopi word for "tall house." Built originally as a small pueblo near the only spring in the area, it became the largest, probably during the 1100s, containing more than 100 rooms and three stories high in places. Beside the ruin, purposely protected from the prevailing desert winds, is an open-air amphitheater used for ceremonials.

A striking feature of the Wupatki Ruin is the method of utilizing the natural walls of red sandstone, constructed above and around the buildings so that the latter appear almost as a part of the surrounding terrain. There are many features similar to the Pueblo culture of that period, such as the rectangular kiva at the southeast corner, the T-shaped doors, and the small ventilator in the outside wall of the first row of rooms.

Foot trails lead from the road to Wukoki Ruin and Lomaki Ruin, with others—the Nalakihu and Citadel ruins—accessible directly from the road.

Overutilization of the soil and the great drought which began in 1215 forced the Indians to leave, and by 1225 the many villages were completely deserted.

geological wonder
in the midst of the Painted Desert

PETRIFIED FOREST

En route from Gallup, New Mexico to Holbrook, Arizona, the best way to see the Petrified Forest National Park is via U.S. 66 (50 miles west of Gallup) to the north entrance and visitor center. A self-guiding road tour circles the Painted Desert, then turns south through the forest to the Rainbow Forest entrance at the south end. Continue to Holbrook northwest on U.S. 180.

Geologically, the history of the forest extends back in time some 200 million years, to the late Triassic age, and its human history started over 1,500 years ago—the more than 300 Indian ruins in the park bearing silent homage to these early inhabitants. But the natives were unaware of the origin of the petrified wood, while recognizing that it was "different" from ordinary rocks. John Wesley Powell, an early explorer of the Colorado River and this region of the Southwest, recorded that the Paiutes of southern Utah were convinced that the petrified logs were the arrow shafts of their thunder god, Shinuav. The forest was also part of the Navajo legends, for they believed the strange, stonelike logs were the bones of Yietso, the "great giant" killed when their forefathers first ventured into the region.

At one time, this portion of Arizona—now a virtual desert—was a low-lying swampland, with numerous meandering streams and twisting, slow-moving rivers that carried great trees and fallen logs into the bogs and muddy marshes, which also snared thousands of prehistoric animals that became trapped by the encircling waters. And the reptilians—primarily the phytosaurs—which required the wet swamp country for survival, died as an extended dry period turned the bogs into arid islands.

According to the geologists, the low-lying valley during the Triassic period predated the Sierra Nevada, and a long plain sloped gradually west to the Pacific. Over the centuries, the flooding of the streams and runoffs from the highlands filled the valley with sand and silt, covering the trees and vegetation to a depth of nearly 3,000 feet. Minerals in the water seeped into the tree trunks, fossilizing them. Finally, during a period of great upheaval some 60 million years ago the basin rose from 3,000 feet below sea level to 5,000 feet above. As water carried the sand and silt into the Puerco and Little Colorado rivers, the remains of the trees, now petrified, were uncovered.

The self-guiding tour—most worthwhile as a combination auto-hike trip—starts with a 6-mile circle of the Painted Desert, with sweeping overlooks from Kachina, Pintado, and Lacey points. A picnic area has been established at Chinde Point, just west of Kachina. Five miles south of the Painted Desert is the Puerco Indian Ruin, which originally included approximately 150 rooms arranged in a square surrounding a large plaza. From their communal dwelling place the natives went to the nearby flood plain along the Puerco River and cultivated the land, raising such crops as squash, corn, and beans. Early in the 15th century, as the hot desert sun baked the soil and no rains came, the pueblo was aban-

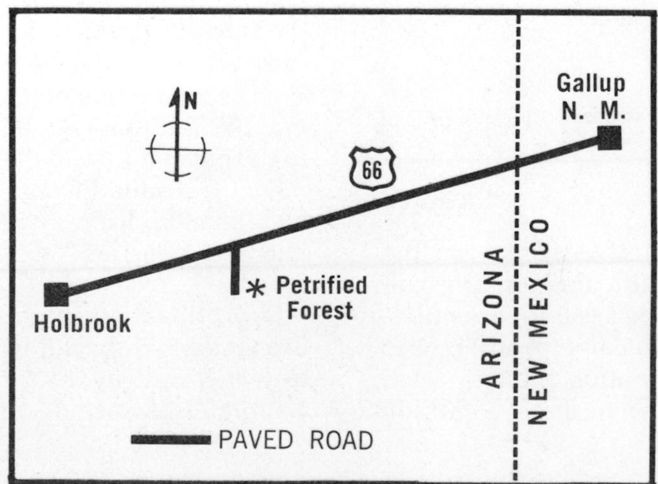

Petrified Forest National Park

doned, its people moving northward, never to return.

A short distance beyond, on a side road (right), is Newspaper Rock, a large sandstone mass covered with numerous petroglyphs (Indian art carved into the surface). Four miles south a side road (left) leads to Blue Mesa, starting point of a foot trail into an area prolific with petrified logs, graphically illustrating how soil erosion has gradually exposed the petrified tree sections.

At Agate Bridge (2 miles from the Blue Mesa junction), south along the park road, more than 100 feet of the Agate Bridge log are exposed, with both ends still encased in the sandstone in which the log was buried. A 40-foot-wide ravine has eaten away the sandstone, with the log spanning the narrow draw.

Another spur road (right) leads to the Jasper Forest Overlook, and a view of great masses of log sections that litter the valley floor. Some of the more spectacular fossil logs are found at Crystal Forest (1.5 miles from the Jasper spur), with beautiful clear and amethyst quartz crystals having filled the cracks and hollows of the wood.

At the Rainbow Forest Museum are some exceptional exhibits, and a park ranger is on duty to answer questions and provide more information about the forest. Behind the exhibit hall is Old Faithful log, one of the largest and most famous in the park.

The Rainbow Park Entrance Station is 2 miles from the park boundary on U.S. 180, 19 miles from Holbrook.

where a bit of the heavens made a 3-mile hole in the earth

METEOR CRATER

Flagstaff is the starting point for the adventure tour of Meteor Crater, a phenomenon of nature that dwarfs by comparison such man-made wonders as the Washington Monument and Egypt's Great Pyramid of Cheops. Take U.S. 66 east 35 miles and turn right on a surfaced road for 5 miles to the crater site.

The meteoritic mass from outer space that gouged out Meteor Crater—possibly a wandering asteroid or the head of a disintegrated comet—struck the earth with a force equalling that of a multimegaton hydrogen bomb (hundreds of times more powerful than the bomb dropped on Hiroshima), splashing nearly half a billion tons of rock from the crater and destroying all plant and animal life within a 100-mile radius. The size of the crater gouged out of the earth is 4,150 feet from rim to rim, 3 miles in circumference, and 570 feet deep.

If early man had lived in northern Arizona at the time, he must have watched in awesome fear the blinding flash and earth-shaking explosion of the meteorite's impact. Recent dating tests using the radioactive carbon isotope method indicate that the meteorite, weighing more than a million tons, struck the earth at least 12,000 years ago—possibly at a time when great glaciers still covered much of the northern part of the continent. From the time of the earliest known Indians, 1,500 years ago, the crater has been both a landmark and a part of the Indians' tribal customs and legends.

Meteor Crater, known also as Barringer Crater, was first discovered by the white man in 1871. In the beginning, the common theory advanced by scientists of the day was that it was volcanic in origin. It was in 1903 that Daniel Moreau Barringer, a Philadelphia mining engineer, initiated a series of studies of the crater. Shortly before his death in 1929 he had established that the crater was actually the result of the impact of a huge meteoritic mass from outer space. This discovery spurred further scientific investigations at the crater. Through identification of its peculiar features, such as shatter cones and rare minerals formed by the impact, coesite and stishovite, other craters were subsequently discovered in various parts of the world, ranging in size from 130 miles in diameter and 250 million years old (the Vredevert Ring in South Africa) to the Sikhote-Alin' group of 200 craters and pits formed by a meteoritic shower in Siberia in 1947.

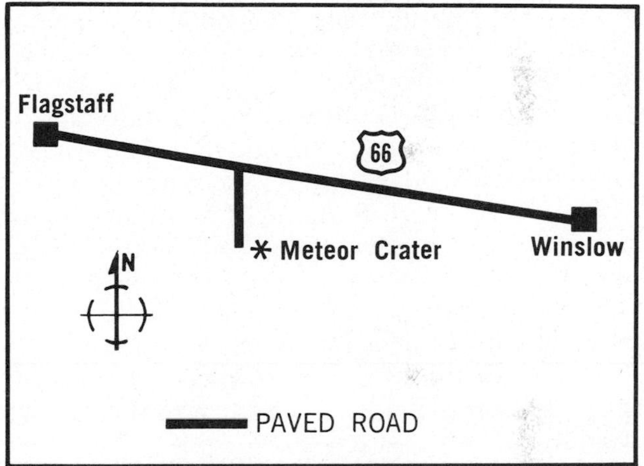

America's astronauts used Meteor Crater as an important training ground for their walks on the moon. This is the only geological formation on earth that even closely approximates the great craters on the lunar surface.

The museum at the site is open all year from sunrise to sunset, with a brief talk concerning the crater being given on the veranda overlooking the dramatic phenomenon. A second lecture is given at the summit of Moon Mountain, the highest point on the crater's ragged rim. A high-powered telescope at the site provides a superlative view of the Painted Desert, the towering San Francisco Peaks, and the remote Hopi Mesas.

A trail winds around the 3-mile rim of the crater, and trails also lead from the museum to the bottom of the crater for the more adventurous.

THE TONTO BASIN ROAD

From Flagstaff, the Tonto Basin Road branches southeast from Interstate 17 at 2.4 miles south of the city, continues to junction with State 87, and goes south on this route for 47 miles, then left on State 188 to Roosevelt. Total length of the tour is 144 miles. The trip can be continued on the Apache Trail to Phoenix.

This adventure byway winds entirely through national forest country, starting in Coconino, skirting the edge of Sitgreaves, and finally going through Tonto National Forest. A graveled road at 33 miles leads right to Stoneman Lake (5 miles), providing boating facilities and campgrounds. A small lake only a half-mile wide, it is in the midst of a tranquil pine setting.

The junction with State 87 is at Clint's Well (54 miles). At 72 miles the Mogollon Rim Road takes off to the left, a spectacular trip through rugged and heavily wooded mountains abounding with wildlife. This unpaved scenic road continues for 42 miles to a junction with State 160. Turn right on State 160 for return to the Tonto Basin Road.

State 87 climbs to Mogollon Rim (9,998 feet) and then begins its descent into Pine (78 miles), an isolated Mormon settlement on Pine Creek established by pioneers from Salt Lake City in the 1870s.

At 83 miles an unimproved road to the right leads to Tonto Natural Bridge (3 miles), a remarkable wonder of nature. This tremendous travertine arch, reaching 183 feet in height as it crosses Pine Creek, is so vast that a five-acre farm is located on its top. Beneath the arch a labyrinth of caves leads far into the mountain. Among the mysterious grottoes and chambers evidence has been found of aboriginal habitation. The caves have never been completely explored. A trail leads from the top of the arch to the bed of Pine Creek below. The arch was discovered in 1877 by Dave Gowan while seeking refuge from pursuing Apaches.

Returning to the highway, the route continues through Payson (95 miles), an authentic cow town when it was originally settled that still preserves this image. Until recently, an annual rodeo was held on the main street with horse racing by day and dancing by night. The rodeos remain a part of Payson life, but are now presented in a rodeo ground the last week in August.

At the junction with State 188 (105 miles), turn left for the continuation of the Tonto Basin Road. Between this point and Roosevelt the Mazatzal Mountains rise along the horizon. Four Peaks, a group of rocky spires in the southern part of the Mazatzals, are viewed almost due south of the junction. According to legend, these peaks ended the migration from Mexico of a tribe of Indians who considered "four" a mystical number meaning the end of life. When the Indians arrived at the Salt River Valley and observed these four distinct peaks of almost equal height, they decided this was the barrier marking the edge of the world of the living.

Tonto Basin (127 miles) is the center of a triangle of primitive beauty, deep in the valley surrounded by the Mogollon Rim, the Mazatzal Mountains, and the Sierra Ancha. From the basin the northern shores of Roosevelt Lake can be seen and, for the fortunate traveler, thousands of pelicans may be observed using the lake as their feeding grounds.

At 143 miles is the Seiber Monument, commemorating the life and activities of Al Seiber, one of Arizona's most famous scouts. He came to Arizona in 1868 and served under Generals Crook, Howard, and Miles as chief of scouts. Using his innate virtues—including firmness, justice, and a belief in fair play—he was able to negotiate with and control bands of mutinous Apaches. The Indians respected him and called him "Man of Iron." As late as 1907, when they were hired to work on the Roosevelt Dam, Al Seiber was called on to supervise their activities.

Tonto Basin Road joins State 88 (the Apache Trail) at Roosevelt (144 miles). See The Apache Trail, also under Arizona.

144-mile tour of rugged wilderness and natural wonders

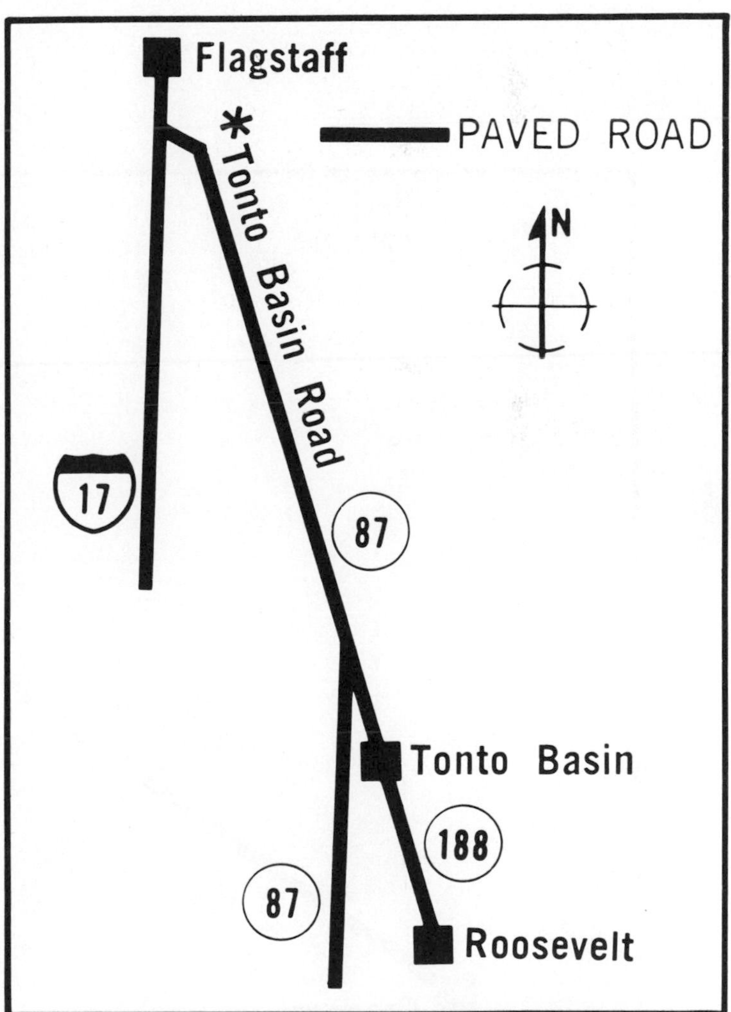

JEROME

copper mining town with a mine museum and home of the famous Traveling Jail

The one-time copper mining town of Jerome, still boasting a population of 243, is reached from Flagstaff via the Oak Creek Canyon Highway. Take U.S. 89A south on this spectacular route which traverses the Coconino and Prescott national forests, winding down the gorge of Oak Creek Canyon from an altitude of 7,000 to 2,500 feet. The highway twists its way through broad, red-walled gorges thick with growths of pine, aspen, sycamore, oak, maple, and fern.

A side trip (right) from Sedona (29 miles) leads to Ruins of Red Rocks, 25 miles distant, on the upper Verde River.

The route continues through Cottonwood (50.7 miles) to Clarkdale. Another side trip via a dirt road to the right leads to Tuzigoot National Monument (2.4 miles), an ancient pueblo which has been partially restored. Relics found in the ruin indicate the Indians, antecedents of the modern Hopi, had achieved a high degree of culture.

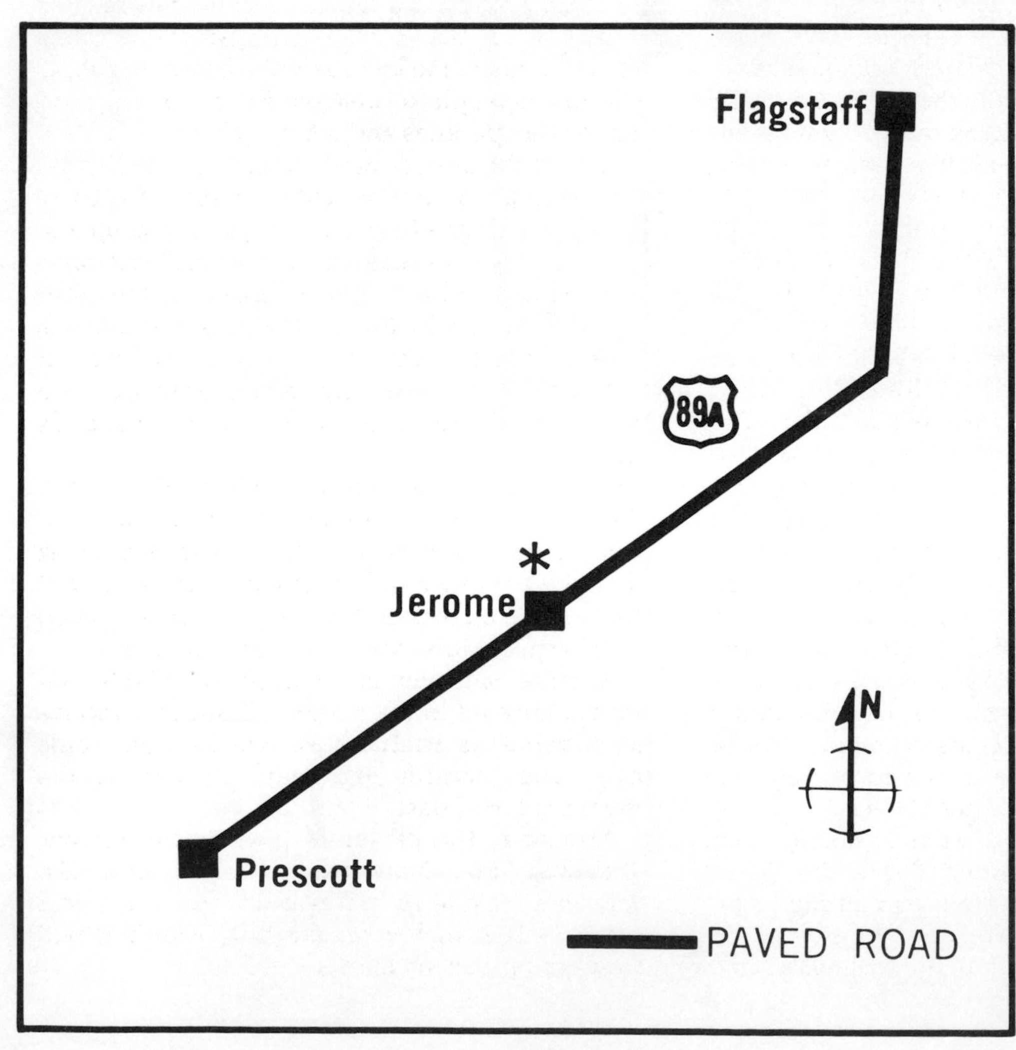

The Tuzigoot Museum, patterned after the ruin, displays several varieties of pottery, beadwork, shell and turquoise mosaics, and ollas 24 to 27 inches in height.

Jerome can be seen from a distance as it appears to hang precariously on the side of Mingus Mountain, its frame houses looking slightly ridiculous on their stilted porches, trying, it would seem, to climb to the top of the mountain. The town actually starts near the bottom of the Verde Valley, rising upward until the buildings at the top are 1,800 feet above the valley floor.

This amazing town had its origin in the 1870s when a small group of prospectors led by John O'Dougherty and Captain John Boyd traveled from Prescott to the Verde River in January of 1876. They discovered outcroppings near the head of Bitter Creek, but did not stay to develop their findings. Later that same year John Ruffner and August McKinnon, two ranchers, prospected the same area, and Ruffner staked the claim which was eventually known as United Verde. Ruffner leased his claim to Territorial Governor Frederick A. Tritle, who, in turn, obtained financial support to develop the property from Eugene Jerome, a New York lawyer, who made one condition: that the mining town be named for him.

The difficulties seemed insurmountable and little was done to develop the claims until 1882, when a railroad, the Atlantic and Pacific, reached Ashfork. Tritle had to construct his own road in order to bring in a smelter and, later, the coke required for fuel. Although the town was officially born in 1883 when the United Verde Copper Company was incorporated, it was little more than a cluster of shacks until W. A. Clark purchased the mining properties in 1886. At this time the railroad was built to Jerome Junction, and Clark constructed a narrow-gauge road into Jerome proper.

Clark also started building attractive frame houses, hoping to develop a more solid community. To eliminate the shacks, he promoted in 1888 the construction of the Montana House, capable of housing 1,000 men and at that time the largest stone structure in Arizona.

His great vision and sound management brought prosperity to United Verde, the richest copper mine in Arizona from its humble beginnings as a Clark property until its sale to the Phelps Dodge Corporation in the mid-1930s.

Unfortunately, Jerome suffered from a serious lack of water and, after fire had swept through the town three separate times forcing its population to camp on the nearby hills, only the frontier spirit and determination kept the town alive. Ironically, Pancho Villa, the notorious Mexican revolutionist, profited greatly from the town's adversity, by providing 200 burros to bring water to the town in 1900.

It was a wild and woolly place to live, populated by rough, hard-working miners who felt entitled to shake up the town as part of their relaxation. In 1917 the Industrial Workers of the World led a strike that involved such bitterness that several hundred miners were ousted from their company-owned homes and loaded on boxcars as company gunmen stood by, then dumped in some remote point in Arizona's southeastern desert.

The peak was reached in the 1920s, and a semblance of respectability and civic pride began to show itself, with ladies proudly holding box socials and the community leaders erecting stone bleachers in the business district to enable the townspeople to observe Fourth of July and Labor Day parades and other activities.

In 1921 the annual production totalled $25,000,000, and its population had climbed to 15,000 by 1929. Then, as the price of copper dropped, people began to leave in droves. After temporary closings during the depression, the mine was purchased by Phelps Dodge and reopened. During World War II there was a flurry of activity, but the ore reserves were finally worn away and the mine at Jerome was permanently closed in 1953.

But Jerome, apparently, isn't ready to die. Recently, as the influx of retired couples into Arizona has skyrocketed, there is an increasing demand for low-cost homes with a view. And in Jerome it's an axiom that every home is a home with a spectacular view from its front porch.

A mine museum is an unusual point of interest. Located in the middle of town, it contains such relics as shaft cages, winches, old mine cars, and pictures and maps illustrating the town's colorful past.

Also near the center of town is the famous Traveling Jail. Now resting askew near the roadside, at one time it was 225 feet away and some 50 feet higher on the hill. Where it will finally stop nobody knows.

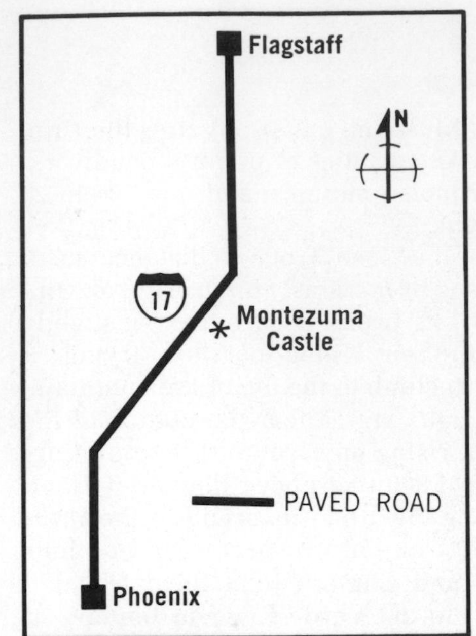

To reach Montezuma Castle from Phoenix, take Interstate 17 north for 91 miles to Montezuma Castle exit. Turn right for approximately a mile to the visitor center. The route continues via the McGuireville Interchange to Montezuma Well, 7 miles northeast.

Montezuma Castle, perched high in a limestone cliff on the north side of Beaver Creek in central Arizona, is one of the best preserved prehistoric Indian structures in the Southwest. It was named by early white settlers who mistakenly believed that it had been built by Aztec

MONTEZUMA CASTLE

Indians on their way to Mexico.

The castle, 145 feet up the face of the perpendicular cliff, was reached by a series of ladders placed against the cliff. The first floor is a row of 8 rooms, possibly the original pueblo. Some of the adobe bricks show the fingerprint impressions of the original mason who lived around A.D. 1250. Roofs were built in typical pueblo fashion of that period, with beams of sycamore over which were laid successive toppings of small sticks, reeds, and a thick layer of adobe that also served as the floor for the unit above.

As the community grew, new families constructed their own additions to the pueblo. Montezuma Castle, containing 5 stories, is 40 feet high, and completely fills the available space in the natural cave.

Actually, there are two units, Montezuma Castle, with 20 rooms and, 100 yards to the west, Castle A with 45 rooms.

It is believed that the Indians who settled at the Montezuma Castle were originally part of the Sinagua people who had moved into the Wupatki area after the last eruption of Sunset Crater. When conditions became crowded, or the fertility of the soil was depleted, some of the Sinagua migrated south and, around 1250, began to erect large, compact structures, frequently on hilltops or in the faces of sheer cliffs.

Obviously the dry-farming Indians immediately saw the potential of this particular cavern-studded limestone cliff along the north bank of Beaver Creek, and only 4 miles from the Verde River and plenty of good land for crops.

The population of the Montezuma Castle region probably reached a peak of about 200, and the length of the Indians' stay is estimated at 200 years. Handcrafts included work in stone, bone, and shell; weaving, basketry, and pottery making. Archeologists disagree as to the ultimate destination of the Montezuma cliff dwellers, but there is evidence they may have migrated north to join the Hopi Indians, since some modern Hopi traditions suggest ancestral origins in the Verde Valley, the region in which the castle is located.

Another example of prehistoric Indian ingenuity can be seen at Montezuma Well, 470 feet in diameter with a water depth of 55 feet. This large, limestone sink appears like a small volcanic crater and, although the water level is 70 feet below the rim, it has a flow of 1.5 million gallons of water per day. This water supply was probably the main reason for the Indians settling in this region. A total of 12 cliff dwellings surround the rocky wall of the well, all in an excellent state of preservation.

Indians with no engineering knowledge diverted the water into irrigation ditches that carried it to farmlands below. A calcareous substance deposited by the water accumulated during long usage until it formed a stone lining and, although the ditches were originally built some 700 years ago, parts of the ditch linings are practically intact.

The monument is open all year long from 8 A.M. to 5 P.M. Although no camping is permitted, limited picnic facilities are available.

dramatic cliff dwellings and irrigation marvel engineered by prehistoric Indians

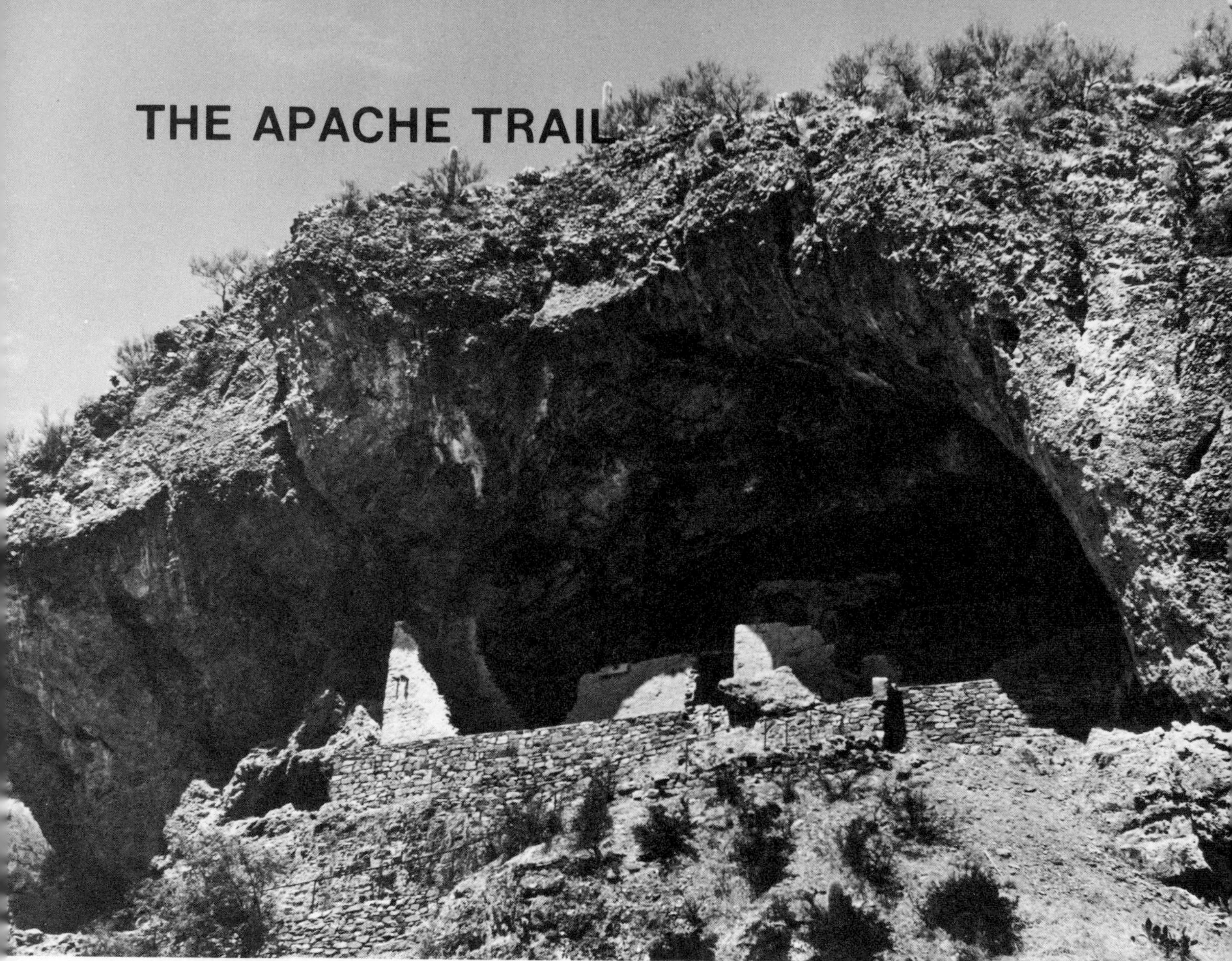

THE APACHE TRAIL

gateway to Apache Lake, mecca for boaters and fishermen

The Apache Trail, sometimes called the Little Grand Canyon, starts at Claypool, 71 miles east of Phoenix, ending at Apache Junction. Officially designated as State 88, the route takes off in a northwesterly direction from U.S. 60-70 and winds its way for 79 miles through beautiful mountain and canyon country. Except for approximately 20 miles south of Roosevelt, the road is paved, although it includes numerous hairpin curves and frequently runs along a ledge cut into the mountainside, with sheer walls above and vertical dropoffs into deep canyons below. Practically the entire tour is within the boundaries of the Tonto National Forest.

Wheatfields (7 miles from Claypool), an agricultural area once cultivated by the Apache, won a page in history as the center of one of the greatest treasure hunts in the Southwest since the Spanish conquistadores set out to find the Seven Cities of Cibola. It all started when Doc Thorne endeared himself to the warlike Apache and spent some time with them healing their sick. When he returned from their country, he told of huge gold and silver nuggets lying in a mountainous area near a hat-shaped butte.

In 1869 A. F. Banta, chief guide and scout at Fort Whipple, organized a party to search for Doc Thorne's treasure. When they reached the vicinity of what is now Sombrero Butte, they were frightened by Indians and rushed onward to Camp Reno. But when, in 1871, a prospector named Miner reported finding a treasure field in the same general direction as Doc Thorne's lost mine, the entire territory was swept by excitement and the lust for gold. Leader of the expedition was Territorial Governor A. P. K. Safford, who had contracted gold fever as a pioneer of Nevada's Comstock Lode days. Joined by a substantial number of hopefuls, Safford and his expedition entered the Apache reservation from the Gila River, crossed Salt River, and continued to Sombrero Butte. They searched the Cherry Creek section and the Sierra Ancha and eventually reached Wheatfields, where the party was dispersed and the old prospector was discredited for spreading false rumors. Ironically, the Safford party had passed completely around the spot where, five years later, a rich silver mine was discovered.

At 13 miles, Smoke Signal Peak can be seen to the right, jutting above the surrounding hills. This was one of several peaks used by the Indians for communicating smoke signals. After passing the junction with Feud Turnoff (17.5 miles), a series of high cliffs (part of the Sierra Ancha Range) appear on the horizon with patches of white below the rims, easily mistaken for snow. Asbestos is still being mined in the area, and the snowlike patches are tailings of abandoned asbestos mines. On the left (21.2 miles) can be seen a huge rock formation called Cathedral Rock, and at 28.4 miles is a junction with the road leading left to Tonto National Monument (1 mile). Two prehistoric cliff dwellings can be seen. The house on the lower level is a two-story structure with 29 rooms. The house at the higher level is much larger and also more irregular, indicating that there were periodic additions in the usual Pueblo custom. The only approach to the dwellings is over a cactus-covered hillside offering no protection to an attacker. These Indian apartments were probably built in the 14th century.

The town of Roosevelt, located at the junction of Tonto Creek and the Salt River, on the shore of Roosevelt Lake, exists primarily as a home for employees at Roosevelt Dam. Started in 1906 as one of the federal government's first reclamation projects, it is the world's highest masonry dam (284 feet) and has created a reservoir (Roosevelt Lake) 23 miles long, offering the angler excellent bass fishing.

To the right, after the road has proceeded southwest of Roosevelt, Apache Lake can be seen in the valley below. Surrounded by mountains, buttes, and mesas, this is a delightful spot for boating and fishing.

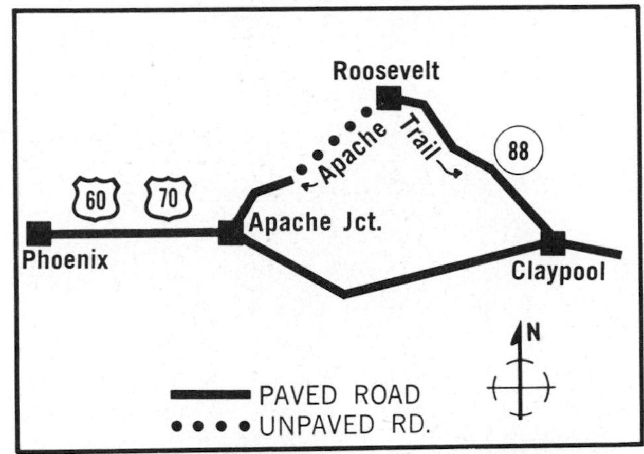

The road begins a steep ascent up Fish Creek Hill into the awesome Fish Creek Canyon (50 miles). High, vertical rock cliffs form the gorge and a narrow passageway for the highway, and the towering walls (called Walls of Bronze because of their color) conceal the way out.

After driving 55.2 miles, a dirt road leads right to Horse Mesa Dam (6 miles). The gorge near the dam is so narrow that it seldom receives any direct sunshine at its base. Partway up the rocky face on the road side of the river is a ledge that provides access to a natural cave behind. It is possible to climb to the cave, but the use of guides is recommended.

The cave was considered by the Apaches one of their safest strongholds and was used for years as a base for attacks on the Army. During General Crook's campaign of 1872-73 against the Apaches the cave was discovered, and a battle ensued in which 76 Indians were killed and 18 taken prisoner.

Surrounding the town of Tortilla Flat (60.1 miles) are the Tortilla, Superstition, and Mazatzal mountains and to the west are forests of saguaros. Superstition Mountain is the supposed site of the Lost Dutchman Gold Mine, found by Jacob Walz in the late 1880s and missing ever since.

The road continues through Goldfield, site of a mine still producing limited amounts of gold, and to Apache Junction, where State 88 again meets U.S. 60-70.

the Praying Padre, the Chinaman's Head, and other weird stone formations

Chiricahua (pronounced cherry-cow-ah), with some of the weirdest stone formations in the Southwest, is located in the extreme southeast corner of Arizona. From Tucson, take Interstate 10 east for 83 miles to Willcox and a junction with State 186. Turn right and continue southeast for 35 miles to Chiricahua National Monument.

This region of strange, grotesquely shaped colored monoliths was accidentally discovered in 1886 by Colonel Hughes Stafford and Sergeant Neil Erickson, who had homesteaded in the area. The renegade Apache Massai and his squaw had stolen one of Stafford's favorite horses and the Colonel, joined by Erickson, took out in pursuit, the trail taking them into a wonderland of rocks. At the formation now called Massai Point they recovered the horse, with Massai escaping. Erickson remained in the region, exploring it, later expending considerable time and much energy in bringing the remarkable country to the attention of public officials.

It was not unusual for Massai to head for Chiricahua, for at one time this was an Apache stronghold and a favorite hideout for Cochise, the Apache chief who waged bitter warfare against the white invaders.

Many of the formations in the 10,530 acres of the monument can be seen from the highway, but the most impressive can be explored only by hiking or on horseback along the 15 miles of trails. From the lookout tower on Massai Point the adventurer can see against the desert horizon, from left to right, the Totem Pole (137 feet high), the Chinese Wall, the Mushroom, and the Balanced Rock. Cochise Head, a massive formation in this same area, was named by some of the early explorers who believed the features resembled those of the fearsome Apache chief.

Some of the more outstanding formations seen from the road are the Praying Padre, the Chinaman's Head, the Bishop, the Ugly Duckling, and Cathedral Rock.

Geologically the origin of Chiricahua goes back millions of years. It was inundated at one period in time (by the same sea that covered the Petrified Forest, probably), and then shaken by violent volcanic activity, creating fantastic rock formations. Gradually, as the centuries passed, water, wind, temperature changes, and frost eroded the softer deposits, resulting in the monolithic spires, columns, and balanced rocks.

Returning to the monument entrance, an unpaved road to the left leads into Coronado National Forest, abounding with large and small game in the forests, and with wily trout in its clear, mountain streams. Continuing on this road for 17 miles takes the adventurer to Paradise, the ghost of a former mining town, with weathered and crumbling frame buildings scattered along the narrow, winding mountain road. North of Paradise three miles is the ghost town of Galeyville, which, following its departure from the scene as a mining camp, became a favorite resort for gunmen, rustlers, and smugglers. Among the notorious characters who found the remoteness and inaccessibility of the place to their liking were Curly Bill Borcius and his right-hand man, John Ringo, whose vicious career ended in mystery, his body being found in Turkey Creek Canyon with a bullet hole through the skull. Killings were frequent in Galeyville, but the law steered clear of the bandit hideout until some rustlers made the mistake of stealing cattle belonging to John Slaughter, sheriff of Cochise County. The sheriff's vengeance resulted in a complete cleanup of the town, which, as it turned out, marked its demise.

Portal, 5 miles east of Paradise, is the location of a ranger station and a source of supplies and guides for Crystal Cave. To reach the cave, proceed west from Portal approximately one mile and turn left on a dirt road. Continue for 2 miles to Cave Creek Canyon. At 5.2 miles from this spot is the starting point of a marked, steep trail leading to Crystal Cave. This should not be explored without a guide.

Some of the points of interest in the cave are Devil's Elbow, King Solomon's Temple, and the Pinnacle, a stalagmite resembling a beehive. Many of the passages in the cave have never been fully explored.

The return to Interstate 10 is made by proceeding north from Paradise on an unpaved road for 22 miles.

Chiricahua National Monumen

Tucson
10
Willcox
186
N
Chiricahua Nat'l Mon.
PAVED ROAD
CHIRICAHUA NATIONAL MONUMENT

Office of the *Tombstone Epitaph*

TOMBSTONE

where Wyatt Earp's guns spoke with authority at the O.K. Corral

Tombstone, as famous as a frontier town as Jerome is as a ghost town, rests in the middle of the desert of southeastern Arizona. From Tucson, the starting point for this adventure tour, take Interstate 10 east to Benson (49 miles) and turn right on U.S. 80 for 26 miles to Tombstone.

Remembered for its historic gunplay, particularly the dramatic Earp-Clanton clash at the O.K. Corral, Tombstone began as a mining camp in one of the region's richest silver lodes. When Ed Schieffelin decided in 1877 to prospect in that Apache-infested country, he was warned that the only thing he'd find would be his tombstone. Later, as he scoured the hills east of the San Pedro River and discovered a ledge of silver ore, he recalled the warnings of his friends and called his claim the Tombstone. A subsequent claim was called the Graveyard and a third, the Lucky Cuss. There was disappointment when the Tombstone and Graveyard proved to be insignificant pockets of ore, but the Lucky Cuss was exactly that, with ore assaying $15,000 a ton.

News of the strike swept the territory like a prairie fire, and Tombstone, laid out about a mile from the first Schieffelin camp and incorporated in 1879, was made the county seat of Cochise County in 1881. By the end of 1879 there were about a thousand residents in town and another thousand miners who camped around the fringes.

Shady operators who followed the mining camp circuit moved into town to open gambling halls, eager to siphon off the miners' new-found wealth. Two out of every three businesses in the district were gambling establishments or saloons, and some of the better known, the Crystal Palace and the Oriental Bar, were on Tombstone's Allen Street. Lawlessness became the rule and, as the population of the rip-roaring silver camp neared 10,000, it became synonymous throughout the territory with everything that was wild, reckless, and unlawful.

The liveliest street battle that ever occurred in Tombstone took place in front of the O.K. Corral on October 27, 1881. It only lasted a few seconds, but when the smoke cleared three men were dead and two others were wounded. The gunfight climaxed the feud between the Earp brothers and some outlaw cowboys led by Ike Clanton. Virgil Earp, though his background was shady, was the city marshall. When he received some open threats from Clanton and his crew, he sent for his brothers, Wyatt and Morgan, and the fabulous card-dealing Doc Holliday to meet the challenge.

An account of what happened at 2:30 that afternoon is recorded by the *Tombstone Epitaph* of October 27, 1881: "They started toward the O.K. Corral on Fremont Street, and a few doors below the Nugget Office, saw the Clantons and the McLowery brothers talking to Sheriff Behan, who had requested them to disarm. He cried out, 'Boys, throw up your hands; I want you to give up your shooters.'

"At this Frank McLowery attempted to draw

his pistol when Wyatt Earp immediately shot him, the ball entering just above the waist. Doc Holliday then let go at Tom McLowery with a shotgun, filling him full of buckshot under the right arm. Billy Clanton then blazed away at Marshall Earp, and Ike Clanton, who it is claimed was unarmed, started and ran off through the corral to Allen Street. The firing then became general, and some thirty shots were fired, all in such rapid succession that the fight was over in less than a minute.

"When the smoke cleared away it was found that Frank McLowery had been killed outright. Tom McLowery lay dead around the corner on Third Street. Billy Clanton lay on the side of the street, with one shot in the right waist and another in the right side near the wrist. He was taken into a house and lived half-an-hour in great agony.

"Morgan Earp was shot through both shoulders, the ball creasing the skin. Marshall Earp was shot through the fleshy part of the right leg. Wyatt Earp and Doc Holliday escaped unhurt.

"The shooting created great excitement and the street was immediately filled with people. Ike Clanton was captured and taken to jail...The feeling of the better class of citizens is that the marshall and his posse acted solely in the right in attempting to disarm the cowboys and that it was a case of kill or be killed."

As fabulous as it was, Tombstone's career was a brilliant flash on the frontier horizon, and by 1890 the population had dwindled to less than 1,900 and remains today a fairly stable 1,300. A lack of water, decline in silver prices, and a fire destroying the works of the Grand Central and Contention mines were all factors that caused Tombstone to be little more than an epitaph.

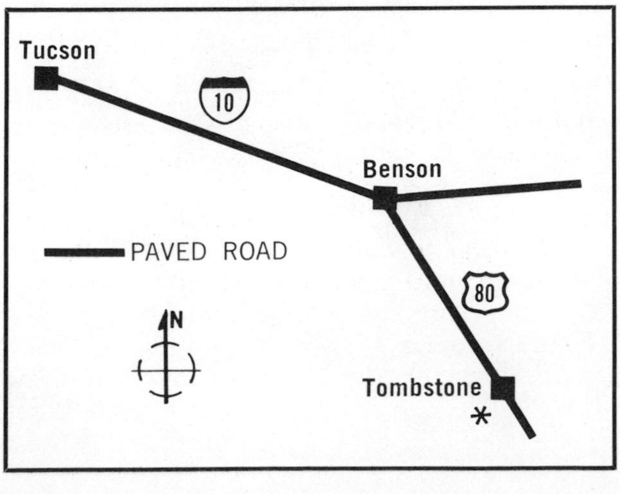

Several of the old historic buildings and sites still remain. The Bird Cage Theatre, at Sixth and Allen streets, is open to visitors. When built in 1881, it was the town's variety house, saloon, gambling house, and brothel. During its first three years, the Bird Cage never closed, day or night.

The office of the *Tombstone Epitaph*, the oldest weekly continuously published in Arizona, is located on Fifth Street between Fremont and Allen streets. The O.K. Corral site, on Fremont Street between Third and Fourth streets, is indicated by a marker. The Crystal Palace Saloon on Fifth and Allen streets was probably Tombstone's most luxurious saloon and gambling house. Across from the Crystal Palace was the Oriental Bar, famous as a hangout for Deputy Marshall Wyatt Earp. So many shots came from across the street that the saloon owners moved their bars about 20 feet back from the front doors to preserve their elaborate mahogany fittings and plate glass mirrors. The Oriental Bar is now a drugstore.

Boot Hill Graveyard is located at the northwest city limits adjoining U.S. 80. The marker over the three McLowery-Clanton graves bears this epitaph: "Tom McLowery, Frank McLowery, Billy Clanton, murdered on the streets of Tombstone." Another marker: "John Heath taken from County Jail and lynched by Bisbee Mob in Tombstone, February 22, 1884."

Dutch Annie, queen of Tombstone's red light district, is also buried there in an unmarked grave. Her funeral in 1883 was attended not only by the lesser element of the community, but by businessmen and city officials. In total, the procession to the cemetery included 1,000 buggies and was second in size only to that of Ed Schieffelin, the town's founder.

An annual Helldorado celebration is held each October, with simulated gunfights, parades, and old costumes to provide a re-enactment of the Tombstone that was. All of the residents become involved, with the men growing beards and joining vigilante committees or arranging gun battles and hangings. While the celebration is in progress, the town's population is boosted by thousands of outsiders and once again, for a few days, it becomes the Tombstone of yesterday.

roaming

Nevada is where the action is—whether on the neon jungle strip of Las Vegas or in a mountain playground. It is also where the silence is—whether in the intriguing desert, or the crumbling ghost towns of Belmont or Candelaria. Nevada is a land of many moods and many faces. It is the Comstock Lode and the rush for riches in the silver-laden hills of Virginia City, and the later rushes at Tonopah and Goldfield's Columbia Mountain. Nevada is fishing at historic Pyramid Lake or sailing on Lake Mead or touring giant Hoover Dam. Nevada is looking up at the diamond-studded night sky that reaches from horizon to horizon, and watching the sun rise over the Ruby Mountains and the golden rays dancing on the aspen leaves.

Scenic and natural wonders await the traveler leaving Las Vegas, whether his direction be north or south, east or west. To the north the wide highway sweeps through Pahranagat Valley, flanked by mountain ranges, passing almost within sight of one of the largest Joshua forests in America. This is rock-hunting country, and an opportunity for the adventurer to trek the wilderness and possibly experience the thrill of seeing a band of freedom-loving wild horses. To the east of Las Vegas is the Valley of Fire, a brilliant array of desert and rock formations, so changeable in color and hue that the ancient Indians were convinced the valley was controlled by their gods. Nearby, cut into the slope of the Frenchman

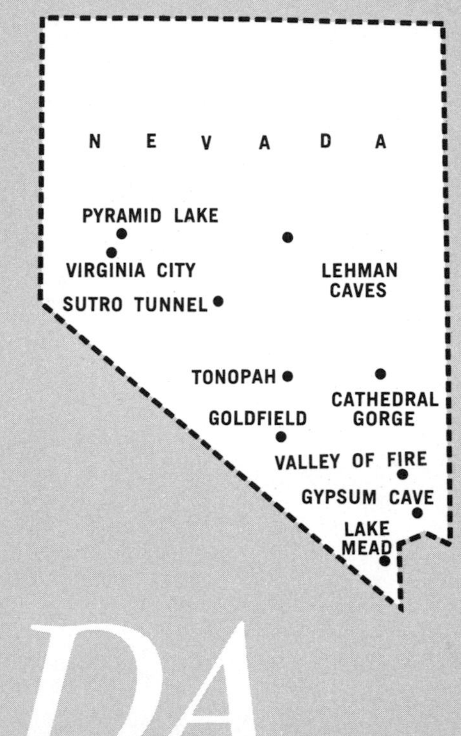

in NEVADA

Mountains, is Gypsum Cave, a great cavern providing evidence that some form of man lived in this mountain shelter at the same time prehistoric animals were wandering about the area.

There are other caves to explore, such as the Lehman Caves, on the eastern flank of the Snake Mountain Range, with a labyrinth of colorful tunnels and passageways leading to weird and awesome caverns. There is also a famous man-made hole drilled in a mountain —the Sutro Tunnel which drained the Comstock mines, started in 1869 and completed nine years later. Considered one of the great construction and engineering feats of the 19th century, the tunnel project ended with an ironic twist. By the time it was ready for operation, the Comstock boom was virtually over.

Travelers in search of adventure can find it in Nevada, land of the last frontier, desert wonders, snow-capped mountain ranges, and the fabulous Las Vegas strip—Nevada, where the action is.

mystic prehistoric inland sea
and the world's largest pelican rookery

PYRAMID LAKE

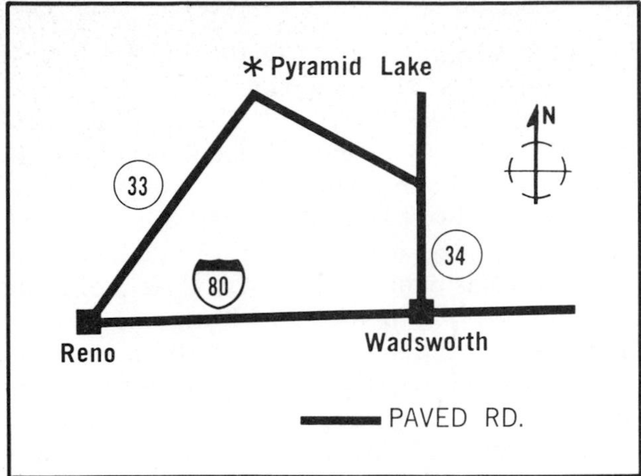

Pyramid Lake, one of the last remnants of a vast body of water which covered most of Nevada in prehistoric times, is reached from Reno by taking State 33 north approximately 30 miles to the lake shore. By turning left at this point, a picturesque drive can be taken along the west side.

A primitive, strangely beautiful desert lake located entirely within the Paiute Indian Reservation, Pyramid Lake is famous for its giant cutthroat trout. Swimming and water-skiing are popular activities at the lake, with unusual opportunities for rock hunters and artifact-seekers along the shores and in the nearby mountains rising to 8,000 feet elevation.

Once a part of a great inland sea known as Lake Lahontan, Pyramid Lake has changed little since the time when giant sloths and primitive men wandered along its shorelines. Today, as millions of years ago, the azure blue water in the midst of sagebrush-covered hills and rock-strewn gullies creates an unusual, almost mystic, panorama. Named for a 600-foot pyramid-shaped tufa formation on the southeast shore, the body of water is actually owned by the Paiutes, but access is free, with a small charge made for fishing and boating privileges. For many miles around the lake there are long stretches of white, sandy beaches and sheltered coves.

Discovered and named by Captain John Fremont in 1844, it was the scene of violence during frontier days. In May of 1860, during the bloody battle of Pyramid Lake, the Paiutes massacred over 100 white troops to win the most decisive Indian victory in Nevada history.

At that time, it was thought to have more fish in its waters than any other inland lake its size, and today is the only known source of a prehistoric sucker-type fish called "cui-ui," once the basic food of Nevada Indians who caught them by snagging.

Another unique feature of Pyramid Lake is the world's largest pelican rookery on Anahoe Island in the southern portion of the lake. Pelicans have come to Anahoe Island from prehistoric times, and each year some 5,000 birds make it their temporary home and sanctuary, protected by federal law from encroachment by man.

The picturesque Truckee River, which bisects downtown Reno, roughly parallels State 33 and empties into Lake Pyramid. Excellent fishing can be enjoyed from several points along its banks.

Pyramid Lake, overshadowed by the fabulous resort areas of Reno and Lake Tahoe nearby, is often overlooked by the traveler.

In Reno are many points of interest hiding behind the facades of the gambling casinos. Harrah's Automobile Collection, for one, contains more than 750 vintage autos restored to their original condition and is the largest collection in the world. The Museum of the Old West on the second floor of Harolds Club exhibits hundreds of firearms and other valuable and rare weapons.

On the northeast shore of Lake Tahoe is the Ponderosa Ranch, surrounded by towering ponderosa pines. Here is a western museum, a frontier town, riding stables, and a trading post. Transportation to the ranch is provided by horse-drawn wagons, narrow-gauge railroad, or antique autos.

Carson City, a few miles east of Lake Tahoe, once known as the nation's smallest capital city, has grown rapidly in recent years, although it retains much of its historic charm. When the western frontier was being settled, Carson City was an important station for Wells Fargo and the Pony Express and a takeoff point for the West's most famous mining camp, Virginia City.

ufa formation in Lake Pyramid

VIRGINIA CITY

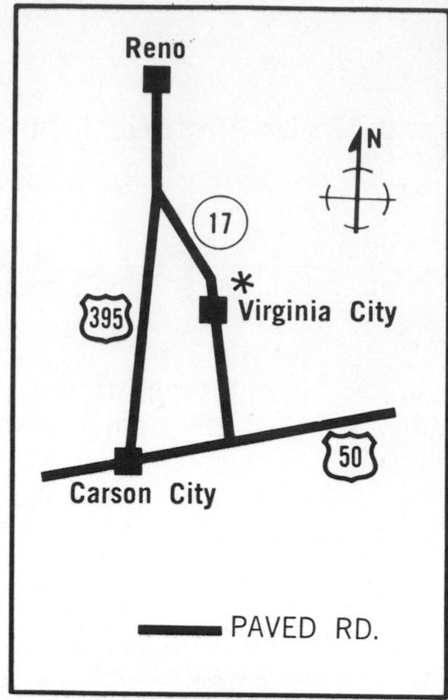

bonanza town of the Old West comes back to life

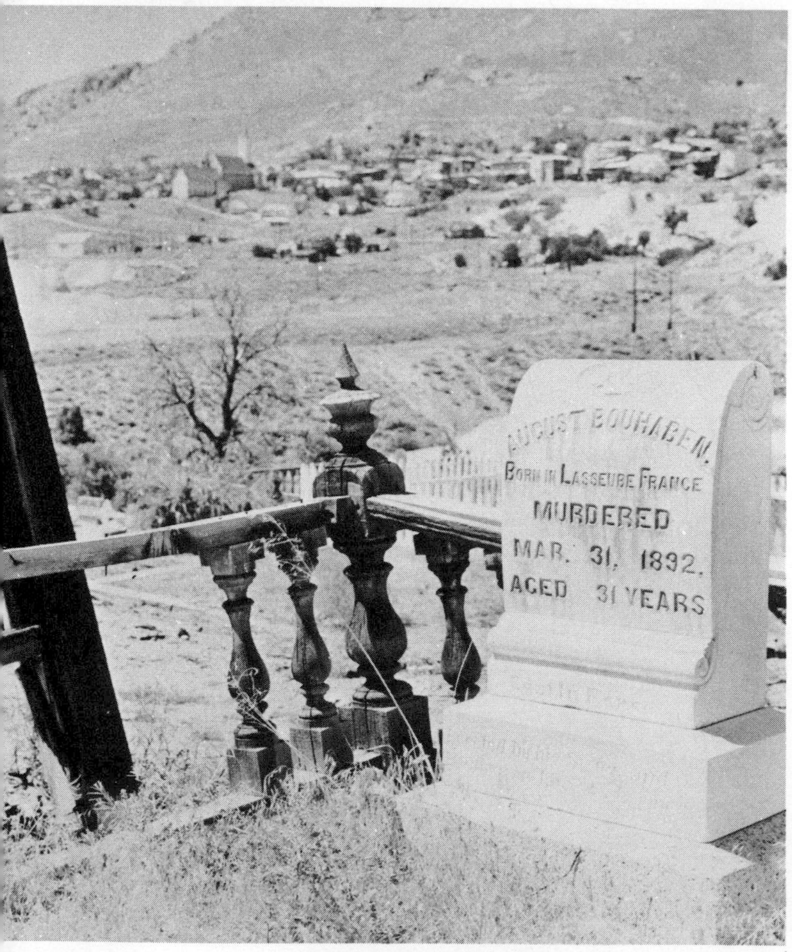

Cemetery near Virginia City

To reach Virginia City, Nevada's liveliest ghost town, take U.S. 395 from Reno south for 9 miles to the junction with State 17. Turn left and proceed 12 miles to Virginia City. It was here, in 1856, that Ethan Allen and Hosea Ballou Grosch, two brothers, discovered the Comstock Lode, without question the greatest silver mine the world has ever known, with a yield of some $900 million, of which a half-billion was in silver and the remainder in gold. Unfortunately, both brothers died shortly after, and Henry Comstock, a Canadian trapper and adventurer, laid claim to the land in 1859, although he actually played no part in its discovery.

By the end of 1859 prospectors were swarming over the countryside, staking claims on Sun Mountain, on which present-day Virginia City is located. And within a year nearby Gold Canyon and Sun Mountain were dotted with primitive cabins, tents, and dugouts. A telegraph line was hurriedly extended from Genoa, and the prices of lots in Virginia City skyrocketed. By 1862 some 40 companies had erected shaft houses and an even dozen had installed machinery for pumping water and hoisting rock from the mines. In that year alone more than $12 million was taken from the region.

Construction of the Virginia and Truckee Railroad started in 1869 and reached the silver city eight months later. Production was increasing, doubling between 1872 and 1873, and the population of Virginia City was 35,000. The great bonanza was roughly oblong in shape, a body of high-grade ore more than 1,300 feet in length. One drift, a crosscut through the heart of the Comstock, was over 100 feet long, with top, bottom, and sides all high-grade ore worth $1,000 a ton. One of its owners, John W. Mackay, claimed it was the "longest, richest drift anybody in the world ever saw, or ever would see."

But in 1875 temporary adversity struck. In the fall of that year William Sharon began to manipulate Comstock shares, and the following spring financial panic hit the Pacific Coast with a disastrous break in the price of Comstock stock. By August the Bank of California was forced to close its doors. Then, late in the year, Virginia City had one of the worst fires in the history of the West, with more than 2,000 buildings burned to the ground and losses exceeding $10 million.

The silver capital of the West made a come-

back, with production exceeding $35 million annually for the next two years. But as the mines grew deeper and ventilation became difficult and water seepage began to flood the workings, production costs began to increase. The ore veins narrowed and profits diminished. By 1880, the two largest mines, the California and the Consolidated-Virginia, were no longer paying dividends. After the mines had yielded profits of $75 million, the companies were pouring money back into development, hoping to find another bonanza. Gradually the mines shut down and the jobless miners began to move out, seeking their fortunes in other boom towns in Colorado, Montana, and Arizona.

At one time larger than the San Francisco or Chicago of that era, Virginia City's population dwindled to a scant 2,500. But its history would live on as a part of the heritage of the gold rush days of the West. There would always be the memory of Piper's Opera House playing host to such stars as Lillian Russell, Edwin Booth, Maude Adams, and Lola Montez. During its heyday, C Street was lined with saloons, and virtually any gambling game the thirsty miner preferred was never more than a few steps away. Partway down the hill on D Street was a row of white cottages where the ladies of pleasure were always available, presided over by Julia Bulette, Virginia City's first and most famous madame. In 1880 five breweries supplied the town's 100 saloons, justifying the comment made only half in jest that there was "a whisky mill every 15 steps."

There are still plenty of landmarks for the ghost town adventurer to see. A large number of the old Victorian houses have survived, as well as numerous mine offices, schools, and public buildings. Three churches have survived (there were only four), at least for a time. The Presbyterian Church on C Street is an empty shell, wrecked by vandals as much as by the ravages of nature. St. Mary's in the Mountains is still in use, and the Catholic church built in 1876, with its tall steeple and redwood columns, remains an outstanding landmark even today.

SUTRO TUNNEL

engineering feat of the century deep in the heart of Comstock Lode country

From Reno to the Sutro Tunnel, one of the great construction and engineering feats of the nineteenth century, take U.S. 395 south to Steamboat Springs (9 miles). Turn left on State 17 and proceed through Virginia City to junction with U.S. 50 (20 miles). Turn left and proceed 4 miles to Dayton. A graveled road (left) leads to Sutro Tunnel (7 miles). From Carson City, proceed northwest on U.S. 50 to Dayton (11 miles) and continue as above.

The pathway to the whitewashed brick facade is nearly obliterated now, but the lettering on the portal is still visible. It says, "Sutro Tunnel. Commenced October 19, 1869." Designed to drain the hot waters from the lower levels of the Comstock mines, to reduce fire hazards and to enable easier removal of ores, it was one of man's most ambitious—and most costly—projects of its time.

As more and more valuable ore was removed from the Comstock Lode and the mines burrowed deeper and deeper into the mountains, serious technical problems had developed, not only increasing costs but threatening to close down the operations. Expensive machinery was required to bring the ore up from the depths, water seepage causing flooding required pumps, and temperatures in the deep mines rose as high as 120 degrees.

Adolph Sutro, a California emigrant who was operating a small mill in the Carson Valley, conceived the idea of a drainage and ventilation tunnel. What started as a hopeful dream became an obsession, then a nightmare, and finally a reality. The tunnel, some 4.5 miles in length, would travel from the 2,000-foot level of the mines to a place near the banks of the Carson River. Not only would it drain off the water and ventilate the mines, but it could also be used to move ore directly to the new mills which had been constructed along the Carson River.

Strangely enough, the opposition was overwhelming, which only added to Sutro's determination. He fought his case in the newspapers, in the courts, and in the Congress of the United States. His opposition came from the powerful Bank of California, which controlled the Comstock mines and mills and also the prosperous Virginia and Truckee Railroad. William Sharon, the bank's representative in Virginia City, turned against Sutro and his idea for hauling ore in the tunnel, since it would be in direct competition with the railroad.

Sutro's personal lobbying resulted in an 1866 decision by Congress that all mines which would benefit (a total of 19) would pay Sutro a royalty of $2 per ton of ore removed.

It was generally agreed that the idea was sound, but politics and opposition forces delayed the project for five years. But when, in 1869, the big Yellow Jacket Mine had a terrible fire that killed 40 miners and aroused the wrath of the entire community, the union advanced $50,000 to get the project underway. On October 19, 1869, Sutro himself broke ground on the tunnel site.

Over the next nine years Sutro engaged in an unrelenting search for new capital to keep the project alive. And, as the dream finally neared reality, Sutro, stripped to the waist, fired the blast that broke the tunnel through the lower level of the Savage Mine on July 8, 1878. The total cost of the project has been estimated at $5 million.

By the time it was completed, ironically, the

Comstock was well into its decline, although royalty payments over the next few years more than surpassed the cost. Within a year Sutro sold most of his stock in the Tunnel Corporation for $2 million and invested the money in San Francisco real estate. He invested heavily in the central business district and acquired large tracts of then vacant land. He built the famous Cliff House and was elected mayor of San Francisco in 1895.

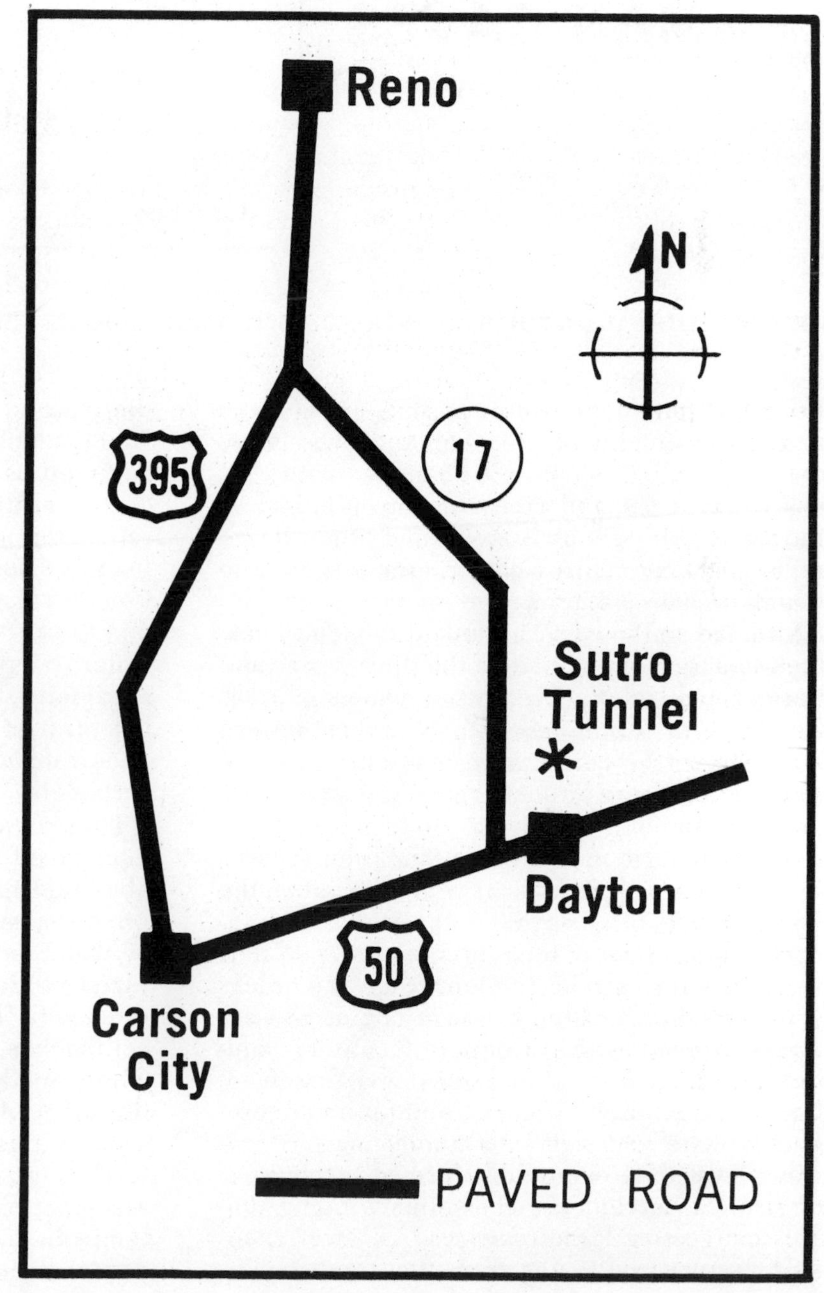

LEHMAN CAVES

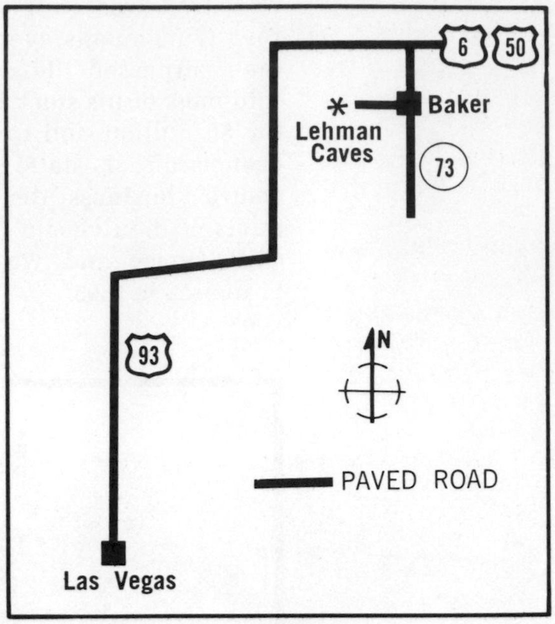

underground wonderland whose formation began tens of thousands of years ago

From the man-made wonder of Las Vegas to the geological wonder of the Lehman Caves is 290 miles, via U.S. 93 north to the junction with U.S. 6-50. Turn right and continue for 30 miles. At junction, turn right on State 73 and proceed five miles to Baker. Turn right on entrance road to Lehman Caves National Monument.

Situated on the eastern flank of Wheeler Peak, the 640-acre monument is in the pinyon pine and juniper belt, at an average elevation of 7,000 feet. Only a few miles from Nevada's eastern boundaries, the caves were discovered by Absolom S. Lehman, a rancher, and declared a national monument in 1922.

The first stage in the formation of the caverns started tens of thousands of years ago, when the Snake Range, of which Wheeler Peak is the pinnacle, was lower and less rugged. Water, charged with carbon dioxide, filled the cracks and joint planes of the rocks, widening and enlarging them as the process of solution continued. The more soluble rock was dissolved, leaving large vaulted rooms, and fault and joint planes were widened into connecting passageways until they eventually formed a labyrinth of straight corridors and smaller winding tunnels connecting larger caverns. As lower channels drained the water from the upper levels, the second stage began. The calcium-laden water, seeping down through the overlying rock, gathered as drops and spread out in thin films on the roofs and sides of the caverns. Evaporating, the water deposited some of its dissolved load as dripstone. As a result, myriads of stalactites developed from the roofs, growing longer and thicker through the ages. At the same time, water dripping from stalactites built up stubby stalagmites from the floor. In places, water seeping through the walls built graceful draperies and translucent, ribbonlike strips of calcium carbonate.

Thin round disks of calcite form the uncommon cave formations called shields or pallettes, abundant throughout Lehman Caves, and these remain a geologic puzzle. In some places, pools of water are held in place by beautifully terraced miniature dams around them. One such room with fluted columns reaching from floor to ceiling has been named the Cypress Swamp, while another, dominated by a large, mirrorlike pool of water that reflects the formations around it, is called Lake Como. On many of the formations, as well as on the walls and ceilings, are twisting helictites, peculiar mushroomlike lumps in varying colors from buff, chocolate, or red to a creamy white.

The conducted tours through the caves require about 1.5 hours. Since the temperature averages only 50 degrees, a warm sweater is recommended. Picnic facilities and meals are available in the headquarters area, but overnight camping is not permitted. Campsites are located in Humboldt National Forest, adjacent to the monument.

Throughout the monument many varieties of wild flowers bloom, changing as the seasons change. In spring and early summer, the slopes are dotted with lupine, yellow aster, larkspur, locoweed, columbine, prickly poppy, and cactus. As the season advances, blossoms appear high on the mountains until by late summer the flowers bloom in profusion in the high country and along the clear, fast-flowing streams. In autumn the mountain slopes are streaked with the brilliant gold of the aspen.

Mule deer can occasionally be seen feeding in the higher meadows or bounding away through the forests of pine, spruce, and fir.

A short distance south of Baker on State 73 are Baker Creek and Snake Creek Recreation Area. Fishing is excellent and camping facilities are available.

Lehman Caves National Monument

TONOPAH

the mining town that started Nevada's silver revival

The route from Reno to Tonopah (240 miles) is via Interstate 80 east to the junction with U.S. 95A (34 miles), south on U.S. 95A through Silver Springs to Schurz and the junction with U.S. 95, and along the western edge of Walker Lake to the start of the long climb to the historic mining town. Flanked on one side by Mount Butler and on the other by Mount Oddie, Tonopah was forced to grow for the most part along a single, main street that shoots sharply upward.

As with many of the mining towns of the West, Tonopah started by accident. For if old Jim Butler, a lackadaisical rancher born in the mining country of California, had decided to get up early that May morning in 1900, and returned to the ranch as his partner had done, he might never have located the outcroppings that started one of the greatest silver booms in Nevada's history. Butler, with a natural curiosity in a new strike not too far from his place, wandered down to look over the Southern Klondyke, discovered in 1899. He camped overnight at Tonopah Springs ("Little Water"), only to find the next morning that his mules had meandered off. While searching for them, he noticed an outcropping and chipped off a few likely looking pieces of rock.

He arrived at the Southern Klondyke that night and showed one of his samples to Frank Hicks (or Higgs) and asked him to assay it. But production was poor at the Klondyke and Hicks wasn't inclined to trouble himself. Butler went on the next day, and eventually had the samples assayed. They were rich in silver content, but when Butler received the report he merely went

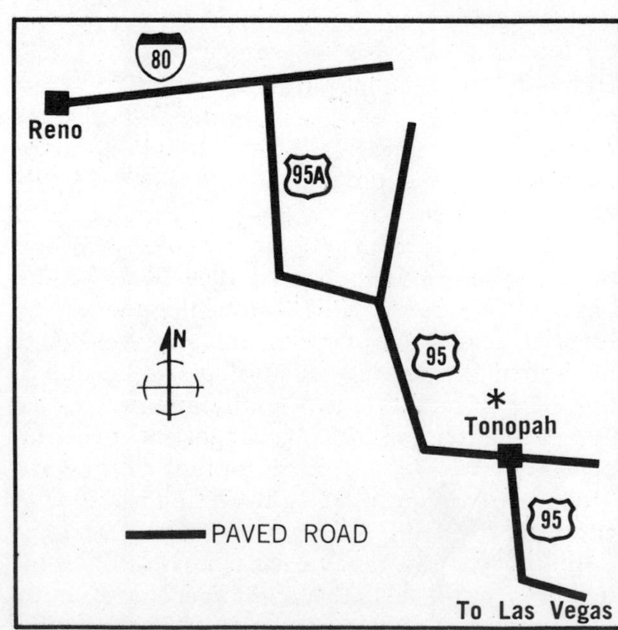

on with his haying, not convinced that the one small sample meant very much.

His wife was impressed and managed to prod her husband into establishing a claim. They went to nearby Belmont and tried to get Tasker L. Oddie, a friend who had helped with the assay and an attorney, to go with them, but he was too busy. Nevertheless, one of the eight claims they staked was in his name. Mrs. Butler happened to stake the Mispah, which turned out to be the richest producer of all.

When Frank Hicks heard of the assay reports on Butler's specimen, he hurriedly assayed the sample Butler had left with him many weeks before and was amazed when it showed a value of $500 to the ton.

A partnership was formed between the Butlers, Oddie, and Wilson Brougher, one of the Southern Klondyke miners who happened to have a badly needed wagon and mules. Oddie and Brougher did the digging, Mrs. Butler did the cooking, and Mr. Butler gave advice. The first ore had to be hauled north almost 100 miles to Austin, and there were many anxious moments before the jubilant news that the smelter had paid $800 for the first ton. It was the beginning of the silver rush.

Walter Gayhart, the Austin school superintendent, laid out a town and by 1900 Tonopah was developing rapidly, while facing the acute problems of getting the ore out and supplies in. At the end of 1901 there was a lull, caused partly by the expiration of leases and partially by the Tonopah Sickness, a lung congestion probably caused by the high silicate content of the rock. Many men died and many more fled rather than risk their lives.

But there was a renovation when Philadelphia interests purchased the eight discovery claims and organized the Tonopah Mining Company. Later the Tonopah-Belmont Company, the Jim Butler, the North Star, the Montana-Tonopah, and the Tonopah Extension were organized, and regular freight and stage service between Tonopah and Sodaville was established.

The real rush came in 1902, with new streets climbing the mountainsides and bigger and better buildings appearing in the business district. The population grew to 20,000, and the restaurants served expensive oysters, quail, and champagne. By the spring of 1903 there was a new opera house, and the Tonopah Club became the city's rendezvous, with gambling stakes running to fabulous sums. It seemed that the whole world was rushing to Tonopah and its fledgling to the south, Goldfield (see Goldfield, also under Nevada). Even Wyatt Earp, Tombstone's notorious lawman, arrived to start a saloon. And on July 24, 1904, the Tonopah and Goldfield Railroad extending to Sodaville reached Tonopah.

It was a wild affair, with the governor and his wife joining in the celebration and a beauty queen and her court riding in a parade, while there were champagne toasts by the dozens to Tonopah, "the greatest camp on earth." But following 1913, when production reached $9,500,000, the road was downhill, the mines were closing, and the population declining steadily until, by 1930, it was little more than 2,000. Today it remains at less than 1,800.

For the ghost town adventurer, Tonopah remains an interesting place, situated in a dramatic setting. The mine dumps and mills still rise behind the tired, frame houses. The Tonopah Club is in business, and the Butler Theatre and the Mispah Hotel are still there. And surely, the memory of Tonopah's exciting past is still there.

U.S. 95 continues south through Goldfield and to Las Vegas through a flowering desert country.

tarnished, tired remnants of a town where lots sold for $45,000

With Las Vegas as the starting point to the historic mining camp of Goldfield, take U.S. 95 northwest across the flat and endless desert country 114 miles. As the route nears Goldfield, Joshua trees are seen in great numbers, with large, creamy blossoms flourishing in the spring. And all along the route the snow-capped mountains of California rim the southern horizon.

Goldfield is surrounded by mountainous terrain, but the town itself lies on a broad, flat plain. From a distance its large buildings loom out of the desert, suggesting a thriving rural village, but there is, instead, an awesome silence, a ghostliness about the empty shells and deserted streets. The town still exists, the Esmeralda Courthouse and the firehouse alive and active. The Goldfield Hotel, built in 1910 as a showplace for this growing, progressive city of 20,000, still stands, empty and boarded up. In this high brick structure with an ornate recessed entrance and beautiful mahogany woodwork in the lobby, thick flowered carpets covered the floors of suites that rented for $20 a day.

GOLDFIELD

Without Tonopah, the mining town 22 miles north, old-timers say there would have been no Goldfield. For when Shoshone Tom Fisherman brought in his rich specimen found a few miles away, he would have found no one around to appraise it. And Tom Kendall, owner of the Tonopah Club, would not have had the money he'd accumulated in the silver boom and would not have been able to grubstake Billy Marsh and Harry Stimler so that they could search for the place where Tom Fisherman had found his rich nugget. Without the hordes of prospectors who had originally descended on Tonopah, there would not have been enough people interested in the Marsh and Stimler claim of December 4, 1902, with ore that assayed only $12.60 a ton. But there was excitement because the ore was not silver—and this was a silver state—but gold.

From the north came the influx from Tonopah, which had come on the scene only two years earlier (see Tonopah, also under Nevada), and was suffering from the malady known as the lull after the storm. Marsh and Stimler filed some additional claims and other grubstakers moved into the area. When the first discoverers were forced to let some of their earlier claims lapse through lack of funds, Charles Taylor claimed the Jumbo, which eventually produced $1,250,000 in ore.

A combine of eleven men surveyed the land and laid out the town, and thus started one of the most sensational real estate booms in history, with lots at one time selling for $45,000 each. Claims covered the country for miles, and new stock issues were being offered as fast as certificates could be printed. With the arrival of eastern interests and the development of bigger mines, friction developed between the miners and the operators. Federal troops were sent in to

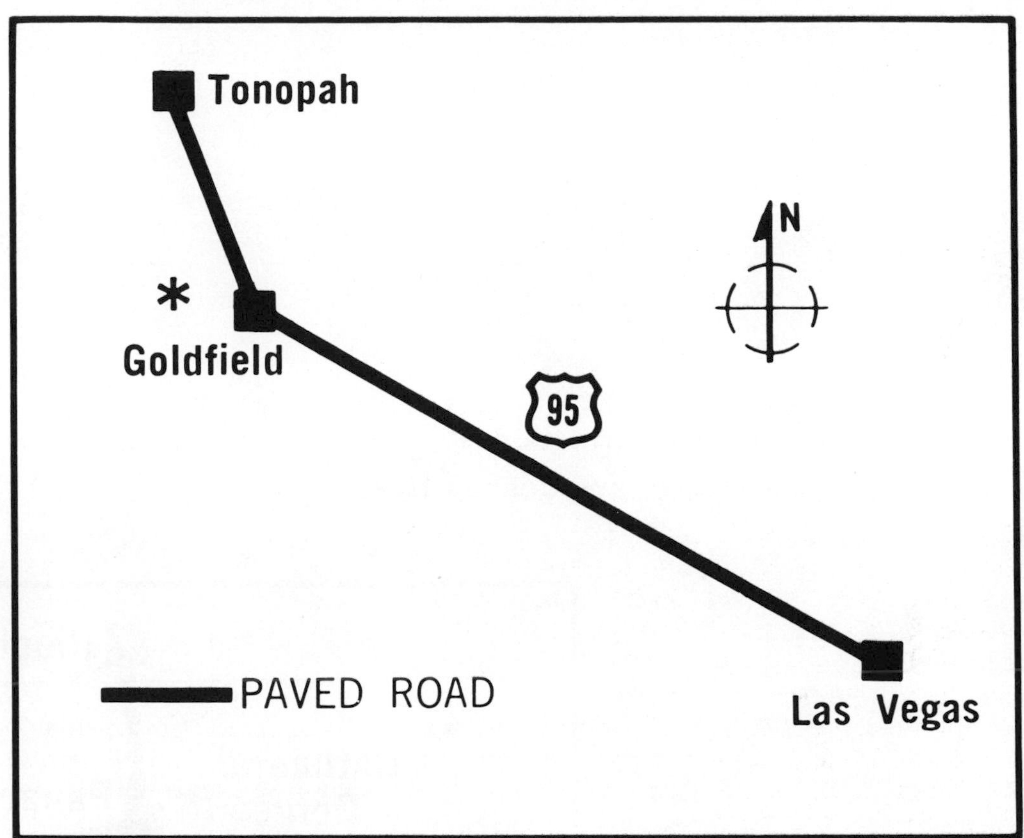

quell the disturbances late in 1907, remaining until March, 1908.

With the mines operating in three shifts, Goldfield production reached its peak in 1910, with ore mined and processed valued at more than $11 million at that time.

And as the wealth of the community increased, so did the social life. Parties were frequent and lavish. As part of the grand opening of Goldfield's new theater, Nat Goodwin and Edna Goodrich, top comedy team of the day, were on hand to perform. In 1906 the town promoters arranged for Goldfield to host the light heavyweight world championship fight between Gans and Nelson. Billed as "the battle of the century," it focused national attention on the one-time gold mining camp until the 46-round match was over, with Gans crowned as the winner.

But the great days were running out, and by 1912 mine production had slumped by $5 million. Production in 1920 was less than $150,000, and the dreams of a great metropolis of the desert vanished along with the former residents.

Fifty-two blocks of the town burned in 1923, the flames fanned by desert winds and a dying town with neither the water, facilities, or inclination to try to halt the conflagration. When another major fire hit in 1943, destroying or gutting most of the buildings before it was finally controlled, Goldfield became, not a ghost town perhaps, but more accurately a town that died and remains in limbo.

tour with weird rock formations,
a remote ghost town, and Joshua trees

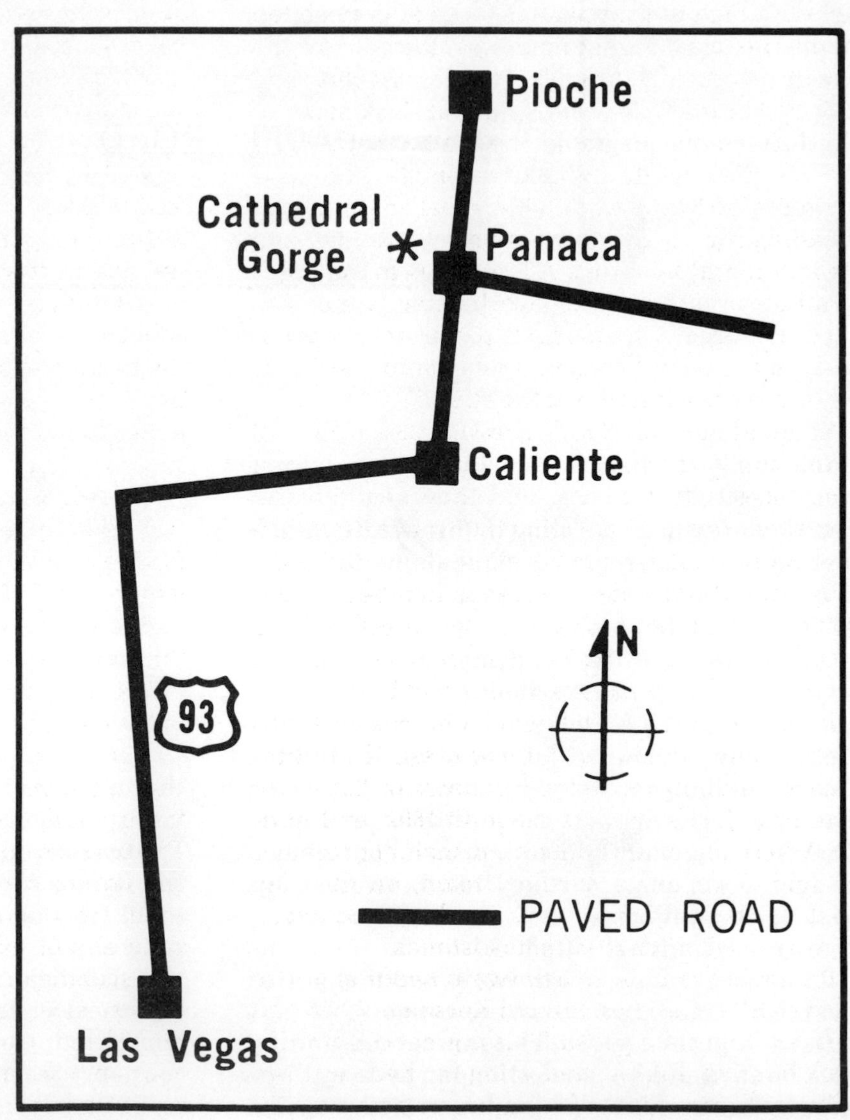

CATHEDRAL GORGE

From Las Vegas, U.S. 93 sweeps northward across low sandy hills where most of the flora is cactus and mesquite, en route to Cathedral Gorge, the heart of Lincoln County's recreational and historical area. The route continues through the Pahranagat Valley, walled by black and denuded ranges, the Clover Valley Mountains to the east and the Pahranagat Range on the west. At 143 miles, where the small town of Panaca joins State 25 with U.S. 93, is the site of Cathedral Gorge State Park.

The dramatic gorge features weird rock formations and varying colors. This long, narrow valley with high perpendicular walls of grayish tan bentonite clay formations was formed as the result of erosion through the ages. Arches and spires dominate the scene, and at dusk some of the formations resemble the Gothic cathedrals of Europe, while others resemble the skyscrapers of Manhattan. One great mass is outstanding for its great symmetrical columns and its innumerable spires. A few miles to the north is an observation tower overlooking Upper Cathedral Gorge, a spectacular panorama, particularly in the desert sunset. Both camping and picnic areas are available at the site.

South of Panaca 26 miles on U.S. 93 a side road turns south through one of the largest Joshua tree forests in America, and then continues to the ghost town of Delamar (18 miles from the highway). As the route continues from the highway, the Joshua trees increase in number. In late spring the carpet flowers in the forest include pink and verbena, white primrose, and various others in delicate shades of pink and lavender.

Before reaching Delamar, the road climbs steeply and, rounding the low crest of the hill, comes suddenly upon the remnants of the town. The first discovery was made in 1892, and until 1900 this camp was the state's principal producer of gold. Two miles north of town, on the way back to the main highway, is a large, enclosed cemetery with interesting headstones.

Returning to U.S. 93 and again heading north, turn right at Caliente toward Kershaw-Ryan and Beaver Dam state parks. This is great country for rock hunting, hiking, and going far back into the hills for a rare view of wild horses roaming the desert. Kershaw-Ryan Recreation Area, 3 miles south of Caliente, provides camping and picnic facilities amid surrounding cliffs and canyons. Beaver Dam, 38 miles northeast of Caliente, encompasses 1,713 acres high in the mountains, in a beautiful setting of pine forests and lofty cliffs. There are picnic facilities, 52 camping units, hiking, lake fishing, and boating all year round.

Continuing north on U.S. 93, the route enters the town of Pioche, one of the oldest mining camps in eastern Nevada and the only one that has survived as an active community for 100 years. Silver was discovered in 1863, but there was little development until the town's namesake, F. L. A. Pioche, a banker from San Francisco, became interested. Although the district produced more than $100,000,000 worth of ore, Pioche became noted, not primarily as a mining center in the frontier days, but as the wildest and toughest camp in the West. According to the old-timers, guns accounted for 75 deaths before anyone in town died of natural causes. It is no wonder that the cemetery on the town's lower hillside became the pride of Pioche, with the townspeople bragging far and wide of its Murderers' Row and Boots' Row, where several dozen hired assassins were laid to rest after they died with their boots on.

As with many of the mining camps, its growth was directly related to its production of ore, and Pioche managed to survive when other, boomier towns like Goldfield, did not. Even today some residents refer to their community as "the camp that came back."

Pioche is a mixture of old and new; its most notorious achievement, perhaps, is its Million Dollar Courthouse, built in 1872 and still standing, although it was condemned in 1933, just three years before the final payment was due. The cost exceeded half a million dollars, though the actual construction expenses were only a small fraction of that amount. It remains in Nevada annals as one of the state's greatest financial scandals. The town remains as the Lincoln County seat, and several mines are still operating. There are various buildings, including the opera house, standing today that date back to the early boom years.

where sandstone changes color with each hour and a city lies under a lake

VALLEY OF FIRE

With Las Vegas as a starting point to the adventure tour of the Valley of Fire, one of Nevada's outstanding geological wonders, take Interstate 15 northeast for 35 miles to the junction with State 40. Turn right and proceed on State 40 for 24 miles to Valley of Fire State Park.

Including some 18,000 acres, the Valley of Fire is one of the most forbidding, yet brilliantly colored desert and rock formations to be found anywhere in the world. So dramatic, so unusual were the brilliant red sandstone formations, seemingly changing both in form and hue with each hour of the day, that the Pueblo Indians living in the region hundreds of years ago considered the valley as being under control of their gods. Of all the weird formations in the park, perhaps the best known is Elephant Rock, bearing a definite resemblance to the behemoth elephant which roamed the earth in prehistoric times.

Evidence indicates that the area has been occupied as far back as 300 B.C., and that a number of different peoples and cultures came and went, with no indication that there was a permanent occupation of the valley. While the Anasazi people were the predominant users, the pottery which has been found indicates that various cultures from western and southern Utah, western and northern Arizona, and the region below the present Hoover Dam were present in the valley. Evidence also exists indicating that people lived in the Lost City (which is now under water in Lake Mead and is truly lost) for 2,000 years and were certainly travelers into the valley during that period. More recently, the valley was occupied at intervals by the early Paiute Indian tribes, who left their mark in the form of petroglyphs etched onto the face of the sandstone some 1,500 years ago.

One of the best areas for viewing the petroglyphs is Atlatl Rock, near the center of the park. The word "*atlatl*" (at-ul-at-ul) is Aztec meaning "spear-launcher." The petroglyphs of the valley contain design elements similar to those considered typical of the Great Basin. Geometric design elements include straight lines, rectangles, zigzag lines, crosshatching, stars, circles and concentric circles, sun disks, and mazes. Natural designs include hand- and footprints, human figures, rows of human figures with hands joined, mountain sheep, birds, snakes, and centipedes.

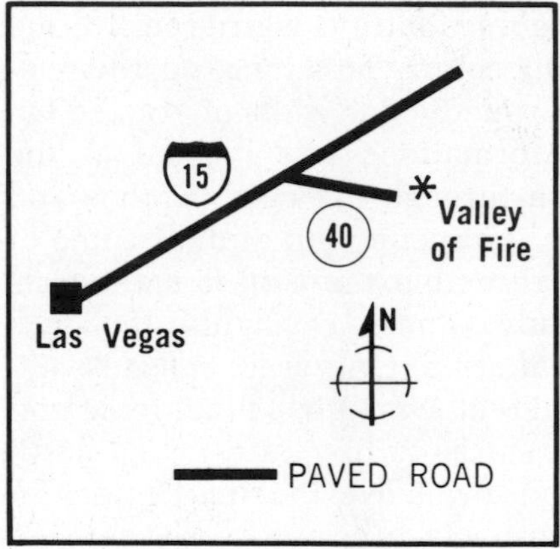

It was common for the primitive people to practice imitative magic by drawing the animal they wished to kill, and the many times the mountain sheep designs appear seem to bear out this conclusion. Some designs bear a resemblance to simplified maps, but archeologists have been unable to explain their meaning.

Considerable areas of the Valley of Fire are covered by a thin accumulation of rock dust, but wherever washes have reached, the undersurfaces become quite colorful, exhibiting many hues of red, yellow, brown, and gray.

Most of the plant life of the region is confined to desert saltbush, mesquite, barrel cactus, Joshua trees, and sunflowers. At one time mountain sheep frequented the area, but very few, if any, remain. Except for various species of snakes and lizards, the wildlife is confined to jackrabbits and cottontails, chipmunks, ground squirrels, and coyotes.

Complete camping facilities and some cabins are available, with most campsites situated to provide a spectacular view.

Elephant Rock in Valley of Fire State Pa

GYPSUM CAVE

Gypsum Cave, one of nature's wonders that man tried to capitalize on by staking a claim to the mineral rights, is located northeast of Las Vegas. Take Interstate 15 to a side road (16 miles) and turn right to Gypsum Cave. Just beyond the turn-off is a dry lake bed (left).

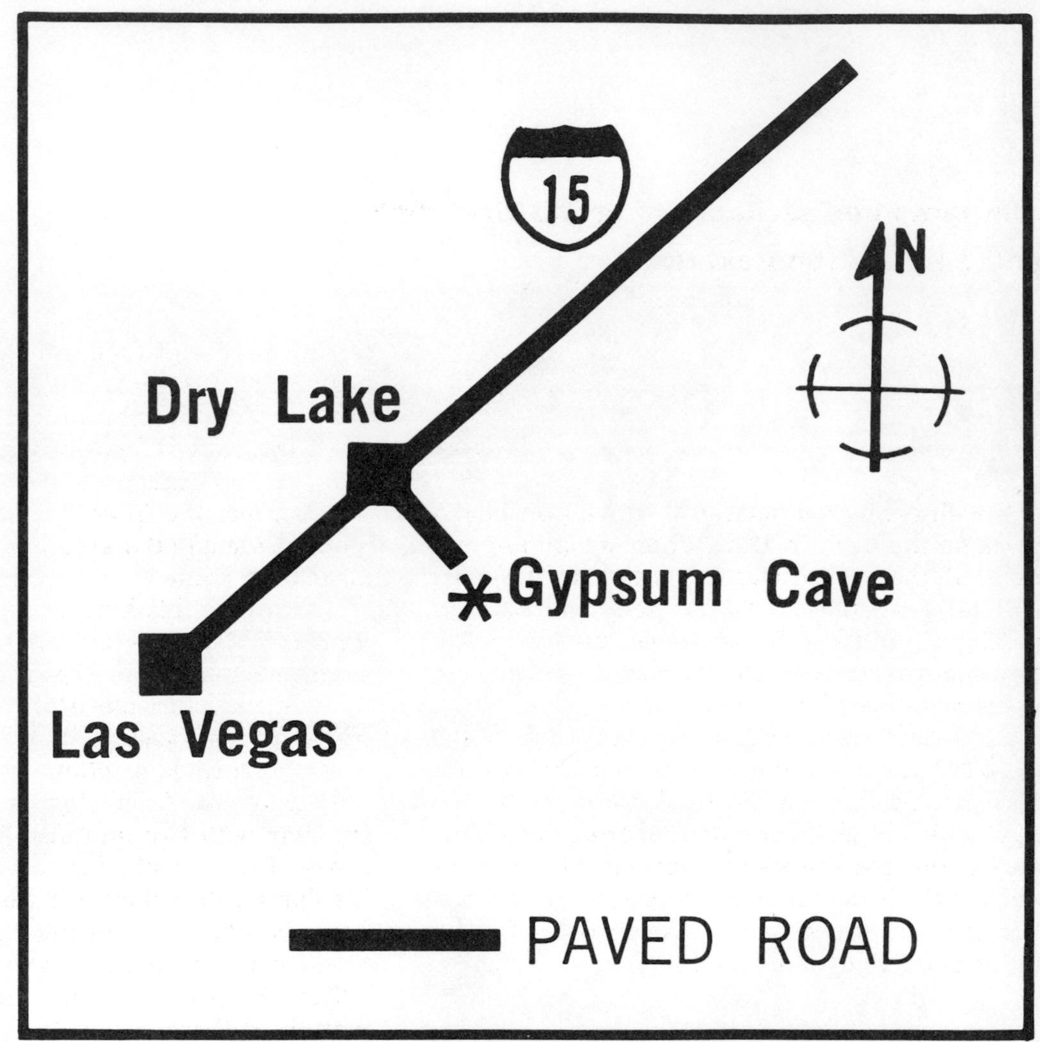

Located in a limestone spur of the Frenchman Range of mountains about 2,000 feet above sea level, the cave was originally discovered by the early settlers, who attached no great scientific significance to this massive hole in the mountain. It was not until recent years that its full import was realized, following the great find of a number of artifacts and bones indicating that both prehistoric man and animals lived there at the same time.

remnants and artifacts of prehistoric man and animals long extinct

A well-organized scientific expedition began work on the cave in 1930. When completely excavated, the cavern was found to have 6 rooms. In total area, it was 300 feet long and 120 feet maximum width. The entrance, measuring 70 feet high by 15 feet, sloped steeply downward to the openings of the inner rooms.

Geological evidence indicates that some 20,000 to 30,000 years ago the present state of Nevada was passing through the final phase of the Ice Age, with a thick layer of ice covering the higher mountains and the valleys turned into tremendous lakes from the melting process. In such a humid atmosphere, tropicallike growths of vegetation abounded on the land.

With plenty of food and water, wild animals roamed profusely. In the beginning there were the hairy mammoth, the caribou, and musk-ox. Fossilized bones from a later period appear to provide proof that an early version of the horse, camels, and the huge, lumbering hairy ground sloth also made the area in and around Gypsum Cave their home.

It was into this kind of country and climate, with this kind of animal environment, that early primitive man came. The date and manner of his arrival and characteristics are all part of the mystery. Spears, darts, or javelins—hurled with a throwing stick, or *atlatl*—were apparently his only weapons. Archeologists are certain he was familiar with fire and also had some primitive sense of the artistic, for he painted the shafts of his darts with colors. He would hunt down the animals who lived in the caves and, at times, would camp in their caves himself.

The explorations of the early 30s reveal that man lived there before the prehistoric animals were extinct. Weapons, strings, forked sticks, fragments of chipped flint and other artifacts, together with deposits of sloth dung and a skull from this prehistoric animal, have been found and are considered irrefutable bits of evidence.

Although dozens of shattered darts have been uncovered in the cave, along with other specimens of man's handicraft—flutes, basket and pottery fragments, a flint knife with a wooden handle—the great unanswered question remains: Why have no human bones ever been unearthed?

exploring, boating, fishing, and scenic wonder at the site of the tallest dam

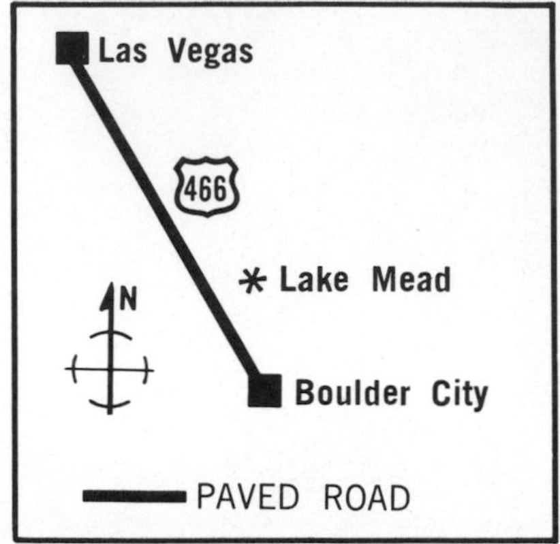

LAKE MEAD

From Las Vegas to Boulder City, gateway to the Lake Mead Recreation Area, is 23 miles via U.S. 93-466. Boulder City is the starting point for various tours. A left turn from the visitor center leads to the north shore road skirting the north edge of Lake Mead. A right turn leads to spectacular Hoover Dam.

The complete area consists of two vast lakes surrounded by a rugged terrain of colorful deserts, deep canyons, and lofty plateaus—a total of more than 3,000 square miles in Arizona and Nevada.

Work on the Hoover Dam was started in 1931, with its dedication in 1935. It is the tallest dam in the Western Hemisphere, rising 726.4 feet from base rock to the roadway on top. Davis Dam, 67 miles south, was completed in 1952. This earth-and-rockfill structure is 200 feet high and 50 feet thick at the top, with a 1,600-foot crest. Lake Mohave was formed behind Davis Dam, extending nearly 70 miles to the base of Hoover Dam. Its 45-square-mile surface affords many recreational opportunities, including boating, water-skiing, fishing, and swimming. Along the canyon walls bordering the shore can be seen many interesting geological formations and ancient Indian petroglyphs. And when the canyons fade away, sandy beaches provide excellent campsites or sunbathing spots.

Lake Mead, 115 miles long, has an area of 229 square miles at maximum capacity and a depth of 589 feet. Wide sandy beaches, shadowed coves, and steep canyon walls carved long ago by the Colorado River make up the 550-mile-long shoreline.

Geologists have found the canyons of the Colorado of great interest from the time of its earliest exploration by Dr. Newberry in 1857. This interest was heightened further following Major John Wesley Powell's thrilling expedition from the Green River in Wyoming through Utah and into Arizona, where the great Hoover Dam now stands.

From the Pierce Ferry road, along which is one of the largest Joshua tree forests in the Southwest, a spectacular panorama unfolds, highlighting the pinyon- and juniper-covered plateaus. And from the Temple Bar approach road, the Grand Wash Cliffs near Pierce Ferry appear as an unbroken vertical wall several thousand feet high. Actually, they are rugged, steplike slopes whose upper edges recede and advance along sharply incised canyons. In contrast to the nearly level plateaus to the east of Grand Wash Cliffs, the country to the west is dominated by broad valleys running north and south between narrow, high mountain ranges.

Along much of the Lake Mead shoreline are sharp promontories and monoliths such as Napoleon's Tomb, Delmar Butte, and the Temple, rising precipitously above the smooth blue water of the lake. These unusual, colorful formations were formed about 10 million years ago by erosion of soft clays and silts which were deposited before the Colorado River began excavating the Grand Canyon.

From the Boulder Basin of Lake Mead southward, the exposed bedrock consists of lavas resting upon ancient granite. In a violent era of mountain making, a wide area was uplifted and subsequent erosion swept away a great thickness of sedimentary rocks. In the Virgin and Muddy mountains to the north these sedimentary rocks still remain.

Many of the sedimentary layers occurring in the walls of the Grand Canyon contain fossil shells in abundance, indicating that the ancient seas in which these animals lived must have been teeming with life. Later sediments, some to be found immediately north of Lake Mead, contain fossil trees and the remains of large amphibians and reptiles.

Man has inhabited this region almost continuously for thousands of years. Ancient campsites, believed to be those of the pre-Columbian Indians, have been found in several locations.

Along the Muddy River in Moapa Valley, ruins of extensive aboriginal dwellings have been discovered. These Pueblo ruins are popularly referred to as the Lost City. Although the rising waters of Lakes Mead and Mohave covered many archeological sites, including the Lost City, extensive surveys were conducted to salvage and study this irreplaceable prehistoric evidence before it became lost for all time as part of modern man's definition of progress.

The geological splendor of the area can be seen by the various roadways, such as the route from Kingman Highway north some 50 miles to Pierce Ferry. Or, more exciting for the adventurer may be one of the cruises that leave Lake Mead Marina daily. During the summer season, a park naturalist frequently accompanies the trip and explains the various points of interest.

Both Lakes Mead and Mohave are ideal for swimming, but the waters of the upper section of Lake Mohave are extremely cold. Public beaches are found at Boulder Beach, Las Vegas Wash, and Katherine, open during the summer.

Boating is unexcelled, and free public launching ramps are provided at each developed area on both lakes. Boats and motors can be rented

and mooring sites are available.

Fishing is permitted throughout the year, but a fishing license from Nevada or Arizona is required. The main headquarters for fishermen are Willow Beach on the Arizona side, 28 miles from Boulder City; Eldorado Canyon, 37 miles south; Cottonwood Cove, east of Searchlight, Nevada, and Katherine, 3 miles north of Davis Dam. Both water-skiing and skin diving are permitted on either lake.

The recreation area is open all year, with summer temperatures rising in the daytime above 110 degrees, although the heat is not oppressive because of the low humidity. The best weather lasts from late September through early December and from early February through late May.

California is the Golden State—enchanting, inviting, intriguing. It is a vast land, embracing three-fifths of the West Coast of the contiguous United States, a land of endless topographical variety: mountains, sea, inland lakes, and deserts. The climate varies from mild winters and cool summers along the Pacific and powder snow on the slopes of the Sierra Nevada to boiling heat in Death Valley. Elevation ranges from 282 feet below sea level in Death Valley (lowest point in America) to 14,495 feet above sea level at the top of Mount Whitney (highest point outside of Alaska). And California is an old country, for it was 1542 when Juan Rodríguez Cabrillo, sailing under the flag of Spain, discovered San Diego Bay. Three hundred years later James W. Marshall discovered gold at Coloma on the American River, and the rush that changed a nation's destiny began. California is a four-season paradise, from the High Sierra to the sea. It's camping, fishing, hunting, skiing, beachcombing, ghost town exploring, or mountain climbing.

In northern California, just a few miles south of the Oregon border, the Marble Mountain Wilderness offers 237,000 acres of scenic splendor, an opportunity to escape from the world of freeways and frustrations while hiking its hundreds of miles of trails. Traveling south, it's Shasta Country—boating, fishing, water skiing, or loafing on 28,000-acre Lake Shasta, or climbing 14,162-foot Mount Shasta. And to the east is the Sierra mother lode country, a symphony of grandeur. Pick your own attraction—Lake Tahoe, the restored ghost town of Columbia, or Jim-town or Jackson. Mount Tamalpais offers an unforgettable view of San Francisco Bay, or the traveler can explore nearby Muir Woods, containing redwoods 2,000 years old and rising to heights of 250 feet. Pinnacles, a national monument located a short distance south of San Jose, is a vast cluster of jagged peaks, the last remnants of an ancient volcano now criss-crossed by adventure trails. In southern California, the idyllic Ojai Valley basks in quiet beauty, a sanctuary almost within sight of the spreading metropolis of Los Angeles. The rapidly diminishing Joshua trees still flourish in Joshua Tree National Monument; and, in Anza-Borrego, near San Diego, the strange and awesome world of the desert wilderness is preserved for the adventurer.

California—the land that has everything, the glorious land of plenty, the Golden State—beckons you to breathtaking adventure.

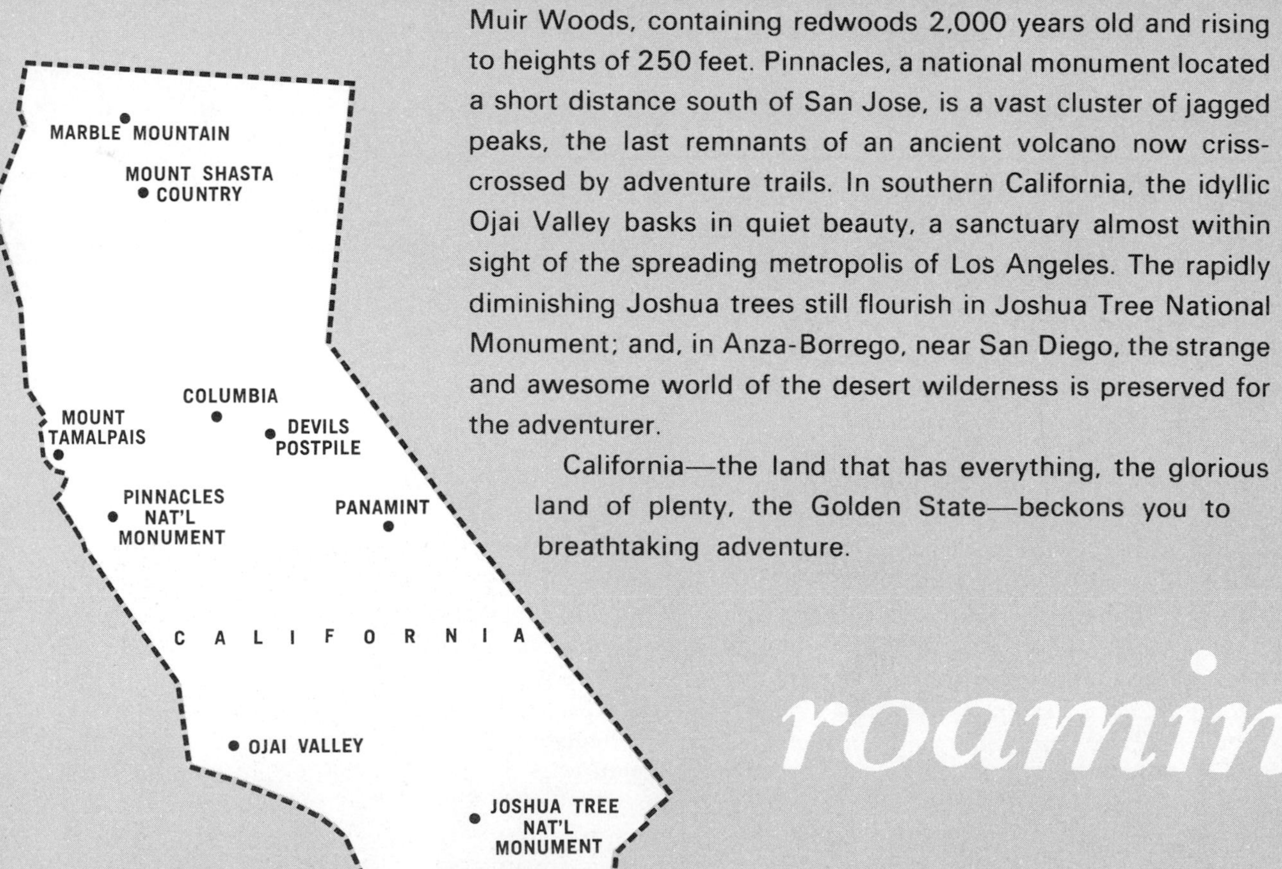

Point Reyes National Seashore

in CALIFORNIA

MARBLE MOUNTAIN WILDERNESS

over 237,000 acres of scenic isolation, and 50 crystal-clear lakes

The Marble Mountain Wilderness, over 237,000 acres of scenic isolation, is reached from Sacramento via State 16 north to join Interstate 5, continuing north through Redding and Mount Shasta to Yreka (approximately 250 miles from Sacramento), then turning left on State 3 and proceeding to Fort Jones, the takeoff point to the Marble Mountain Wilderness. From Eureka, proceed north on U.S. 101 to junction with State 299 (10 miles) and continue 40 miles to junction with State 96. Turn left and follow this scenic route to junction with U.S. 99. Turn right to Yreka and right again on State 3, proceeding as above.

A loop trip of the Wilderness may be made by continuing through Etna, Sawyers Bar, Somes Bar (and junction with State 96), Happy Camp, Seiad Valley, and returning to Interstate 5. From State 96 a dirt road leads to Scott Bar, a ghost town of weathered, crumbling buildings in the deep Scott River Gorge. A typical gold mining boom town, its population spurted in the 1850s following a gold strike, then deserted the camp when the gold was gone, some ten years later. The road continues along a ledge cut into the canyon to Spring Flat, the starting point for a number of trails in the Wilderness.

One of the outstanding features of the region is King's Castle, a stark outcropping of limestone and marble, streaked with a vein of glistening white and rising to an altitude of 7,396 feet. Boulder Peak, the highest (8,317 feet), overlooks some 50 crystal-clear lakes stocked with trout. A dozen streams rush down the mountainside, providing more excellent fishing.

Most of the trails are easy to travel, with the ridges atop gentle slopes and the terrain fairly smooth and open in the meadows, with forests of Douglas fir, black oak, mountain hemlock, and weeping spruce covering the mountainsides.

A number of trails intersect at the Sky High Lakes, almost in the center of the Wilderness, providing an infinite variety of trips in virtually any direction. Extensive pack trips on horseback lasting several days to a week offer the greatest in satisfaction for the Wilderness explorer. Names of outfitters can be provided at the ranger stations located in Happy Camp, Fort Jones, and Sawyers Bar.

The Forest Service maintains five camps: Paradise Lake, Marble Valley, Sky High Valley, Spirit Lake, and Upper Cabin.

From Yreka, it is possible to visit the Lava Beds National Monument by going south to Mount Shasta, turning left on State 89 to the junction with State 299, turning left and continuing to Canby and the junction with State 139. Another left and proceed to the Lava Beds, a 46,000-acre area of startling volcanic features, highlighted by one of the world's outstanding exhibits of lava caves. The roofs and sides of the caves (or tubes) vary in color from a dark chocolate to gray, and the walls are sometimes ribbed; others have small stalactites suspended from the ceilings. Valentine Cave has benches along the walls; and Skull Cave, so called because of the big horn skulls found there, is one of the largest tubes, its roof being 80 feet above the floor.

Fire-hardened spatter cones are found at Black Crater and Fleener Chimneys, and examples of prehistoric Indian art are found in the form of pictographs at Symbol Bridge and in the rock carvings at the Petroglyphs.

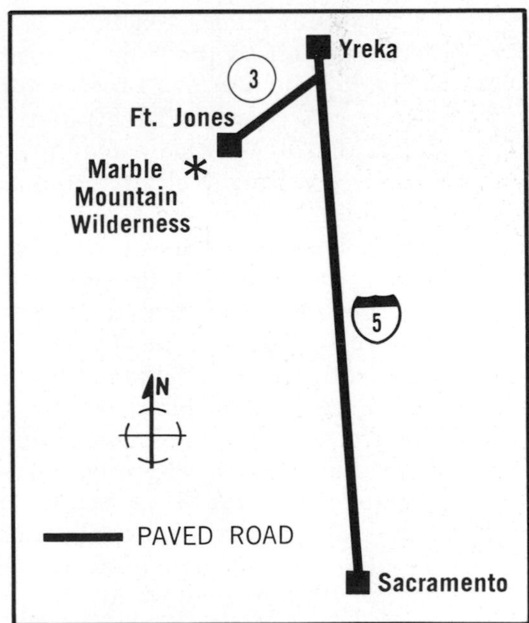

◄Lava Beds National Monument

circle tour to the top of the famous peak and Lassen Volcanic National Park

SHASTA COUNTRY

The town of Mount Shasta, stepping-stone to Shasta country, is reached from Sacramento via State 16 north to Interstate 5 and continuing north for 237 miles. Located near the base of Mount Shasta, its namesake city is the starting point of the Shasta trail to the summit of the mountain (14,161 feet).

Winding upward, at first through stands of chaparral, the narrow, twisting trail provides constantly changing views of the countryside below. At 8 miles is the Shasta Alpine Lodge, a stone rest house. Ascending more rapidly, the trail twists its way beyond the gnarled, dwarf pines near timberline to barren stretches of rough, brown lava, then across the glistening snowfields to the summit (12 miles). Below, a 360-degree panorama of lesser peaks and green valleys rewards the mountain adventurer. As Joaquin Miller wrote, "Lonely as God and white as a winter morn, Mount Shasta starts up sudden and solitary from the heart of the great black forest."

The Mount Shasta Ski Bowl is a popular ski resort, and offers the summer visitor an opportunity to ride the 6,055-foot chairlift (vertical rise from 7,703 to 9,212 feet) and enjoy some of the scenic splendor once available only to those who were willing to climb the spectacular peak.

South of the town of Mount Shasta on Interstate 5, 58 miles, is Shasta Dam, second highest in the world, and to the north the spreading fingers of Shasta Lake, the reservoir created by the dam. Tours of the 602-foot-high structure, showing the inner working of the dam, are conducted every half-hour during the summer, and every hour from Labor Day to mid-May.

The lake, with 365 miles of shoreline, is especially popular as a boating paradise, its placid surface and numerous fingers reaching into the canyons providing a delightful ride spiced with the spirit of adventure. An innovation at the lake is a self-propelled houseboat which can be used for living quarters. These floatels, as they are called, can be rented by the day or by the week.

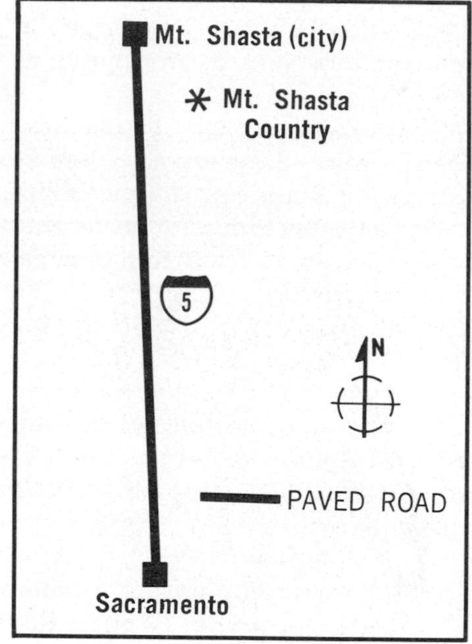

Shasta Lake is well stocked with German brown, rainbow, and Kamloops trout, kokanee salmon, and black bass. More than 20 campsites, many of which have boat ramps, are located along the lake shore.

From Redding, 10 miles south of the dam on Interstate 5, Lassen Volcanic National Park is only 51 miles east on State 44. Surrounding the dormant volcano, Lassen Peak, the 106,000-acre park is living evidence of the violent volcanic upheavals that not only date back to prehistoric time, but which also occurred as recently as 1921, making Lassen Peak the most recently active volcano in the United States, excluding Alaska and Hawaii.

Even today the area seems to be seething, as

Mt. Diller *(left)* **and Lassen Peak** *(right)*

if some underground god were waiting to vent his anger. The boiling lakes, the fumaroles, the jagged cliffs, and steaming mud pots are living features of the park.

State 89, crossing a shoulder of Lassen Peak, winds through the western section of the park, providing endless variety in this strange wonderland of nature's making. More than 20 foot trails crisscross the park, many of them through beautiful mountain meadows and idyllic forests.

There are numerous campgrounds, and accommodations are also available at Manzanita Lake Lodge and Drakesbad Guest Ranch in the park. Most of the park road is closed from November to June.

raucous, oft-burned mining town restored complete with Wells Fargo and Company Express office

COLUMBIA

With Sacramento as the starting point for the adventure tour of Columbia, once known as the gem of the southern mines and now a restored ghost town, take State 16 southeast for 30 miles and the junction with State 49. Continue through Angels Camp. At 15 miles beyond, turn left and proceed 1.8 miles to Columbia.

One of the richest gold mining camps of the

roaring 1850s, it was also one of the noisiest and most sinful in the Mother Lode. With the discovery of rich gold deposits by some Mexican miners in March of 1850, and another strike within a month by a member of Dr. Thaddeus Hildreth's party, the rush to "Hildreth's Diggings" was on, and by mid-April there were 6,000 gold-seeking inhabitants.

The first year almost marked the birth and death of the mining camp, as water, indispensable in placer mining, gave out during the summer months, and the population dwindled to a handful of diehards. Then, in 1851, the Tuolumne County Water Company was formed to bring water into the area. Later, perhaps the first cooperative in the United States was formed when the miners decided to establish their own water company to compete with Tuolumne. The new company started construction of a 60-mile-long aqueduct through the mountains which was not completed until 1858, by which time the richest reserves had been exhausted and the miners were already leaving by the hundreds.

But Hildreth's Diggings, with the more permanent name of Columbia, refused to become a ghost. Streets had been laid out and homes replaced the tents and shanties. By the end of 1852 there were 30 saloons, 143 faro games, 4 banks, 3 express offices, 27 produce stores, and an arena for bull-and-bear fights, once described in the *New York Tribune* by Horace Greeley and said to have been the source for the terms "bull" and "bear" on Wall Street. In 1856, among the cypress trees on Kennebec Hill, St. Anne's Church with its distinctive square brick tower was built. Brick was used more frequently for construction following a fire in 1854 which destroyed everything in the center of the business district except for the one brick building.

In 1857 another fire ravaged the town's business district, wiping out virtually every building in a 13-block area. Rebuilding started immediately. The town formed a volunteer fire department and purchased a fire engine named "Papeete," a small, fancifully decorated hand-pumper.

The Chinese influence was strong in Columbia, as it was in nearly all the gold rush camps. Brought in to work in the mines, many Chinese eventually became businessmen who managed such enterprises as Chinese George's Restaurant, Chan Hang's Laundry, and Wan Hop's drinking establishment.

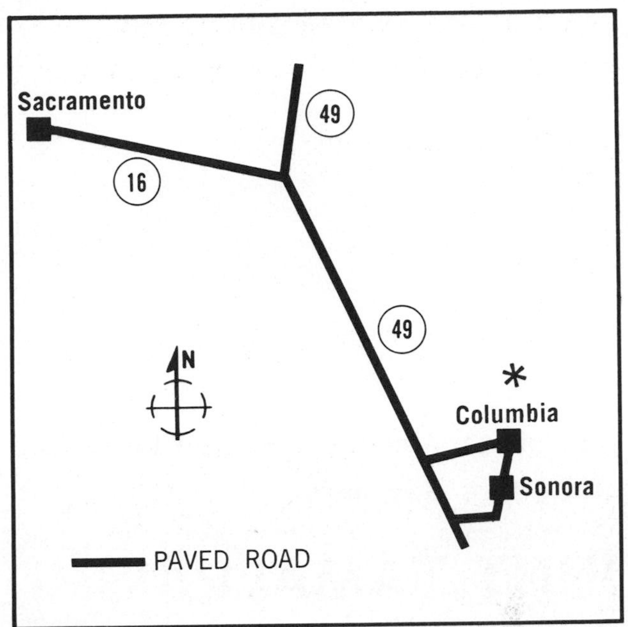

As the community grew, serious attempts were made to raise the level of culture, and billboards proudly announced the appearances of such great names in the theater as Lola Montez, Edwin Booth, and Lotta Crabtree.

In the 1860s Columbia began its decline and many of the buildings were torn down in the 1870s and 1880s, although it never became a true ghost town, since it managed to maintain a population of nearly 500.

With the purchase of the town by the state and its dedication as a historic park, many of the buildings have been restored. Today, the old Wells Fargo and Company Express office can be visited. The schoolhouse has been completely restored, complete with bell tower, pump organ, desks, and pot-bellied stoves.

The Fallon Theatre, once the center of Columbia's social life, is again active during the summer months, as students of the University of the Pacific present a 6-week repertory season.

Other points of interest include the stabilized ruins of a Chinese store owned by Lun Sing, a fandango hall, the town jail, the park museum and orientation center, two miners' cabins, and the Eagle Cottage, once a boardinghouse for the miners.

most spectacular view of San Francisco in the entire Bay area

MOUNT TAMALPAIS

Located adjacent to the beautiful Muir Woods National Monument, Mount Tamalpais is reached from San Francisco via the Golden Gate Bridge, then going west from Marin City to the Panoramic Highway. From Oakland, take State 17 over the San Rafael Bridge, turning south at San Rafael to Mill Valley and the Panoramic Highway.

The mountain (2,608 feet above the Golden Gate Bridge) provides a more spectacular view of San Francisco and its environs than any other point in the entire Bay area. Interesting roads traverse the triple-peaked Mount Tamalpais, with easy trails to the top of East Peak.

From the Muir Woods Road a side route crosses a trestle built over the old roadbed of the Mount Tamalpais and Muir Woods Railway, constructed in 1896. Because of its 281 curves it was known as "the crookedest railroad in the world." Mountain Theater, located along the way, is a natural amphitheater on the lower western side of Mount Tamalpais amid a forest of redwoods and mountain oaks, with San Francisco Bay and the Pacific Ocean as a backdrop for the stage.

Continuing upward, the road twists along the slopes of the three crests: West Peak, Middle Peak, and East Peak. An excellent view is obtained from the picture windows at Mount Tamalpais Tavern.

Muir Woods National Monument was established to preserve the forest of giant coast redwood trees *(Sequoia sempervirens)*, threatened by destruction at the hands of private interests who planned to cut the trees and use the site as a reservoir.

Containing redwoods 2,000 years old and rising to heights of 250 feet, the grove includes 485 acres. It cannot be properly seen without taking the 3/4-mile-long self-guiding nature trail, posted along the way with numerous identifying signs relating to a leaflet describing the forest. With the sunlight filtering through the mighty redwoods onto the shaded trail, the adventurer has the feeling of being in another world, almost cathedrallike in atmosphere.

Carpeting the forest floor is a luxuriant growth of sword ferns, lady ferns, and brackens. Other wild flowers in the monument include shooting star, Oregon oxalis, violet, ginger, fetid adder's-tongue, and trillium, with beautiful, white-blossomed azaleas in the spring.

Most of the paths are fairly level, although two trails wend their way up the canyon wall to lookout points offering spectacular views of Golden Gate Bridge and the Bay.

There are no picnic or camping facilities within the monument, but both picnic and camp sites are located at Mount Tamalpais State Park.

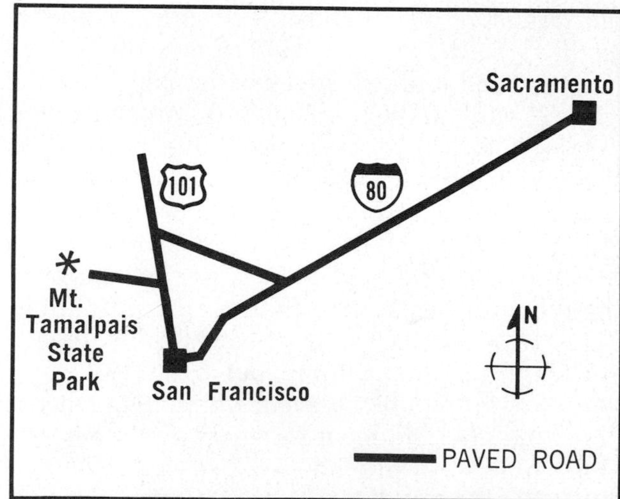

Muir Woods National Monumen

remnant of a basaltic lava flow
that originated 915,000 years ago
carved by glacial action into symmetrical columns

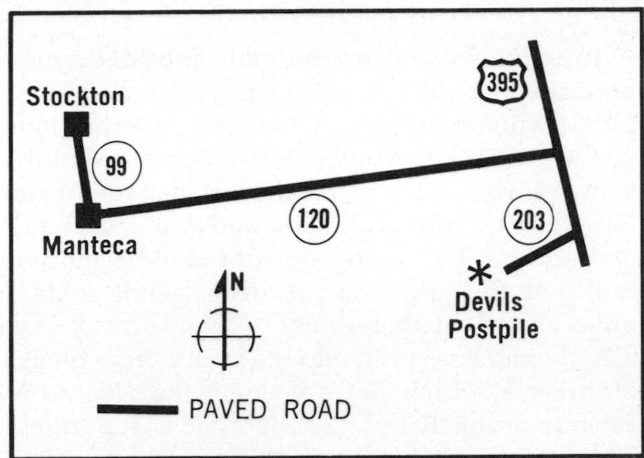

Devils Postpile, located between Yosemite and Kings Canyon national parks, is reached from Stockton via State 99 south to Manteca (10 miles) and the junction with State 120. From there turn left and continue to Sonora (53 miles); then proceed on State 108 over Sonora Pass to the junction with U.S. 395 (82 miles). Turn right and proceed to the entrance road (approximately 74 miles) on the right. Go 10.5 miles to Minaret Summit and then 7.5 miles on an unpaved mountain road to Devils Postpile National Monument.

DEVILS POSTPILE

Located in the magnificent forest and lake country of the Sierra Nevada, Devils Postpile (elevation 7,600 feet) is an extraordinary formation of symmetrical, grayish brown columns, some of which, rising more than 60 feet, fit closely together like the pipes of a tremendous organ.

The Devils Postpile is a remnant of a basaltic lava flow that originated in what is now known as Mammoth Pass and poured for 6 miles down the canyon of the Middle Fork of the San Joaquin River to a point just beyond spectacular 140-foot Rainbow Fall at the monument's southern end. This phenomenon took place during the later interglacial periods in the Sierra Nevada, at least 915,000 years ago.

As the glacier advanced it met the obstructing basalt wall. Being perhaps 1,000 feet thick, the glacial ice poured over the obstruction, wearing the underlying lava smooth and leaving the tops of the basalt columns as a broad, flat area, polished by the grinding action of the glacier until they resembled a mosaic or tile inlay.

During the thousands of years that the ice held sway, the bulk of the basaltic flow was removed, with only the more resistant parts remaining. Of these, the largest is the Devils Postpile, about 900 feet long and 200 feet high.

Another interesting geologic feature of the monument is the pumice found in the northern section. This material, an exceedingly porous volcanic rock so light that it floats in water, was deposited in postglacial times by volcanoes located east and north of the Postpile. Several bubbling hot springs, one located at Reds Meadow, are also evidence of recent volcanic activity.

Two miles down the river trail from the Postpile, the Middle Fork of the San Joaquin makes a sheer drop of 140 feet into a deep green pool. The crashing white water, sometimes dancing with rainbows, contrasts strikingly with the dark basaltic cliffs surrounding the waterfall. A short, steep trail leads to the bottom, where willows, alders, western white pines, and mountain hemlocks form a delightful natural garden.

Park rangers are on duty during the summer, and a campground is available, located near the ranger station.

Devils Postpile National Monument

PINNACLES

Pinnacles National Monument, 10,000 acres of jagged peaks crisscrossed by adventure trails, is reached from San Jose by taking U.S. 101 south 22 miles to the junction with State 25 through Hollister, continuing 35 miles to the monument.

Here the last remnants of an ancient volcano, carved into spectacular pinnacles and spires by rain, wind, heat, and frost, rise against the sky. This cluster of jagged peaks contrasts strikingly with the wide, gently rolling valleys of the surrounding country.

The weird colored rock formations of dark red conglomerate are found nowhere else in the Western Hemisphere. Spires rise from 600 to 1,000 feet, while sharp canyons have been carved into long, twisting caverns between precipitous walls.

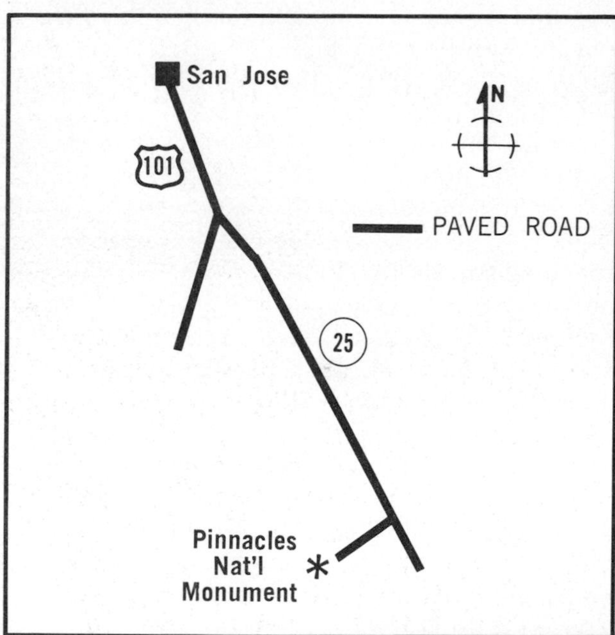

Some 30 million years ago the earth shook as volcanic eruptions belched forth from the mountains of the Gabilan Range and vast quantities of lava poured from cracks in the earth some five miles long. These flows formed a domelike mountain that may have reached an elevation of 8,000 feet—more than three times the height of the Pinnacles today.

As active volcanism gradually subsided in the area, erosion and faulting began to play their part. Two major faults developed on either side of the Pinnacles. Movements along these faults slowly lowered the central mass between Chalone Creek Fault on the east and Pinnacles Fault on the west. These are considered to be splinter faults of the great San Andreas Fault some 6 miles east of the monument.

With water seeping into the joints, large blocks of breccia which have become the fingers of rock or pinnacles of the high peaks separated. Then, perhaps eons later, tilting of the mountain between the faults accelerated the stream-cutting that produced the very narrow gorge seen at Bear Gulch and Old Pinnacles.

To fully appreciate the area, the explorer should take advantage of the many trails throughout the monument, starting with the High Peaks Trail at the visitor center in Bear Gulch. Climbing about 1,300 feet, hikers are rewarded with panoramas of the entire monument. Allow 3 to 4 hours for the 5-mile trip.

Caves-Moses Spring Nature Trail is a self-guiding 1-mile round trip, starting on the Caves Trail, which follows the bottom of Bear Gulch Canyon, winding through dark passages beneath gigantic boulders wedged between the canyon walls. A leaflet, available at the visitor center, is keyed to numbered stakes along the way. The stakes continue on Moses Spring Trail, which returns from Bear Gulch Reservoir to the parking area.

The most difficult, but most worthwhile for the adventurer, is the 8.5-mile round trip from Bear Gulch to the top of North Chalone Peak, the location of a fire lookout. The trail, starting at Caves Trail, wanders uphill through dense stands of chaparral and provides a distant view of Pinnacle Rocks.

Campsites for trailer and tent camping are available, with fireplaces and tables. A park naturalist is on duty, and evening talks are given on summer weekends.

Pinnacles National Monument

adventure trails crisscross
10,000 acres of jagged peaks

rugged, desert land
and the remains of a violent mining town
on the edge of Death Valley

PANAMINT CITY

With Bakersfield as a starting point for the adventure tour of the ghost town of Panamint City, take State 178 east to junction with State 14. Turn left and continue north (State 14 becomes U.S. 395) to Olancha and the junction with State 190. Turn right, passing by the edge of Owens Lake and continuing about 60 miles to a paved side road (right) leading south into Panamint Valley. At approximately 30 miles the route intersects the Emigrant Pass Road. Continue south for approximately 25 miles to an unpaved road (left) leading to Ballarat, into Surprise Canyon and the site of Panamint City. The road is too difficult for passenger cars, but can be ridden by 4-wheel drive vehicles during dry weather.

Panamint Valley country is rugged, desert land that marked, for the early pioneers moving west into California, the end of an arduous battle across the vastness of Death Valley. It was William Alvord who sought gold on the west side of the Panamint Range and who named the mile-long passageway between the high rock walls Surprise Canyon. His third trip to the area proved to be his last, as a berserk partner, perhaps driven mad by the ghostly canyon, killed him. A year later a party of prospectors entered Wildrose Canyon to the north (the site of picturesque charcoal kilns used during gold rush days) and drove a tunnel into the mountainside, finding traces of antimony and silver. But the Panamint Indians, distrusting the white man's motives, ambushed the group, and killed them all.

This marked the end of prospecting in Panamint country for ten years. In 1872 Richard Jacobs, W. L. Kennedy, and Robert Stewart fought their way up Surprise Canyon and to the mountain beyond. Reaching a basin surrounded by greenish blue cliffs, they made tests of the rock and, when their rough assays showed rich copper-silver values, they staked two claims. A year later the three prospectors established a mining district 20 miles long on the crest of the range, extending east to the center of Death Valley and west to the center of Panamint Valley.

It was rough country, difficult to reach and miserable for living. When word reached civilization that there was a strike, the inaccessibility of the place only added to the challenge. A wagon road of sorts was carved through the canyon, but only the toughest of men—or the most foolish—traveled the route. It was natural that it gained a reputation as a violent camp, filled with gunslingers and desperadoes. But with more discoveries, Panamint City was born, and 200 Chinese laborers were imported to improve the road and chip trails to the mines.

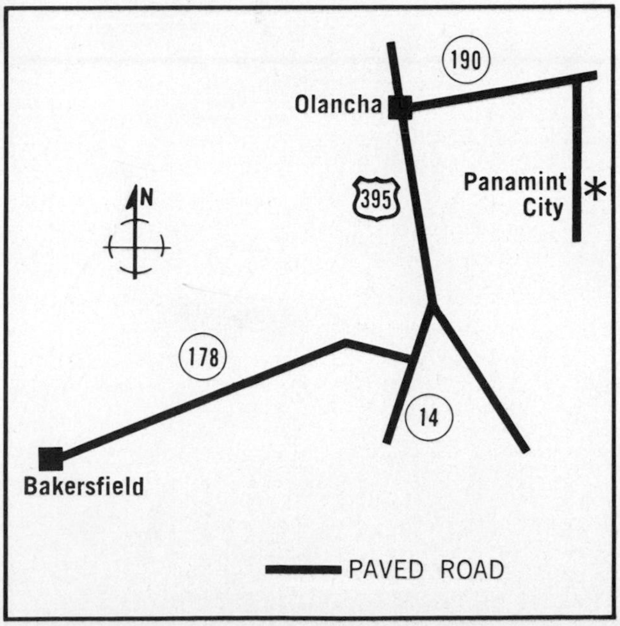

Activity continued to increase, the town prospered, and the main street grew to a mile in length, flanked by more than 200 stone houses and 20 saloons. Neagle's Oriental Saloon was one of the more elaborate, with black walnut bar, separate card rooms, and $10,000 worth of fixtures.

Panamint reached its peak population of 5,000 in 1875. All of the mines were producing heavily and 10 tons of ore were being taken out of the hills each day. Holdups were so frequent along the rugged route from Panamint that Wells Fargo refused to handle bullion shipments. But one ingenious shipper finally foiled the bandits by casting his silver in 750-pound balls, too heavy for the highwaymen to carry. This became the normal method of shipping bullion from that time on.

The first issue of the *Panamint News* was published on November 26, 1874, and the last issue on October 21, 1875. The boom was dying and with it the town. Some of the rich veins were playing out and when, on July 24, 1876, a torrential rainstorm hit the town, sending torrents of water rushing down the valley into the main street, the inhabitants fled to the mountainsides. When the storm had ended, the town had been demolished, the buildings nothing but flotsam and jetsam, ending up, along with the bodies of 15 miners, on the desert floor below. That was the end of Panamint City; it died as it had lived, violently.

Still remaining are the tall brick stack and foundations of one of the big mills, the remnants of stone-walled buildings, and, in Sour Dough Canyon, a few graves.

Death Valley National Monument is just a few miles away, via Emigrant Canyon road to State 190, then right into the monument. Several roads and hiking trails traverse this spectacularly beautiful desert country where the land rises from a point 282 feet below sea level (the lowest point in the United States) to Telescope Peak, 11,049 feet above sea level, just 15 miles away.

There are numerous campgrounds in the monument, most open only in the winter months, and accommodations are available at Furnace Creek Inn from November 1 to Easter, and at Stove Pipe Wells Hotel from October 15 to May 1.

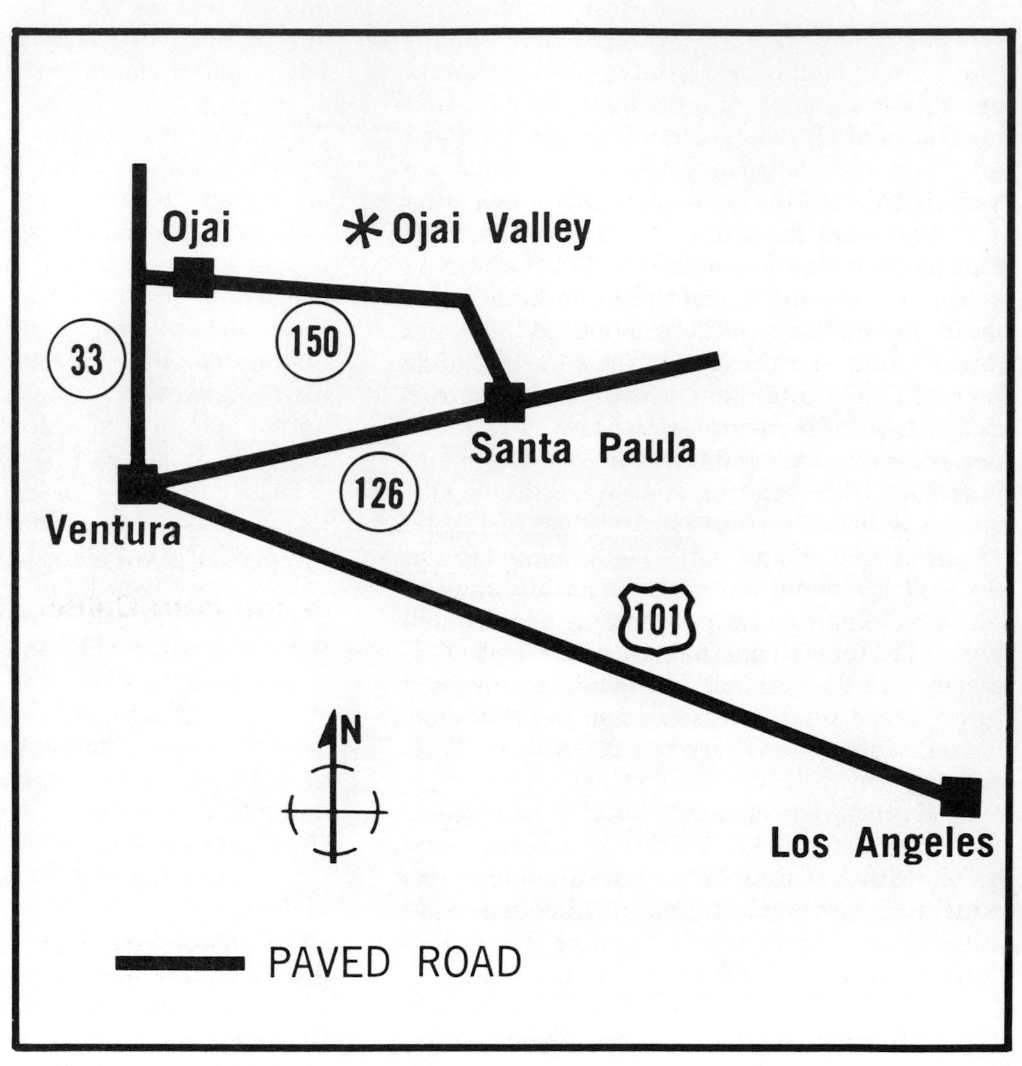
Ojai
Ojai Valley
33
150
Santa Paula
126
Ventura
101
N
Los Angeles
PAVED ROAD

OJAI VALLEY

one of the most beautiful circle trips in southern California

A circle tour of the Ojai Valley, only a few miles from Los Angeles, is one of the most beautiful trips in all of California. Take U.S. 101 or State 1 to Ventura (50 miles), turn right on State 126 to Santa Paula, then left on State 150 through Steckel Park and the Upper Ojai Valley to the town of Ojai. Continue to junction with State 33 and turn left for return to Ventura. The entire loop is less than 100 miles and is a leisurely four-hour trip, with time for several stops and side trips.

From Santa Paula north, the route passes pleasant Steckel Park, situated on a sprawling 190 acres with a picnic and camping area located in an oak grove beside Santa Paula Creek. Also nearby are a baseball diamond, an archery range, badminton courts, and an outdoor theater. A small zoo and aviary are also a part of the park.

At 11 miles (from Santa Paula) is Sulphur Mountain Road (left), a narrow winding route leading into the oak and toyon forest covering the slopes of Sulphur Mountain. The paved road ends at 5 miles and the next 11 miles are impassable for passenger vehicles when the weather is wet. Winding along the top of the ridge, the route offers dramatic views of the deep canyons nearby and, toward the horizon, of the coast and offshore Channel Islands. The road zigzags its way down the mountain to a junction with State 33 north of Ventura.

Continuing on State 150, the route passes several other interesting small canyons, with dead end side roads skirting the canyon rims for a few miles. At the high point of the road is Dennison Park, a delightful setting providing barbecue pits and picnic tables under the shade of a grove of oak trees, and a spectacular panoramic view of beautiful Ojai Valley. From the park, the road switchbacks its way rapidly downward into the valley and into the town of Ojai.

The community is enchanting. The buildings of its business district are of Spanish architectural design and add a certain quiet charm amid a pleasant setting.

On the return to Ventura, the route passes near Lake Casitas Recreation Area. At Foster Park, turn right on Casitas Pass Road, which ends at the Casitas Dam. The lake, opened for fishing for the first time in 1961, is now a favorite spot for anglers. The camping area is open all year, and there is a 14-day camping limit.

North of Ojai, on State 33, a side road leads to Matilija Hot Springs, featuring hot sulphur baths which are open all year, and a large swimming pool open during the summer. At nearby Matilija Lake, reached by a steep, narrow road (paved), is a campground in a particularly pleasant setting, hidden by a grove of giant oaks.

exploring this once inhabited desert wonderland by foot trails and auto tours

Joshua Tree National Monument, located in beautiful high desert country of southern California, is reached from Los Angeles via Interstate 10 east for 78 miles to the junction with State 62. Turn left and continue over San Gorgonio Pass through Joshua Tree to Twentynine Palms, the north entrance.

One of the most spectacular features of the monument is the rapidly diminishing Joshua tree, bearing creamy, white blossoms in clusters 8 to 14 inches long at the ends of angular, erratic branches. It attains heights of up to 40 feet and is at its best in March or April, although it does not bloom every year.

Found mostly above 3,000 feet in the higher central part of the area, the Joshua tree is sometimes confused with the Mohave yucca, another large member of the lily family which is more common at lower elevations. The leaves of the Mohave yucca are much longer and are distinguished by the abundance of light-colored fibers along their edges.

Numerous roads allow exploration by auto throughout the 870 square miles of the monument, and there are also foot trails providing the adventurer with considerably more knowledge of this vast desert wonderland. Maps and leaflets available at the visitor center at Twentynine Palms are very helpful.

The outstanding scenic point is Salton View, reached by a paved road that runs south from Hidden Valley. From an elevation of 5,185 feet, an unforgettable sweep of valley, mountain, and desert is combined in one magnificent panorama from the Salton Sea, 241 feet below sea level, to the summits of San Jacinto and San Gorgonio, over 10,000 feet high.

The road leading to Hidden Valley passes through the Wonderland of Rocks and is perhaps the most scenic portion of the monument. Great rock outcroppings burst skyward, like giant castles surrounding the valley, and hiding the entrance are scrambled rock formations, with narrow passageways between huge granite boulders.

Another dramatic panorama may be viewed from the top of Ryan Mountain, reached by a 3-mile (round trip) trail. The climb, 2 to 3 hours, is a strenuous one, but the scenic splendor of Hidden, Queen, Pleasant, and Lost Horse valleys makes it worth the effort.

The longest trail, Lost Palms, starts at Cottonwood Spring and is 4 miles long, leading to an oasis of more than 100 native palms.

A large number of campsites found along an ancient river terrace in the Pinto Basin provides evidence that this region was once inhabited by primitive man. Crudely fashioned stone weapon

Twentynine Palms
Los Angeles
10
62
Joshua Tree Nat'l Monument *
N
PAVED ROAD

Joshua Tree National Monument

points, distinctive in shape, were discovered lying along the banks of the old stream bed.

More recent Indians lived in the monument area, mainly around waterholes and springs. When the first white man came he found two groups of Indians: the Serrano and the Chemehuevi. Their campsites, with grinding holes, metates, manos, pottery, and other artifacts have been found throughout the monument.

The topography of the region consists mainly of a series of mountains separated by nearly flat valleys, the results of shifting of segments of the earth's crust along great fractures. Over the centuries, weathering and erosion have combined to wear down the mountains and fill the intervening valleys.

Scattered over a large part of the monument, particularly in the higher central part, are hundreds of outcrops of massive, light gray or pinkish quartz monzonite which solidified perhaps 150 million years ago.

Seven campgrounds with tables and fireplaces are provided within the monument, though campers must bring their own water and firewood and should be prepared for wide temperature fluctuations. Conducted trips and campfire talks are scheduled principally during the winter.

JOSHUA TREE NATIONAL MONUMENT

ANZA-BORREGO DESERT STATE PARK

state park preserving desert wilderness intact with fossil footprints made by giant mastodons

Anza-Borrego, a half-million acres of wrinkled wasteland and twisting, rocky canyons, is reached from San Diego via U.S. 80 east for approximately 33 miles to the junction with State 79. Turn left and proceed to Julian (21 miles) and the junction with State 78. Turn right

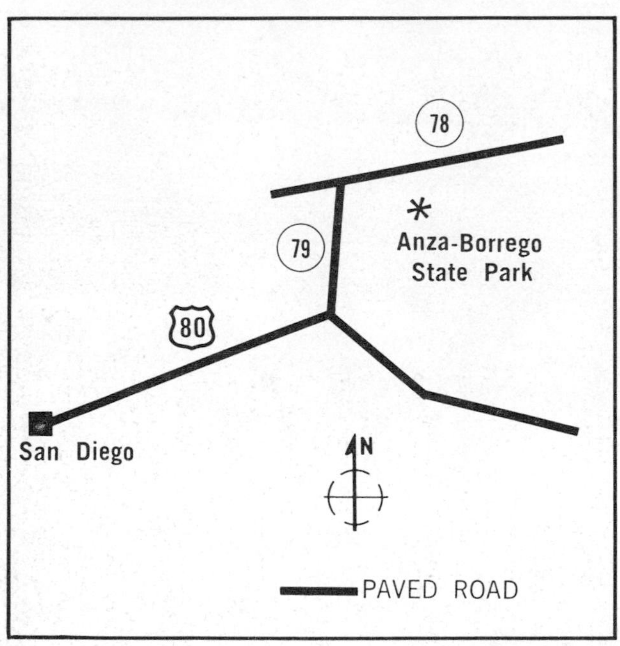

and continue to Anza-Borrego Desert State Park.

Appearing like a section of the moon's surface transplanted, Anza-Borrego is an endless stretch of folded hills, a strange and bizarre desert land relieved now and then by a row of palms along a canyon flow and an occasional oasis of desert shrubs and wild flowers.

The largest state park in California, it extends almost the entire length of San Diego County's eastern edge between Riverside County and the Mexican border. In elevation, it ranges from 100 feet below sea level near the Salton Sea to the peak of San Ysidro, 6,000 feet high.

Established as a park to preserve a portion of desert wilderness intact for future generations, most of the area is open only to the hiker or the 4-wheeler using the network of dry washes as his highway. One of the few roads suitable for passenger cars takes off 4.5 miles below Scissors Crossing and leads toward the pinnacle of Pinyon Mountain. In early spring, some of the most beautiful displays of desert wild flowers are in bloom along this stretch—Mohave yucca, ocotillo, desert agave, and nolina. From Pinyon Mountain are some excellent views of Borrego Valley and some good campsites.

Some of the most rugged portions of the park's badlands are found en route to Fish Creek Wash, reached by taking the oiled road south from State 78 at Ocotillo Wells, then to the Anza-Borrego Desert State Park sign. About 2 miles beyond is Fish Creek Wash, which can be traversed by 4-wheel vehicles. Up the wash is a narrow cleft through the mountain ridge extending for some 3 miles. Continuing on, the route leads to some extensive fossil beds with some shells 3 feet or more in thickness.

Near the eastern edge of the park another road takes off from State 78 (right) and leads to a gypsum mine in the Fish Creek Mountains, with a trail through the canyon to an area covered with fossil footprints, apparently made by giant mastodons that came to a prehistoric watering hole to drink.

November through May is the best time to explore Anza-Borrego, and camping in the desert is most enjoyable in the early spring. Excellent facilities are available at Borrego Palm Canyon and Bow Willow, and there are numerous more primitive camps scattered throughout the park.

Anza-Borrego Desert State Park

roaming in

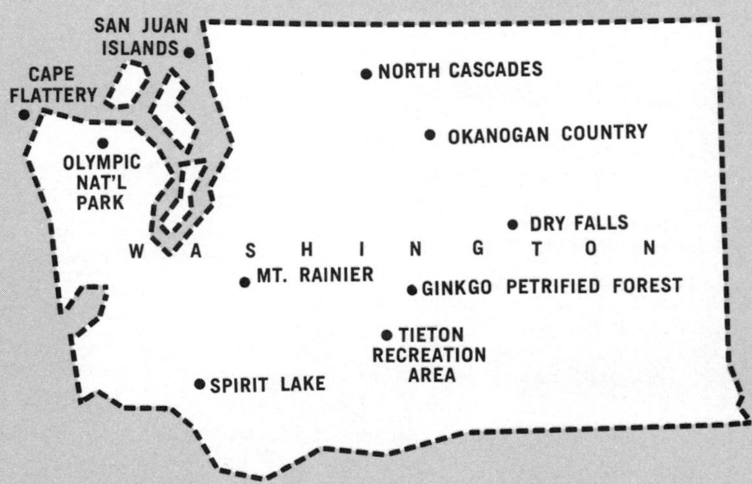

Explore the wonderful world of Washington—from the towering snow-clad peak of Mount Rainier to the jewellike San Juan Islands, from the luxurious growth of sitka spruce to the ageless logs of Ginkgo Petrified Forest, from clamming on the Pacific shores to fly-fishing for trout in the North Cascades, from picnicking on the slopes of the Blue Mountains to a hike through the enchanted rain forests of the Olympic Peninsula.

Cape Flattery, the most northwesterly point on the United States mainland (excluding Alaska), instills an excitement never to be forgotten as one stands on this tip of land and listens to the roaring surf pounding the rocks 100 feet below. In north-central Washington

WASHINGTON

is Okanogan country, with roadways passing through a forest wonderland and trails winding through a primitive wilderness, leading to lakes and streams that tempt the fisherman's appetite. And not too far removed from Okanogan is the North Cascades, the only national park whose primary access is via a water route. A spectacular boat trip runs the 55-mile length of Lake Chelan, leading to the jumping off point for the Cascades, an untamed wilderness of snow peaks, glacier-filled slopes, and forests of fir, red cedar, and western hemlock. In central Washington, in the vicinity of Grand Coulee Dam, is Dry Falls, an ancient waterfall that was three times higher than Niagara. And a few miles south the bizarre Lenore Caves, once used as shelters by prehistoric man, invite the adventurer.

For the hiker, it's Wonderland Trail in Mount Rainier National Park, with unparalleled vistas at every turn in the path. Or it's the Paradise Glacier trail for those who wish to visit the Paradise Ice Cave. The Tieton Recreation Area is a fisherman's delight, with an abundance of cutthroat trout at Cirque Lake and eastern brook trout at Pear Lake, and a scenic wonderland all along the easy, upward-winding trails. Spirit Lake, a blue emerald in the shadow of legendary Mount St. Helens, is in the midst of 173,000 acres of undefiled wilderness, a potpourri of pleasure in the great outdoors.

This is Washington, hub of the historic Northwest, land of scenic beauty on a giant scale.

SAN JUAN ISLANDS

"America's most beautiful boat trip" leads to a fascinating paradise

To reach the San Juan Islands, located north of the Puget Sound and midway between the Strait of Juan de Fuca and the Strait of Georgia, it is necessary to take a boat or a ferry from one of the various points on the mainland, the most popular being Anacortes and Bellingham. The route to Anacortes from Seattle is via Interstate 5 to junction with State 536 at Mt. Vernon. Turn left and proceed 13 miles to the port city. To reach Bellingham, continue on Interstate 5 for 26 miles.

There are several ways to explore the hundreds of islands which are a part of the San Juan chain. Launches, cruisers, or yachts can be chartered, or the visitor can select from dozens of different cruises that run on a schedule. For sightseeing on an independent basis, it is best to take the ferry trip and drive around the larger islands.

One of the most interesting boat tours is the 3-hour ferry trip between Anacortes, Washington and Sidney, British Columbia. This is a leisurely cruise, winding its way through the islands and stopping at some of the small communities on San Juan, Lopez, Shaw, and Orcas islands. Another cruise of 5 hours, called "America's most beautiful water trip," also starts at Anacortes and penetrates the very heart of the San Juans. The run provides endless variety and scenic excitement as it skirts the wooded shores, dips into the sheltered coves, and then swings away from rugged coastlines.

Orcas Island is the largest and is noted for its many attractive resorts and beautiful beaches. Moran State Park is located on the island, offering excellent campsites and good swimming in Cascade Lake, the focal point of the 5,035-acre park. There is trout fishing at Cascade and also in Mountain and Twin lakes. Mt. Constitution rises 2,409 feet above sea level and is the highest point on the island. A good paved road leads to the summit.

San Juan, west of Orcas, is the most populous of the islands, but this does not interfere with extensive stretches of green trees, fertile valleys, and rolling green hills.

On the island is American Camp, the site of a boundary dispute facetiously referred to as the Pig War between the United States and Britain in 1859. The British-American treaty of 1846 was so vague concerning the islands that both countries claimed them, and citizens of both countries settled there. The bloodless "war" began when an American farmer shot a pig belonging to the Hudson's Bay Company. British

Historic Hotel de Haro at Roche Harbor in the San Juan Islands

Blockhouse memento of the Pig War

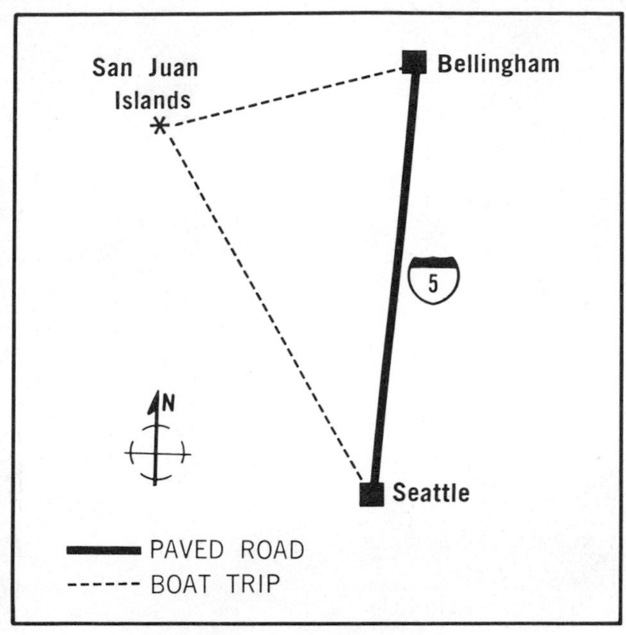

residents demanded that he be tried for his crime in Victoria, with Americans countering that the pig had been uprooting an American garden. The British sent warships to the island, and the United States dispatched Captain George Pickett with a detachment of troopers, to defend American rights. The matter was settled when Emperor William I of Germany, as arbiter, awarded the archipelago to the United States.

After touring the islands and before leaving the area, a few hours can be well spent cruising Puget Sound. Take the ferry (without car) to Bremerton Navy Yard and enjoy a conducted tour by the Navy of the battleship U.S.S. *Missouri.* Or, for a unique experience, take a Bremerton or Winslow ferry at the Seattle Ferry Terminal in the early evening and experience the splendid views of the port cities and Mount Rainier by twilight.

see gray whales at play at the most northwesterly point on the U.S. mainland

CAPE FLATTERY

Neah Bay, the stepping stone to Cape Flattery, the most northwesterly point on the mainland of the United States (excluding Alaska), is reached from Port Angeles by taking State 112 west for 72 miles. The highway twists its way along the Strait of Juan de Fuca, the blue horizon broken by the shores of Vancouver Island and the misty San Juans.

Neah Bay, the center of the Makah Indian Reservation, is far more renowned for its salmon fishing than for its Indian culture. Historically, the Makah Indians were once a fierce tribe of canoe builders and whale killers, and even today an occasional dugout canoe can be found on the beach.

From the town, there is only one road that leads west, a narrow winding passage through a pleasant wooded lane for approximately 6 miles. From the end of the road Cape Flattery is a bit less than a mile away by foot trail, a tranquil path through rain forest foliage. At the cape, the roaring surf pounds away 100 feet below, and to the north is the hazy outline of Vancouver Island, to the west the endless Pacific, and to the south the rugged, menacing cliffs, while a half-mile offshore looms the lonely, rockbound Tatoosh Island, crowned by a lighthouse station.

Tatoosh Island, a meteorological station, was a menace to ships in the early days, until the lighthouse was erected in 1857. The island, with no wharves or quiet coves, is dependent for its supplies on the weekly boat from the mainland. The supplies have to be lifted from the boat by an overhanging crane, and a 6-month reserve of food is maintained on the island, since ships cannot approach it during heavy weather.

After leaving Cape Flattery, State 112 can be taken from Neah Bay for 28 miles to a junction with a side road, right, that leads to a meeting with U.S. 101 at Sappho. Turn right on U.S. 101 and continue 10 miles to another side road (right) that leads to La Push, a spectacular ocean resort. Located on the Quillayute Indian Reservation at the mouth of the Quillayute River, the town overlooks one of the most beautiful portions of the Washington coast.

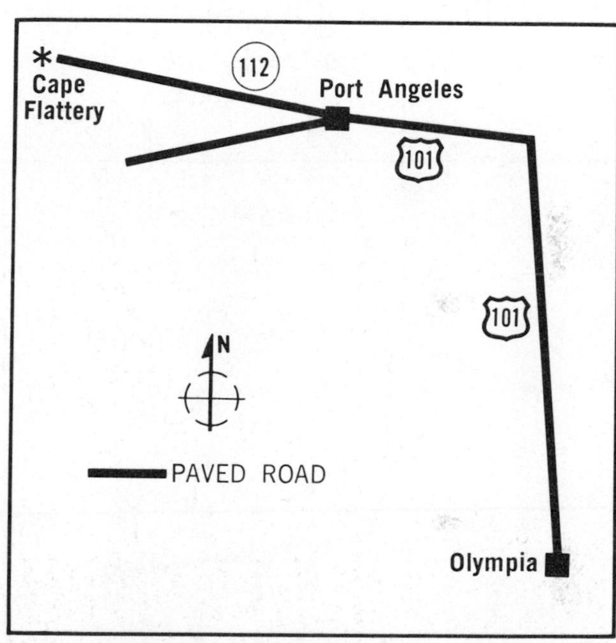

There are numerous beach and forest trails in the area, and excellent ocean fishing or steelhead fishing in the nearby streams. Between the months of March and May, schools of gray whale move in close to shore and can be seen spouting and playing in the ocean.

Offshore at the mouth of the Quillayute, James Island erupts from the ocean, its clifflike banks reaching 183 feet in altitude. The island, with several acres of brush and trees on its flat summit, can be reached over the sand beach at low tide. Numerous smaller, wooded islands lie immediately north of it, on the edge of heavily forested Quillayute River valley. A favorite with artists is The Needles, a series of jagged rocks extending for more than a mile out to sea.

Beach at La Push

OKANOGAN COUNTRY

follow the route of fur traders and prospectors in a country of badlands and saw-toothed mountain pinnacles

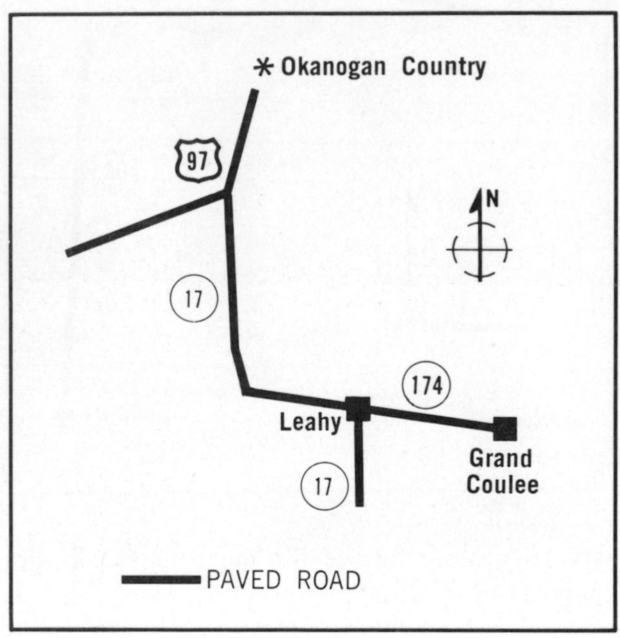

The town of Okanogan, in the heart of a recreational, scenic, and historical bonanza in north central Washington, is reached from Grand Coulee via State 174 west to Leahy (22 miles), then continuing on State 17 west to junction with U.S. 97 (25 miles). Turn right and proceed 22 miles through the picturesque Okanogan Valley to Okanogan.

En route to the town, an unpaved road at Monse, 3 miles north of the junction with U.S. 97, leads (right) to a stone tower marking the site of old Fort Okanogan. In 1811 the Astor fur interests built a crude fort at a bend in the river and raised the first American flag to wave over a permanent settlement in the Northwest. In 1815 the original buildings were replaced by a complex including living quarters, two houses for the men, and a trading post. Armed with brass 4-pounders at strategic points and surrounded by palisades, it discouraged attack. It was abandoned after the Treaty of 1846 fixing the boundary between Canada and the United States, and a flood in 1894 swept away most of the timbers of the old fort.

The town of Okanogan began as an old trading post in 1886, and remained as little more than that until irrigation was obtained from a reservoir constructed at Conconully in 1906 and the countryside became dotted with fruit orchards.

A paved road northwest from Okanogan leads to the Conconully Reservoir and Dam, passing en route (13 miles) the old ghost town of Ruby, at one time the only incorporated town of Okanogan County. Known as "the liveliest little town in a lively county," it had its start in 1886, when claims were staked on Ruby Mountain in a rush after Chief Moses' land was declared public domain. The mines kept working until the silver crash of 1893, when overnight the population dropped to a few dozen. Nearby ranchers salvaged the lumber from the buildings, and a fire in 1900 wiped out what was left. Today, Ruby's main thoroughfare consists of a few weathered foundations hidden in the brush and grass.

From Okanogan north, U.S. 97, also known as the Cascade International Highway and the Okanogan-Cariboo Trail, roughly follows the route over which the fur brigades of the Hud-

son's Bay Company carried pelts from Canada to Fort Vancouver on the Columbia River. Then, in 1858, the Cariboo Trail was used by prospectors seeking their bonanza along the Fraser River. The country to Oroville and the Canadian border offers endless variety, from rugged badlands set beside level plains to saw-toothed mountain pinnacles rearing above rolling foothills. In places the highway passes through a forest wonderland, only to emerge on a bare and rocky landscape.

But it is still rugged, primitive country, with untold clear, fast-flowing streams and lakes and reservoirs. Just a few yards or at most a few miles off the road are the Okanogan River, Spectacle, Whitestone and Wannacut lakes, Blue and Salmon lakes (improved by man-made dams), and Conconully Reservoir, with excellent camping facilities. It is a country for hikes, exploring, and legendary trout fishing.

Douglas fir trees in Olympic National Park

over 600 miles of trails through rain forests and a glacier wonderland

OLYMPIC NATIONAL PARK

Olympic National Park, which includes more wilderness area than any other national park in America, is located in northwest Washington. U.S. 101 from Olympia roughly skirts the perimeter, and at Port Angeles reaches the park headquarters and one of three visitor centers. Continuing on U.S. 101, a second visitor center is located on the south side of Lake Crescent. The third is south of Forks on the Hoh River Rain Forest road into the park.

Containing nearly 1,400 square miles, Olympic is a unique wilderness of rugged mountains, coniferous rain forests, wildlife, glaciers, lakes, streams, and seascapes. To explore this wilderness, over 600 miles of trails have been developed; to fully appreciate the grandeur of this rich mountain country, backpack hiking or horseback riding provide the most satisfactory mode of transportation.

But there is much to be seen from the major highway that frequently dips into the park and occasionally ascends to such heights that the snowy summits of the Olympic and Bailey ranges can be enjoyed. And there are numerous secondary (but paved) roads leading into the park. State 111 leads south from Port Angeles to the Hurricane Ridge (17 miles from the visitor center); the road winds through deep forest as it climbs to the Ridge (5,225 feet), affording in places a vast panoramic view of the Strait of Juan de Fuca and the San Juan Islands to the north and the distant Mount Baker and Glacier Peak to the east.

The route continues to Obstruction Point, starting point of the trail to Grand and Moose lakes. The lodge at Hurricane Ridge has a lunchroom and a souvenir shop. Open all year long, the excellent skiing and sledding at Hurricane Ridge has made this the most important winter sports center on the peninsula.

Of the many fascinations in the park, the rain forests are perhaps the most delightful. Centuries of extreme wetness in the western valleys have produced an extraordinary forest growth, the great trees seeming to drip with mossy, fern-like vegetation. It is not a dark and gloomy woodland, but rather is filled with a soft translucent green light. Sitka spruce and western hemlock dominate, but Douglas fir and western red cedar are also common, some reaching heights of 300 feet. Near the streams bigleaf maple, red alder, and cottonwood are found. Mosses carpet the forest floor and upholster tree trunks and fallen trees. The Hoh River Rain Forest is one of the most accessible, reached by a nature trail that starts at the end of the Hoh River Road.

Some 56 species of wild mammals inhabit the park. While they are difficult to see, particularly in the densely forested valleys, visitors in the high, open mountain country can expect to see various kinds of wildlife. Blacktailed deer frequently appear in the lowlands as well as in the mountain meadows, especially during mornings and evenings when they are feeding. From certain high vantage points the black bear is frequently seen. About 6,000 American elk live in the park, mostly in the western region.

Wild flowers are found everywhere. In the meadows near timberline and above, they reach their greatest abundance, blooming from June to October. The northern side of the park, around Hurricane Ridge and Mount Angeles, is especially rich in mountain wild flowers.

The trails within the park have been improved and are safe, not too steep, but narrow, few being more than 18 inches wide. For those who lack the stamina for backpacking or trail-riding, the lowland trails, starting in the river bottomlands and extending up the valleys, are recommended. The terrain is occasionally smooth and level, but more often the trail traverses a series of spurs and dips.

For the more experienced and more adventurous, the longer trails up the mountainsides are rewarding, as they pass through forests of hemlock, Douglas fir, western white pine, and Alaska cedar, treading over conifer cones and needlelike leaves of fir and hemlock. Sunlight shafts sift through the forest canopy, and the silence is broken only by the murmuring of mountain brooks or the persistent call of a grouse.

The trails switchback ever upward as the tree growth thins and the conifers become smaller until, with dramatic suddenness, the high meadows appear. From the open, grassy country vast vistas appear in great panoramas. On clear days the distant peaks shimmer in the sunshine and at other times the valleys below are misty, filled with fog, with only occasional glimpses of glaciers, snowfields, or mountain ranges.

The Olympic Mountains, uplifted from an ancient sea in some prehistoric time, rise generally to heights of 5,000-6,000 feet, although Mt. Olympus, the highest, is 7,965 feet. The rugged characteristic of the range results primarily from erosion by ice and water. Precipitation in portions of the park is estimated at 200 inches a year, much of it in the form of snow, some of which does not melt, accumulating and becoming a part of the great glaciers that have scoured the Olympic Mountains for thousands of years.

Separated from the main body of the park, but a part of it, is a 50-mile-long strip of Pacific coastline, one of the most primitive remaining in the contiguous United States. The encroaching sea has produced a scenic oceanscape here with many shoreline needles and offshore rocks and islands. Wild animals roam the forests, and offshore seals are frequently seen.

The park is open all year, with summer and early autumn the best seasons. Fishing is permitted, and the streams contain cutthroat, rainbow, brook, Dolly Varden, and, in winter, steelhead trout. No license is required in the park, but regulations should be obtained from park headquarters or at ranger stations.

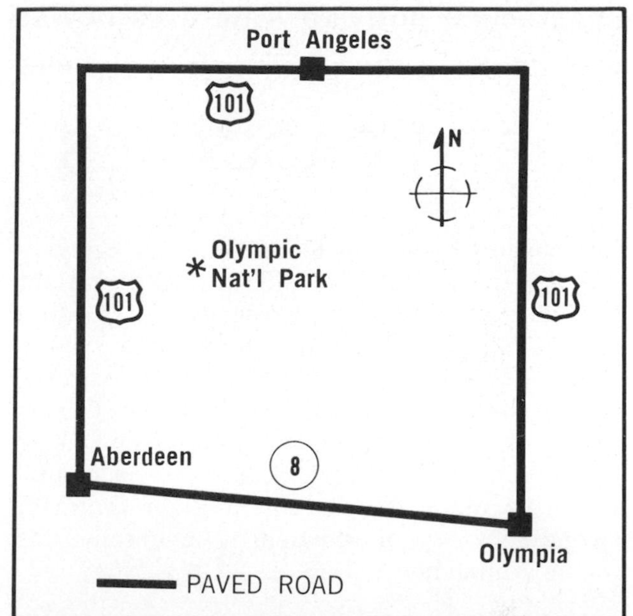

Rain forest in Olympic National Park

spectacular entry to America's newest national park and its more than 150 active glaciers

NORTH CASCADES

The North Cascades is one of America's newest national parks (established in 1968), and the only one with its primary access via a water route. For the adventurer visiting the North Cascades, a motor launch leaves Chelan and travels the entire 55-mile length of Lake Chelan to Stehekin at the northern tip. To reach Chelan from Wenatchee, take U.S. 97 north, a beautiful drive along the Columbia River featuring sweeping views of the nearby mountains and fertile Wenatchee Valley.

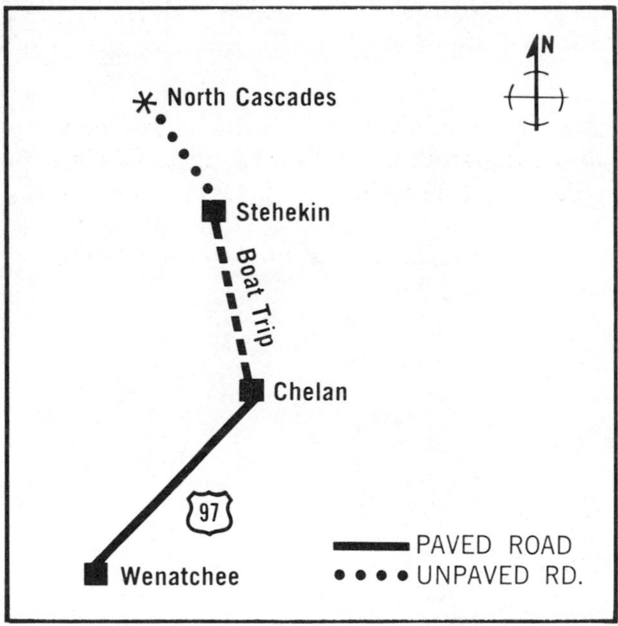

By 1973 the North Cross Highway (State 20) will bisect the North Cascades, from Marblemount on the west to Winthrop on the east. By the end of 1969 the route was completed as far east as Diablo Dam, with a trail from this point following Thunder Creek south toward Stehekin.

Stehekin, in the heart of the Lake Chelan National Recreation Area, is the most popular starting point for exploring the North Cascades. Rental cars are available, and a road runs north to the head of Stehekin Valley in the park.

That portion of the Cascade Range encompassed by the national park has an array of alpine scenery unmatched in the Pacific Northwest: deep glaciated canyons, more than 150 active glaciers, hundreds of jagged peaks, mountain lakes and streams, and innumerable species of plant and animal life.

Formed of weather-resistant rocks, the high stretch of the Cascades intercepts some of the continent's wettest prevailing winds, with the resulting precipitation producing a region of hanging glaciers and icefalls, great ice aprons and ice caps, hanging valleys, waterfalls, alpine lakes nestled in glacial cirques, and glacier-carved canyons like Stehekin at the head of Lake Chelan.

Including more than 1.5 million acres, divided into a north unit (north of the Skagit River and west of Ross Lake), and a south unit (between the Skagit River and Lake Chelan National Recreation Area), the major feature of the Park is the Picket Range, a silhouette of severe jagged peaks: Watcom, Phantom, Crooked Thumb, Mount Challenger, and Mount Terror, all but one rising more than 8,000 feet above sea level.

Geologically, the Cascade Mountains are perhaps 6 million years old. Between the Pacific and the present range, known scientifically as The Weaver Plain, the land underwent a series of undulating movements, with the ocean reaching the present-day mountain country. The climate cooled and the plains warped into a series of ridges. As the earth became restless and volcanic activity increased, pouring hot lava over 200,000 square miles of the North Cascade region, the uplifting began. About 10,000 years ago, with the coming of the Ice Age, the great glaciers gouged the slopes, leaving the precipitous mountainsides and sharply ridged summits, today the Cascades' outstanding feature.

Below the snowy peaks and the glacier-filled slopes, the mountainsides are covered with Douglas fir, western red cedar, and western hemlock. Each fall a spectacular island of flaming gold comes to Stehekin Valley, created by the turning of the leaves of the pure stands of western larch which grow below the summits

Liberty Bell Peaks at eastern entrance to North Cascades National Park

Rainbow Falls in Lake Chelan National Recreation Area

and above Lake Chelan.

Wildlife abounds throughout the park, including black bears, mountain goats, whitetail and mule deer, bobcats, lynxes, coyotes, red foxes, marmots, porcupines, gold-mantled ground and flying squirrels, raccoons, and mink.

About 345 miles of hiking and horse trails exist throughout the park, and in Ross Lake and Lake Chelan recreation areas. Horses and pack mules are available at towns surrounding the park, as are professional guides and packtrain services. One of the more exciting ways to see the North Cascades is by taking a chartered plane flight, available at Bellingham, Anacortes, Seattle, Tacoma, Omak, Chelan, and Yakima. A chartered flight for two persons is $100 to $150 for the 3-hour round trip.

Fishing is excellent in Lake Chelan and Ross Lake, and also in the many small mountain lakes and streams. The principal game fish are trout: rainbow, Eastern brook, cutthroat, and Dolly Varden.

Lake Chelan, seen both approaching and leaving the park if one takes the launch, is perhaps the most beautiful in the West, the gentle terrain of the foothills at the south giving way to rugged gorged walls of the untamed wilderness. In places the lake is less than a quarter-mile from shore to shore, and its maximum width is barely a mile.

Motels and restaurants are available at Stehekin, and campgrounds will be found at Chelan State Park and 25-Mile Creek. Only primitive backcountry campsites are available within the park, though more complete facilities are being developed.

DRY FALLS

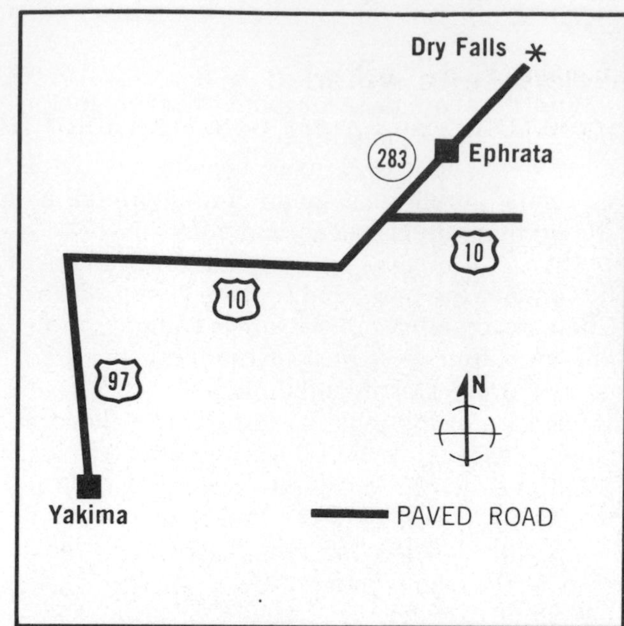

Dry Falls, the skeleton of one of the greatest waterfalls in geologic history, is reached by Ephrata via State 28 northeast for 5 miles to Soap Lake. From Soap Lake, take State 17 for 18 miles to Dry Falls, just west of Coulee City.

Included as part of Sun Lakes State Park, Dry Falls is 3.5 miles wide with a drop of over 400 feet. The world-famous Niagara Falls, a mile wide and with a drop of only 165 feet, would be dwarfed by Dry Falls. As a power source, it has been estimated that Dry Falls would have generated 100 times the energy of Niagara.

Sometime during the Ice Age, with the cooling temperatures resulting in the formation of extensive ice fields over much of the continent, pressures on the ice caused it to start moving southward. This vast continental glacier reached a thickness of about 4,000 feet in some areas. As it moved south out of Canada, it blocked the Columbia River and forced a change in its course, somewhere in the vicinity of the present Grand Coulee Dam.

The Columbia River at that time was much larger than it is today, and the dammed water, flowing like a broad, moving lake, began to spill out across the southward-dipping lava plateau. Ultimately, the more erosive soil fell prey to the waters and the coulees which characterize the region today were formed.

As the main stream raced southward, two major cascades were formed, one just north of Coulee City and the other near Soap Lake. The larger cataract was that near the Upper Coulee, where the river roared over an 800-foot precipice. The eroding power of the water caused the falls to retreat 20 miles and eventually destroy itself upon cutting through to the valley of the Columbia near what is now the Grand Coulee Dam.

The other major cataract started near Soap Lake, where the basalt layers were gradually worn away by this tremendous torrent, and the great waterfall subsequently developed. As in the Upper Coulee, the raging river tore the basalt from the face of the falls, causing it to retreat to its present location.

When the climate moderated, the ice retreated northward and thousands of years later, following a disintegration of the ice dam, the waters of the Columbia returned to their original channel around the edge of the lava plateau in Big Bend country. The Grand Coulee and network of other watercourses across the plateau were left high and dry, several hundred feet above the level of the present Columbia River.

The Dry Falls, as well as the numerous coulees and small lakes on the plateau, remain as a reminder of these tremendous changes wrought by nature in some prehistoric time.

Ten miles south of Dry Falls on State 17 are the Lenore Caves, used as shelters by prehistoric man. A trail leading to some of these caves has been developed near the north end of Lake Lenore.

Throughout this Grand Coulee country, much of it included in Sun Lakes State Park, are numerous lakes providing boating, swimming, water-skiing, and fishing. Other facilities include riding stables, various riding and hiking trails, cabins, campgrounds, and picnic tables.

Soap Lake, 20 miles south of Dry Falls on State 17, is in a picturesque setting at the end of a rugged canyon. Indians called it Smokiam (healing waters), later changed to Soap Lake by the white man, who noticed the suds that formed along its shores on a windy day. This spa supposedly contains 16 life-sustaining minerals, and visitors from all over the world have taken advantage of its therapeutic values.

skeleton of a waterfall
once 100 times more powerful than Niagara

Dry Falls

Ginkgo Petrified Forest, a unique discovery made in 1932, is located 3 miles west of Vantage. From Yakima, take U.S. 97 to Interstate 90 and turn east, continuing for 25 miles to the Forest.

Although the white man was unaware of this geologic wonder until George Beck's fairly recent discovery, the Indians frequently wandered into the area, using the chips of exposed trees for arrowheads and stone tools. Some of their work pits, with scattered fragments of quartz flakes remaining, are found throughout the area.

The ginkgo, last surviving member of a family of trees which first appeared more than 200 million years ago, is now a popular ornamental tree. This "living fossil" apparently escaped extinction only because the Chinese Buddhists cultivated it for centuries in their temple grounds.

Geologists believe that the Ginkgo Petrified Forest was formed when molten rock covered log jams in streams and lakes some 10 million years ago, which explains why many of the trees dip at a 45-degree angle, and also why they appear to have been bruised. Since none have been charred, as would normally have happened when surrounded by molten lava, the theory of the trees being under water appears justifiable.

The trees are embedded in 6 to 15 layers of soil and rock, some lying separately, others grouped together. Some are found in peat bogs amid roots and stumps, others in a clearing in whole or partial sections. In total, there are between 5,000 and 10,000 logs in the 7,000 acres included in the forest.

A museum at the site contains polished specimens, microphotographs of the grains of petrified wood, samples of shells and rock specimens, as well as an illustrated history of the ginkgo tree and fossilized forest.

The area is reached by a short canyon trail, marked on the north side of the highway.

To the west 25 miles on Interstate 90 is Ellensburg, a progressive little town that has attempted to preserve much of its early western atmosphere, including an annual rodeo held in late August or early September. The first settlement at this location was referred to as Robber's Roost. Growth was rapid with the coming of the long-awaited Northern Pacific Railway in 1886, and it became a boom town when the Milwaukee Road arrived in 1907.

geological wonder

formed 10 million years ago

GINKGO PETRIFIED FOREST

Six miles south on U.S. 97 the highway enters Yakima Canyon, a spectacular multicolored high-walled gorge. The road winds along a shelf carved from solid rock, at times barely above the Yakima River, at others 100 feet above it. Prior to construction of the highway, the only route between Yakima and Ellensburg was by the railroad.

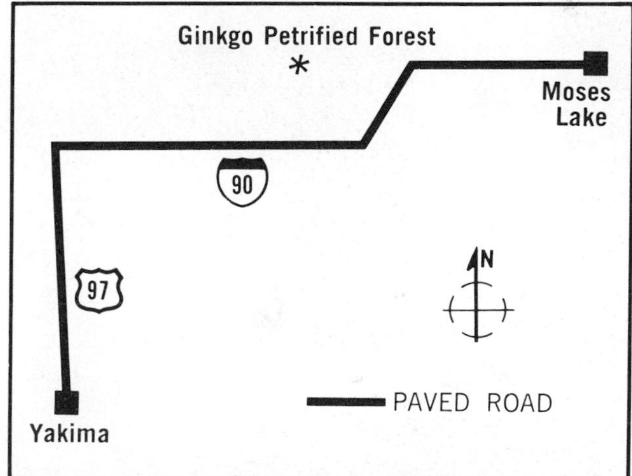

Petrified tree in Ginkgo Petrified Forest

to the top of one of the largest extinct volcanoes in the United States

MOUNT RAINIER

With Tacoma as the starting point, Mount Rainier National Park is reached by taking State 7 south for 35 miles to Elbe. Turn left on State 706 to Paradise Valley within the park (park entrance 14 miles from Elbe).

There are numerous trails available for the hiker, from the short 3-mile Pinnacle Peak Trail (round trip) to the Wonderland Trail, a loop of 90 miles around the spectacular mountain for which the park is named. One of the most exciting is the Paradise Glacier Trail (6 miles round trip) starting just west of the Paradise Ranger Station. It is well marked, and guided tours are also conducted. Along the way are numerous wild flowers, including bear grass, western pasqueflower, American bistort, and rock spiraea. Reaching Mazama Ridge, a Mount Rainier lava flow, the wooded wilderness spreads out below in a memorable panorama, and toward the horizon are the jagged mountains of the Tatoosh Range. When the weather is clear, Mount Saint Helens, 40 miles to the southwest, can be seen.

Suddenly the trail reaches a great cave, the mouth completely surrounded by ice and snow. The roof of the cave appears as a deep iridescent blue, the result of the bright sun shining through. A rushing stream on the floor of the cave reflects the blue of the ceiling. As the trail goes deeper, the colors become deeper and more pronounced. The Paradise Ice Cave is considered one of the most beautiful sights in the park.

Seven different roadways reach points of interest within the park, some leading to the starting place of the hiking trails. The Sunrise Road takes off from State 410, and descends gently for a mile through heavy timber. The road follows a twisting route up the side of an ever deepening canyon, frequently along the nearly perpendicular ledge, reaching Sunrise Point (6,400 feet), the highest point in the park attainable by car. From Sunrise, many trails lead to dramatic scenic locations and to spectacular glaciers. Emmons Glacier, one of the

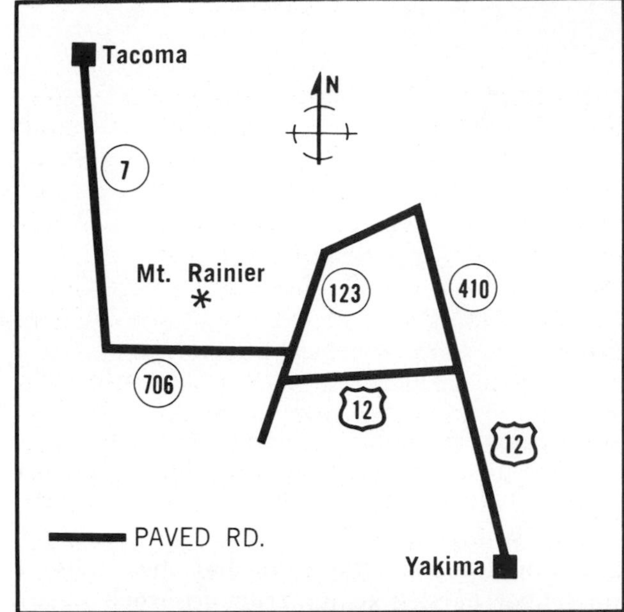

largest in the United States, covers the eastern slope of the mountain with formidable ice cascades 5.5 miles long and almost 2 miles wide. The Emmons Glacier Vista embraces a dramatic sweep from the mountain summit to the reaches of the White River far below.

Sourdough Trail, leading into the Sourdough Range, offers some colorful panoramas to the southwest.

The West Side road (turn north from Nisqually-Paradise road 1 mile after entering park) winds along the western boundary, offering a potpourri of views of Mount Rainier, with the road ending at Klapatche Point near the west base of the mountain. Most spectacular from this point is the hanging Puyallup Glacier. Above the canyon at an elevation of 12,000 feet, the glacier rises in a great cirque in the Sunset Amphitheater. Along this road are numerous trails leading to fishing lakes and campground areas.

Except for a climb to the summit, the Wonderland Trail is probably the most satisfying way of exploring Mount Rainier. Because it intersects the road at several points, it is not necessary to hike the entire 90 miles. There are overnight shelters and fireplaces, in addition to campgrounds, generally found close to the roadways.

A climb to the summit requires two days, and climbers must register with a park ranger, giving evidence that they are physically capable, have proper equipment, and have had experience in climbing similar hazardous peaks.

Mount Rainier, rising 14,410 feet, is one of the largest volcanoes in North America, and more glaciers are found on its slopes than on any other mountain on the continent. As mountains go, Rainier is fairly young, not having been in existence during the Eocene Epoch, 60 million years in the past. The mountain probably started some hundreds of thousands of years ago with a vent in the earth through which molten lava flowed, followed by continuous eruptions of fragmental lava, steam explosions, and lava outpourings that swept as far as 10 miles before cooling. Intermittent quiet periods were followed by more eruptions until Mount Rainier reached its present height.

Paradise Ice Cave

The land around Mount Rainier is a series of lesser ranges, with wide variations in the flora and fauna as one moves from the icy summits to the flower-filled mountain meadows. In the low country the slopes are covered by Douglas firs, western red cedars, and lodgepole pines. From 5,000 to 6,500 feet are subalpine firs, mountain hemlocks, and whitebark pines.

Larger campgrounds in the park are found at Paradise, Cougar Rock, White River, Sunrise, and Ohanapecosh; smaller campgrounds are located at Sunshine Point and Carbon River. No charge is made for camping, but there is a 14-day limit from July 1 through Labor Day.

Park headquarters is at Longmire (Nisqually entrance), with a visitor center, cafeteria, service station, post office, and gift shop.

Sunrise Park in Mt. Rainier National Park

TIETON RECREATION AREA

myriad fishing streams in the land where legend turned Indians into mountains

The Tieton Recreation Area, at the southern end of Snoqualmie National Forest, is reached from Yakima by taking U.S. 12 northwest through Naches, then turning left at 19 miles (from Yakima) and continuing for 20 miles to Tieton Dam and Rimrock Lake. The route follows the Tieton River through a spectacular canyon marked by massive rocks and bizarre columns.

It is possible to take an interesting trip along the south edge of the lake back to U.S. 12. West of Clear Creek Dam, at the west end of Rimrock, is the Goat Rocks Wilderness Area, highlighted by some rugged peaks, extensive glaciers, and mountain meadows carpeted with rare alpine flowers.

Several of the mountains in the region were held in awe by the Indian tribes and were part of their legends and myths. Chiefs from near and far sent their daughters to dance before Chief Me-ow-wah, one of the most eligible bachelors in the area, hoping he would succumb to their charms. Instead, to preserve the chastity of the tribe, he decided to sacrifice himself and the maidens. When they came before him, Me-ow-wah and the young Indian girls were turned to stone. Kloochman Mountain, on the south, is the Spokane maiden; Wildcat Mountain on the north is the Okanogan, Bethel Ridge to the west is the Cowlitz, and Goose Egg Mountain is Chief Me-ow-wah.

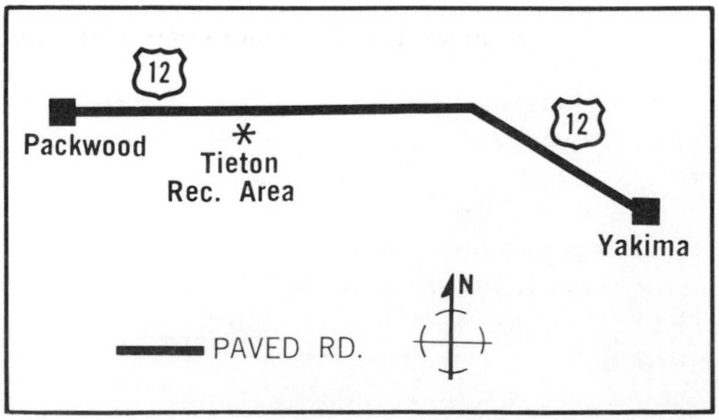

Various roads, unpaved but passable in passenger cars, take off from Rimrock Lake's south edge, leading into the Recreation Area and joining with foot and horse trails to hundreds of fishing streams, lakes, and mountain peaks.

A medium-to-difficult trail takes off from the end of Bear Creek Mountain Road and leads to Bear Creek Mountain (elevation 7,335 feet). This is a 2-hour trip covering 7 miles round trip. The first 2.5 miles is an easy grade through mountain meadows and across frequent clear mountain streams. The last mile climbs abruptly, usually through snowfields. From Bear Creek Mountain is an excellent view of the Goat Rocks Wilderness, Mt. Rainier, and surrounding peaks and valleys.

Excellent fishing for cutthroat trout is found at Cirque Lake, reached by a trail from the end of a road taking off from the south side of Rimrock Lake. The round trip is about 8 miles and requires 2.5 hours. The first 1.25 miles climbs steeply; then the trail levels off for 1.5 miles before climbing to the ridge overlooking the lake. The trail descends to the edge of the cirque and campsites are available. While hiking, it is not unusual to see Columbia blacktail deer, Yellowstone elk, and black bear.

From the end of Indian Creek Road (north of Rimrock Lake), a 5.5-mile hike can be taken to Pear Lake. Except for the first creek crossing which may be difficult during the early part of the season, it is an easy trail. Fishing is good at Pear Lake for Eastern brook trout and camping is available. Pear Lake makes an excellent base for side trips to other nearby lakes: Apple, Blankenship, and Twin Sisters.

Rimrock Lake in Tieton Recreation Area

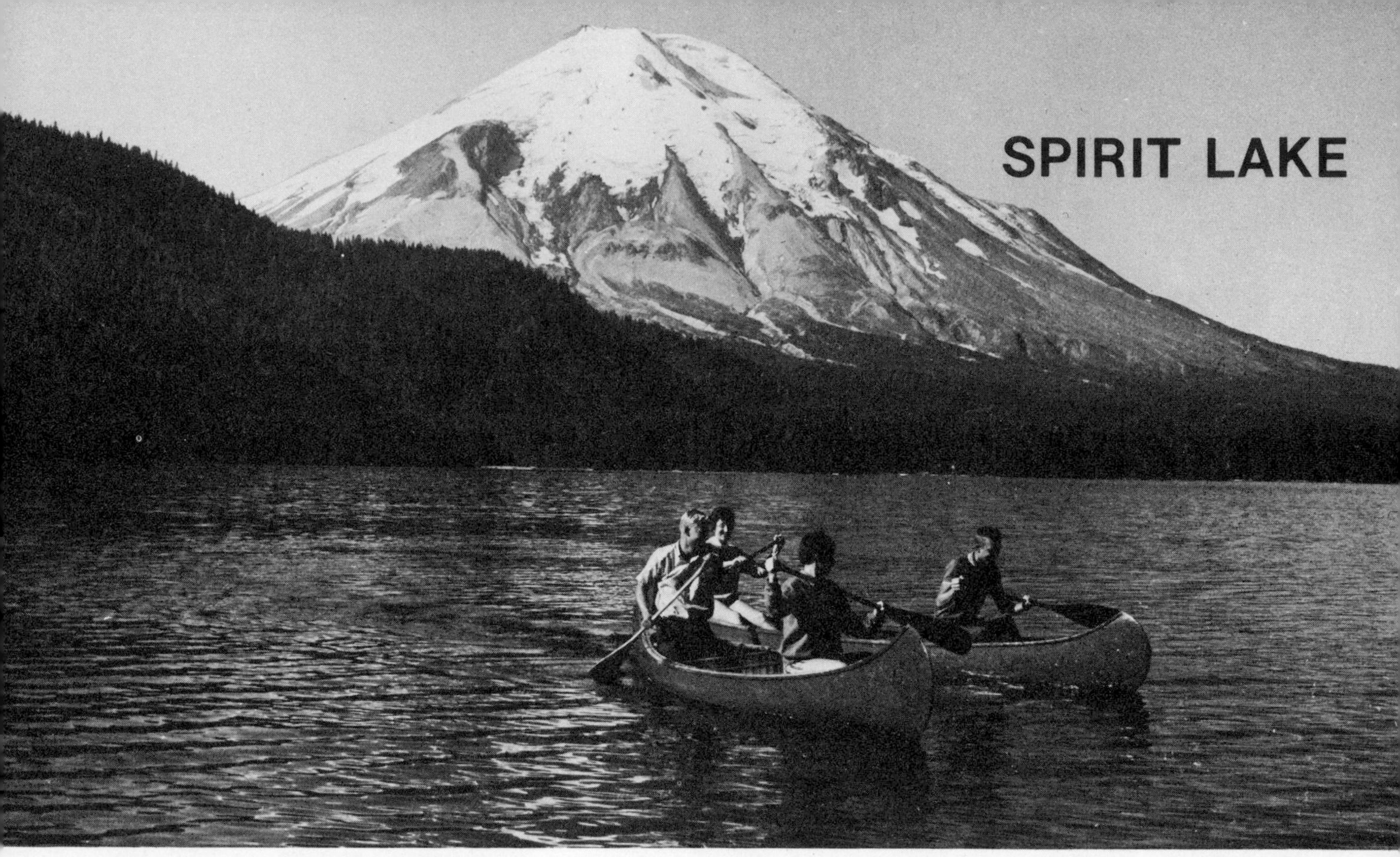

SPIRIT LAKE

Spirit Lake and Mt. St. Helens

sportsman's playground hallowed in Indian legend

From Olympia to Spirit Lake, one of the most picturesque bodies of water in the Northwest, is 98 miles. Interstate 5 leads south through Centralia to Castle Rock (52 miles). Turn left on State 504 and proceed 46 miles to Spirit Lake, located in Gifford Pinchot National Forest.

The lake is a part of an area generally referred to as the Mount Saint Helens-Spirit Lake region, including some 173,000 acres of undefiled wilderness, exciting recreational opportunities, and fascinating glimpses of natural wonders. Mount Saint Helens is the youngest volcanic peak in the United States; Spirit Lake, the largest in Gifford Pinchot National Forest, is one of the most spectacular in the state, and the Saint Helens Lava Caves, the most recently discovered and in many ways the most interesting in the United States.

Mount Saint Helens (9,677 feet) was discovered in 1792 by Captain George Vancouver, who named it in honor of His Majesty's British Ambassador to the Court of Madrid. Because of the mountain's symmetrical shape, it is sometimes called "the Fujiyama of the West."

Early accounts of Mount Saint Helens and Spirit Lake are found in Indian legends. One of the myths relates that an Indian brave, seeking food for his starving tribe, trailed a giant bull elk to the lake, only to be led to his death by a phantom spirit. Each year, according to the story, both of them appear over the lake on a certain night. Another legend tells of two Indian braves who were lost on the lake when a strong gust of wind upset their canoe. When their bodies were not recovered it was believed that spirits rose from the depths and claimed them. It was this belief that gave the lake its name.

During the later 1800s, the gold rush period of the frontier, widespread interest developed in mineral deposits north of the mountain and several mines were established, but none became operational.

Considered one of Washington's most interesting geological features, the Lava Caves are located in a lava flow that covers approximately 7,000 acres, from Mount Saint Helens to the Lewis River (8 miles).

Fiery lava cascaded down the raw slopes of

newly formed Mount Saint Helens. Then, consuming the forest in its path, it flowed slowly toward the Lewis River valley. The surface of the lava hardened, but beneath the cooled crust the still molten material flowed on, leaving hollow tubes in its wake. As new flows occurred they also ran through the open tubes, adding layers to the walls.

Five large lava tubes or caves have been discovered with a combined length of over 5 miles. Ape Cave, extending 2 miles, is the longest; in fact, it is the longest lava tube in the United States.

Easily accessible by stairs, the cave is open for exploration. Any spelunkers planning to explore the caves should be equipped with warm clothing, heavy shoes, headlights, lanterns, and protective headgear.

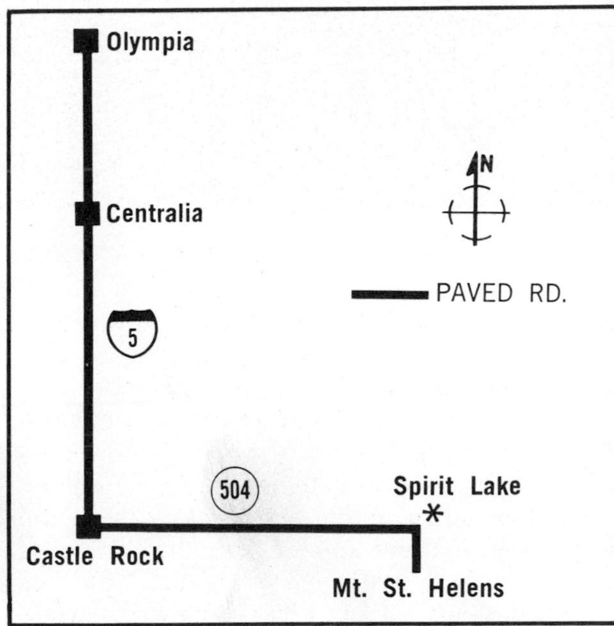

The lake developed as the result of volcanic action, with successive eruptions blocking the headwaters of the Toutle River. The lake was increased in size in the early 1920s when Coe's Dam was built at the outlet, raising the water level by 2 feet. The lake now covers 1,262 acres and has a maximum depth of 184 feet.

Along the forested shores of Spirit Lake are three camp and picnic grounds. Spirit Lake, the largest, consists of 170 family units. Two smaller campgrounds, accessible only by boat or trail (Donnybrook and Cedar Creek), are located on the east shore of the lake.

Spirit Lake provides for water sports of all kinds, with a public boat launching site at Duck Bay, a mile east of the information center. There is excellent fishing for rainbow, not only in Spirit Lake, but in Saint Helens Lake and other high lakes in the backcountry.

One of the largest elk herds in the state inhabits the forest surrounding Mount Saint Helens. During the spring, Roosevelt elk and deer are seen frequently along the highway. Black bear are also common among the berry patches and may be encountered along the trails. They are usually harmless unless provoked.

The Lava Caves, on the south side of Mount Saint Helens, are reached by returning to Interstate 5, going south to Woodland, and turning left on State 503. Proceed to Cougar (30 miles) and continue east for 6 miles to Forest Road N83. Follow N83 about 2 miles to Forest Road N816 and continue for 1 mile to the caves.

One of the Mt. St. Helens Lava Caves

Oregon is a land of spectacular coastlines, high plateaus and forests, alpine lakes and magnificent gorges, sand dunes and ghost towns, sea lions and white water running, scenic splendor and spectacular skiing. Oregon is a land of cascades and caves, waterfalls and wilderness, forests and fantasy. This is the stamping ground of Lewis and Clark. It is the site of the first seat of government in the United States west of the Mississippi, and of the hunting ground of Chief Joseph and the Nez Percé Indians. And Oregon is famous for its great dams and huge irrigation projects, forest timber country, cattle ranches, broad wheat fields, fossils, and fishing.

Along the Upper Coast, just off the beach, the wreck of the *Peter Iredale* still remains, and a few miles south is one of the largest sea lion rookeries off the continental mainland. A highlight of the Middle Coast is Sea Lion Caves, a bizarre hideout created by

roaming in OREGON

nature for these intriguing animals. More spectacular is the 50-mile stretch of sand dunes, reaching as much as two miles inland, including a part of the Siuslaw National Forest. Hidden in another wilderness forest are the Oregon Caves, a maze of caverns decorated with intricately sculptured clusters of marble and pendants of crystal chandeliers, all a product of nature's mysterious handicraft. In the heart of Rogue River country is beautiful Lake of the Woods, well stocked with wily trout.

To the north is Crater Lake, once thought by the Indians to be the battleground of the gods. Serene and quiet, geologists assert that it was probably formed in one of nature's most explosive, violent moods. And beyond is the Willamette National Forest, including more than 1,600,000 acres of untrammeled wilderness, a haven for the skiier, the fisherman, the hunter, or the adventurer. The streams abound with brook, rainbow, German, and cutthroat trout; and the forest is the refuge for the Columbia black-tailed deer and Roosevelt elk.

Between the states of Oregon and Washington is the spectacular Columbia Gorge, one of the longest stretches of magnificent panoramas in the Northwest. And in eastern Oregon, where the land is harsh and the scenery dramatic and expansive, are many ghost towns, remnants of the Northwest's counterpart to California's and Colorado's gold rushes.

From the wonders of nature to the imposing artifacts of man, Oregon is a state of enchantment.

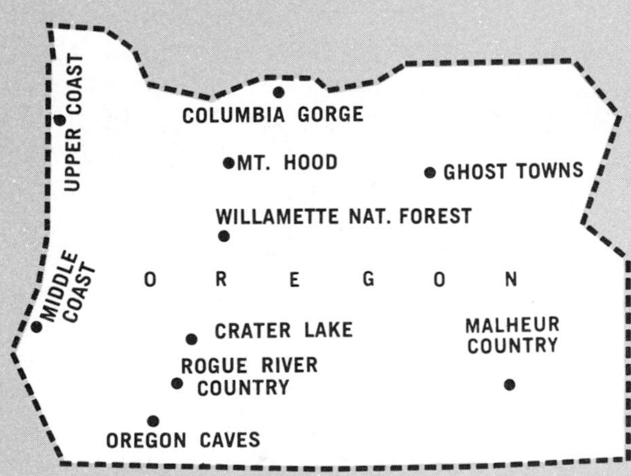

a famous shipwreck, historic forts, scenic tours, and bottom fishing on this ocean shore route

THE UPPER COAST

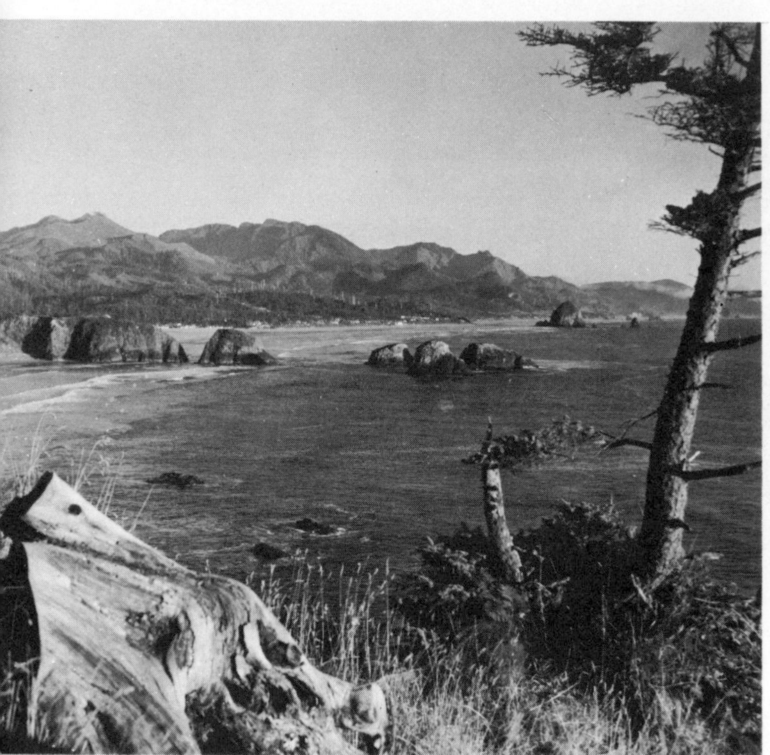

Seascape from Ecola State Park

The Oregon coast stretches 395 miles from the state of Washington on the north to California on the south. It is, without question, the most spectacular, most rugged, and most dramatic coastline found in the United States. Starting from Astoria, the adventure tour of the Upper Coast is primarily along U.S. 101 from Astoria to Tillamook.

Fort Clatsop, a national memorial to the Lewis and Clark Expedition, is south of Astoria on U.S. 101. At 5.7 miles the route crosses the Lewis and Clark River, and at 6.5 miles is the junction with the road leading to Fort Clatsop (left). It was on December 8, 1805 that the expedition, after spending nearly a month on the north side of the Columbia River, searched for and found "an eligible place for our winter residence," some 7 miles southwest of present-day Astoria. The rugged explorers built a large fort, 50 by 50 feet, consisting of 7 rooms, and cleared an area for a parade ground. And when it was done, they named it Fort Clatsop for a neighboring Indian tribe.

Captain William Clark described his first Christmas at the fort: "At daylight this morning we were awoke by the discharge of the fire-arms of all our party—a Salute, Shouts and a Song which the whole party joined in under our windows, after which they retired to their rooms . . . After breakfast we divided our Tobacco which amounted to 12 carrots one half of which we gave to the men of the party . . . The Indians leave us in the evening all the party Snugly fixed in their huts. I received a present of Capt. L. of a fleece hosrie, Shirt Draws and Socks, a pr. Mockersons of white weazils tails of the Indian woman, & some black root of the Indians before their departure . . . The day proved showerey wet and disagreeable . . . our Dinner concisted of por Elk, so much Spoiled that we eate it thro' mear necessity."

The expedition remained until March 23, 1806, leaving the fort for the Clatsop Indians. When settlers arrived in the 1840s, Fort Clatsop was little more than a pile of rotting logs. Eventually it was reconstructed by the National Park Service in 1955 and dedicated as a national monument in 1963. The site is open daily and includes a visitor center and museum.

Returning to U.S. 101, continue south for another 1.4 miles and turn right on road leading to Fort Stevens, built in 1863 and surrounded by a moat with an entrance tunnel. Designed to protect the Columbia River from Confederate gunboats, there were emplacements for 29 guns. Fort Stevens, enlarged both during World Wars I and II, has never fired a hostile shot and is the only military installation in the United States fired upon by a foreign power since the War of 1812. On June 21, 1942, a Japanese submarine made an unsuccessful attack on the installation, with only one of 12 shells landing close to the

Saddle Mountain State Park

mark—approximately 200 yards from Battery Russell. The fort is no longer active, but the emplacements and buildings remain.

Adjacent to the installation is Fort Stevens State Park, one of Oregon's largest and most attractive. There is excellent swimming and boating at Lake Coffenbury as well as swimming and an attractive beach on the ocean. Just offshore is the wreck of the *Peter Iredale*, one of the few shipwrecks that can still be seen, and one of the most photographed attractions along the entire Oregon coast. A British bark of 2,075 tons, it was stranded on Clatsop Beach October 25, 1906. The park includes more than 300 camp and trailer sites and picnic facilities.

Four miles south of the resort community of Seaside on U.S. 101, turn left on U.S. 26 to Necanicum, then left on graded road for 8 miles to Saddle Mountain, a state park of more than 3,000 acres located in a game refuge where deer and elk abound. A trail leads from the camping and picnic area to a U.S. Forest Service lookout at the top of 3,284-foot Saddle Mountain.

Approximately 6 miles south of Seaside (on U.S. 101), Ecola State Park stretches southward from Tillamook Head, providing a breathtaking elevated view for miles of the entire Cannon Beach area. Less than a mile offshore is a rookery of sea lions which can be observed at most seasons. Within the park itself deer and elk roam at will. Along the 6 miles of coastline included in the park, numerous rocky fingers push out into the sea. Many interesting trails are waiting for the adventurer in the park's 1,100 acres.

A legendary buried treasure may be hidden on nearby Neahkahnie Mountain. According to Indian folklore, the crew of a wrecked Spanish galleon buried a fortune in gold and jewels on the slopes of the mountain. True or false, Oregonians have been searching fruitlessly since pioneer days.

Tillamook, world-famous for its cheese, is also the hub of one of the more scenic areas of Oregon. An excellent 18-mile scenic tour, called the Cape Meares Loop Road, starts at the west edge of town and continues around Tillamook Bay. At Cape Meares State Park there are tours to the lighthouse, some pleasant trails along rain forest paths, and a chance for driftwood collectors to have a field day along Short Beach.

At Cape Lookout State Park, 11 miles south of Tillamook, there are year-round camping facilities on this densely wooded fingerlike peninsula.

All along the coastal area fishermen will find an abundance of steelhead and cutthroat in the nearby streams, regardless of season. Bottom-fishing is also a year-round sport, both in bays and in the ocean.

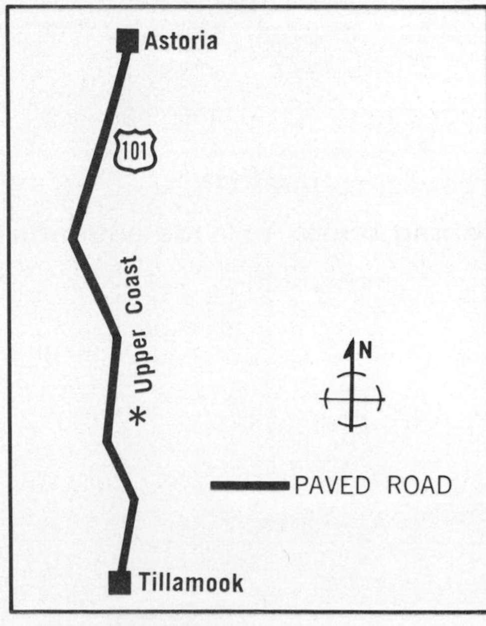

THE MIDDLE COAST

From Newport on the north to Coos Bay on the south, U.S. 101 hugs the ocean; seldom is the Pacific shoreline out of sight.

The Sea Lion Caves, 38 miles south of Newport, are at sea level, with the highway at this point adjacent to the coast but some 300 feet above it. One of the great sea grottoes of the world, it has a floor area of about 2 acres and a vaulted rock dome about 125 feet high. In all, there are 3 main passages, with the main cave continually under water and the lowest passageway being washed by the ocean during high tide. A third passage enters some 50 feet above the floor of the sea cave and provides an elevated observation window through which the entire underground system may be observed. The sea level portion of the caves and the sea cliff rocks just outside have become the only known mainland rookery of the Steller's sea lion, and to a lesser extent the smaller California sea lion.

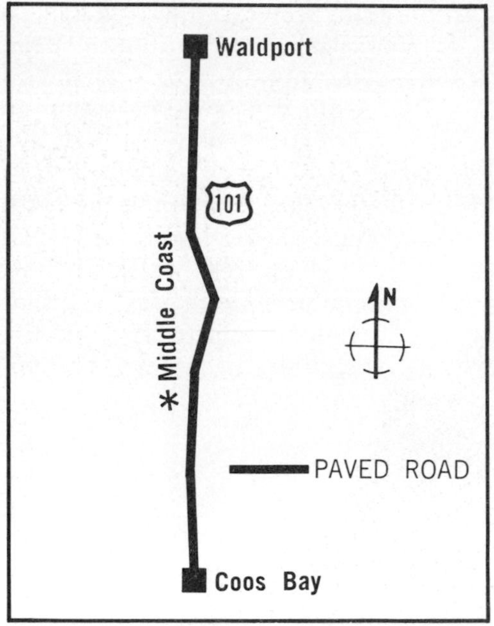

sea lion caves, rugged cliffs, and marching dunes provide adventure

At Sea Lion Caves geologists believe a combination of earth fault and a stratum of more vulnerable rock may have opened the way to the inroads of the sea. When the restless work of the water was done, the vast Sea Lion Caves remained, with their remarkably colored walls, odd formations, and their unique acceptance by the huge sea lions as a safe and suitable rookery.

The caves are almost as well known as a bird rookery as they are for the sea lions. Gulls, cormorants, and an unusual bird called the pigeon guillemot are all seen in numbers during their nesting seasons. The last named actually nests within the caves, with as many as 300 building their nests on the ledges inside the grotto.

Three miles south of Florence on U.S. 101 is Honeyman State Park, a favorite camping facility with excellent swimming and beaches at Cleawox Lake. A mile hike across the sand dunes leads to the beach and swimming facilities on the Pacific Ocean.

The entire park area is an ancient sand dune formation, low and undulating. The ever shifting sands are almost free of growing vegetation. The dunes still are being built up by the ocean winds and are constantly moving inward, first covering the herbs, grasses, and shrubs and finally enveloping the tops of tall trees.

Siuslaw National Forest is one of the most unusual in the Forest Service system, being noted primarily for some of the outstanding sand dunes in the nation, called the Oregon Dunes, extending from Sea Lion Point on the north to Coos Bay on the south, a distance of some 50 miles along the coast, and extending an average of 1.5 to 2 miles inland.

Sea lion rookery at Sea Lion Caves

An interesting side route along the Umpqua River starts at Reedsport (State 38) and winds inland to Elkton and a junction with Interstate 5. From June 1 to Labor Day a jet-propelled excursion boat cruises up and down the Umpqua from Scottsburg, 2 miles east.

All along the Dunes are excellent camping facilities. Eleven sites have been established and many more are now being developed. Frequently located near timbered groves of firs, spruce, or hemlock, the campsites are takeoff points for long and short hikes through sand dune country.

In the vicinity of Coos Bay are several state parks and other points of interest. Charleston, at the mouth of the Bay, is at the head of the route leading to Shore Acres, providing one of the magnificent ocean views on the Oregon coast. There is excellent ocean fishing along the rocks of Cape Arago and from boats chartered at Charleston, as well as from the shores of Coos Bay itself.

Sunset Bay State Park, closest to Charleston, offers excellent swimming facilities, and provides both camping and picnicking in picturesque surroundings.

OREGON CAVES

hiking trails
surrounding caverns of marble

With Grants Pass in southwestern Oregon as the starting point to the adventure tour of Oregon Caves, take U.S. 199 west through Wilderville (13 miles) and Selma (25 miles) to a junction with State 46 at Cave Junction (34 miles). Turn left and proceed for 20 miles to Oregon Caves National Monument.

From Crescent City, California, Oregon Caves may be reached by taking U.S. 199 northeast to Cave Junction (46 miles) over Summit Pass.

Surrounded by the Siskiyou National Forest, the 480-acre monument is 4,000 feet above sea level, on the slope of Mount Elijah. This unusual wonder of nature was formed millions of years ago when lime was deposited at the bottom of the ocean existing at that time. Eventually the lime was turned to stone and, perhaps eons later, as the earth began a great upheaval, creating both tremendous heat and pressure, the limestone was converted to marble.

Later in geologic time, water filled with carbonic acid seeped through the cracks and dissolved the marble, leaving the cavities which were to become the Oregon Caves. Within the caves are numerous caverns in which clusters of intricately sculptured marble hang from the frescoed ceilings, and stalagmites and stalactites join together to form columns not unlike giant organ pipes. The route leads over chasms, down corridors that wind snakelike through narrow openings and into broad, high-ceilinged chambers. The names of the various formations are sometimes descriptive, sometimes mysterious. Niagara Falls is a one-time waterfall now frozen eternally into marble. Paradise Lost, deep within the mountain, is a high-vaulted chamber with pendants of crystal chandeliers hanging from the roof, while Dante's Inferno is a yawning chasm which resembles the contents of a boiling cauldron.

The setting for the monument is idyllic, a wild preserve within a forest of Douglas fir, western hemlock, sugar pine, and Port Orford cedar, while ferns and rhododendrons form a carpet on the forest floor. Numerous hiking trails twist through the mountain country, most of them starting near the caves entrance. Wildlife that roams the vicinity includes mule deer, bobcats, black bears, raccoons, and gray foxes. Birdwatchers might observe western tanagers, California and mountain quail, Steller's jays, chestnut-backed chickadees, and varied thrushes.

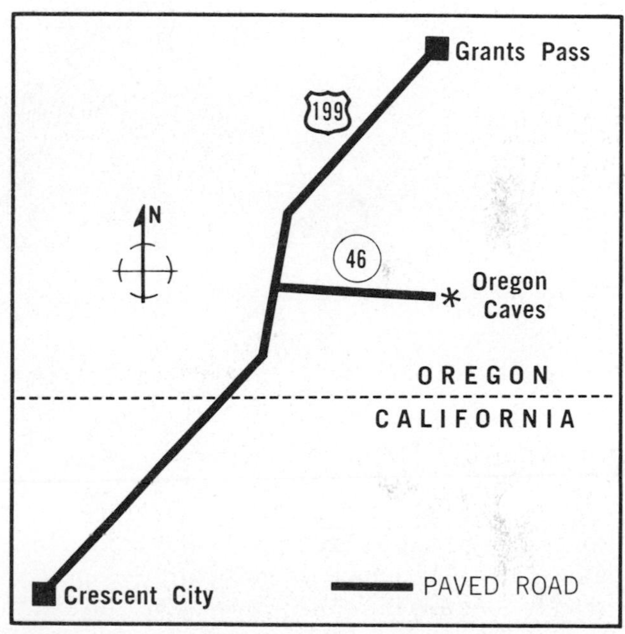

President Taft proclaimed the area a national monument in 1909, and for years the Oregon Caves were publicized by a group of public-spirited ambassadors called the Grants Pass Cavemen. Within the monument accommodations are available at the Oregon Caves Chateau or in cabins on a nearby hillside. No camping facilities exist within the monument, but Grayback Campground is just eight miles north of the entrance in Siskiyou National Forest.

On the return route, there is a junction at 17.2 miles from the monument entrance with a dirt road. Turn left and continue 2.5 miles to the abandoned ghost town of Althouse. Also near Althouse is the site of Browntown, scene of a placer strike that yielded, as part of its gold production, a single nugget valued at $1,200.

The Ghost Chamber, largest "room" in Oregon Caves National Monument

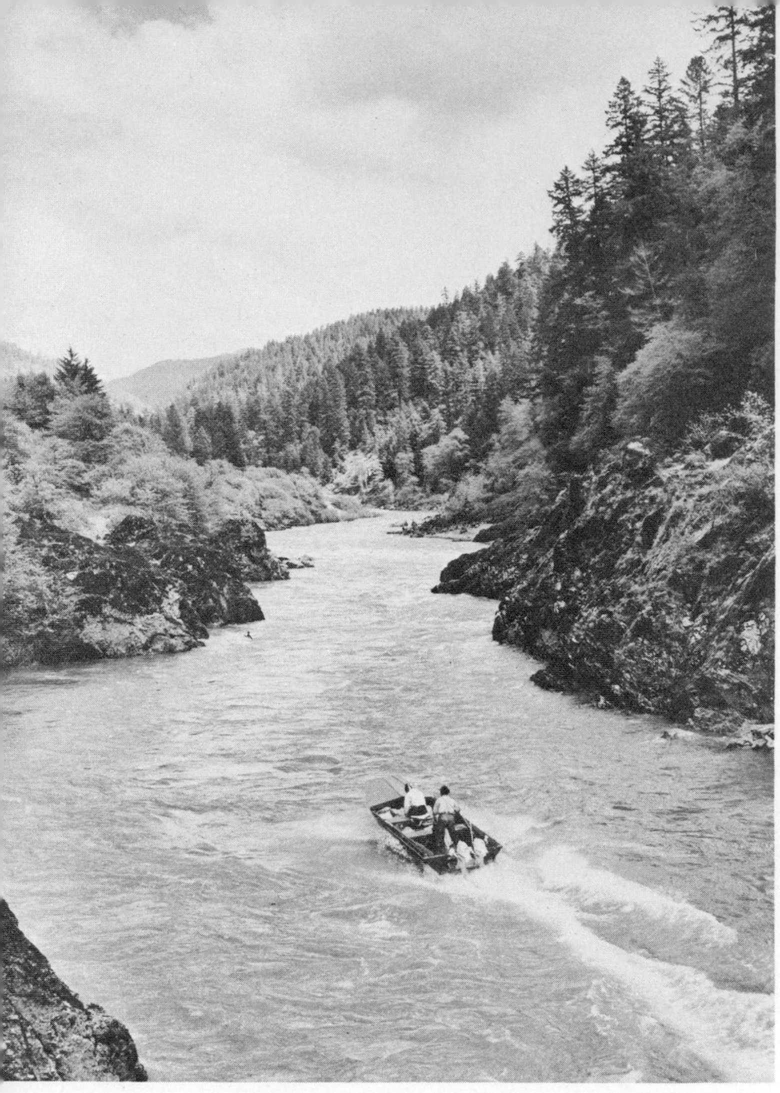

steelhead fishing and whitewater trips in a land of gold rush towns

ROGUE RIVER COUNTRY

Rogue River country extends roughly from a few miles west of Grants Pass eastward for approximately 30 miles in southwest Oregon. The small town of Rogue River, 7 miles east of Grants Pass, is located on the south bank of Rogue River. First christened Woodville and located at one of the early ferry sites, the town lies partially hidden among the heavy growths of pine in the fertile Rogue River valley.

The river and its tributaries, the Applegate and Illinois, are world-famous for the steelhead fishing found in their cool waters. Best times for catches occur in September, early October, and between mid-January and March in the Grants Pass area of the river.

Part of the Rogue River country includes the Lake Selmac Recreation Area, reached from Grants Pass by taking U.S. 199 west to Selma (20 miles) and turning left on paved road to Lake Selmac (4 miles). The State Game Commission has planted the lake with black bass and bluegill, making it the only lake in the area on which the public may fish for spiny-ray fish. Boat-launching facilities are excellent and rental boats are also available. Lake Selmac provides swimming, and there are easy trails in the region for hiking. Picnic and camping facilities are good.

Another favorite fishing spot is located on the Rogue, 8 miles west of Grants Pass. Called Whitehorse Park (because of the whitehorse riffle on the water), there are complete trailer and camping facilities.

River trips can be made from Grants Pass to spectacular Hellsgate Canyon in special jet-propelled boats (allow 2.5 hours). A more exciting trip is a whitewater adventure from Grants Pass to the ocean, ending at Gold Beach. Kayaks may be used, or a specially built Rogue River boat for two passengers and the boatman may be rented. Transportation from the ocean back can be arranged through the boat operator.

East of Medford, in the Rogue River National Forest, numerous small lakes provide various recreational activities. One of the most beautiful is Lake of the Woods, located on State 140 east from Medford 42 miles.

Two of Oregon's better-known gold rush towns are in Rogue River country. Gold Hill, 6 miles east of the town of Rogue River on State 234, was the scene of early placer mining. Before the day of bridges, prospectors sometimes forded the river or, when too high, would swim across, hanging on to their horses' tails. The town's greatest growth occurred following the discovery of quartz deposits, and started to die as the reserves began to dwindle. Today it is a modern town, with none of the old mining camp buildings existing.

Jacksonville, also dating from the 1851 gold discoveries in the region, is one of the best preserved towns from that era. Between the time the first two prospectors washed gold from Rich

Lake of the Woods in Rogue River National Forest

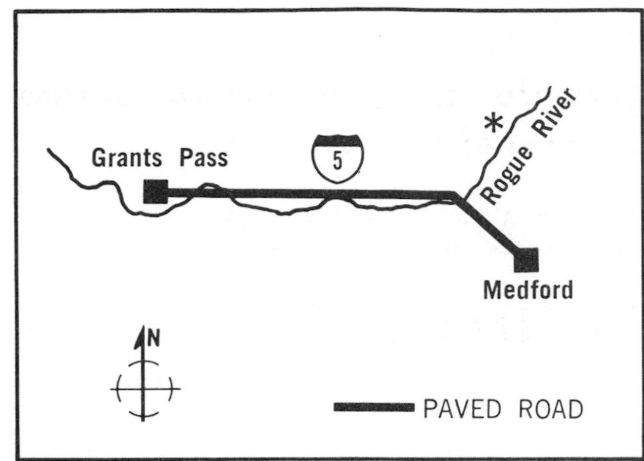

Gulch in December and the next summer, over 1,000 men invaded the territory.

The early days of Jacksonville's history were marked by numerous Indian assaults. When, in 1855, the Rogue River Indian War started, the men began to leave Jacksonville to fight in the volunteer companies then being formed, leaving the women and children to fend for themselves. The indignant women held a private meeting, excluding all the men, who resented the affront; and that night they hung a petticoat from the flagpole in front of the express office. The women demanded it be lowered, and the men refused until one of the hardy pioneer females threatened to chop down the flagpole. The feud continued, with the men determined to maintain their superiority. Following the petticoat episode, a strange vigilante party assembled beneath the town's favorite hanging tree. And the next morning, to the women's dismay, they saw two effigies—one male and one female—hung from the branches with the male being hung higher than the female to indicate his higher status, at least in the eyes of his countrymen, if not in the eyes of God.

Today's residents have dedicated themselves to preserving the old buildings as well as the memories. The county courthouse is now a museum, and the Wells Fargo office, on one of the side streets, could pass for a modest brick home if it were not for the sign over the door. The J. A. Brunner building, the oldest brick structure in town, was erected in 1855, and across the street is the two-story I.O.O.F. hall, built in 1856 and still used as a meeting place.

Part of Jacksonville's charm is the Jacksonville stage, a colorful replica of the Concord stage, used to take visitors on a 15-minute tour of the historic points of interest.

Each year, in August, Jacksonville is the setting for the world-famous Peter Britt Music Festival, with afternoon and evening concerts. Peter Britt started as a gold prospector in Jacksonville in 1852 but became a photographer of some repute, recording for posterity much of the color of early-day Jackson County.

where hikers can walk down the wall of a volcanic crater

CRATER LAKE

With Klamath Falls as a starting point to the adventure tour of Crater Lake, take U.S. 97 north 23 miles. Bear left on State 62 for 34 miles to Crater Lake National Park entrance.

The peaceful and serenely beautiful lake for which the park was named was created in one of nature's more violent moods. Several thousand years ago mighty Mount Mazama, a great and violent volcano, stood where Crater Lake now lies. After a tremendous discharge of ash and lava, thousands of feet of the mountaintop collapsed, producing one of the largest craters known to man. Wizard Island, at the west end of the lake, is a giant cinder cone that rises over 2,700 feet from the crater floor and towers some 760 feet above the surface of the lake.

The Klamath Indians knew of Crater Lake before its discovery by the white man but seldom visited it, regarding the lake and the mountain as the battleground of the gods. John Wesley Hillman, a young prospector leading a party in search of a "lost cabin mine," discovered the lake on June 12, 1853. Nine years later Chauncey Nye happened upon it and named it Blue Lake. A third discovery was made August 1, 1865, by two soldiers who called it Lake Majesty. Finally, in 1869, the name was changed to Crater Lake by visitors from Jacksonville.

Before 1885 the lake was virtually unknown. On August 15 of that year, William Gladstone Steel stood for the first time on its rim and conceived the idea of preserving it as a national park. For 17 years he dedicated himself to this project. Typical of his devotion to and interest in Crater Lake was his singular effort to plant fish in it. In 1888 Steel carried 600 Rogue River fingerlings from that stream over the rugged mountains to the lake. To enable the delicate fish to withstand the journey, he stopped at every stream to freshen the water, and part of the way he carried a bucket of fish in his own hands, releasing the fingerling trout at the lake's edge. Only 37 of them survived long enough to swim away. Apparently the survivors flourished, and today, with the help of subsequent plantings, the fish population is in the hundreds of thousands.

The water of Crater Lake is the accumulation of rain and snow. The average annual precipitation is 66 inches. Except for seepage, the lake

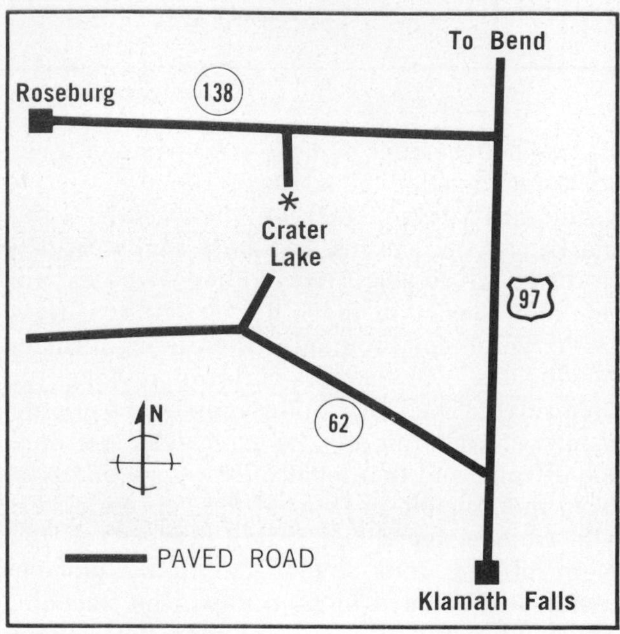

has no inlet and no outlet; yet evaporation, seepage, and precipitation are so balanced that the water level is virtually constant. The intense blue of the lake is the result of its extreme depth of some 2,000 feet, making it the seventh deepest lake in the world.

The best way to see the outstanding features of the park is via Rim Drive. Turn right from State 62 and proceed 4 miles to the park headquarters and information center. Continue 3 miles, then turn right 0.7 miles to Rim Village, which includes Crater Lake Lodge, sleeping cabins, cafeteria, store, campground, and picnic ground. A short foot trail leads to Sinnott Memorial atop Victor Rock. This vantage point offers an excellent view of Wizard Island. A trail leads from the shore of the island to its crater, which is approximately 90 feet deep and 350 feet in diameter.

Right from Rim Village the spectacular Crater Wall Trail slopes steeply down to the edge of

the lake (1.6 miles, 2-hour round trip). During the summer season (June 15-September 15 approximately) a 2.5-hour launch trip around the lake is made daily, leaving the boat landing at 9 A.M. Private boats are not permitted on the lake, but rowboats may be rented at the boat landing.

Also from Rim Village a 1.7-mile trail, east of the lodge, leads to Garfield Peak (elevation 8,060 feet). From its summit, there is a magnificent view of the lake and surrounding region.

To continue Rim Drive, return to park headquarters at 3.7 miles; then turn left. The narrow road winds its way through a tall forest of hemlock trees, skirting the edge of Sun Canyon, offering a magnificent view. At approximately 7 miles (from Rim Village) a small stream tumbles down the face of Vidae Cliff. From Kerr Notch (12 miles) is an excellent view of the Phantom Ship, an island rising 160 feet above the waters of the lake and resembling a giant ship under sail.

A side road to the left leads to Cloudcap Viewpoint, affording the most spectacular view on the entire Rim Drive. To the right from the junction with the Rim Drive, a foot trail leads to Mount Scott (2.5 miles). This is the highest point in the park, 8,938 feet.

Watchman Peak (35 miles from Rim Village) on the west rim may be reached by a half-mile trail from Rim Drive. A rare panorama of the park and surrounding country may be viewed from the fire lookout, 1,850 feet above the lake.

There is more than sightseeing at Crater Lake. Angling for trout and kokanee salmon in the midst of the grandeur of this setting is an experience to remember.

With the park open year-round, it has become an exciting ski resort, with two trails from Rim Village to park headquarters maintained for skiers. There are no overnight accommodations in the park from September 15 to June 15, but warming house facilities are provided at Rim Village. Also, during the winter only the west and south entrance roads to the park are open.

There are four free campgrounds within the park, open from about July 1 to September 30, limited to 30-day stays.

WILLAMETTE NATIONAL FOREST

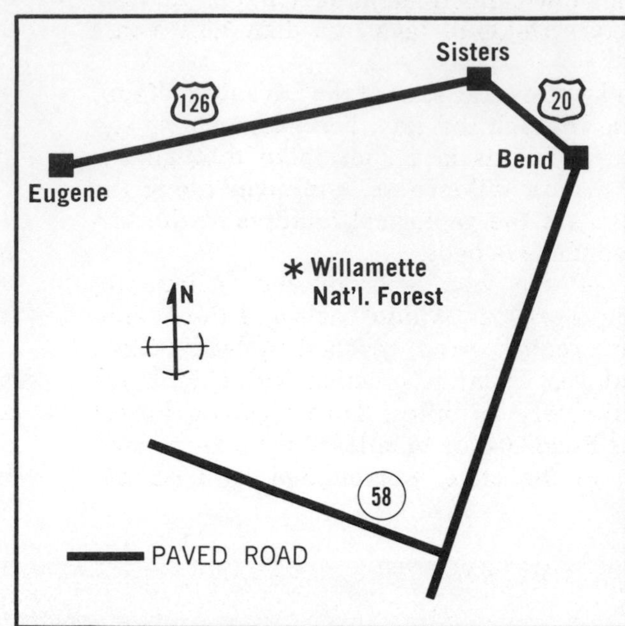

the Oregon Skyline Trail and four wilderness areas for explorers, hikers, and mountain climbers

Willamette National Forest stretches for 110 miles along the western slope of the Cascade Mountain Range in central Oregon. Access highways are State 22 starting 52 miles east of Salem, U.S. 20 from Bend, and State 58 southeast from Eugene.

Four Wilderness Areas—the Three Sisters, the Mount Washington, the Diamond Peak, and the Mount Jefferson—occupy more than 15 percent of the 1,600,000 acres of the forest. These wilderness preserves, defined by Congress as areas "where the earth and its community of life are untrammeled by man, where man himself is a visitor who does not remain," offer the explorer, the hiker, and the mountain climber challenging opportunities. The Oregon Skyline Trail, part of the National Scenic Trails System, traverses the four wildernesses.

For the fisherman, the streams and lakes abound with Eastern brook, rainbow, German brown, mature cutthroat, golden, and Dolly Varden trout, and kokanee salmon. For the hunter, the forest is the home of Columbia blacktail deer, Roosevelt elk, bear, and mule deer.

Two ski areas are located in the forest. Hoodoo Ski Bowl at the summit of Sanitam Pass has three chairlifts, a day lodge, several rope tows, a snow-play area, and a variety of trails. Willamette Pass Ski Area (State 58 east of Oakridge) has a pomalift and several rope tows.

More than 197 miles of state highways wind through the forest, with hundreds more miles of county and Forest Service roads providing the traveler with a continuous opportunity to enjoy some of the Northwest's most beautiful mountain country.

Going east from McKenzie Bridge on State 242, the route passes Proxy Falls on the edge of Three Sisters Wilderness. These two beautiful waterfalls tumble 200 feet over moss-covered lava cliffs.

A half-mile trail leads through an open lava field into a mixed conifer forest, with the forest floor decorated with rhododendron and bear grass in early summer and fall. The trail crosses White Branch Creek over a log bridge. A fork to the left leads to the crystal-clear water pool at the base of Upper Proxy Falls. The fork to the right leads to a viewpoint opposite Lower Proxy Falls.

The highway twists and turns along Deadhorse Grade, past Alder Springs Campground to Scott Lake, a photographic point of interest, with the peaks of the Three Sisters reflected in the blue, mirrorlike water. Near the summit of McKenzie Pass, the route reaches the Dee Wright Observatory, with striking vistas of

North and Middle Sister from Scott Lake

ancient snow-capped mountains across the jumbled, stark fields of lava less than 3,000 years old.

At this point is the start of the Lava River Trail, winding through the lava beds adjacent to the observatory. This is a short hike through the Three Sisters Wilderness, and signs along the trail explain the geological features of the terrain and the lava beds.

One of the highlights of the Willamette National Forest is Waldo Lake and the Waldo Lake Recreation Area, reached by taking State 58 northwest from the junction with U.S. 97 for approximately 25 miles. Turn right on Forest Service Road 204 for 10 miles to the lake, second largest in the state. Surrounded by a 32,000-acre recreation area, Waldo Lake lies near the crest of the Cascades. The eastern shore is completely accessible, with three major campgrounds. The western shore is kept in a primitive state, accessible only by trail or by boat. The Oregon Skyline section of the National Trail System passes just east of Waldo.

Several trails head from this area, one of the more picturesque leading to Bobby Lake (2 miles), a fairly level hike to good fishing for rainbow and Eastern brook trout.

In total there are 72 campgrounds in the forest, most of them with trailer facilities, and all located on picturesque sites. Most areas are open all year, but the weather is best from June through September.

access to Pacific Crest Trail and the Scenic Highway that winds among 11 waterfalls

COLUMBIA GORGE

The Columbia Gorge, from The Dalles on the east to Portland on the west (83 miles), is one of the longest continuous stretches of magnificent views and spectacular panoramas found in the Northwest. Although Interstate 80N is a high-speed route, there are many stopping points along the way, and the high-level Scenic Route between Bonneville and Troutdale offers some of the most awe-inspiring vistas of the gorge.

The Dalles was named by the French trappers of the Hudson's Bay Company who noted the resemblance between the basaltic walls of the Columbia Narrows and the flagstones (*les dalles*) of their hometowns in France. Lewis and Clark stopped at The Dalles on their way west, and later, with the establishment of fur trading stations on the lower Columbia, the town became a rendezvous for traders and Indians.

In 1838 a Methodist mission was constructed, marking the beginning of the white settlement, and three years later a Catholic mission was started. The Methodist mission so declined in popular favor that it was sold to Dr. Marcus Whitman, Presbyterian missionary, in 1847. Later that year, when the entire Whitman family was wiped out in the Whitman Massacre, the mission was abandoned.

Points of interest include Fort Rock, which can be reached by a marked foot trail from the town. This promontory, used by Lewis and Clark as a camp, affords an excellent view of the Columbia River. Pioneer Cemetery, on the Scenic Drive out of The Dalles, is the burial place of many of the first citizens of the town. The earliest graves date back to 1859.

The highway west of The Dalles starts its sweep through the Cascade Range. Towering Mount Hood can be seen to the southwest and Mount Adams across the Columbia to the north. At Hood River, the bridge across the Columbia to the popular Mount Adams Recreation Area makes possible an interesting side trip. Also at Hood River is the starting point for the Mount Hood Loop trip (see Mount Hood, next under Oregon).

The Pacific Crest Trail takes off to the south along the east fork of Herman Creek, approximately 3 miles east of Cascade Locks. This trail continues to Casey Creek (4 miles). South of this point it continues to the base of Mount Hood, then to Wahtum Lake, Buck Peak, and Lost Lake (22.5 miles).

Bonneville Dam, stretching for 1,400 feet between Bradford Island (an old Indian burial ground) and the Washington shore, is open to the public daily during daylight hours. A visitors' building, including numerous displays and visual representations concerning the operation of the dam, is located near the parking area.

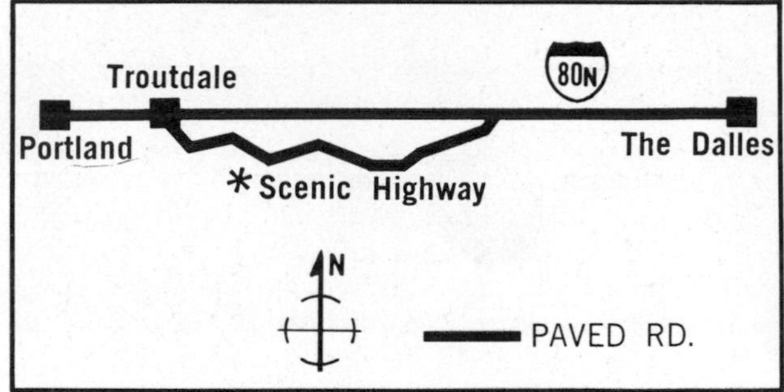

Fish ladders, actually a series of pools stepped up at 1-foot intervals, have been constructed at each end of the spillway to enable migratory fish to return to their spawning grounds upriver. Walkways are provided so that visitors can watch the fish in the pools and counting stations.

Approximately 8 miles east of Bonneville is the start of the old Columbia River Highway, now called the Scenic Highway. Also near this point is Multnomah Falls, plunging 620 feet into an evergreen glen. The second highest in the United States, it is but one of 11 waterfalls on the Scenic Highway. Several trails lead through woodland country to points on the rim of the gorge. Wahkeena Falls are considered by many to be the most beautiful in the region. There is no sheer drop, as the waters hurl downward in a series of fantastic cascades.

The Scenic Highway reaches its peak at Crown Point, 725 feet above the river on an overhanging rocky promontory. The highway begins its descent, joining the Interstate at Troutdale.

Multnomah Falls

family climbing trails to ice fields, smoking rocks, the inn anchored by cables

MOUNT HOOD

To reach Mount Hood from Portland, take U.S. 26 east for 55 miles, turn left and continue for 6 miles to Timberline Lodge at the base of the mountain. From Hood River, take State 35 south for 41 miles, turn right and continue for 6 miles to Timberline Lodge.

The Mount Hood loop trip starts at Portland, goes east on Interstate 80N to Hood River, through the Hood River valley on State 35, and returns to Portland on U.S. 26 (170 miles total).

State 35 winds its way through the narrow Hood River Gorge, crosses the Hood River valley, and threads its way through the deep canyons along the eastern base of Mount Hood, then climbs the Cascade Divide before joining with U.S. 26.

An interesting side trip starts 6.7 miles south of Hood River. Turn right on paved road to Odell, continuing through Dee, site of a large sawmill. The West Fork of the Hood River is bridged at its confluence with Lake Branch, a crystal-clear mountain stream. Trout fishing is excellent in both streams. From this valley, the road climbs upward to Lost Lake (24.2 miles) at 3,140 feet altitude. At times during the day the shimmering reflection of Mount Hood can be seen in Lost Lake. This is perhaps the most beautiful view of Mount Hood from any point in

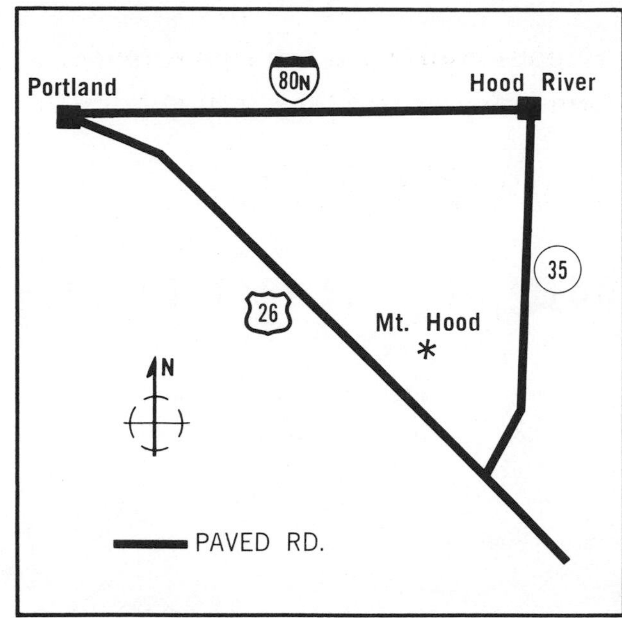

Oregon.

According to legend, the shores of Lost Lake were the favorite summer and fall campgrounds of the Indians. One night while the tribe was gathered for a potlatch, after the squaws had brought in their well-filled baskets from the berry patch and the men had carried in their venison, the feast was being prepared. Suddenly a snow-white doe, pursued by wolves, broke from a thicket, plunged into the lake, swam to the middle, and disappeared. A medicine man decreed that this was an omen of bad luck and the Indians left hurriedly, never to return.

Many years later, in 1912, a young Indian couple, educated in the East and inclined to ridicule the superstitions of their elders, came to Lost Lake to camp. During a storm a bolt of lightning struck the tree under which they were standing and killed the bride. Today many Indians refuse to visit the lake.

The road passes Sahale Falls, a delightful cascade of the East Fork of the Hood River, then rises to the summit of Bennett Pass, drops down to White River, and climbs once again to cross Barlow Pass (4,158 feet), used by the first wagon train into the Willamette Valley.

Near the junction with U.S. 26 a side road, right, leads to Timberline Lodge, switchbacking its way up the south shoulder of Mount Hood. Climbs to the summit of the mountain start from this area.

The East Trail is a relatively easy climb and offers more beautiful views than the West Trail as it winds through forests and alpine meadows to Iron Creek (8 miles) and, at 18 miles, reaches Cloud Cap Inn, a historic old hotel first opened in 1889 and anchored to the mountain by cables to resist the winter winds. The trail continues through the thick forests to Elk Cove (22 miles) and Eden Park (25 miles), where it meets the West Trail.

The South Side climb to the summit requires 8 to 10 hours. Starting from Timberline Lodge (6,000 feet altitude), the trail heads in a northerly direction to Palmer Glacier (1.5 miles) at 7,500 feet altitude. Although it is an active ice field, it is not difficult to cross, as it is fairly flat and devoid of crevasses. From Triangular Moraine to Make-up Rock is a steep climb, rising 1,500 feet in a half-mile. The route continues to Crater Rock (10,000 feet altitude), 3.1 miles from the Lodge.

The route veers sharply westward to Hot Rocks, so called because of the sulphurous fumes that come from hundreds of vents in the rocks. Devils Kitchen is at the center, where temperatures a few inches below the surface reach 200 degrees. At this point Steel Cliff extends to the summit. A trail leads up the cliff, but should only be attempted by expert mountaineers.

The trail continues across another ice field to the southern end of The Chute, where the trail has a slope of 34 to 45 percent. The route winds eastward along a narrow ridge to Summit Cabin (11,245 feet altitude), an abandoned fire lookout. This unimposing structure provides shelter from storms and bunks for campers. In the cabin is the register book for those who have scaled the peak.

The view from the summit is unparalleled, with Mount Jefferson rising almost to the same height as Mount Hood in the foreground, and beyond are seen the Three Sisters. Along the Cascade slopes is the vast panorama of the forests, a green carpet stretched between the towering peaks. To the west is the Willamette Valley with the Coast Range as a backdrop, and to the north the white-capped peaks of Mount Adams, Mount Saint Helens, and Mount Rainier.

Returning to U.S. 26, the route proceeds west down Laurel Hill, crosses Zigzag River, and proceeds through Rhododendron, Sandy, and Gresham into suburban Portland.

hideout caves, vast dry craters, lava-covered beaches, Basque life, and more

MALHEUR COUNTRY

Malheur country in southeastern Oregon is a strange and barren land, with lava-covered terrain broken now and then by giant solitary buttes, vast dry craters, weird mystic caves, and lakes with black lava beaches. The adventure route starts from Burns, proceeding due south on State 205 for 32 miles to the Malheur Wildlife Refuge. Including 180,000 acres, it is the largest refuge in the United States, and more than 248

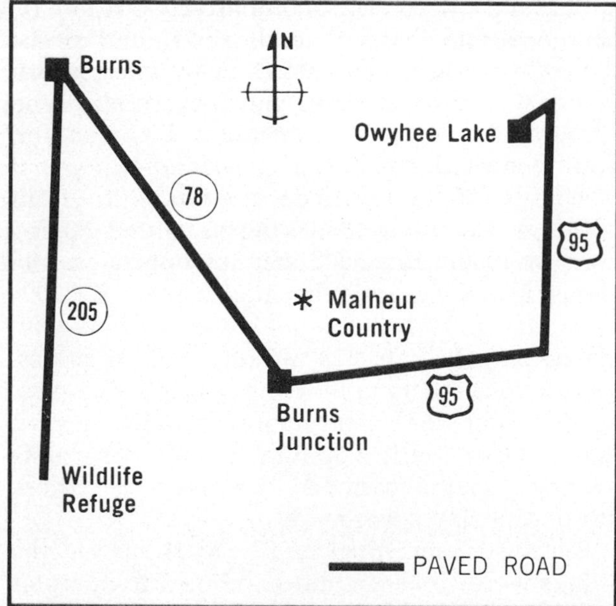

species of birds either make the area their home or a migratory stopover. From mid-March through May, and during October and November, the migrations are at a peak, and trumpeter swans and sandhill cranes mingle with thousands of ducks and geese at the refuge.

From this point, it is necessary to return to Burns and swing southeast on State 78 for 52 miles to reach Malheur Cave. Turn left for 2.8 miles to Indian Creek and the cave. This tunnel-like passage is nearly a mile long, 50 feet in width, and from 10 to 25 feet high. From the entrance the floor slopes for approximately 200 feet before turning a few degrees and ending in a freshwater pool of incredibly clear water. The Paiute Indians at one time used the cave for defense against their enemies. When the cave was first discovered, numerous arrowheads, spearheads, and other Indian artifacts were found nearby.

Continuing on State 78, take U.S. 95 left at Burns Junction toward Jordan Valley. From Rome, a graveled road (left) leads to the Walls of Rome, stark, buttelike formations that are actually vertical walls of a dry tributary canyon of the Owyhee River.

Jordan Valley, settled in the 1870s and 1880s by Basques from Spain, had its beginnings in 1863 when Michael Jordan led a party to a gold discovery on Jordan Creek. At one time Jordan Valley was one of the greatest sheep grazing regions in the West, with 150,000 sheep roaming the nearby hills and valleys. Though the sheep have largely disappeared, many of the Basque traditions persist. Festivities are still held to celebrate Three Kings' Day, observed on January 6 in honor of the kings who visited the Christ Child.

The route proceeds north at Jordan Valley. At 6 miles, an unpaved road (left) follows Cow Creek, reaching Cow Lakes at 13.7 miles and continuing 4.3 miles to Jordan Craters, the result of violent volcanic action as recent as 500 years ago. The field covers 60 square miles, with the most spectacular volcanic cones at Jordan Craters. A road leads partly up the slope of the largest of these, leaving a short hike to the lip of the crater.

South from Jordan Valley to Three Forks (37 miles) on an unpaved road is one of the least known and most spectacular canyons in the state. With chasms as deep as 2,000 feet, the formations are both dramatic and colorful, a magnificent wonder of nature for the back-road explorer.

A rock hunter's paradise exists some 18 miles north of Jordan Valley, along the narrow floor of multicolored Succor Creek Canyon. This area has produced some excellent finds—red and green agates, petrified wood, jasper, thunder eggs, white crystals, and fire opal.

Owyhee Lake is eastern Oregon's most popular recreation area, featuring a setting of unbelievable beauty and primitive isolation. But since it was created as part of the Owyhee Dam in 1932, it has become a favorite spot for motorboating and racing, fishing, camping, hiking, and exploring. Extending for 52 miles in length, the lake snakes its way into numerous bays and inlets, at times meeting a rugged, clifflike canyon wall and at other times washing up on a smooth, black lava beach.

The lake can be reached by continuing north on U.S. 95 into Idaho, then joining State 201 and proceeding 3 miles beyond Adrian, turning left for 4 miles, then left again for 23 miles to Owyhee Dam and Lake Owyhee State Park. Two campgrounds are located here, with public boat ramps both at the park and at the dam. A private marina and resort is located at the end of the paved road, offering boat rentals, lodging, a general store, and restaurant.

Owyhee Lake

circle tour of yesterday's gold-country boom towns

Starting point for a tour of Oregon's ghost towns in the northeast portion of the state is Baker, 96 miles south of Pendleton on U.S. 30. Some of the ghosts lurking in the hills are Sumpter, Auburn, Bonanza, Greenhorn, and Granite.

Take State 7 south, crossing site of the tracks of the old Sumpter Valley Railroad, constructed in the 1890s and one of the last narrow-gauge railroads to continue operations in the state. A few miles out of Baker is the site of Griffin Creek, where gold in Oregon was first discovered on October 23, 1861. Turn right on a dirt road at 7 miles and continue for 3.3 miles to Auburn, marked by a historic plaque, a few piles of stones, and some weathered boards half-hidden by a grove of weeping willows.

When gold was discovered at the site in 1861, log cabins and a blockhouse to protect the prospectors from the Indians were erected. By 1862, word of the gold discovery had spread and hundreds of gold-happy miners rushed in. So rich was the area that 1,270 claims were recorded within a year, and two Frenchmen had panned $100,000 worth of gold dust during the last few months of 1862. Auburn was made the county seat of newly created Baker County, and by 1864, when its population rose to 5,000, it was the second largest city in the state.

Typical of the boom towns of the era, it was wild and woolly and jam-packed with gamblers, bunco artists, and promoters of every description. Justice was quick and final in Auburn. When French Pete, a miner, was found guilty of putting strychnine in his partner's flour, he was summarily hanged on Gallows Hill. And Spanish Tom died in the same fashion for wielding a Bowie knife in too deadly a fashion.

With gold discoveries in Idaho in 1867, Auburn began to falter. The county seat was moved to Baker in 1868 and gradually the buildings were deserted, eventually being hauled away by nearby ranchers for firewood.

Returning to State 7, continue south 2 miles and head west on a paved road along the north bank of Powder River. Sumpter (19.6 miles) achieved its birthright when a small group of Confederate soldiers on their way to California in 1862 found gold in the vicinity, erected a log cabin, and named it Fort Sumpter. A flurry of activity resulted as miners moved in and established a placer camp along the banks of the Powder River. And when they left, hundreds of Chinese took over, reworking the region for additional gold.

With the discovery of deep mines in the 1870s and the completion of the Sumpter Valley narrow-gauge railroad, mining operations increased and Sumpter became a town of 3,000 inhabitants. By 1900 the peak was reached, with an output of almost $9 million from 35 mines. And in 1902 the *Sumpter News* asked: "Sumpter, golden Sumpter, what glorious future awaits thee?" Over 12 miles of mine tunnels were being worked, and the town had an opera house where fancy dress balls were held.

But the boom ended and by 1906 most of the mines were closed. What happened to Sumpter after the great fire of 1916 is virtually an unknown chapter in history, except that it was deserted, with pack rats the only occupants of the two former banks. All that remains is a smelter, erected during the last days of the boom.

An unpaved road (right) from Sumpter for 6 miles leads to Bourne, located on the banks of Cracker Creek. It was born in the 1870s as Cracker, the liveliest gold camp in the region, becoming known later as Bourne, notorious for its unusual number of wildcat ventures. Two editions of the same paper were published by an unscrupulous promoter—one edition for home consumption and the other, with glowing

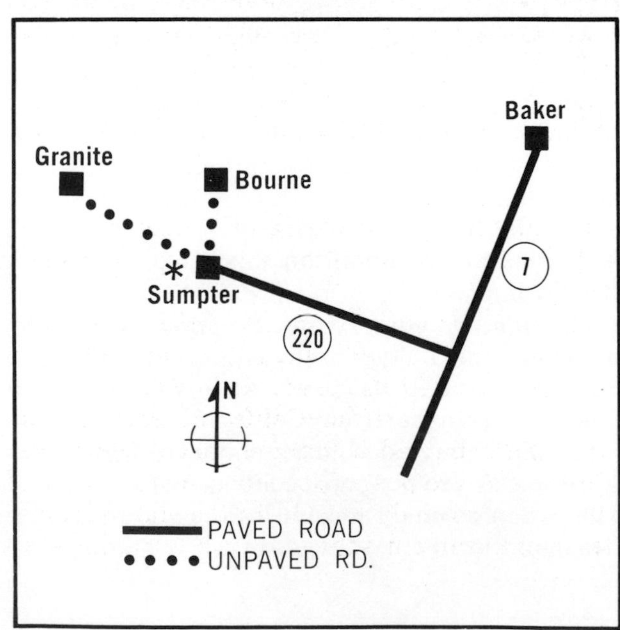

accounts of rich strikes and fabulous mining activities, for distribution to strategic places in the East.

Continuing west from Sumpter, the road reaches Granite (15 miles), the remnant of a town that started its career on July 4, 1862 when the first settlers from California reached the area. They named it Independence, which was rejected by the post office since another town of that name already existed in the state. Granite was not a conventional gold rush town, depending more on trade, distributing, and shipping for its livelihood. But when the other mines in the region played out, the population of Granite dwindled until, according to the latest census, there are but 2 inhabitants. The once ornate Grand Hotel, a 3-story building with 30 rooms, still stands, an empty, weathered shell. All that remains of yesterday in addition to the hotel are some dilapidated cabins, a few graves half-hidden by the tall grass, deserted tunnels, and occasional heaps of tailings.

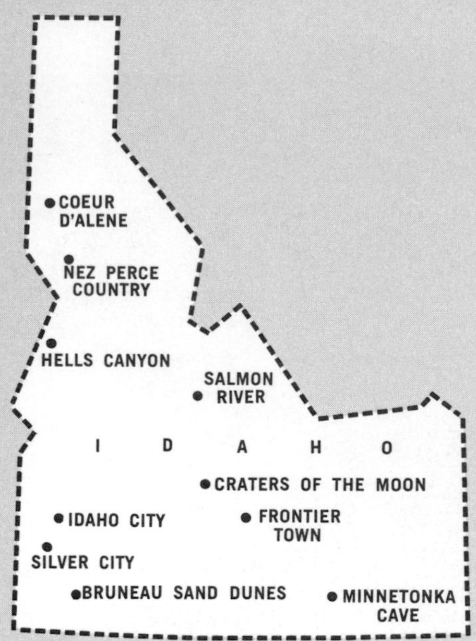

roaming

Idaho is a kaleidoscope of superlatives, from the depths of Hells Canyon (deepest in North America) to the wilderness of the raging Salmon River and the Middle Fork, from the mountains known as the Seven Devils to the colorful sweep of tableland known as Henry's Lake Flat. Historically, Idaho was the home and hunting grounds, the breadbasket and battlefield for various Indian tribes: the Coeur d'Alenes, the Bannocks, the Shoshone, the Sheepeaters, and the Nez Percés. Rugged pioneers and prospectors also left their mark on Idaho—the land of the Oregon Trail and violence in the gold mining camps.

In Coeur d'Alene country of northern Idaho, mountains and lakes far outnumber villages and towns. There's Coeur d'Alene Lake, known as one of the five most beautiful bodies of water in the world, and Lake Pend Oreille, home of the giant Kamloops—king-size version of the rainbow trout. This is Nez Percé country, and in the unique Nez Percé National Historical Park, landmarks, museums, battle sites and frontier forts bring yesterday to life for the adventurer.

To the south and east the Salmon River (the River of No Return) cuts its way through the heart of the state; and from its fast-moving waters fishermen in the spring and fall take their limits of oversized steelheads, while other thrill-seekers maneuver kayaks through its rapids or float a rubber raft down the Middle Fork.

Those who seek adventure amid the crumbling ghost towns of the past travel along the Snake River and swing into the primitive country of Boise National Forest to Idaho City. In less than six years—from 1863 to 1868—forty million dollars' worth of gold was removed from its surrounding hills, and its population approached that of present-day Boise.

In south-central Idaho rise the strange and ever shifting Bruneau Sand Dunes, overlooking an azure lake that provides fishing, swimming, and sunbathing on the fabulous sand dune beach. Along the southeastern edge of the state, the towering Teton Mountains form a backdrop for the meandering Snake River. And nearby is Minnetonka Cave, an underground wonder of nature high in the Wasatch Range.

This is Idaho, wild but friendly country, a land of unspoiled beauty.

Pack trip into the Idaho wildernes

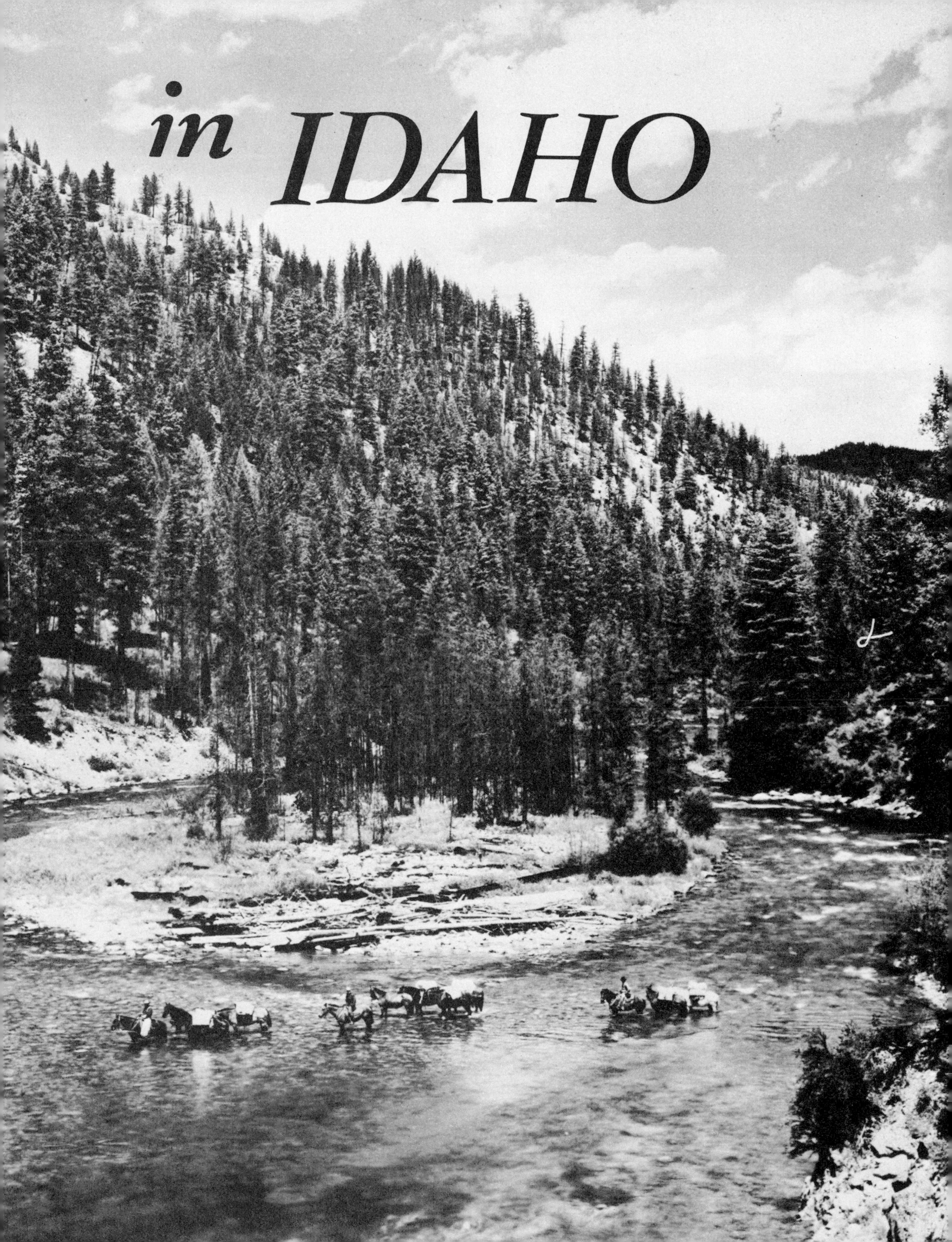
in IDAHO

a shimmering lake, a fly-fishing river, an Indian reservation, and a national forest to explore

COEUR d'ALENE COUNTRY

Coeur d'Alene is more than a city; it's a special part of north Idaho country that includes spectacular Lake Coeur d'Alene, the fly-fishing Coeur d'Alene River, the Coeur d'Alene Indian Reservation, and the Coeur d'Alene National Forest. The city of Coeur d'Alene, situated in the extreme northwest portion of the state, is only 30 miles east of Spokane, Washington.

The area's earliest inhabitants were the Coeur d'Alene Indians, a small tribe numbering perhaps 500, living quiet and peaceful lives. The name, meaning Pointed Heart, was originally bestowed upon the Indians by the French traders. From the beginning, explorers of the region have been impressed with its beauty. Father de Smet wrote, "These plains are surrounded by magnificent forests of pine, fir and cedar . . . You see towering mountains, ridge rising above ridge, robed with snow and mingling their summits with the clouds."

And Isaac I. Stevens, governor of the territory, described the Coeur d'Alene Mountains in 1853 as "clothed with evergreen forests, with here and there an open summit covered with grass; numerous valleys intersecting the country for miles around; courses of many streams marked by the ascending fog."

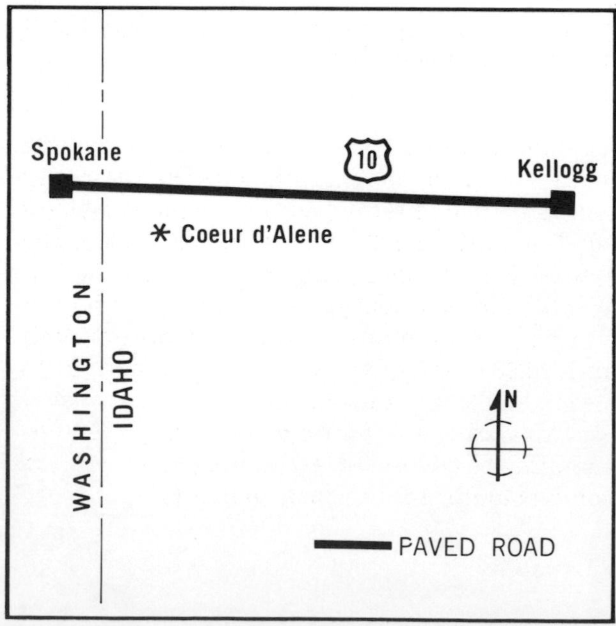

An important lumbering center since the advent of the white man, the Coeur d'Alene country has become increasingly important as a tourist mecca since World War II.

Coeur d'Alene Lake is reached by going south from the city on U.S. 95 Alternate. Entirely surrounded by low wooded hills, the lake stretches out in endless blue, seeming to change in hue and texture depending upon the time of day or the direction from which the lake is being observed. The shimmering surface bends and twists into various coves and bays. It is perhaps the most beautiful lake in the Northwest and is considered by many as one of the loveliest in the world.

Boat cruises are available on the lake from June through the first Sunday in October, leaving Coeur d'Alene at 11:30 A.M. and returning around 6:30 in the evening.

The most spectacular view of the lake is obtained from above it at a point reached by the Mineral Ridge Trail, some 3 miles long and rising 715 feet above the surface of the lake. The trail is located between Wolf Lodge Bay and Beauty Bay in the Mineral Ridge Scenic Area. Several viewpoints, selected by members of a local camera club, offer ample opportunities for picture taking and enjoying the unfolding vista.

Heyburn State Park, located on State Highway 5 off U.S. 95 between Plummer and St. Maries, is the state's oldest and largest park. Its 8,000 acres on the southern end of Lake Coeur d'Alene offer fishing in four lakes, swimming, boating, picnicking, and complete camping facilities.

Going east from the city of Coeur d'Alene on Interstate 10 for 28 miles brings the adventurer to the old Cataldo Mission on the Coeur d'Alene River, a marvel in construction that required 20 years from its beginning to its completion in 1868. Wooden pegs were used for nails in this 90 by 40 foot structure that stands 30 feet high. Willow saplings, interwoven with twisted ropes of wild grass, laced the beams together. Plaster was developed, using mud from the nearby river, and spread on the walls by hand. The attractive portico is supported by 6 massive wooden pillars. Father Ravalli, who helped in

St. Joe River, only river in the world which cuts through a lake, flowing towards Lake Coeur d'Alene

the construction, painted two of the works still hanging in the church. In 1929, when the building was restored, an annual pilgrimage was initiated; and now, on August 15, Indians and whites come back to the Mission to worship.

The Cataldo Mission was a frequent stopping place for Captain John Mullan, who headed the contingent of military men that constructed the Mullan Military Road across northern Idaho en route from Fort Walla Walla, Washington to Fort Benton, Montana. Although it was hardly more than a trail, it did serve to tie the east and west together, playing an important part in early-day travel across the mountains. During an 11-month period of 1866, there passed over the road 5,000 head of cattle, 1,500 head of horses, 6,000 mules loaded with freight, 2,000 miners heading into Montana to prospect, 52 light wagons with families going to Montana, 31 wagons traveling west, and 20,000 persons traveling back and forth. Today this is the route of Interstate 90, the heaviest traveled in the entire state. Today's modern adventurer covers in a day distances that involved months for the early pioneers.

Lewis and Clark, battlegrounds of the Indian wars, early mission, habitation dating back 8,000 years, frontier outposts

Clearwater River

NEZ PERCE

The Nez Percé National Historical Park spreads from Spalding on the west to Lolo Pass on the east, generally follows U.S. 12 (the Lewis and Clark Highway) on the north, and extends to the White Bird Battlefield on the south. To reach park headquarters and the start of the adventure tour in Spalding, proceed northeast from Lewiston on U.S. 12 for 10 miles.

It was in Spalding in 1805 that Lewis and Clark pulled up their canoes on the shore of the Clearwater and first traded with the Nez Percé Indians. The town played an important part in the growth of Idaho Territory. The Territory's first school and church were established in this historic town, the first printing press installed, the first blacksmith shop built. The site of the old Lapwai Mission is commemorated with an 18-ton boulder, bearing a bronze tablet, at the Clearwater River bridge.

The site of Coyote's Fishnet is pointed out by a state historical sign on the south side of U.S.

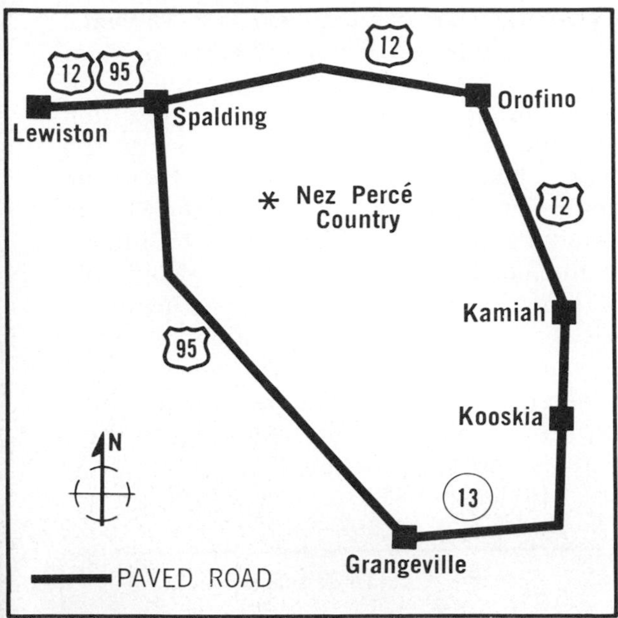

12 and 95, 6.3 miles east of Lewiston and 4.3 miles west of Spalding. The Fishnet formation is on the face of the bluffs on the south shore of the Clearwater River, while a second rock outcrop known as the Bear is high up on the hills on the north side of the river. The legend on the historical sign tells the story: "Coyote, the all-powerful animal spirit, was having a good time until Black Bear, the busybody, began to tease him. Finally losing his temper, Coyote tossed his huge fishnet onto the hills across the river. To teach Black Bear a lesson, Coyote threw him to the top of the hill on this side and turned him to stone. The Nez Percé people know just where to look for the net and unfortunate bear."

Continuing south from Spalding on U.S. 95 for 4 miles, the route passes Fort Lapwai on the Nez Percé Reservation. It was established in 1862 to prevent clashes between the Indians and whites and was the scene of important councils with the Nez Percé which preceded the Nez Percé War. After its abandonment by the army it became the headquarters of the Nez Percé Indian Agency. Idaho's earliest mission was also established here by Henry Harmon Spalding, November 29, 1836. The site is marked by a state historical sign.

At 12 miles (from Spalding) is the Culdesac, a high point that provides an interesting panorama by looking back once the summit is reached. Farms are checkerboarded as far as the Clearwater, closely knit squares and rectangles of rich brown, freshly-tilled soil, green pastures, or yellowish fields of grain.

Cottonwood (46 miles) was the site of a series of skirmishes following the Battle of White Bird. A state historical marker just south of town provides details of one of several attacks: "A Gatling gun firing from the top of the low hill beat off a Nez Percé Attack July 4, 1877. Next day, Indians just east of here surrounded 17 Mt. Idaho volunteers: two were killed and wounded when cavalrymen in Cottonwood did not or could not rescue them. Meanwhile, Chief Joseph's people, screened by this well-planned diversionary skirmish, crossed the prairie to join their allies on the Clearwater. From there the Indians retired across the mountains to Montana, where the Nez Percé War ended three months later."

Eight miles south of Cottonwood, in Grave Creek Canyon, is the Weis Rockshelter, reached by driving south on Grave Creek Road from the hotel. The rockshelter is about 150 yards south of a small spring (on the right). This site is one of the few thus far excavated in the Nez Percé country revealing human occupation dating back 8,000 years.

The White Bird Battlefield, scene of the opening engagement of the Nez Percé War of 1877, is a large area on the north slope of White Bird Canyon, west of White Bird Creek on U.S. 95, 88 miles south of Spalding and 3 miles north of the town of White Bird. Federal troops were ambushed at this location and suffered heavy losses. This victory so convinced the Indians that they could successfully defeat the Army that the war became a prolonged and disastrous conflict for the Nez Percé.

The circle trip continues to Grangeville. Take State 13 to junction with U.S. 12 at Kooskia. Continue to Kamiah (34 miles from Grangeville), location of the Asa Smith Mission site, and the Lewis and Clark Long Camp site. Homeward bound in 1806, the Lewis and Clark Expedition reached the Kamiah Valley in May and, finding the snow too deep in the Bitterroot Mountains to cross on the Lolo Trail, camped on this site from May 13 to June 10.

The route continues to follow the Clearwater River, again rejoining U.S. 95 at Spalding.

whitewater adventures and spawning salmon in "The River of No Return"

From Twin Falls to the Middle Fork of the Salmon U.S. 93 north leads to Stanley (137 miles). Turn left on State 21 and continue approximately 20 miles to gravel road (right) leading to Bear Valley Creek. To float the entire length of the Middle Fork, a total of 110 miles, the boat can be put in the water at Bear Valley, or at various other points farther downstream. From Fir Creek (approximately 3 miles east of Bear Valley Campground) two trails may be taken, one reaching Blue Bunch Mountain and the other, along Bear Valley Creek, continuing along the Middle Fork the entire length of the river.

Float boating down the Middle Fork is an experience alternating between thrills and chills. One moment the boat glides along placid emerald-hued pools and the next is bouncing through the boiling waters of dazzling white rapids. The river drops 60 feet to the mile during the first 40 miles, and the rest of the way 16 feet per mile. It flows through one of the deeper canyons in the West and is within the Idaho Primitive Area including a portion of four national forests. Normally, a 4-man rubber boat capable of hauling 3 passengers plus the oarsman is used (motorboats are not permitted). Information concerning an outfitter may be obtained by writing Idaho Outfitter and Guide Association, P. O. Box 95, Boise, Idaho 83701.

The river, born at the confluence of Marsh and Bear Valley creeks, swells as it progresses, nourished by numerous streams. For miles in every direction the landscape of rugged peaks is marked only by an occasional landing strip, a solitary ranch, or a Forest Service station.

Designation by Congress as part of the National Wild and Scenic River System guarantees that the river shall be preserved in a free-flowing condition and that both it and its immediate environment shall be protected for the benefit and enjoyment of present and future generations.

Explorers and trappers found Shoshone Indians living in the nearby Salmon Mountains in the early 1800s; and bone chips, tools, and mussel shells found in rock shelters along the rugged canyon walls confirm that primitive man once lived there, perhaps as long ago as 8,000 years.

The many pools and deep holes along the river provide outstanding fishing for salmon, steelhead, cutthroat, rainbow, and Dolly Varden from spring through fall. Almost a third of the Chinook salmon spawning nests (redds) in the Salmon River drainages are found in the Middle Fork and its tributaries. The mighty Chinook leave the ocean to migrate up the Columbia River from March through July, spawning in the Middle Fork during August and September. Their young spend from one to two years in fresh water, then go back to the sea, where they live up to four years before returning to their ancestral waters to spawn and die.

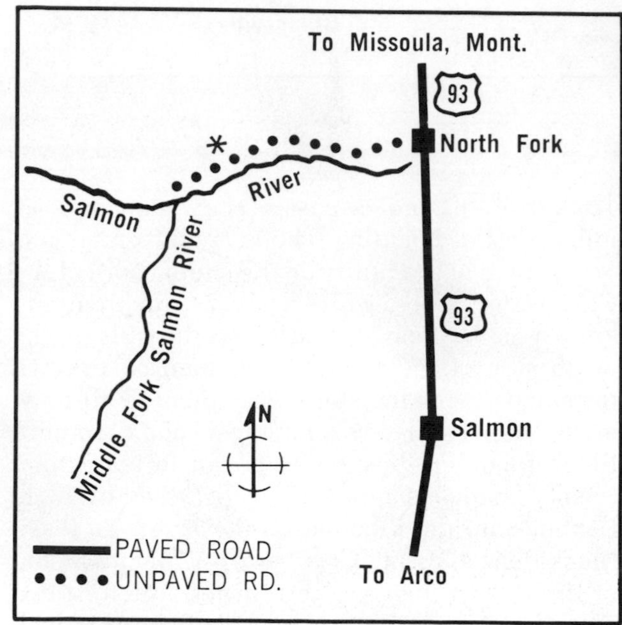

The Middle Fork country also abounds in game. Deer, bighorn sheep, mountain goat, elk, and bear may be hunted in season. To avoid the rugged hike by foot or horseback, many hunters boat down the river after flying in to a nearby landing strip.

Prominent points of interest include the fish ladder at Dagger Falls to assist the salmon in the final stages of their Middle Fork journey; Sheepeater Hot Springs, named after the Sheepeater (Shoshone) Indians; Parrot Diggings, left by Earl Parrot, an old hermit-prospector who sought his fortune among the Middle Fork's rugged cliffs; several Indian caves with paintings and

Float boating on the Salmon River

writings, and the Bighorn Crags, one of the most awe-inspiring ranges in the Northwest.

The Salmon River, originating in the Sawtooth and Lemhi valleys of eastern Idaho, is 425 miles long, rising at an elevation of more than 8,000 feet and cascading downward to 905 feet at its confluence with the Snake.

The 79-mile stretch of river between the end of the road west of North Fork and the end of the road from Riggins is generally known as "The River of No Return." For more than 150 years after the first white man came to the valley, only one-way trips were possible. Even today, with power boats, traveling up the river requires experience, skill, and considerable courage.

The Salmon, a challenging waterway through a vast wilderness, flows through the second deepest gorge on the continent (only the Snake River Canyon is deeper). Approximately 180 miles of the Salmon Canyon is more than a mile deep.

As in the Middle Fork, rubber rafts can be used to float the river. Kayaks, power boats, and flat-bottomed barges are also permitted and provide exciting adventure through the more than 40 stretches of rapids on the Salmon. Some of the more dangerous are Ruby, Salmon Falls, Bailey, Big and Little Mallard, Little Elk Horn, and Gun Barrel rapids.

A considerable amount of breathtaking scenery along the Salmon can be seen by taking a graveled road east from Riggins to French Creek, or by taking a graveled road west from North Fork (21 miles north of the town of Salmon) for approximately 50 miles.

THE SALMON AND MIDDLE FORK

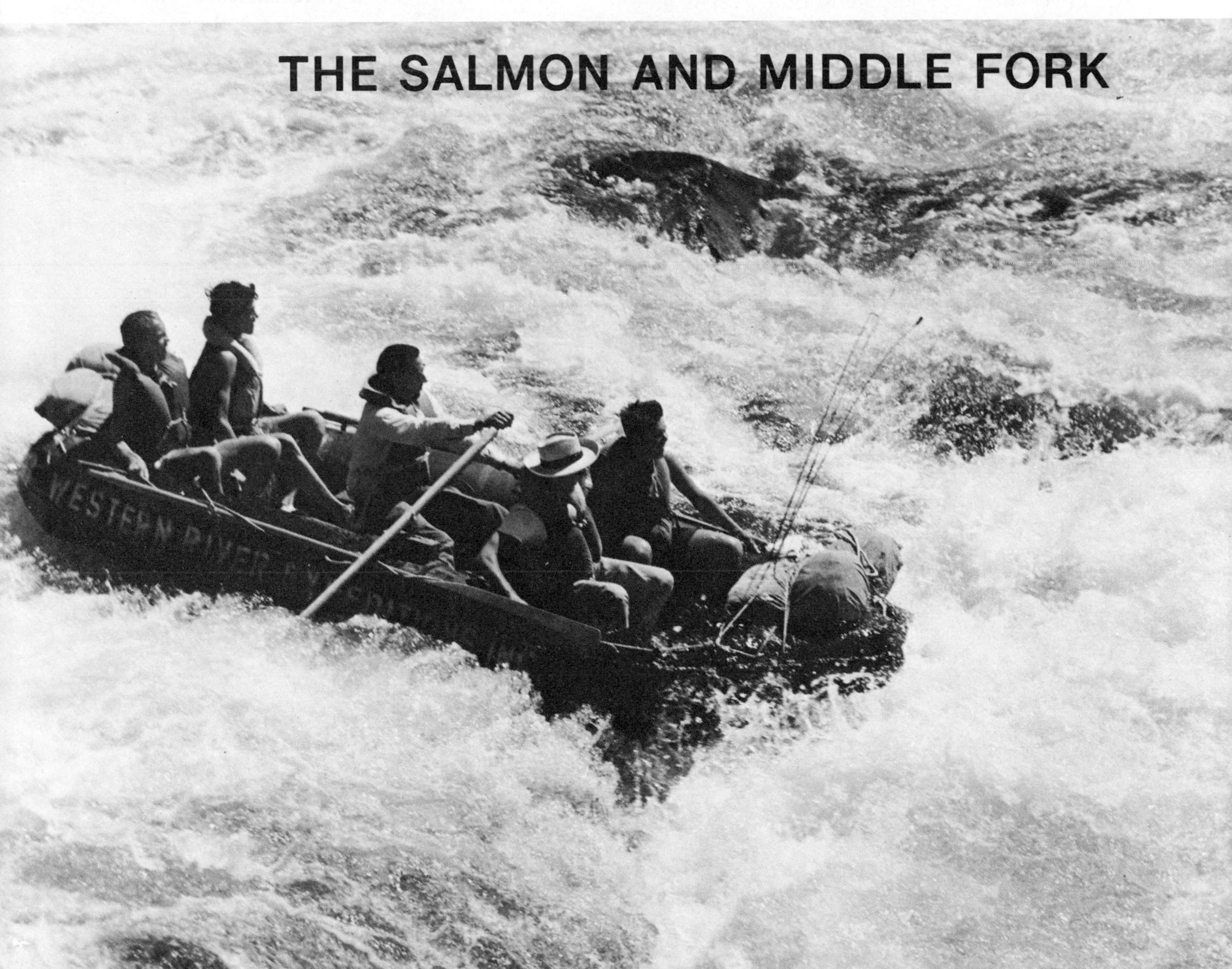

deepest gorge on the North American continent and mirrorlike lakes in wild, primitive country

HELLS CANYON

Hells Canyon, the deepest gorge on the North American continent, is reached from Weiser (pronounced Weezer) by proceeding north on U.S. 95 to Cambridge (29 miles), turning left on State 71, crossing the Snake just north of Brownlee Dam, and making a second crossing north of Oxbow Dam. Proceed 23 miles to Hells Canyon Dam.

An alternate route from Cambridge is to re-

main on U.S. 95 to Council (21 miles), turning left on a paved road for 8 miles, at which point the paving ends. The route goes up a narrow valley, gradually climbing through a logged-off area in which stately yellow pine trees remain. Take the left fork at Bear toward the old ghost town of Cuprum. An interesting switchback road winds downward from Cuprum into Snake River Canyon. Or, from Cuprum there is a road leading to Horse Mountain Lookout and to Kinney Point and Sheeprock, where the 7,000-foot canyon rim overlooks the Snake River.

Until recently, Hells Canyon and the Seven Devils area north of Cuprum were virtually unknown—part of a wild wilderness cut through by a raging stream that, according to one early French explorer, was an "accursed, mad river...." An old-time navigator wrote in 1891 that "the river winds like a serpent, whooping itself to gather strength for greater speed. The wall-rock towers so high that it shuts out the sun—and the fury of the torrent whips the surface white with foam and fills its labyrinthian passage with perpetual rain."

But today Hells Canyon is a recreational paradise, an area of calm, mirrorlike lakes against a backdrop of some of America's most magnificent scenery. The transformation resulted from a complex of dams—the Brownlee, Oxbow, and Hells Canyon—started in 1959 and completed in 1968 at a cost of $230 million.

Hells Canyon Lake, filled in 1967, is proving equally as popular with sportsmen as Oxbow and Brownlee lakes, two areas considered as among the state's best fishing grounds. Excellent camping and picnic facilities as well as trailer parks are located along the shores of all three lakes.

Still much of the primitive Snake River country remains in its rugged, virgin state. Hells Canyon excursions down the Snake River are operated out of Lewiston, from full-day tours to 2-day 240-mile river cruises (between April 1 and October 31). As seen from the boat, the towering peaks and almost perpendicular walls of the canyon appear in weird and mystic beauty.

The Seven Devils—a range of rugged mountains along the Snake—were named, so legend has it, by an Indian brave who became lost among the high crags while on an annual hunt. He wandered for days, becoming more and more confused. Eventually, probably on a night when the moon was full, he encountered a devil, then a second, a third, and, in total, seven. He ran in wild fright, and before any harm had come to him, he found his tribe and recounted his experiences. Thenceforth the mountains were known as the Seven Devils.

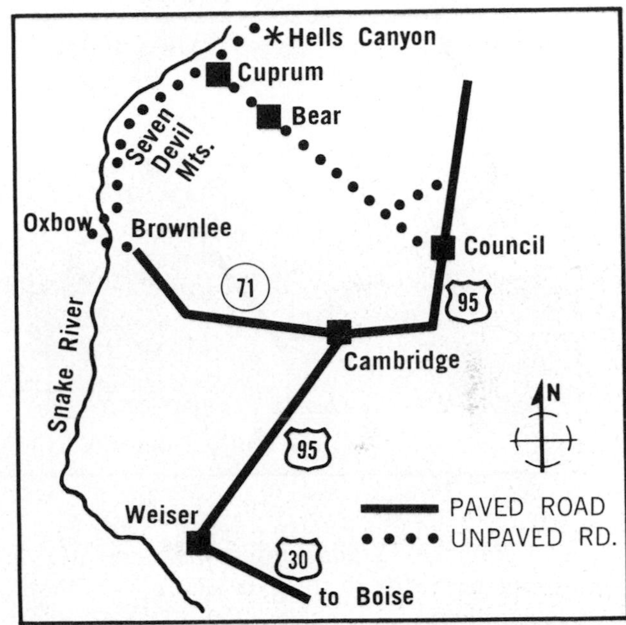

It is a land of violent contrasts. From the depths of Hells Canyon to the peaks is a distance of 8,000 feet. The lower slopes are meadowlike, covered with grass. At higher elevations the vegetation changes to mountain flowers, then to alpine and, among the lofty crags, the delicate tundra of the high country.

Wildlife in the Hells Canyon-Seven Devils scenic area includes deer, bear, wild turkey, mountain goat, and numerous small game animals and birds: the bald and golden eagle, quail, grouse, chukar, and Hungarian partridge. Good fishing for cutthroats can be found in several of the lakes in the Seven Devils, including Big Baldy, Triangle, and Gem, with rainbow in the Upper Hanson and Seven Devils Lake.

Numerous hiking and horse trails are located throughout the area, with stables at Seven Devils and Lower Cannon lakes. Guided pack trips are also available. For information contact the Idaho Outfitters and Guides Board, State Office Building, Boise, Idaho.

IDAHO CITY

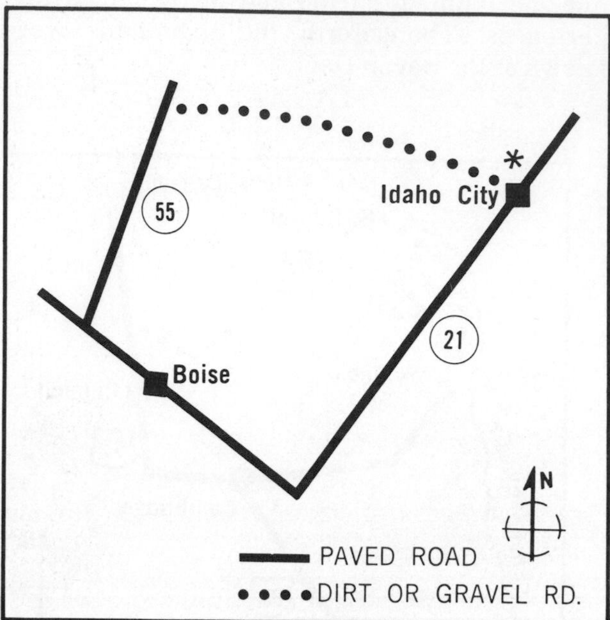

From Boise to the ghost town of Idaho City, more famous for its dead than its living, take State 21 east, following the curve of the Boise River for the first 19 miles before swinging northward into the Boise National Forest to Idaho City (42 miles from Boise).

At its zenith, Idaho City reportedly had a population approaching that of Boise today. Certainly it has a past that is probably the most colorful of any frontier boom town in Idaho, if not in the entire West. The origin of the old mining camp is surrounded by legend and fantasy, some old-timers insisting that a group of men searching for the lost Blue Bucket mine in 1862 traveled up the Boise River and discovered the Boise Basin diggings, resulting in a tremendous influx of prospectors into the area. Among the communities that sprang up were Pioneer City, Placerville, and Bannack City, renamed Idaho City a year later.

By 1865 the Idaho City Directory listed 250 business houses, with 4 breweries, 41 saloons, 5 billiard parlors, 10 Chinese washhouses, 4 hotels, 36 grocery stores, and 23 law offices. Its citizens did not lack for the finer things in life, as four theaters—the Jenny Lind, the Temple, the Forrest, and the Idaho—were operating, and the touring theatrical troupes from New York always included Idaho City in their itinerary.

The Idaho City jail was the first in the territory, and some of the tales concerning its occupants are hair-raising, with many of the stories climaxing at the end of a rope. One of the local characters was Ferd Patterson, known gambler, gunman, and murderer, as well as a flashy dresser. He affected high-heeled boots, plaid trousers, a fancy silk vest spanned by a heavy gold chain, and a frock coat of beaver trimmed with otter. Some of his exploits included killing the captain of a boat in Portland, scalping his ex-mistress, and, to show disdain for law and order, shooting to death the sheriff of Idaho City. Since the sheriff was considered an honorable upholder of the law, a thousand men gathered in town bent on lynching the well-dressed scoundrel. But the deputy managed to get his prisoner safely into the jail. Not to be denied, the mob met in the graveyard to discuss strategy, went to Boise, and obtained a cannon, resolving to attack. But the deputy also had a cannon and cut portholes in the jail wall. With the help of his desperadoes, the deputy won the battle, though the jail suffered somewhat. And the final irony: Patterson went to trial and was acquitted.

The *Idaho World*, a spritely biweekly newspaper whose office is still standing on Main Street, reported on the second major fire to sweep Idaho City on May 18, 1867: "Just after noon this day, flames were seen issuing from the roof of John Cody's saloon, southwest corner of Main and Wall Streets. At the time it was reported in our office, we had just completed an article in which we referred to the fact that this would be second anniversary of the great fire of May 18, 1865, which laid this city in ashes, and recommending to our citizens a greater degree of watchfulness, during day and night, to guard against a repetition of the calamity. The ink was not dry upon the paper when the alarm of 'Fire!' reached our office."

The amount of gold taken from the hills surrounding Idaho City has been estimated at $40 million between 1863 and 1869, the greatest boom, and since that time at $100 million. Other experts believe that the entire Boise Basin produced over $300 million in gold dust between 1862 and 1886.

once Idaho's most populous boom town, today more famous for its dead than its living

Some of the historic buildings remaining in Idaho City include the present courthouse (Idaho City is still the county seat), originally one of the old hotels; Weigle's Place, previously the Miner's Exchange Saloon; the Catholic church built in 1867, and the Buena Vista Bar across Elk Creek and once connected to the business district by a swinging footbridge.

By 1886 the boom was past and Idaho City began to die. In the 1930s, when the price of gold was increased to $35 an ounce, there was a revival in the Boise Basin until World War II restrictions forced a suspension of mining activities. Today there are less than 200 residents in the town, many of whom have become active in their efforts to preserve the relics and historic places that are reminders of a wild and glorious past.

foot trails snake through this wasteland of lava and cinder

CRATERS OF THE MOON

Starting point for the adventure tour of the Craters of the Moon is Twin Falls in southern Idaho. Take U.S. 93 north to Shoshone (26 miles); then go right on U.S. 93A for 66 miles to the entrance. From Arco, take U.S. 93A southwest 17 miles to the entrance to the Craters of the Moon National Monument.

With man's landing on the moon, the strange, vast area of lava flows, cinder cones, and large depressions has become of even greater interest, both to the scientist and the twentieth-century adventurer. In this region formed from massive lava floods, all vegetation within 83 square miles was originally destroyed. As centuries passed, many determined plants took root and now exist throughout the monument.

A 7-mile loop drive, starting at the Visitor Center, with several side trips en route, provides an overall view of the intriguing wonder. By taking all or some of the 5 trails leading from the roadways, a far better understanding of the monument will be otained. The drive, including several short hikes, takes about an hour.

The first stop, North Crater Flow, is interesting because it is one of the youngest formations in the region. The eruption creating it ceased only 1,600 years ago, a fact determined by scientists who counted the rings on an ancient pine called the Triple Twist Tree.

From North Crater the road skirts the edge of Paisley Cone. Beyond is a short spur road leading to Devils Orchard, a weird-appearing group of lava fragments from a crater wall. A nature trail, including a closeup inspection of Devils Orchard, takes off from this point. The cinders at the site are hardened lava froth, formed by expansion of gases within the molten rock and then shot into the air as giant fire fountains. The vegetation seen here and in other parts of the monument includes such desert plants as antelope bitterbrush and rubber rabbit brush in the older lava flows, while mock orange and tansybush fill the deep crevices of the younger flows. In the spring silvery pads of dwarf buckwheat, topped with yellow or pink pompom flowers, dominate the open cinder

Arco
93A
Craters of the Moon
Carey
Shoshone
93
N
Twin Falls
PAVED ROAD

Spatter cones in Craters of the Moon National Monument

slopes.

At Inferno Cone Viewpoint is a fascinating panorama encompassing the distant mountain ranges with a volcanic landscape of cinder cones in the foreground. A short distance from Inferno Cone is the Big Craters-Spatter Cones area. From the rim to the south can be seen the cinder cone chain along the Great Rift, dominated by Big Cinder Butte towering 800 feet above the lava plain. To the east of Inferno Cone across the road a trail leads to Indian Tunnel, Dewdrop, Boy Scout, and Beauty caves. A wayside exhibit demonstrates how lava tubes form, resulting in various-sized underground caverns.

The drive continues to a spur leading to Broken Top, a ruptured cinder cone. A roadcut here reveals numerous cinder layers, indicating that eruptions took place at intervals, while layers of soil provide evidence of long periods of inactivity in between. From Broken Top a 1.5-mile trail leads to Great Owl Cavern and the Tree Mold Area.

The Great Owl Cavern is a lava tube 500 feet long, 40 feet high, and 50 feet wide. The opening to the tunnel is the original source of a lava dome, created by the hardening of the surface while molten lava continues to flow underneath. A stairway leads into the cavern, but a lantern or flashlight is necessary for exploration.

There is considerable evidence to prove that the Indians were familiar with the lava flows. An ancient Indian trail followed the Great Rift, with caves along the route providing temporary shelter. A semicircular arrangement of stones at Indian Tunnel apparently was an attempt to keep the wind from howling through the cave.

Campground facilities are available within the Monument (April 15 to October 15) and naturalists are on hand to answer questions. Each evening during the summer an illustrated program on the geology, plants, and wildlife of the region is given at the campground site.

replica of an old frontier town, with boot hill cemetery, pioneer fort, and western relics that have eluded museums

TRESSL'S FRONTIER TOWN

To reach Tressl's unique Frontier Town from Idaho Falls, take Interstate 15 southwest to Blackfoot. Turn right on U.S. 26 and proceed approximately 3 miles to Groveland Road. Turn right and continue past the Groveland store. Continue to the second road (approximately 1 mile) and turn left to Frontier Town.

More than 20 years ago Adolph "Addie" Tressl and his wife started gathering together bits and pieces of clothing, equipment, supplies, and relics of the early West. By 1959, Tressl began to build his personal memorial to the old frontiersman. A year later he had completed his project: an authentic replica of an old frontier community, complete with Main Street and a village square.

Today, Frontier Town includes a school, drugstore, dentist, trading post, saloon, town hall, barber shop, assay office, Chinese laundry, hat and dress shop, hotel, blacksmith shop, chapel, Fort Apache (at the end of the square), and boot hill.

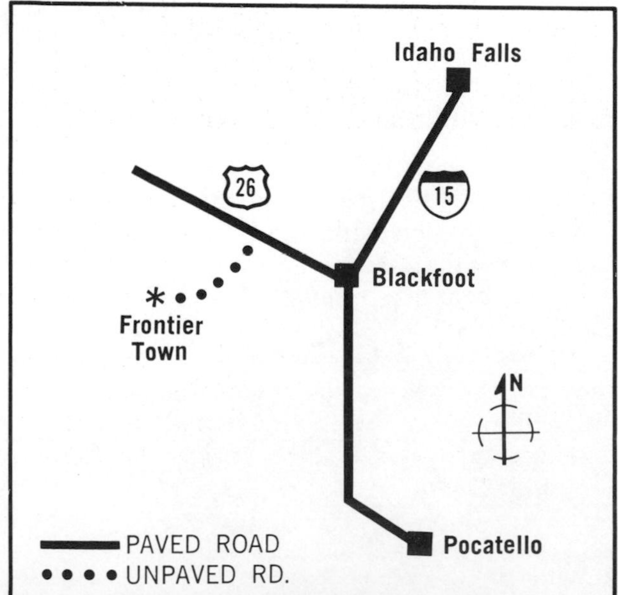

Many of the western relics he has gathered are so rare they cannot be found even in museums. In the trading post stand wooden egg cartons and a jar half-full of 90-year-old mincemeat preserved with rum and brandy.

Found in the millinery shop is a collection of hats that represent high styling of those bygone days. Adding to the authenticity is the busy milliner seated at an ancient sewing machine.

In the manner of the day, the barber shop

provides the quarters for a court of law, an itinerant dentist's chair and treadle drill, and apothecary. A mustachioed barber leans over a bewhiskered frontiersman, with razor poised above the bristling beard.

Next door to the barber shop the old-time assayer bends over his ore samples collected by the Tressls from historic mines all over the West.

Occupying the north end of Main Street is Fort Apache, its log gates closed and barred against attack and with a pair of cannon leering through peepholes in the walls, ready and primed in case of an attack by unfriendly Indians. Beyond the Fort are boot hill cemetery, Alder Gulch, and an Indian camp.

Visitors are welcome during the summer and early fall, but queries should be made at the Blackfoot Chamber of Commerce prior to making the 4-mile drive to Tressl's fabulous Frontier Town.

SILVER CITY

crumbling remains of a gaudy past where mine owners fought each other to the death

From Boise, the adventure trip starting point, to the ghost town of Silver City is 63 miles. Take U.S. 30 west to Nampa, turn left on State 45 to Murphy, the smallest county seat in America (population 50), and then proceed on a graded road southwest for 20 miles to Silver City.

Not quite deserted, the faded, crumbling buildings of Silver City seem to blend into the low, rolling, sage-covered hills that reach toward the horizon. A lonely town in vast, lonely country (some say the jackrabbit population of Owyhee County is greater than its human population), Silver City was once a booming mining town and, from 1886 to 1935, the county seat.

The construction of the courthouse was announced in the June 1, 1867 edition of the *Owyhee Avalanche:* "The contract for building a courthouse and jail for Owyhee County was let last Wednesday. The jail is to be 30 feet by 22 feet, running back into the hill, built of hewn lumber set on end and lined with two-inch planks spiked on; floors and ceilings to be of hewn timber. The courthouse will be two stories on top of the jail, running back ten feet further into the hill. The first floor will contain offices for the county officers, lined and papered. The upper story will contain three rooms—the courtroom, the District Clerk's office and a jury room. There will be two porches in front and stairs on the side." All that remains is the empty shell, its two upper stories and its interior completely gone, and the stone arches of its once ornate facade.

The headwaters of the Jordan Creek are found at Silver City; it was the discovery of gold in the creek in 1863 that provided the lifeblood for the mining camp. Almost at once the new boom town began to threaten the community of Ruby City, which was at that time the county seat of Owyhee County. In typical frontier fashion, there was bitter competition between the two towns, a battle for survival. With its proximity to the mines and its natural protection from the high and violent winds in its favor, Silver City triumphed, winning both the county seat and much of Ruby City's population. So completely annihilated was its rival that the exact location of Ruby City is no longer known.

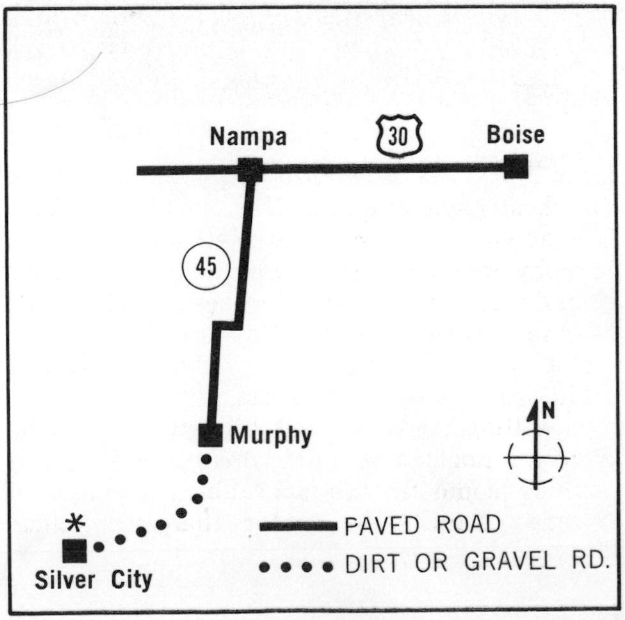

The original placer deposits played out after the first few years, but with the locating of important quartz lodes in 1864 the growth of mining and Silver City was assured. At the first of 30 mining operations on War Eagle Mountain, the Oro Fino, quartz assayed $7,000 in silver and $800 in gold to the ton, yielding almost $3 million in its first 6 years of operation. Ore from the Poorman Mine, discovered in 1865, assayed between $4,000 and $5,000 to the ton, and a mass of solid ruby-silver crystals weighing a quarter of a ton was found at a depth of 100 feet. When some of these crystals won a gold medal at the Paris Exposition in 1866, Silver City became internationally famous. The Poorman, plagued by vicious ownership fights further inflamed by a fantastic production record, was closed down in 1875 when the secretary of the company absconded with the funds. Its total production had exceeded $4 million.

Violence was the rule during the mining heyday. The Ida Elmore and Golden Chariot mines hired gunmen to solve a boundary dispute, and in the ensuing battle at the Ida Elmore, the owner of the mine was shot through the head. Fighting continued for 3 days, finally quelled when a squad of cavalry was sent in from Boise.

At its peak Silver City had its own newspaper and the first telegraphic news wire in the territory, a Catholic church, 6 general stores, a brewery to supply its numerous saloons, a photographer's gallery, 2 lumber shops, a tailor shop, and 3 barber shops. It boasted 2 hotels, the Idaho being the more magnificent, with 50 rooms and a grand bar with impressive mirrors and polished mahogany furnishings. The Idaho remains intact today, its exterior badly in need of paint and its long porches a bit swaybacked. Its competitor, the War Eagle, haunted by the ghost of a young girl who died there, was deserted and collapsed in 1917. What remains stands on Washington Street, a crumbling structure entirely surrounded by sagebrush.

Silver City had its big slump in the 70s and a subsequent revival in the late 80s. But in 1935 the county seat was moved to Murphy, and in 1942 the last of the mines shut down, telephone service was ended, and the post office closed its doors.

BRUNEAU SAND DUNES

swimming, boating, biking, playing amidst the world's tallest sand dunes

The starting point for the Bruneau Sand Dunes and the spectacular Bruneau Gorge is Boise, the capital of Idaho and its largest city. Take U.S. 30 southeast to Mountain Home (43 miles) and turn right (south) on State 51 for 17 miles to Bruneau Dunes State Park, the highest sand dunes in the world. Situated on the northern edge of Owyhee County, the natural wonder is in an area of vast desert and towering peaks.

Strangely, with dunes rising 452 feet (surpassing the Sahara Desert's highest by 150 feet) and extending over a vast area, the region is becoming popular as a swimming and boating resort. Dunes Lake, covering 160 acres, was formed by seepage through the sand from the Snake River a few miles to the north.

Around the lake the dunes form a high serpentine range nearly 2 miles long, shaping a natural amphitheater of sand. The unusual height results from the reaction of the hot desert air hitting cool air over the adjacent marshes, causing air currents that tend to move the sand towards the top from both sides.

The great dunes come alive on windy days, when the air is suddenly filled with long streamers of flying sand. Although the dunes are very dry on the surface, just a few inches under the top layer is a substantial amount of moisture, occasionally visible following a windstorm. Around the lake marsh grasses and a few trees manage to survive, and some of the lesser rolling sand hills support bunch grass and sagebrush.

A hike to the top of one of the larger dunes is difficult, because of the soft sand and the steep slopes, but the 15- or 20-minute workout has its rewards; the view from the top is superbly beautiful, with the blue-green lake directly below, the white dunes rolling away to the brown desert floor, and, 20 miles to the south, the snowcapped peaks of the Owyhees, rising to nearly 9,000 feet.

Overlooked by tourists and natives alike until someone discovered that the dunes were the highest in the world, they are now a source of pleasure to the trail bike and dune buggy enthusiast. The best time of year for trail biking is in the late winter when the sand is moist, providing traction and enabling the rider to make great sweeping slides over the level areas and climb to the top of the highest dunes. In fact, so popular are the dunes that motorized vehicles are now restricted to areas not used by the general public.

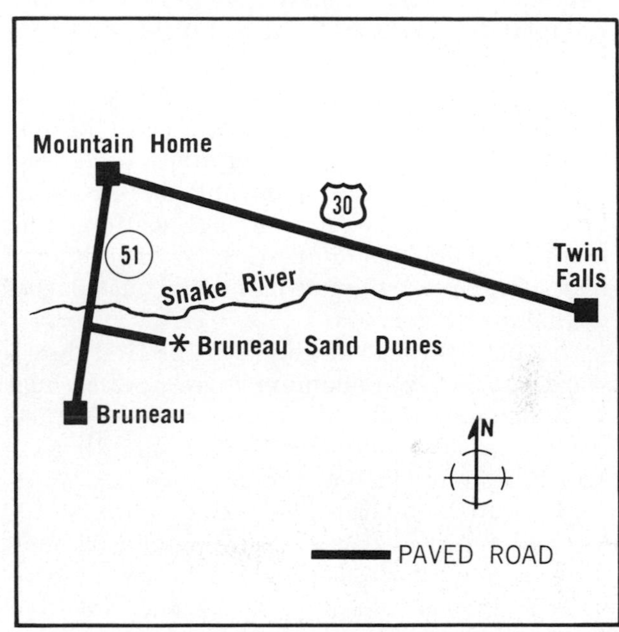

To reach Bruneau Canyon, return to State 51 and continue to the small town of Bruneau. Just to the south, spur roads lead to the canyon. Extending along the Bruneau River for 67 miles, the gorge is one of the deepest narrow canyons in the world. It is possible for a man to hurl a rock from rim to rim in places where the canyon is 2,000 feet from the top to the river, with walls almost perpendicular. In the upper reach is Jarbridge Canyon, whose name is a Shoshone word meaning devil. According to Indian legend, the devil claimed a sacrificial offering from the tribe when any member offended the Great Spirit. The medicine man would select the prettiest maiden of the village, kill her, and lay her body on the brink of the gorge. During the night, Jarbridge would come to possess the offering.

Eight miles southeast of Bruneau is an indentation from the canyon into which pours steaming water from Hot Creek. It's a popular spot for a picnic and a quick swim.

MINNETONKA CAVE

underground giant chambers and grotesque formations once part of a prehistoric sea

Minnetonka Cave, at the 8,000-foot level in the Wasatch Range, is reached from Pocatello via Interstate 15 south to McCammon (25 miles), turning left on U.S. 30N through Soda Springs (46 miles), and proceeding to junction with U.S. 89 at Montpelier (30 miles). Turn right on U.S. 89 and continue for 18 miles to graveled road leading up St. Charles Canyon into the Cache National Forest. At 9.5 miles is the Minnetonka Campground and parking area for those wishing to explore the cave.

Temperature in the cave is always at 40 degrees, and a warm sweater is advised. Minnetonka is a remarkable underground wonder, not only for the vast chambers and the grotesque formations, but because numerous fossils of plants and marine animals have been found inside the cave, evidence that it was once part of a great prehistoric sea.

The path through the cave leads first downward, into a large chamber, then upward over a conglomeration of huge glazed stones, resembling a mystic cemetery of some bygone era, lying undisturbed for centuries under its high vaulted ceiling. The trail then winds through a narrow passage, coming to a 100-foot-deep gorge. Impressive boulders, as large as houses, appear along the trail and, in other places, crystal-clear water falls upon the large, round stones. Beyond this point is a mammoth blade of stone resembling the cleaver of some prehistoric giant. The path enters a long, serpentine corridor, leading to the Bride. The Bride is a huge stalagmite seven feet high, her delicate trousseau draped around her, while the unfortunate Bridegroom hangs from the ceiling by his heels.

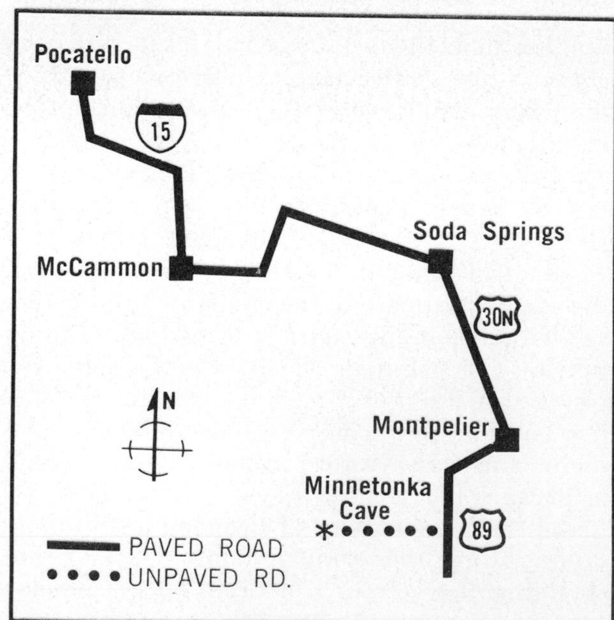

Returning from Minnetonka Cave, turn right at U.S. 89 to Bear Lake (see Logan Canyon under Utah), half of which belongs to Idaho, the southern half to Utah. There is a state park with picnic facilities on the north shore and a Utah state park a few miles farther south. Frequent stiff afternoon breezes during the summer make Bear Lake especially popular with sailboat buffs.

Every winter an unusual mystery of nature occurs when the Bonneville cisco, a small white fish, make a spawning run in Bear Lake. During the frigid days of January, fishermen wade offshore to net these small but tasty fish. Generally the run lasts about 12 days and is limited to the 1.5-mile stretch of shore 9 miles north of Laketown on the Utah side.

Nonresidents can use either Idaho or Utah special 2-day licenses. Catching cisco is a simple procedure, requiring only an 18-inch hoop net with a long handle.

Skiing is an ever growing wintertime sport in southeastern Idaho's 3 ski areas: Skyline, located 15 miles southeast of Pocatello via Interstate 15; Caribou, just 6 miles east of Pocatello, and Home Canyon, 8 miles north of Montpelier via U.S. 30N.

An interesting return route from Minnetonka is via U.S. 89 northeast through Ovid and Montpelier, then north on U.S. 30N through Soda Springs and Lava Hot Springs (used by the Indians for centuries before white settlers appeared), to McCammon and a junction with Interstate 15 north to Pocatello.

Formations in Minnetonka Cave

INDEX

(Note: Page numbers in italic type refer to photographs.)